*Introduction
to Mathematical Psychology*

Introduction to
MATHEMATICAL PSYCHOLOGY

FRANK RESTLE · *JAMES G. GREENO*
Indiana University   *University of Michigan*

ADDISON-WESLEY PUBLISHING COMPANY

Reading, Massachusetts · Menlo Park, California · London · Don Mills, Ontario

This book is in the

Addison–Wesley Series in

BEHAVIORAL SCIENCE: QUANTITATIVE METHODS

Frederick Mosteller, *Consulting Editor*

In this book we try to introduce and define the broad spectrum of mathematical work in experimental psychology. To serve as an introduction, a book should be broad in coverage and relatively easy to read, but to serve as the definition of a new field, the book must cut deeper and seek the organizing principles that can unify research.

We have sought to do both tasks in a single book because we find that students of mathematical psychology are willing and able to study serious presentations of the subject, provided only that the logic of the theories is presented fully so they can follow the whole argument. We do not think it necessary to make the book easy by leaving out the "hard parts" of the proofs, for that merely makes the theory unintelligible. Our approach is almost the contrary—we have assiduously sought out the difficulties of mathematical psychology and tried to bring them to the attention of the reader—where possible, with satisfactory solutions.

When one tries to write a survey of a new research area and at the same time provide a critical examination of concepts, it becomes necessary to achieve economy somewhere. This has been done in three ways; first, by writing concisely. This serves to save pages rather than time, and the inexperienced reader must be prepared to read slowly and work along with the text. Asterisks follow some headings. These mark sections of some difficulty which may be skipped by a reader interested mainly in concepts. Second, we have attempted to handle our topics with simple mathematics rather than introducing more powerful methods. The cost, here, is that the student will want to make use of the more advanced techniques learned in a mathematics department. As teachers, we are happy if students find the book unsatisfactory and find better and simpler ways to do the problems discussed here. We hope that the large number of exercises will be used, either as individual or class projects, to fix ideas, develop skills, and challenge the ingenuity and creativity of the students.

Our third economy is to delete large parts of mathematical psychology, and give only a brief treatment to others. We take it as our prerogative and responsibility to decide what is important and what is not, and to predict what parts of mathematical psychology will be most fruitful in future years. These decisions are forced by the requirement of reasonable economy, so that the book can be used as an introduction, but may also serve as the basis of defining the field.

The book may be divided into three main parts. First are three chapters on learning, the topic that has received the major attention from mathematical psychology for many years. The first chapter shows how learning curves are used to decide theoretical questions, the second chapter works out the all-or-none theory, and the third chapter is devoted to the more detailed quantitative predictions made from hypothesis-selection theories. The detailed developments of linear learning models and stimulus-sampling theory are under-represented, because we believe the student should move forward from them rather than relive the birth-pangs of this area. We also have the theoretical prejudice that the detailed theories of reinforcement schedules served more to explicate that particular theory, than to press forward our knowledge of psychology. It seems to us that the future will lie, not with those who develop a given theory, but with those who pursue particular psychological questions wherever the facts may lead.

A second section of the book deals with perception, psychophysics, and choice. Here we begin with Helson's work on adaptation. Our efforts deviate somewhat from Helson's, mainly in that we work out a narrow spectrum of problems intensively, whereas most of the theoretical work in perception has been more panoramic. Our discussion of detection and discrimination is based on the theory of signal detection, and centers around the concept of noise and sources of noise, particularly the controversial concept of internal noise. Our discussion of the process of choice builds around the Thurstone theory and the ideas introduced by R. Duncan Luce in his choice theory, and develops a critique of both "strength" theories by analysis and demonstration of the effects of complexity of objects on choice.

Each of the first six chapters is built around one or more psychological issues. By an "issue" we mean a question admitting of two or more possible answers, each having a rationale and each tied in with other facts and other theoretical commitments. Psychology has advanced by framing issues, deciding them by experiment and analysis, then proceeding to new issues. Mathematical methods have helped to formulate issues, often by showing just where two theoretical positions are different and where they are not. Mathematical methods have helped to design the experiments to decide between issues, as for example by mediating the deduction of consequences. When two alternative hypotheses stand naked, it may be difficult to decide between them, but when each has been made to yield its consequences in detail, the possible experiments to decide the issue become more obvious and more powerful. Finally, mathematical methods help in the analysis of data and in bringing the observations directly to bear on the factual question at hand.

The last section of the book provides the mathematical foundations upon which the remainder of the book should rest. We put the mathematics last, despite its logical priority, because we find that our students readily pick up the mathematics once they are clear about the problem to be solved.

Our four mathematical chapters begin with an introduction to logic, set theory, and probability. In this chapter we attempt to give a coherent account of the foundations of probability as the notion should be applied in psychology. There are some controversial matters in this chapter, and we often find that our "logical" theory of probability gives rise to lively class discussion. Our formulation will work, and serve as a suitable basis for the remainder of this book. The teacher may either accept our formulation and get on, or may encourage discussion and debate, thereby deepening the students' appreciation of these issues in psychological theory.

The second chapter extends this discussion to stochastic processes, giving a more complete account of sample spaces and the general ideas underlying most of the models given earlier. The importance of a theoretical, logical understanding of these issues cannot be overestimated. The student who can calculate but does not understand his own calculations may make errors, and even more likely may find himself unable to proceed in a calculation because he cannot decide whether what he has already done is correct or incorrect.

The third technical chapter gives a thorough elementary treatment of the neglected subject of estimation of parameters, an important process in psychology, and one that is barely touched in most statistics courses. We aim at a balance between practical methods that can be used in emergencies, and those optimal methods, particularly maximum likelihood, that serve as a beacon even when they cannot be applied directly.

Our fourth technical chapter deals with identifiability and observability. As psychological questions become more complex and less obvious, it becomes more and more difficult to determine whether a given experiment can or cannot decide a given issue. A part of that question can be embedded in simple models and in a kind of statistical context, and the detailed solution to that part of the question, given here, should be valuable in efforts to solve the general question of the relevance of experimental data to theoretical questions.

A book like this must strike many balances, and the authors can only indicate what they think they have done. In the balance between mathematics and psychology, we have leaned as heavily as we could toward psychology. Within psychology, we have stayed as near as possible to what we take to be the "central" topics of learning, perception, and choice, leaving all interdisciplinary problems to others.

Finally, we find that we have not "applied mathematics to psychology." That is, we have not taken mathematical systems, already built for another purpose or from another set of concepts, and then searched out corners of psychological fact or theory that could serve as examples of the system. Instead, we have developed distinctly psychological ideas in such a way that the formal, general, and mathematical aspects could emerge into view. Therefore it is not natural for us to organize our discussions around Markov chains, linear algebra, noise theory, measurement theory, or compound distributions, but instead around the all-or-none question of learning, relativity of perception, sources of noise in detection, the processes of choice, and the combining of partial decisions. In our opinion, since these questions arise from the heartland of psychological theory, they are most likely to benefit psychologists and to contribute unique and valuable insights to the rest of the scientific community.

Bloomington, Indiana   F.R.
Ann Arbor, Michigan   J.G.G.
January 1970

Contents

CHAPTER ONE

Learning: Accumulation or Replacement

The first three chapters of this book are devoted to learning theory. Although the process of learning is notoriously mysterious, it has served as the subject of a voluminous research literature, both experimental and theoretical. The basic problem of learning theory is that, although behavior changes and improves, the process of learning itself is never observed. For this reason, psychologists have tried to determine the necessary and sufficient conditions for learning to take place, and have developed procedures to find out just what it is that a subject has learned.

Mathematical models of learning are a relatively recent development, and this discussion begins with work done by Estes and by Bush and Mosteller about 1950. Earlier work by Thurstone, published as early as 1919, is also used, however, and the basic theoretical work of Clark L. Hull exists as an inspiration to all who would attempt a definite and logically organized account of learning.

During the history of learning theory, many issues have been brought up and debated. Many issues are those of fact: Does a rat learn a place or a response? Can a response be conditioned without being performed? How broad is the "cognitive map"? What events are, in general, reinforcing? Other questions are broadly programmatic: Should learning theory explicate underlying physiological mechanisms? Should it refer only to observables such as stimuli and responses, or should it take into account states of mind, sensations, drives, and tensions? Should it be concerned with the simplest behavior of simple organisms, or attempt to handle socially significant behavior of humans?

The issues of learning theory that concern this book lie somewhere between factual questions and general programs; basically, they are those issues that concern the proper form of a learning theory. We have chosen, for this first chapter, to discuss several experiments on simple human learning, and to ask in each case whether the subject is accumulating habits, or replacing wrong tendencies by correct ones. Different situations may yield different answers. For example, learning a list of German vocabulary words seems to be mainly the accumulation of new associations, whereas correcting a golf swing is mainly a matter of replacing some movements with others. Still other problems in learning, such as teaching a child to read, may be some unknown mixture of accumulation and replacement.

It is likely that some experiments will produce replacement, some accumulation, others mixtures or even entirely different processes. A general decision among these possibilities will not be made, but instead four special experiments will be analyzed to determine which idea, replacement or accumulation, applies in each case. The methods developed in these analyses can be used in general to investigate the structure of interesting learning tasks.

This chapter is mainly a study of the learning curve, the simplest and oldest analysis of learning data. A learning curve gives a measure of performance P as a function of training time or trials n. Time is always a positive variable, which may be continuous or discrete. The dependent variable, performance, may be a measure of production, such as words typed per minute; it may be a physical measurement, such as strength or accuracy of response; it may be a clock measurement, such as rate or latency of response. Experiments using these different measures will be considered, but the fundamental measure is the probability of success. It is easiest to think of P as the probability of the correct response in a multiple-choice problem.

It is important to distinguish clearly between two different abstractions, each of which may be called a "learning curve." One is the empirical learning curve: the fraction of correct responses on each trial as calculated from a set of data. The other is the theoretical learning curve: a mathematical function P as derived from assumptions about the learning process. The discussion here will be based on theoretical curves. These provide useful summaries of learning processes if the assumptions used in the derivations are approximately correct.

Our first task is to present the basic mathematical ideas involved in a simple replacement model and a simple model of accumulative learning.

REPLACEMENT LEARNING[1]

In a replacement learning system, some habits or expectancies are replaced by others. The simple and ideal process of replacement leaves the total number of entities constant, and substitutes one for one.

---

[1] The model given here has been used widely. This version is equivalent to that of the linear operator model studied by R. R. Bush and F. Mosteller, *Stochastic Models for Learning* (New York: Wiley, 1955), and it is similar to stimulus sampling models like those applied by W. K. Estes and J. H. Straughan, Analysis of a Verbal Conditioning Situation in Terms of Statistical Learning Theory. (*J. Exp. Psych.*, 1954, **47**, pp. 225–234), and by C. J. Burke, W. K. Estes, and S. Hellyer, Rate of Verbal Conditioning in Relation to Stimulus Variability. (*J. Exp. Psych.*, 1954, **48**, pp. 153–161).

Habits, hypotheses, or stimulus elements may have many properties, but for present purposes it is possible to abstract the single property of leading to one or another response. Then the process of learning is summarized, in its quantitative aspects, by the number of elements of each type and the transfer of elements from one state to another. The transfers occurring in learning can be visualized easily by use of a model consisting of one or more urns and marbles, and calculations from such model correctly represent the flow of hypotheses or habits, provided that the necessary basic hypotheses hold, namely, hypotheses of random sampling.

Think of a subject in a learning experiment as having an urn containing red and white marbles. On each trial a marble is taken from the urn. If the marble taken is red, a correct response occurs; if it is white, there is an error. Let M be the total number of marbles in the urn. According to the replacement idea M is a constant, and learning is a process by which white marbles are replaced by red ones.

Call the subject's urn S, and suppose that there is a second urn E used by the experimenter. Suppose that the experimenter's urn has a very large number of marbles, and that it is an inexhaustible source of new habits or expectancies. A certain proportion a of the marbles in E are red, and this proportion does not change. If a is less than one, then the training process is imperfect and sometimes teaches errors.

We are now using a simple replacement learning process in which some number k of marbles are taken from S on each trial, discarded, and replaced with an equal number of marbles from the training process E. Suppose that the samples from S and E are chosen at random. Let R_n and W_n be the numbers of red and white marbles in S on trial n. Then, on the average, the marbles taken from S will include kR_n/M red marbles and kW_n/M white marbles. The marbles put into S will include ka red marbles and $k(1 - a)$ white ones. On trial $n + 1$, then, the number of red marbles will be

$$R_{n+1} = R_n - k\frac{R_n}{M} + ka, \tag{1}$$

on the average.

Suppose that k, the sample size, is 5, and that E consists of $a = 0.8$ red marbles, and $1 - a = 0.2$ white ones. On a certain trial, say, trial $n = 12$, let $R_n = 30$ and $W_n = 20$ so that $M = 50$. Then, on the average, the marbles taken from S include 5 times $R_n/M = 5(30/50) = 3$. The number of white marbles taken from S is 5 times $W_n/M = 5(20/50) = 2$. The marbles put into S include $ka = 5(0.8) = 4$ reds, and $k(1 - a) = 1$ white. Therefore on trial $n + 1 = 13$, there will be $R_{n+1} = 30 - 3 + 4 = 31$, and $W_{n+1} = 20 - 2 + 1 = 19$.

The probability of a correct response on trial n is equal to the proportion of red marbles in urn S;

$$P_n = \frac{R_n}{M}.$$

Therefore, dividing by M in Eq. (1),

$$P_{n+1} = \frac{R_{n+1}}{M} = \frac{R_n}{M} - \left(\frac{k}{M}\right)\left(\frac{R_n}{M}\right) + \left(\frac{k}{M}\right)a$$

$$= P_n - \left(\frac{k}{M}\right)P_n + \left(\frac{k}{M}\right)a.$$

If we let θ stand for the proportion sampled from S, k/M, then

$$P_{n+1} = (1 - \theta)P_n + \theta a. \tag{2}$$

Equation (2) provides the basis for what is called the linear model, since P_{n+1} is a linear function of P_n. There will be some initial level of performance, P_1, and there will be an asymptote of performance, P_∞. The asymptote will be equal to a.

One way to see this last point, that the asymptote equals a, is to realize that at asymptote the probability does not change with learning. Therefore, at asymptote, $P_{n+1} = P_n$ and this quantity may be called P. Then Eq. (2) becomes

$$P = (1 - \theta)P + \theta a,$$

whence, by simple rearrangement, $P = a$.

It is also important to see what happens over a sequence of trials. If all trials are alike, we can analyze a sequence by applying Eq. (1) repeatedly, each time to the result of the previous application. For simplicity we let $P_1 = 0$. Then

$$P_2 = (1 - \theta)P_1 + \theta a = \theta a,$$

$$P_3 = (1 - \theta)\theta a + \theta a = a(2\theta - \theta^2) = a[1 - (1 - \theta)^2],$$

$$P_4 = (1 - \theta)a[1 - (1 - \theta)^2] + \theta a.$$

All these results are consistent with the hypothesis that

$$P_n = a[1 - (1 - \theta)^{n-1}]. \tag{3}$$

This is true for P_2.

Now apply mathematical induction. Suppose that Eq. (3) is correct for some n. Then, according to Eq. (1),

$$P_{n+1} = (1 - \theta)a[1 - (1 - \theta)^{n-1}] + \theta a$$

$$= a[1 - (1 - \theta)^n].$$

This, however, is Eq. (3) with n replaced by $n + 1$. Therefore,[2] Eq. (3) must hold for all n.

Suppose that P_1 is not 0, but some other constant, say, b. Then

$$P_1 = b, \qquad P_2 = b + (a - b)\theta,$$

and, in general,

$$P_n = a - (a - b)(1 - \theta)^{n-1}. \tag{4}$$

This is the general solution to a single linear operation applied $n - 1$ times.

Application to Data

As an illustration, in an experiment by G. H. Bower,[3] college students learned to give the response "1" or "2" to each of a list of pairs of consonants by the method of *paired associates*. Since there were two responses, a subject should have probability 0.50 of being correct at the beginning of the experiment. Therefore, we let $b = 0.50$ by hypothesis. Further, since college students can be expected to master so simple a task perfectly after enough practice, the assumption may be made that $a = 1.0$. This specializes Eq. (4) and results in

$$P_n = 1 - \tfrac{1}{2}(1 - \theta)^{n-1}. \tag{5}$$

This formula is fairly simple in form, but contains an unknown parameter θ. (Note that n is not an unknown, but is the symbol denoting trials. The equation holds for all trials, but the value of θ for which it holds is still not known.)

A value of θ based on the data shall be selected. It would be nicer to have an hypothesis about θ, as was possible about a and b, but it usually happens that at least one parameter of a model is not known in advance. This parameter must be estimated from the data, and this involves fitting the model to at least some of the data at hand as closely as possible.

The present estimation makes the expected total correct responses, from the theoretical learning curve, equal the mean total correct responses made by subjects on the first N trials. To do this, a simple expression for the expected number of correct responses on trials $1, \ldots, N$ as a function of θ is necessary.

---

[2] The argument behind the inductive proof may be stated as follows. Since Eq. (3) holds for P_2, it then holds for an initial sequence of trials $1, 2, \ldots, m$ for some m. Suppose that it does *not* hold for all m. Then there must be a trial on which Eq. (3) is first incorrect. However, it has been proved that if Eq. (3) is correct on m, it also is correct on $m + 1$; hence $m + 1$ is not the trial on which Eq. (3) first fails to hold. But since m was chosen without restriction, there can be no trial on which Eq. (3) fails to hold.

[3] G. H. Bower, An application of a model to paired-associate learning. *Psychometrika*, 1961, **26**, pp. 255–280.

The expected, or theoretical mean number of correct responses on the first N trials is calculated as follows. The expected total correct on trials $1, \ldots, N$ is the sum of the expected correct on each trial:

$$E_T = E_1 + E_2 + \cdots + E_N.$$

The expected number of correct responses on trial N is, however, just the probability of a correct response, as given by Eq. (5). Thus

$$
\begin{aligned}
E_T &= P_1 + P_2 + \cdots + P_N \\
&= 1 - \tfrac{1}{2} + 1 - \tfrac{1}{2}(1 - \theta)^1 + 1 - \tfrac{1}{2}(1 - \theta)^2 + \cdots \\
&\quad + 1 - \tfrac{1}{2}(1 - \theta)^{N-1} \\
&= N - \tfrac{1}{2}[1 + (1 - \theta) + (1 - \theta)^2 + \cdots + (1 - \theta)^{N-1}].
\end{aligned}
$$

To reduce this further, let

$$S = 1 + (1 - \theta) + (1 - \theta)^2 + \cdots + (1 - \theta)^{N-1}$$

so that

$$E_T = N - \tfrac{1}{2}S.$$

Now,

$$S - (1 - \theta)S = 1 - (1 - \theta)^N,$$

for

$$S = 1 + (1 - \theta) + (1 - \theta)^2 + \cdots + (1 - \theta)^{N-1} \qquad \text{(From above)}$$

$$(1 - \theta)S = (1 - \theta) + (1 - \theta)^2 + \cdots + (1 - \theta)^{N-1} + (1 - \theta)^N$$

(Multiplying by $1 - \theta$)

$$\theta S = 1 - (1 - \theta)^N \qquad \text{(Subtracting)}$$

From this it follows that

$$S = \frac{1 - (1 - \theta)^N}{\theta}$$

and

$$E_T = N - \tfrac{1}{2}\frac{1 - (1 - \theta)^N}{\theta}.$$

In the empirical curve, Fig. 1.1, by trial $n = 11$, P_n is near 1.0. If so, Eq. (5) shows that the term $\tfrac{1}{2}(1 - \theta)^{11}$ is very small, and $(1 - \theta)^{11}$ can probably be neglected in an approximation. Then

$$E_T = N - \frac{1}{2\theta}.$$

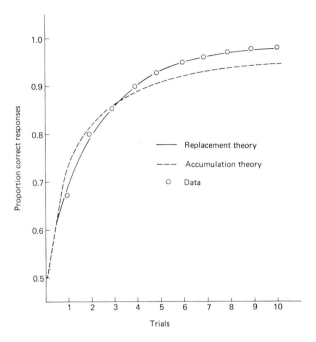

Figure 1.1

Although E_T is not known exactly, the goal is to choose a θ that makes E_T equal the obtained mean number correct, O_T. Setting

$$O_T = E_T, \qquad O_T = N - \frac{1}{2\theta},$$

and solving for θ, we have

$$\theta = \frac{1}{2(N - O_T)}. \tag{6}$$

Table 1.1 lists the results of Bower's experiment. The mean number correct over the 11 trials of the empirical data, given in Table 1.1, is

$$O_T = 9.5.$$

Substituting this value into Eq. (6), we have

$$\theta = 0.333.$$

Substituting this value into Eq. (5) yields the completely specified expression

$$P_n = 1 - \tfrac{1}{2}(1 - 0.333)^{n-1}.$$

This equation, calculated for $n = 1, 2, \ldots, 11$, yields the theoretical values of Table 1.1.

Because of the method of estimation, the theoretical curve must have the same total correct as the data; geometrically, the area under the theoretical curve will equal the area under the empirical curve. Since both start from about 0.50, and both approach 1.0 and have the same area, it is not surprising that they look much alike.

Table 1.1 Experimental learning curve and theoretical learning curve from the linear model [Data from Bower (1961)]

Trial	Observed proportion correct	Theoretical P_n
1	0.50	0.50
2	0.67	0.67
3	0.80	0.78
4	0.85	0.85
5	0.90	0.90
6	0.93	0.93
7	0.95	0.96
8	0.96	0.97
9	0.97	0.98
10	0.98	0.99
11	0.99	0.99

The preceding section gives a simple replacement theory and develops the corresponding urn scheme. The urn scheme led to a learning curve, and from that a formula for total errors. To compare the model with Bower's data on paired-associates learning, the learning-rate parameter θ was estimated by making the theory's expected total errors equal the observed total errors per item. The learning curve deduced from the theory follows the empirical learning curve closely. The alternative theory, that of accumulation, now receives a parallel study.

LEARNING AS ACCUMULATION[4]

In accumulative learning, habits or expectations are added to those that were there before. Consider two urns, S and E, as before. Recall that E contains an inexhaustible supply of marbles, a of which are red and lead to

[4] The model given here leads to the same learning curve as that given by L. L. Thurstone, The Learning Curve Equation (*Psychological Review Monograph Supplement*, 1919, **26**, No. 3). The assumptions are similar to those developed later by Thurstone in The Learning Function (*J. Gen. Psych.*, 1930, **3**, pp. 469–491). More recent work on this class of models has been done by R. D. Luce, and some of his results are given in *Individual Choice Behavior* (New York: Wiley, 1959).

correct responses. In the accumulation model, samples of marbles are moved from E to S, but no marbles are removed from S. Suppose that a constant number of marbles k are transferred on each trial. Then the number of red marbles will increase so that on the average,

$$R_{n+1} = R_n + ka.$$

Meanwhile, the number of white marbles also increases:

$$W_{n+1} = W_n + k(1 - a).$$

The proportion of red marbles in S is again assumed to be equal to P_n:

$$P_n = \frac{R_n}{R_n + W_n}.$$

At trial n, after $n - 1$ units of practice,

$$P_n = \frac{R_1 + (n - 1)ka}{R_1 + W_1 + (n - 1)k}. \tag{7}$$

Equation (7) can be put into a form that makes comparison with the linear model easy. First, divide the numerator and denominator by $R_1 + W_1$:

$$P_n = \frac{\dfrac{R_1}{R_1 + W_1} + \left(\dfrac{k}{R_1 + W_1}\right)a(n - 1)}{1 + \left(\dfrac{k}{R_1 + W_1}\right)(n - 1)}.$$

As before, let $b = P_1 = R_1/(R_1 + W_1)$. Also, let θ be related to the rate parameter k: $\theta = k/(R_1 + W_1)$. Now,

$$P_n = \frac{b + \theta a(n - 1)}{1 + \theta(n - 1)}, \tag{8}$$

which can be compared with Eq. (4) for the linear model. As with the linear model, the asymptote of performance is a. This can be shown by dividing the numerator and denominator by $n - 1$. This gives

$$P_n = \frac{\dfrac{b}{n - 1} + \theta a}{\dfrac{1}{n - 1} + \theta}.$$

As n increases, $b/(n-1)$ and $1/(n-1)$ decrease toward zero. Therefore, in the limit,

$$P_\infty = \frac{\theta a}{\theta} = a.$$

The two theories thus give learning curves starting at b and approaching an asymptote equal to a. They differ, however, in the form of the curve between b and a.

Application to Data

We will now apply the accumulative model to the data of Bower's experiment, used before to illustrate the replacement model. As in the replacement model, let $P_1 = \frac{1}{2}$. When $n = 1$,

$$P_1 = \frac{R_1}{R_1 + W_1},$$

so if P_1 is $\frac{1}{2}$, $R_1 = W_1$. Further, the terminal level of performance in the Bower experiment should be 1, so let $a = 1$. This gives a special case of Eq. (8), namely,

$$P_n = \frac{0.50 + (n-1)\theta}{1.0 + (n-1)\theta}. \tag{9}$$

The next problem is to estimate θ.

A value of θ can be selected that makes the mean of the theoretical function P_n on trials $1, \ldots, N$ equal to the observed mean, as was done for the linear replacement model. Again the expected total correct is just the sum of P_n, and

$$E_T = \sum_{n=1}^{N} P_n$$

$$= 0.50 + \frac{0.50 + \theta}{1 + \theta} + \cdots + \frac{0.50 + (N-1)\theta}{1 + (N-1)\theta}. \tag{10}$$

Unfortunately this summation does not yield to any simple solution. The common denominator is very complex, so computing the sum in compact form to give an estimate of θ will be difficult.

A simple approach is to insert trial values of θ in Eq. (10) to find a value that produces the correct result. The obtained mean correct response is 9.50, and a few trial calculations lead to the value $\hat{\theta} \approx 0.93$. Using this value in Eq. (9), the predictions given in Table 1.2 are obtained. The accumulative theory seems not to agree with the data as well as the replacement theory shown in Table 1.1. Both sets of predictions and the empirical learning curve are shown in Fig. 1.1.

The nature of the difference between the theories is interesting. In the accumulative theory, the change in performance tends to be quite rapid early

Table 1.2 **Bower data and accumulation theory**

Trials	Observed	Predicted
1	0.50	0.50
2	0.67	0.74
3	0.80	0.84
4	0.85	0.87
5	0.90	0.89
6	0.93	0.91
7	0.95	0.92
8	0.96	0.93
9	0.97	0.94
10	0.98	0.95
11	0.99	0.95

in training since not many habits have accumulated at that point. However, later in training many habits are accumulated, and the addition of a constant number per trial makes a smaller difference in the proportion of correct habits. Thus the accumulative curve rises relatively sharply at the beginning, and relatively slowly at the end of practice. In the situation studied here, the initial rise in the accumulative curve is too sharp, and the curve is not high enough at the end. In this situation, the course of improvement is described better by a theory that implies a constant rate of approach to the asymptote. (See Exercises 6 and 7 for expansion of this point.)

STATISTICAL COMPARISON OF MODELS*

The difference in goodness of fit between the two theories does not seem very large, though it seems evident which is better. Realize, though, that the data points are randomly variable—if the experiment were repeated exactly, the data points would not fall exactly at the same values. Therefore, there is some uncertainty as to whether the replacement theory is really better than the accumulation theory.

This situation would be somewhat better if an objective measure of the goodness-of-fit of the two theories were available—something better than mere visual judgment. The question is asked as to whether one theory agrees as well with the data as another theory, and raises an important question about the estimation of parameters. Recall that for the linear model θ was estimated by matching the mean proportion correct of the theoretical and experimental learning curves. With θ estimated in this way, the replacement theory gave an excellent fit to the data. Similarly, a value of θ was found in Eq. (10) so that the theoretical accumulation learning curve had a mean value equal to the observed mean correct trials. It might be that for one theory, an estimate which matches mean values of the theoretical and experimental learning curves results in about as good an overall fit as can be achieved, but for another theory the technique of matching mean values is not very efficient for producing good overall fits. The comparison should be a fair one, and that means that each theoretical learning curve must be calculated with parameter values that give the theory a good chance to agree with the data.

The problem is to obtain optimal estimates of parameters, that is, estimates which make the agreement of each theory with data as good as the theory permits. The problem becomes well defined only when an index is specified by which the agreement between the theory and the data will be measured. In the case of the learning curve, a natural index is the sum of squared deviations between the theoretical and experimental curves. For each trial n, define a discrepancy

$$D_n = P_n - O_n,$$

where P_n is a point on the theoretical learning curve and O_n is the corresponding point on the experimental curve. If a theory agrees well with a set of data, then $\sum_n D_n^2$ will be small. The method of *least-squares estimation* is simply the selection of a set of parameter values which will yield the smallest possible value of $\sum D_n^2$. If least-squares estimates for the parameters of two theories are obtained, then each theory has been given the best possible chance to fit the data, at least with respect to the criterion of the summed squared deviations. Then if one theory has a much higher value of $\sum D_n^2$ than the other, a reason for choosing the better-fitting theory is indicated.

Now to return to the case at hand. It would be good to compare the linear substitutive model and the simple accumulative model, using the data from Bower's experimental learning curve. For each theory, it is necessary to use parameters which give the best fit in the sense of least-squared deviations. Thus, for the accumulation theory, we minimize the function

$$\Delta = \sum_n \left[\frac{b + (n-1)a\theta}{1 + (n-1)\theta} - O_n \right]^2. \tag{11}$$

That is, values of b, θ, and a need to be found that will give the smallest possible value of Δ. Similarly, for the linear model we must minimize the function

$$\Delta = \sum_n \left([a - (a - b)(1 - \theta)^{n-1}] - O_n \right)^2. \tag{12}$$

At this point it is necessary to comment briefly on the technology of estimation. In the earlier estimation of θ for the linear model, we could obtain an easy formula for estimating θ for any mean number correct that might be obtained. However, θ was estimated for the accumulative model by trial and error. In the earlier discussion, a value of θ was needed that would make the theory agree with the data in mean number correct. Now a somewhat more complicated criterion exists. There are cases where the method of least squares leads to simple algebraic formulas to use in calculating parameter estimates, as was true for the earlier estimate in the linear model. However, this is not true in general, and the present examples involve two cases where convenient expressions cannot be derived.

It is necessary to find optimal parameter values by trial and error. This was not hard with a single parameter, but now there are three. It would be impractical in the extreme to try to find values of three parameters giving the minimum value of Δ using hand calculation. The solution is to use a computer to do the job. Computer methods are now available which make it quite easy to find the desired parameter values. Many different values of the parameters are tried, and for each combination the corresponding value of Δ is calculated. The parameter values finally selected are those that give the lowest value of Δ.

One efficient computer program that was available for use by the authors was written by John P. Chandler and is titled STEPIT.[5] This program was used to select parameter values yielding minimum values of Δ for each of the two theories discussed here. In the accumulation theory, the parameter values giving the best fit to the learning curve were

$$\hat{a} = 1.0, \qquad \hat{b} = 0.48, \qquad \hat{\theta} = 0.93.$$

The sum of squared deviations obtained with these parameters was

$$\Delta = 0.011.$$

It seemed most interesting to compare the theories by estimating all the parameters of both of them. Therefore we fit the linear replacement model to the data with all three of its parameter values free to vary. In the linear model, all three of the parameters are probabilities, so they were limited to values in the unit interval. The estimates were

$$\hat{a} = 0.99, \qquad \hat{b} = 0.50, \qquad \hat{\theta} = 0.36.$$

The minimum value of Δ which corresponds to these estimates is

$$\Delta = 0.00042.$$

---

[5] The program will find values of up to 20 parameters which minimize any smooth function. The program is written in FORTRAN and can be obtained by writing to Quantum Chemistry Program Exchange, Indiana University, Bloomington, Indiana, 47401. Request Program QCPE 66.

The theoretical learning curves obtained with these optimal parameters are not noticeably different from those graphed in Fig. 1.1. The graph makes it clear that the replacement theory fits the results better than the accumulative theory. This is also reflected in the large difference between the minimum values of Δ. It is possible to be confident now that the better fit obtained with the replacement model was not the result of a statistical artifact that made the estimation method work to the advantage of the replacement theory.

Application: Learning to Type*

The comparison of replacement with accumulative theories based on simple paired-associate learning may not be a fair test of the accumulative theory. The idea behind the theory involves an accumulation of habits, and there seems to be little that can accumulate in the learning of a simple association.

In his original presentation of the accumulation model, L. L. Thurstone[6] analyzed the learning curve obtained for 55 students learning to type. On the face of it, skill at typing seems a more promising application of accumulative theory than paired-associate learning, since typing involves a complex combination of habits and responses.

In a typing class, practice does not occur on fixed trials as it does in a paired-associate learning experiment. Instead, each student works at his own rate, and different students practice different amounts in the same period of time. In Thurstone's analysis, the unit of practice was considered to be a typed page. After every 10 pages of practice, each student had a test to measure how well he could type, and performance was measured in words typed per minute.

It is necessary to think of the learning process in a new way to correspond to the changes in learning method and form of data. The main change involves going from fixed trials to practice taking place in free time.

Think of an urn S containing red and white marbles, as before, but assume now that sampling occurs very rapidly. When a white marble is drawn, there is a wrong response or nothing happens (time simply elapses), whereas when a red marble is drawn a correct response occurs. Let π be the probability of a correct response during any unit of time. Then π is equal to the proportion of red marbles in the urn. If the system is observed for m intervals, then the number of responses observed should be $m\pi$.

Now a learning assumption for the accumulative model is given. Suppose that during the performance of one unit of practice, a number of marbles k are added to urn S from another urn E. As before, E contains a very large number of marbles, and α is the proportion of red marbles in E. After typing $n - 1$ units of practice, the numbers of red and white marbles will be

---

[6] The analysis is given in Thurstone's 1919 article, cited earlier.

approximately equal to

$$R_n = R_1 + k\alpha(n - 1),$$
$$W_n = W_1 + k(1 - \alpha)(n - 1),$$

and the proportion of red marbles will be

$$\pi_n = \frac{R_n}{R_n + W_n} = \frac{R_1 + k\alpha(n - 1)}{R_1 + W_1 + k(n - 1)},$$

just as in Eq. (7).

Now, however, a proportion of correct responses is not directly observed, but instead the performance measure P is the rate of correct responding per unit of time. But then,

$$P_n = m\pi_n = m\left(\frac{R_1 + k\alpha(n - 1)}{R_1 + W_1 + k(n - 1)}\right)$$

$$= \frac{m\left(\dfrac{R_1}{R_1 + W_1}\right) + \left(\dfrac{k}{R_1 + W_1}\right)m\alpha(n - 1)}{1 + \left(\dfrac{k}{R_1 + W_1}\right)(n - 1)}. \tag{13}$$

The initial rate is

$$b = m\left(\frac{R_1}{R_1 + W_1}\right),$$

and the asymptotic rate is

$$a = m\alpha.$$

This last point is proved by dividing every term of Eq. (13) by $n - 1$, then taking the limit as $n \to \infty$.

As before, let $\theta = k/(R_1 + W_1)$. Then substitution in Eq. (13) gives Eq. (8), the learning curve for the accumulative model. But now the performance measure is a rate of responding, and the parameters b and a also refer to rates of responding.

For the replacement model, just assume that during each unit of practice k marbles are taken from urn S and replaced by a sample of k marbles from urn E. An argument just like the one given above will show that Eq. (4) applies, but with P_n, a, and b interpreted as rates of responding rather than probabilities. (The student is asked to give the argument as Exercise 14.)

The data are presented in Fig. 1.2, along with theoretical curves calculated from Eqs. (4) and (8) for the accumulative and replacement theories, respectively. The parameters for the theoretical curves were estimated by the

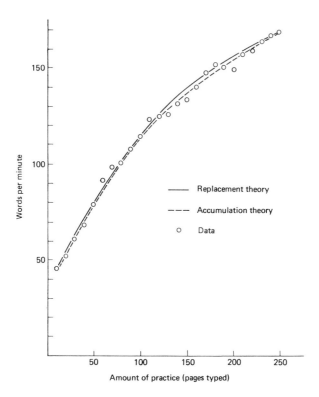

Figure 1.2

least-squares method, using the computer program mentioned previously. The parameter values for the accumulative model were

$$a = 216.8, \qquad b = 26.8, \qquad \theta = 0.0068.$$

For the replacement model, the parameter values were

$$a = 163.0, \qquad b = 0.3, \qquad \theta = 0.0080.$$

As Fig. 1.2 shows, the two theories fit the data about equally well. The minimum sums of squared deviations were nearly the same: 85.2 for the accumulative theory, and 97.8 for the replacement theory. Therefore the criterion of goodness of fit does not help us decide which theory is more accurate.

However, there is another basis for choosing between the models. If the accumulation theory is correct for these data, then the asymptotic level of performance is over 200 words per minute. This is quite unreasonable; 150

words per minute is considered expert, and 200 words per minute is faster than the winning speeds in most speed competitions. The value of the asymptote estimated for the linear replacement model is much more reasonable, and to that extent the replacement theory gives a better account of these data.

It is necessary to resort to consideration of the parameter values, because not enough observations were taken to produce a detectable difference between the theoretical curves for the time of the study. In the paired-associate experiment, practice was continued until the subjects knew all the items. Then in order to agree with the relatively slow rate of change in P in early trials, the accumulative theory predicted a curve which was considerably below the data on later trials. For the typing task, data are not available to show what the limit of performance was. Therefore each theory can be made to fit the data quite well by an adjustment of parameter values. However, in the accumulative theory, the good fit is obtained at the cost of having an unreasonably high estimated asymptote of performance.

AN ALTERNATIVE FORM OF THE LEARNING CURVE*

We have considered both response probability and response rate as a function of amount of practice. In Bower's experiment, the unit of practice was fixed in the experiment, so the amount of practice was equal to the number of trials. However, in the application involving learning to type, the amount of practice depended on the subjects' performance, so the amount of practice and the time spent did not correspond in a simple way. In the typing case, as is usually true when practice occurs in free time, a unit of practice took a relatively long time earlier in training and a shorter time as the subject became more expert.

Thurstone's typing data were presented with performance plotted against amount of practice, a form that is convenient for the theory. However, in many experiments it is more convenient to plot performance against time spent practicing. We will now derive expressions for the learning curve in this alternative form, based on the assumptions of the simple replacement model and the simple accumulative model that has been under study. The derivations are somewhat more complicated than those given before, and approximate methods are needed.

To begin, the time to perform a response as a function of P, the performance measure, is given. As in the preceding section, suppose that a marble is sampled from an urn at fixed short intervals of time. If a red marble is sampled at the beginning of an interval, a correct response occurs during that interval. If a white marble is sampled, a correct response does not occur during that interval. Let π be the proportion of red marbles in the urn. Let x be the number of intervals which elapse before the response is completed. (That is, x includes the interval in which a red marble is sampled.) It is shown in Chapter 2 that the probability distribution of x is

$$P(x = j) = (1 - \pi)^{j-1}\pi,$$

and the mean value of x is

$$E(x) = 1/\pi.$$

Now let δ be the amount of time per sampling interval, and let Δt_n be the time taken between the nth and the $n + 1$ correct responses. Then the average value of Δt_n is

$$\Delta t_n = \frac{\delta}{\pi_n},$$

where π_n is the proportion of red marbles in the urn after the nth correct response.

Two measures of performance have been considered: probability and rate of response. In each case, Δt_n can be considered as

$$\Delta t_n = \frac{c}{P_n}. \tag{14}$$

When response probability is being measured, $P_n = \pi_n$, so $c = \delta$. When response rate per unit of time is being measured, $P_n = m\pi_n$, so $c = \delta/m$.

Now for the replacement theory.[7] Let a unit of practice be the performance of a single correct response, so that P_n is the value of the performance measure after $n - 1$ correct responses have occurred. From Eq. (2),

$$P_{n+1} = P_n + \theta(a - P_n).$$

The average rate of change in P per unit of practice is

$$\frac{\Delta P}{\Delta n} = \frac{P_{n+1} - P_n}{(n + 1) - n} = \theta(a - P).$$

And the average increment of time per unit of practice is

$$\frac{\Delta t}{\Delta n} = \frac{c}{P}.$$

Dividing the increment in P per unit of practice by the corresponding

---

[7] The derivation given here follows closely the one given by W. K. Estes, *Toward a Statistical Theory of Learning*, *Psych. Rev.*, 1950, **57**, 94–107.

increment in t per unit of practice, we have

$$\frac{\Delta P}{\Delta t} = \left(\frac{\Delta P}{\Delta n}\right)\left(\frac{\Delta n}{\Delta t}\right) = \frac{\theta(a - P)P}{c}. \tag{15}$$

Now invoke an approximation. Equation (15) is correct for discrete units of time, and ΔP and Δt are both considered as averages. If very small intervals of time are considered, the change in P per unit of time will correspond to the quantity given in Eq. (15):

$$\frac{dP}{dt} = \lim_{\Delta t \to 0} \frac{P_{t+\Delta t} - P_t}{\Delta t} = \frac{\theta(a - P_t)P_t}{c}. \tag{16}$$

With this assumption, Eq. (15) becomes a differential equation. It has the general solution

$$t = \frac{c}{a\theta} \log \left(\frac{P}{a - P}\right) + k, \tag{17}$$

which can be verified by differentiating Eq. (17) with respect to t:

$$\frac{dt}{dt} = \frac{c}{a\theta}\left[\frac{d}{dt} \log P_t - \frac{d}{dt} \log (a - P_t)\right] + \frac{d}{dt} k,$$

$$1 = \frac{c}{a\theta}\left[\frac{1}{P_t} \frac{d}{dt} P_t - \frac{1}{a - P_t} \frac{d}{dt} (-P_t)\right] + 0.$$

From Eq. (16), we have

$$\frac{d}{dt} P_t = \frac{\theta(a - P_t)P_t}{c},$$

$$1 = \frac{c}{a\theta}\left[\frac{1}{P_t} + \frac{1}{a - P_t}\right]\frac{\theta(a - P_t)P_t}{c},$$

$$1 = 1.$$

It is necessary to have an expression in terms of the parameters a, θ, and b. Recall that b is the initial performance measure—that is, the value of P when t is zero. Then, setting $t = 0$ and $P_t = b$ in Eq. (17),

$$-k = \frac{c}{a\theta} \log \left(\frac{b}{a - b}\right),$$

and then, replacing k in Eq. (17) by the new value just derived,

$$t + \frac{c}{a\theta} \log \left(\frac{b}{a - b}\right) = \frac{c}{a\theta} \log \left(\frac{P_t}{a - P_t}\right). \tag{18}$$

This can be put into more convenient form by multiplying both sides by $a\theta/c$ and rearranging to yield

$$\left(\frac{a\theta}{c}\right)t + \log\left(\frac{b}{a-b}\right) = \log\left(\frac{P_t}{a-P_t}\right).$$

Taking exponentials of both sides, we have

$$e^{(a\theta/c)t}e^{\log[b/(a-b)]} = e^{\log[P_t/(a-P_t)]},$$

and since $e^{\log x} = x$,

$$\frac{P_t}{a-P_t} = \frac{b}{a-b}\,e^{(a\theta/c)t}.$$

Rearranging terms, we obtain

$$P_t = \frac{a}{1 + [(a-b)/b] - e^{(a\theta/c)t}}. \tag{19}$$

This belongs to a special family of growth curves called the family of logistic functions, and is the explicit learning curve relating the rate P_t to the total time t.

The next step is to derive the expression corresponding to Eq. (18) using the accumulative theory. This begins with the rate of change in t per unit of practice:

$$\frac{\Delta t}{\Delta n} = \frac{c}{P_t}.$$

Now, substitute using Eq. (8), the learning curve for P: (Recall that t_n is the time for the $n+1$ response.)

$$\frac{\Delta t}{\Delta n} = \frac{c(1 + \theta n)}{b + a\theta n}. \tag{20}$$

Equation (20) gives the average amount of time added by the $n+1$ correct response. The total time consumed by the first n responses is

$$t_n = \sum_{i=0}^{n-1} \frac{c(1 + \theta i)}{b + a\theta i}.$$

If every term, numerator and denominator, is divided by $a\theta$, and the term $cb/a\theta$ is both added and subtracted from the numerator,

$$t_n = \sum_{i=0}^{n-1} \frac{c[i + (b/a\theta) + (a-b)/a\theta]}{a[i + (b/a\theta)]};$$

separating out the term $i + (b/a\theta)$,

$$t_n = \sum_{i=0}^{n-1} \left[\frac{c}{a} + \frac{c(a-b)}{a^2\theta[i + (b/a\theta)]} \right]$$

$$= \frac{nc}{a} + \frac{c(a-b)}{a} \sum_{i=0}^{n-1} \frac{1}{b + a\theta i}.$$

The sum is unpleasant, but an approximate answer is obtained by substituting x for i and taking the integral:

$$t_n = \frac{cn}{a} + \frac{c(a-b)}{a} \int_0^{n-1} \frac{1}{b + a\theta x} \, dx$$

$$= \frac{cn}{a} + \frac{c(a-b)}{a^2\theta} \log\left(1 + \frac{a\theta(n-1)}{b}\right) \tag{21}$$

if $b \neq 0$. Equation (21) relates total time to total practice. To relate time to performance, return to Eq. (8) and solve for n:

$$n = \frac{P - b}{\theta(a - P)} + 1.$$

Substituting into Eq. (21), we have

$$t = \frac{c}{a\theta}\left\{\frac{P-b}{a-P} + \theta + \frac{a-b}{a} \log\left[\frac{P(a-b)}{b(a-P)}\right]\right\}. \tag{22}$$

Equation (22) is not pleasant, by any means, but it can be computed.

Investigation of the derivatives of Eqs. (19) and (22) shows that in both theories the learning curve expressed as a function of time or fixed trials (with varying amounts of practice per trial) is monotonically increasing, but with positive acceleration early in the learning process. An initial interval of positive acceleration often appears in experimental learning curves, especially those involving complex tasks. For example, Thurstone presented the data from his typing study, showing words per minute as a function of weeks of practice. Figure 1.3 has these data, along with the curves obtained from Eqs. (19) and (22). The parameters for the theoretical curves were those obtained in fitting the data in the other form, which probably accounts for the seeming poorer fits in this case. The important point is the different appearance of the curves, attributable not to a change in the data, but only to a change in the manner of graphing.

Application to a Tracking Task

As a final example, we apply the results just obtained to an experiment on sensory-motor learning. In the experiment, a rotating target is presented to a subject who has a stylus which he uses to track the target. His success is

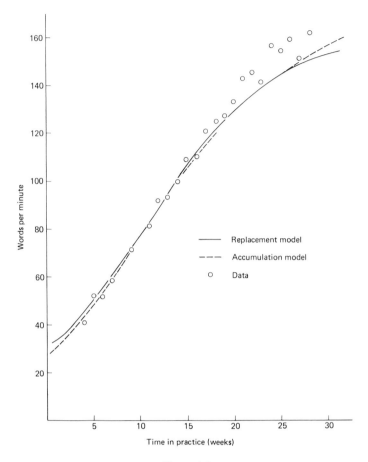

Figure 1.3

measured in terms of the amount or percentage of time that his stylus is in contact with the rotating target. (The data were taken from an experiment by Bilodeau and Rosenquist.[8])

The data are presented in Fig. 1.4, and are again compared with the learning curves derived from the two theories [Eqs. (19) and (22)]. The parameter values were estimated by the least-squares method, as before. The parameter values and resulting sum of squared deviations for the replacement theory were

$$a = 0.810, \qquad b = 0.403, \qquad \theta = 0.00933,$$
$$c = 6.57, \qquad \Delta = 0.00099.$$

---

[8] I. McD. Bilodeau and H. S. Rosenquist, Supplementary Feedback in Rotary-Pursuit Tracking, *J. Exp. Psych.*, 1964, **68**, pp. 53–57.

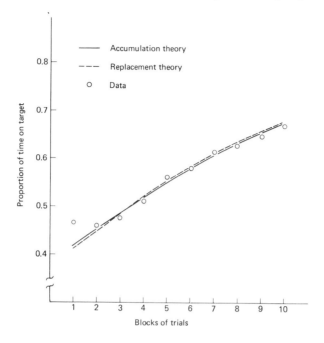

Figure 1.4

For the accumulative theory the parameters and Δ were

$$a = 0.999, \quad b = 0.397, \quad \theta = 0.00804,$$

$$c = 7.2, \quad \Delta = 0.0011.$$

Again, goodness of fit does not help us decide between the theories. However, the parameter values indicate a reason for choosing the replacement theory here as in the typing data. The problem for the accumulation theory again involves the limit a. It would be surprising if subjects in a tracking experiment achieved performance as nearly perfect as that estimated as the limit of the performance for the accumulative theory.

COMPLEX TRAINING SEQUENCES

Thus far, the evidence seems to be slightly in favor of the replacement theory. However, an important factual issue, such as whether simple learning is accumulative or by replacement, should not be decided on the basis of small quantitative differences if it is possible to obtain clearer data.

There is a central difference between the concepts of accumulation and replacement. An accumulation process becomes "stiffer," more resistant to change, as elements accumulate. A replacement process, keeping always the same number of elements, does not stiffen with training. This means that if a subject is trained for a long time to respond in one way, and then the situation is changed so that a different response is appropriate, the two theories would lead to quite different expectations. According to the accumulative theory, the initial training would make the subject resistant to change, and adjustment to the new schedule would be slow and difficult. According to the replacement theory, the only way the initial training can interfere with learning the second phase is to start the second response at a low probability.

To pursue this line of argument, analysis of the learning curve needs to be expanded to consider changes of experimental procedure in various segments of training.

In one kind of experiment, one procedure is used for a block of trials, and then the procedure is shifted. Separate learning-curve equations can be derived and applied to the various segments of training. For example, if a response is established and then extinguished, a second learning curve which continues in the negative direction is introduced at the beginning of extinction.

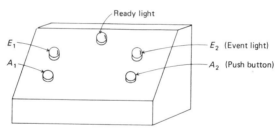

Figure 1.5

In another kind of experiment there are two or more types of trials interspersed randomly. For example, in a *partial reinforcement* experiment, conditioning and extinction trials are interspersed. An important case of this procedure is called probability learning, or a *prediction* experiment. The subject is seated before a panel with two lights, two push buttons, and a ready light, as shown in Fig. 1.5. On each trial the subject must predict which light will come on next. The assumption is that when the light on the left (reinforcing event E_1) comes on, the tendency to push the button on the left (response alternative A_1) is strengthened; similarly, event E_2 strengthens the tendency to push button A_2.

In this chapter we will analyze probability learning at face value, as an example of the mixture of two kinds of reinforcing events. An alternative possibility is that subjects turn the procedure into an elaborate form of problem-solving, as will be discussed in Chapter 3.

In analyzing experiments with mixed procedures, assume that each type of trial leads to a characteristic change in performance. Before, the effect of a trial was thought of as taking k marbles from an urn E and either adding them to the subject's urn S or having them replace k marbles from S. Now suppose there are two urns, E_1 and E_2, corresponding to the two types of trials. There are red and white marbles, as before; the proportion of red marbles in E_1 is a_1, and the proportion of red marbles in E_2 is a_2. Further, it is possible that different numbers of marbles will come from the two urns. When E_1 is used, k_1 marbles are taken, and when E_2 is used, the number of marbles is k_2.

Mixed Events in the Replacement Theory

Suppose that learning is accomplished by replacement. On trials when E_1 is used,

$$R_{n+1} = R_n - P_n k_1 + a_1 k_1,$$

$$W_{n+1} = W_n - (1 - P_n)k_1 + (1 - a_1)k_1.$$

On trials when E_2 is used,

$$R_{n+1} = R_n - P_n k_2 + a_2 k_2,$$

$$W_{n+1} = W_n - (1 - P_n)k_2 + (1 - a_2)k_2.$$

Then after E_1 is used,

$$P = \frac{R_{n+1}}{R_{n+1} + W_{n+1}} = \frac{R_n - P_n k_1 + a_1 k_1}{R_n + W_n}.$$

Define

$$\theta_1 = \frac{k_1}{R_n + W_n},$$

and since $R_n + W_n$ is a constant in the replacement model,

$$P_{n+1} = (1 - \theta_1)P_n + \theta_1 a_1. \tag{23}$$

A similar argument shows that after E_2 trials,

$$P_{n+1} = (1 - \theta_2)P_n + \theta_2 a_2. \tag{24}$$

Equations (23) and (24) are to be applied depending on the E event, and the point to be studied is the effect of a sequence of such applications. As attention shifts from trials (n) to the effects of particular trial events, it is helpful to think of Eqs. (23) and (24) as *operators* acting on a variable P. The general equation is written:

$$P = o(P),$$

and there are two linear operators, o_1 and o_2;

$$o_1(P) = (1 - \theta_1)P + \theta_1 a_1$$

is applied on type-1 trials, and

$$o_2(P) = (1 - \theta_2)P + \theta_2 a_2$$

is applied on type-2 trials.

The operator notation gives a convenient description of a sequence of trials. If the first trial of a series is of type 1, then

$$P_2 = o_1(P_1) = (1 - \theta_1)P_1 + \theta_1 a_1.$$

If the next trial is of type 1 also, then

$$P_3 = o_1(P_2) = o_1(o_1(P_1))$$
$$= (1 - \theta_1)[(1 - \theta_1)P_1 + \theta_1 a_1] + \theta_1 a_1.$$

If the third trial is of type 2, then

$$P_4 = o_2(P_3) = o_2(o_1(o_1(P_1)))$$
$$= (1 - \theta_2)\{(1 - \theta_1)[(1 - \theta_1)P_1 + \theta_1 a_1] + \theta_1 a_1\} + \theta_2 a_2.$$

In experiments involving a mixture of events, there are many possible arrangements of events in the sequence. The complexity of the problem is seen when it is recognized that at, say, trial 20, there are $2^{20} = 1,048,576$ different possible arrangements of type-1 and type-2 trials. A simplification to reduce the difficulty of calculation would be very desirable.

One simplification is possible if the operators are commutative. Operators o_1 and o_2 are said to be commutative if for all P, $o_1(o_2(P)) = o_2(o_1(P))$. For example, the addition of several different numbers is commutative. Let r_1 and r_2 be operators defined as

$$r_1(P) = P + 3, \qquad r_2(P) = P + 5.$$

Now,

$$r_1(r_2(P)) = (P + 5) + 3 = P + 8$$

and

$$r_2(r_1(P)) = (P + 3) + 5 = P + 8,$$

so r_1 and r_2 are commutative.

However, let $r_3(P) = P^2$. Then

$$r_1(r_3(P)) = P^2 + 3$$

and

$$r_3(r_1(P)) = (P + 3)^2 = P^2 + 6P + 9,$$

so r_1 and r_3 are not commutative.

Two linear operators commute if (a) one or the other θ-value is zero, or (b) the asymptotes are equal, $a_1 = a_2$. The first is easy to see intuitively, for if $\theta_1 = 0$, operator o_1 is just an identity operator, $o_1(P) = P$. It does not matter how an identity operation, which changes nothing, is mixed with another operation. If θ_1 and θ_2 are positive, then

$$o_2(o_1(P)) = (1 - \theta_2)(1 - \theta_1)P + (1 - \theta_2)\theta_1 a_1 + \theta_2 a_2$$
$$= (1 - \theta_1)(1 - \theta_2)P + \theta_1 a_1 + \theta_2 a_2 + \theta_1 \theta_2 a_1, \qquad (25)$$

$$o_1(o_2(P)) = (1 - \theta_1)(1 - \theta_2)P + (1 - \theta_1)\theta_2 a_2 + \theta_1 a_1$$
$$= (1 - \theta_1)(1 - \theta_2)P + \theta_1 a_1 + \theta_2 a_2 + \theta_1 \theta_2 a_2.$$

These expressions are equal except for their last terms, $\theta_1 \theta_2 a_1$ and $\theta_1 \theta_2 a_2$; hence they are equal if $\theta_1 = 0$, $\theta_2 = 0$ or if $a_1 = a_2$.

If o_1 and o_2 commute, then the value of any expression like

$$o_1 o_1 o_2 o_1 o_2 o_2 o_1(P)$$

is unchanged if any two operators are interchanged. By a series of such interchanges the expression can be transformed into a segregated form,

$$o_1 o_1 o_1 o_1 o_2 o_2 o_2(P),$$

which can be written

$$o_1^4 o_2^3(P).$$

In the linear replacement theory, this holds only if o_1 and o_2 have the same asymptote, or if one of the operators is an identity operator.

Mixed Events in the Accumulation Theory

In the accumulative model, marbles are taken from E_1 or E_2 and put into S, and none are removed from S. Then after an E_1 trial,

$$R_{n+1} = R_n + k_1 a_1, \qquad W_{n+1} = W_n + k_1(1 - a_1). \qquad (26)$$

And after an E_2 trial,

$$R_{n+1} = R_n + k_2 a_2, \qquad W_{n+1} = W_n + k_2(1 - a_2). \tag{27}$$

Then after n_1 trials using E_1 and n_2 trials using E_2, the probability of response will be

$$P_{n_1+n_2+1} = \frac{R_1 + n_1 k_1 a_1 + n_2 k_2 a_2}{R_1 + W_1 + n_1 k_1 + n_2 k_2}.$$

Letting

$$\theta_1 = \frac{k_1}{R_1 + W_1}, \qquad \theta_2 = \frac{k_2}{R_1 + W_1},$$

we obtain

$$P_{n_1+n_2+1} = \frac{P_1 + a_1 \theta_1 n_1 + a_2 \theta_2 n_2}{1 + \theta_1 n_1 + \theta_2 n_2}. \tag{28}$$

It is easy to see that the order of presenting the two types of trials is irrelevant. In other words, the accumulative theory implies that the effects of two kinds of trials will be commutative in general.

Random Sequences and Average Operators

A common procedure in the *prediction* experiment mentioned above is to use a random sequence of the two lights with some fixed probability π of the E_1 light. We first give the analysis in terms of the replacement theory. We construct the learning curve operator from

$$o(P) = \begin{cases} o_1(P) & \text{with probability } \pi, \\ \text{or} & \\ o_2(P) & \text{with probability } 1 - \pi. \end{cases}$$

The mean operator is, therefore,

$$\overline{o(P)} = \pi o_1(P) + (1 - \pi) o_2(P)$$

$$= \pi(1 - \theta_1)P + \pi\theta_1 a_1 + (1 - \pi)(1 - \theta_2)P + (1 - \pi)\theta_2 a_2. \tag{29}$$

This formula uses two asymptotes, a_1 and a_2. Note that if trials of the first type were given repeatedly, the behavior would stabilize near a_1. In simple probability-learning experiments, trials of the first type are trials in which the left light, E_1, comes on all the time. As everyone would expect, if E_1 comes on for any large number of uninterrupted trials, the probability of response A_1 increases toward 1.0. The conclusion is that $a_1 = 1.0$. Similarly, if the right light comes on all the time, the probability of the response A_1 goes to zero; that is, $a_2 = 0.0$. Assume further that $\theta_1 = \theta_2 = \theta$. Inserting these values in Eq. (29), we have

$$\overline{o(P)} = (1 - \theta)P + \theta\pi.$$

This appears to be a linear operator on P, but all is not so simple. The value of P in the right-hand side is a single value; its value on the left-hand side is an average. If P is known, the mean of $o(P)$ can be computed. However, this process cannot be repeated over and over to derive the learning curve, because it is not yet known how to apply this operator to the mean of a distribution of values of P.

In the experiment in question, all is well, but this must be proved. Suppose that in some way, various subjects have been scattered (perhaps by random pretraining) so that a proportion f_i of them are at performance level P_i. Then with probability f_i,

$$\overline{o(P_i)} = (1 - \theta)P_i + \theta\pi.$$

Now take the expectation[9] of both sides and obtain

$$\sum_i f_i[\overline{o(P_i)}] = \sum_i f_i[(1 - \theta)P_i + \theta\pi]$$

$$= (1 - \theta)\sum_i f_i P_i + \theta\pi$$

or

$$[\overline{o(P)}] = (1 - \theta)(\bar{P}) + \theta\pi. \tag{30}$$

The difference between Eq. (29) and Eq. (30) is that in Eq. (30) there is an expectation as a function of the previous expectation. This expression is sometimes called a recursive equation in the means.

Equation (30) can be solved, using the methods given on p. 4, to yield

$$\overline{P_n} = \pi - [\pi - P_0](1 - \theta)^n. \tag{31}$$

The proof is exactly that from Eq. (2) to Eq. (4) above. The new parameter π has exactly the same location in the equation as the asymptote a. This means that π will be the asymptote of learning, or the subjects will

---

[9] Note that $\sum f_i = 1$, since the f_i are probabilities. By definition of an expectation, $\sum f_i P_i = \bar{P}$; this is an expected probability, an unusual but acceptable concept. If $o(P_i)$ is the expected P after a randomly-chosen operator applied to P_i, then $\sum f_i \overline{o(P_i)}$ is the expectation over the P_i's of that expectation, and is in fact the expectation of P after a random operation. It is written $\overline{o(P)}$.

"probability match," making response A_1 on the average with the same frequency with which E_1 occurs.

It is not hard to give the corresponding analysis in terms of the accumulative theory. Assume that the rate-of-learning parameters are equal:

$$\theta_1 = \theta_2 = \theta,$$

and that the asymptotes of the two processes are 1.0 and 0.0:

$$a_1 = 1.0, \qquad a_2 = 0.0.$$

Assume also that there is a fixed probability π, and that a trial will be of type E_1. Then after n trials, the total number of elements will be

$$R_{n+1} + W_{n+1} = R_1 + W_1 + nk$$

irrespective of the specific number of left and right events.

If there are n trials, and the probability of an E_1 event on each trial is π, then the mean number of E_1 trials is π_n. Therefore

$$\overline{R_{n+1}} = R_1 + k\pi_n.$$

The mean of P_n is given by

$$\overline{P_n} = \overline{R_n}/(R_n + W_n) \tag{32}$$

since the denominator is a constant. (The mean of the ratio of two random quantities is not generally equal to the ratio of their means; Eq. (32) holds because the denominator is not a random quantity.)

As n becomes large,

$$\lim_{n \to \infty} P_n = \frac{\dfrac{R_1}{n} + \dfrac{n\pi k}{n}}{\dfrac{R_1}{n} + \dfrac{W_1}{n} + \dfrac{nk}{n}} = \frac{\dfrac{n\pi k}{n}}{\dfrac{nk}{n}} = \pi. \tag{33}$$

This particular extension of the accumulative model to a series of equal and opposite events leads to probability matching. Therefore the asymptotic performance, on this task, cannot help us decide whether learning is by replacement or accumulation of habits.

Sequential Statistics

The difficulty in the analysis above is that the asymptote of performance only depends upon the balance between the two events E_1 and E_2. In the replacement model, both retain a constant potency, and in the accumulation model, both equally lose their effectiveness in changing behavior.

A more incisive test, to determine whether the effects of E_1 and E_2 are or are not diminishing, is through a study of the effects of individual trials. Now the problem is simply one of grouping the data to obtain an accurate estimate of the effectiveness of each event.

In the experiment described above, the events (lights) come on in a prearranged random sequence independent of the subject's responses. Suppose that on any trial n, the probability of response A_1 is some number P_n. Then, if event E_1 occurs on trial n after the response, it follows that

$$P(A_{1,n+1} \mid E_{1,n}) = P_n(1 - \theta) + \theta.$$

If, on the other hand, E_2 occurs on trial n,

$$P(A_{1,n+1} \mid E_{2,n}) = P_n(1 - \theta).$$

The difference, theoretically, is therefore

$$D = P(A_{1,n+1} \mid E_{1,n}) - P(A_{1,n+1} \mid E_{2,n}) = \theta. \tag{34}$$

When the experiment has been run, it is possible to estimate D from the data as follows. First, consider all the trials following event E_1, and total the proportion of A_1 responses made. The relative frequency of A_1 responses is an estimate of $P(A_{1,n+1} \mid E_{1,n})$. A similar relative frequency is totaled for trials after E_2. Finally, the difference between the two relative frequencies is computed and is found to be an estimate of D.

This estimate, in turn, is an estimate of the learning rate parameter θ. Since θ can also be estimated from the learning curve using Eq. (6), we have a consistency check.

If the replacement theory is correct, since θ is a constant from one trial to another, it should follow that D, estimated from early and late trials, should remain the same.

Now consider the accumulation model, assuming that $k_1 = k_2 = k$ and that the asymptotes are $a_1 = 1.0$ and $a_2 = 0.0$:

$$P_n = \frac{R_n}{R_n + W}$$

and, if an E_1 occurs on trial n, then k elements are added to R_n:

$$P(A_{1,n+1} \mid E_{1,n}) = \frac{R_n + k}{R_n + W_n + k}.$$

When E_2 occurs on trial n, the k events are added to W_n, and

$$P(A_{1,n+1} \mid E_{2,n}) = \frac{R_n}{R_n + W_n + k}.$$

The accumulation theory therefore leads to the conclusion that the difference D is

$$D = \frac{k}{R_n + W_n + k}. \qquad (35)$$

As the number of trials n increases, R_n and W_n increase, but k remains the same. Therefore as n increases, the difference D approaches zero.

If we contrast Eqs. (34) and (35), we find that in the replacement theory D is a constant, θ, whereas in the accumulation theory, D decreases toward zero with more and more trials.

EMPIRICAL EVALUATION

We have examined three properties of the two simple models under study. The replacement and accumulative models both show probability matching, but they differ regarding commutativity and sequential statistics. We will look at data from an experimental study of probability learning to see which of the two ideas is supported better.

The data were reported in a study by Estes and Straughan.[10] There were three experimental groups; all had random sequences of E_1 and E_2 lights and were instructed to try to predict which light would go on each time. The groups differed in the values of $\pi = P(E_1)$ used in an initial series. During the first 120 trials, the three groups had sequences with $\pi = 0.85$, 0.50, and 0.30, respectively. During the last 120 trials, all groups had $\pi = 0.30$.

First, consider the question of commutativity. Recall that for this experiment, the accumulative model has commutative operators, but the replacement model does not. The results from Group 3 will not help in the decision as to whether the operators commute, because they had $\pi = 0.30$ throughout the experiment. However, Group 1, with $\pi = 0.85$ in the first 120 trials and $\pi = 0.30$ in the last 120 trials could provide strong evidence regarding commutativity. For this group, there were about $0.85 \times 120 + 0.30 \times 120 = 138$ E_1 trials, and about $240 - 138 = 102$ E_2 trials. If the operators are commutative, then at the end of the sequence the probability of response would not be different from that of a schedule with 138 E_1 trials and 102 E_2 trials mixed evenly throughout. This would have $P_{240} = 0.575$.

---

[10] The results were reported in Estes and Straughan's 1954 article cited earlier.

However, if the replacement model is correct, the value of P_{240} near the second asymptote of 0.30 could easily be obtained. A similar argument holds for Group 2, with π values of 0.50 and 0.30. According to the accumulative model, the value of P_{240} should be about 0.40; and the value of P_{240} for the linear model could be as low as 0.30. Of course, the result for Group 1 is more interesting, since that involves a greater difference between the theories.

The obtained proportions of response A_1 during the last 20 trials were reported. They were 0.28, 0.37, and 0.30 for Groups 1, 2, and 3. The result for Group 3 is quite a strong indication that the operators were *not* commutative.

The second difference between the theories involves the sequential statistic

$$D = P(A_{1,n+1} \mid E_{1,n}) - P(A_{1,n+1} \mid E_{2,n}).$$

In the linear replacement model, the value of D is constant and equal to θ. In the accumulative model, D decreases toward zero. The values of D can be compared between the first and second halves of the experiment. According to the replacement model, the two values should be equal. According to the accumulative model, the values in the second half should be less than those in the first. The obtained values of D for the first half of the experiment in the three groups were 0.13, 0.20, and 0.15. The values for the second half of the experiment were 0.21, 0.29, and 0.23. Neither theory predicted the increase that occurred. However, as the experimenters suggest, the subjects may have started the experiment with tendencies to alternate from the previous light, which caused the initial value of D to be too low.[11]

At least in the Estes-Straughan experiment, the results say that the operators for two kinds of trials do not commute, and that the value of D does not decrease over trials. We conclude, then, that the replacement model probably is closer to an accurate description of human probability learning than is the accumulative model.

LEARNING CURVES AS AVERAGES

The theories studied in this chapter are in agreement that learning is a determinate event. The basic equations of both theories give a particular value of P_{n+1} as a function of P_n. Performance in these theories is probabilistic; but

---

[11] An additional inconsistency with the theory is a large difference between the value of θ estimated from D, and the same parameter estimated from the mean learning curve. (See Exercise 21.) In contrast to the values of D ranging from 0.15 to 0.23, the values of θ estimated from the mean learning curve varied between 0.018 and 0.08. The authors suggested that this might be due to a lack of independence between trials.

the probability P representing the probability of success (or of response A_1) is itself determined.

This solid assumption of determinism was first broken when we took up random mixtures of competing procedures. Learning is a random event when it is a (determinate) function of a random experimental procedure.

As shall be seen in the next chapter, it is possible to think of learning itself as a random event, which may or may not take place on a given trial. So far as the learning curve is concerned, an assumption of random learning is not very complicating.

Consider first a (replacement) all-or-none learning model: the subject may be in the initial, presolution, state S_0, having probability b of being correct, or he may transfer to the final, "learned," state S_1, then reaching asymptote a at once. The subject starts in state S_0 and on each trial there is probability θ that he transfers to state S_1, where he stays. The probability of being correct on trial n is

$$P_n = aP(\text{state } S_1 \text{ on } n) + bP(\text{state } S_0 \text{ on } n). \tag{36}$$

The probability of being in state S_0 on trial 1 is 1; on trial 2, it is $1 - \theta$; on trial 3, it is $(1 - \theta)^2$, and so forth. This is true because the probability of transfer to state S_1 is θ; hence the probability of staying in S_0 is $1 - \theta$. The probability of being in S_1 is just the complement of the probability of being in state S_0. Hence

$$P_n = a[1 - (1 - \theta)^{n-1}] + b(1 - \theta)^{n-1} \tag{37}$$

$$= a - (a - b)(1 - \theta)^{n-1}.$$

Equation (37) is precisely the same as Eq. (4), the corresponding equation for the linear model. The learning curve is not different.

In a second (accumulation) all-or-none learning model, the probability of learning decreases with every trial in which the subject fails to learn. For example, at the beginning the subject must search through M memories looking for the solution to his problem. Each trial increases the number of memories by one, though there is still only one correct. Then on Trial n, the probability of learning is given by

$$P(\text{learn on } n \text{ given no learning before } n) = \frac{1}{M + n - 1}.$$

Now, for simplicity of notation, say that the probability of learning on n, given that one has not learned before, is l_n. Then let L_n be the probability of learning *by* trial n, that is, on trial $1, 2, \ldots, n$,

$$L_n = L_{n-1} + (1 - L_{n-1})l_n. \tag{38}$$

Now,

$$l_1 = \frac{1}{M},$$

$$l_2 = \frac{1}{M + 1},$$

$$l_3 = \frac{1}{M + 2},$$

$$L_1 = l_1 = \frac{1}{M},$$

$$L_2 = L_1 + (1 - L_1)l_2 = \frac{1}{M} + \frac{M - 1}{M} \cdot \frac{1}{M + 1}$$

$$= \frac{2}{M + 1},$$

$$L_3 = L + (1 - L_2)l_3$$

$$= \frac{2}{M + 1} + \left(1 - \frac{2}{M + 1}\right)\frac{1}{M + 2}$$

$$= \frac{2}{M + 1} + \frac{M + 1 - 2}{(M + 1)(M + 2)}$$

$$= \frac{3M + 3}{(M + 1)(M + 2)} = \frac{3}{M + 2}.$$

A natural conjecture is that

$$L_n = \frac{n}{M + n - 1}. \qquad (39)$$

We prove this by mathematical induction.

$$Hypothesis: L_n = \frac{n}{M + n - 1}.$$

Then by Eq. (38), and since $l_{n+1} = 1/(M + n)$,

$$L_{n+1} = \frac{n}{M + n - 1} + \frac{M - 1}{M + n - 1} \cdot \frac{1}{M + n}$$

$$= \frac{nM + n^2 + M - 1}{(M + n - 1)(M + n)} = \frac{nM + n^2 - n + n + M - 1}{(M + n - 1)(M + n)}$$

$$= \frac{n(M + n - 1) + M + n - 1}{(M + n - 1)(M + n)} = \frac{n + 1}{M + n},$$

which is Eq. (39) to be proved.

Equation (39) is a special, slightly simplified case of the learning curve for the accumulative learning model when one element is added to the set W each trial.

Thus it has been shown that there are simple all-or-none learning models that yield average learning curves just like those in the replacement and accumulation models. The all-or-none theories are quite different from the earlier theories, in the concepts used, and in various details of the data to be expected. However, the learning curve does not show any difference.

This is a fairly common outcome of some theoretical investigations. Two theories may be different in important ways, yet make the same prediction regarding some dependent variable X, such as a learning curve. There are two consequences. If we are only interested in variable X, then it does not matter which theory is used, and the choice can be one of convenience. However, if we want to decide between the theories, a different dependent variable must be studied.

EXERCISES

1. Prove Eq. (4) by induction.

2. Using Eq. (4) for the replacement model, assume that $a = 1.0$, $b = 0.25$, and $\theta = 0.20$. Calculate P_n for the first five trials of learning. Find the trial number at which P_n first exceeds 0.90. Carry out the same calculations using Eq. (8) for the accumulative model.

3. Show that, in general, if N is large, an estimate of θ can be obtained for the linear model from the mean proportion correct responses $\bar{o}$ over trials $1, \ldots, N$, as

$$\hat{\theta} = \frac{a - b}{N(a - \bar{o})}. \tag{40}$$

4. In a paired associate learning experiment with three response alternatives, Greeno and Scandura (1964) obtained the following learning curve: 0.327, 0.680, 0.688, 0.714, 0.838, 0.890, 0.930, 0.923, 0.948, 0.972, 0.983. Assume that $a = 1.0$, $b = 0.33$. Estimate θ in the linear model and in the accumulative model, and calculate the theoretical learning curves.

5. Suppose that we let Q_n be the probability of an error on trial n. That is,

$$Q_n = 1 - P_n.$$

Calculate recursive and explicit expressions for Q_n that are consistent with the assumptions leading to Eq. (4), and compare the resulting explicit expressions with Eq. (4).

6. Let $\Delta_n P = P_{n+1} - P_n$. Find the value of $\Delta_n P$ in the linear model. Ordinarily a measure of "learning rate" is desired which is independent of the initial level of P, the asymptotic level of P, and also independent of n. Show that the quantity

$$\Delta_n P' = \frac{P_{n+1} - P_n}{a - P_n} \tag{41}$$

satisfies these criteria. Show that if $\Delta_n P'$ is calculated on each trial and pooled over trials (summing the numerator and the denominator before dividing), the estimate of θ given in Problem 3 is obtained.

7. (*Continuation*) It was just shown that in the replacement model, the change in P per trial is a constant fraction of the difference between P and a. Show that in the accumulation model, the corresponding constant is

$$\Delta_n P' = \frac{P_{n+1} - P_n}{a - P_n - n(P_{n+1} - P_n)}, \tag{42}$$

or putting the point another way,

$$\frac{P_{n+1} - P_n}{a - P_n} = \theta \frac{a - P_n - n(P_{n+1} - P_n)}{a - P_n}.$$

(This says that the fraction by which P approaches a on a trial depends on n in the accumulative model, whereas that fraction is a constant in the replacement model.)

8. For the linear model and the replacement models, with k marbles taken from urn E, the probability that j red marbles are taken is

$$P(x = j) = \binom{k}{j} a^j (1 - a)^{k-j}. \tag{43}$$

By an elementary theorem of probability, the mean number of red marbles is

$$E(x) = \sum_{j=0}^{k} j \binom{k}{j} a^j (1 - a)^{k-j} = ka. \tag{44}$$

Show that Eq. (8) is a correct description of the mean value of P_n.

9. For the linear model with M quite large, the probability of taking i red marbles from urn S is

$$P(y = i) = \binom{k}{i} P_n^i (1 - P_n)^{k-i}. \tag{45}$$

Show that for fixed P_n, Eq. (1) gives the correct mean change in R_n.

10. Consider two subjects at trial n, with values of $P_{n,1}$ and $P_{n,2}$. Show that

$$\bar{P}_{n+1} = (1 - \theta)\bar{P}_n + \theta a,$$

that is, show that Eq. (2) is a correct expression for the change in the mean of a distribution of P_n values.

11. The program STEPIT works by calculating a function of the data using guessed parameter values, then adjusting the parameters and calculating the function again, and repeating this until the minimum is found. The function is calculated by a subroutine that is called in STEPIT. Write a FORTRAN subroutine that calculates Δ as given in Eq. (12) for the linear model.

12. When a computer is not easily available for estimation, or when a rough approximation is desired, a convenient technique is to rectify the learning curve. This is done when an expression is found making a measure of performance linear with practice. Show that for the accumulative model, Eq. (8),

$$\frac{a}{a - P_n} = \left(\frac{a\theta}{a - b}\right)n + \frac{a}{a - b}.$$ (46)

Then the measure of performance becomes $a/(a - P_n)$ rather than P_n. Calculate this new measure of performance for each data point on Bower's experimental curve in Table 1, assuming that $a = 1.0$. Plot the points on a graph, and use a straight edge to estimate the values of $a/(a - b)$ and $a\theta/(a - b)$.

13. Use the method given in Problem 12 to estimate b and θ for the data given in Problem 4. Calculate the theoretical learning curve for those data using these estimated parameters of the accumulative theory.

14. Show that Eq. (4) is correct for the linear model when the performance measure P_n is a rate of correct responses per unit of time.

15. Suppose that a sequence of trials $E_2E_1E_2$ is given. Describe the changes in P in terms of operators o_1 and o_2. Give the expression for P_4, according to the linear replacement model, using the parameters $\theta_1, a_1, \theta_2, a_2$.

16. In connection with Eq. (25), show that if

$$o_1(P) = (1 - \theta_1)P + \theta_1 a,$$

and

$$o_2(P) = (1 - \theta_2)P + \theta_2 a,$$

then if there are n_1 applications of o_1 and n_2 applications of o_2, the value of P will be

$$P_{n_1+n_2+1} = (1 - \theta_1)^{n_1}(1 - \theta_2)^{n_2}P_1 + [1 - (1 - \theta_1)^{n_1}(1 - \theta_2)^{n_2}]a.$$ (47)

Further, show that the result holds for arbitrary ordering of o_1 and o_2.

17. Equations (26) and (27) can be considered as linear operators on the variables R_n and W_n. Show that the operators

$$o_1(R) = R + k_1a_1, \qquad o_2(R) = R + k_2a_2$$ (48)

are commutative. Then show that the accumulative model is commutative, as claimed in connection with Eq. (28).

18. Two experimental sequences are

A. $E_1E_1E_1E_1E_1E_2E_2E_2E_2E_2$,

B. $E_2E_2E_2E_2E_2E_1E_1E_1E_1$.

In a probability learning experiment subjects are brought to $P(A_1) = \frac{1}{2}$, then divided into two experimental groups. Group A gets sequence A of events, group B gets sequence B.

Calculate predictions of performance at the end of this experiment, using the replacement linear model and the accumulation model. Do the two groups differ? In which direction?

If $\theta = 0.10$ and $b = P_1 = 0.5$, give the numerical values of $P(A_1)$ after sequences A and B using the linear model.

Let $R_n = W_n = 5$ at the beginning of the experimental trials, $k = 1$. Calculate $P(A_1)$ after sequences A and B using the accumulative model.

19. Sequential statistics

$$P(A_{1,n} \mid E_{1,n-1}E_{1,n-2}) = [P(A_{1,n-2})(1 - \theta) + \theta](1 - \theta) + \theta$$

$$= P_{n-2}(1 - \theta)^2 + 2\theta - \theta^2,$$

$$P(A_{1,n} \mid E_{2,n-1}E_{2,n-2}) = P_{n-2}(1 - \theta)^2,$$

$$\text{Diff} = D_2 = 2\theta - \theta^2. \tag{49}$$

Now, *find*

$$P(A_{1,n} \mid E_{1,n-1}E_{2,n-2}) - P(A_{1,n} \mid E_{2,n-1}E_{1,n-2})$$

using the linear model above.

20. Using the accumulation model,

$$P(A_{1,n} \mid E_{1,n-1}E_{1,n-2}) = \frac{W_{n-2} + 2k}{W_{n-2} + B_{n-2} + 2k},$$

$$P(A_{1,n} \mid E_{2,n-1}E_{2,n-2}) = \frac{W_{n-2}}{W_{n-2} + B_{n-2} + 2k},$$

$$\text{Diff} = D_2 = \frac{2k}{W_{n-2} + B_{n-2} + 2k}. \tag{50}$$

Now, *find*

$$P(A_{1,n} \mid E_{1,n-1}E_{2,n-2}) - P(A_{1,n} \mid E_{2,n-1}E_{1,n-2})$$

using the accumulation model.

21. Find an estimate of θ in the replacement model based on the mean proportion of predictions of E_1 during trials $1, 2, \ldots, N$ of a probability learning experiment.

22. Ordinarily, the data from a probability learning experiment is given in blocks of trials, with around 20 trials per block. Let t be the number of trials per block, and show that the average probability of response A_1 in the mth block of trials is

$$\bar{P}_m = \pi - \left[\frac{(\pi - b)(1 - \theta)^{t(m-1)}}{t} \right][1 - (1 - \theta)^t]$$

$$= \pi - (\pi - \bar{P}_1)(1 - \theta)^{t(m-1)}, \tag{51}$$

where b is the initial probability of response A_1 (i.e., the probability on the first trial), and $\bar{P}_1$ is the average probability of response A_1 during the first block of trials.

23. In a probability learning experiment by D. L. LaBerge,[12] subjects were given varying amounts of training with $\pi = 0.50$, before a sequence of trials with $\pi = 0.90$. It was found that estimates of θ for the simple linear model depended on prior training; the values were 0.050, 0.028, 0.025, and 0.023 for groups receiving 0, 20, 60, and 200 trials with $\pi = 0.50$. This is evidence against the simple replacement model described in the chapter, and the direction of the effect agrees with the accumulative model. LaBerge extended the linear model by assuming that at the start there is a proportion u_1 of irrelevant or neutral elements. In our urn model, we might think of a number U of clear marbles which do not affect the subject's choice, so that

$$U_n = \frac{U_n}{U_n + R_n + W_n} ,$$

and the probability of response A_1 is

$$P_n = \frac{R_n}{R_n + W_n} .$$

Assume that on an E_1 trial, a random sample of k marbles is taken from urn S and replaced by k red marbles, and on an E_2 trial k marbles from S are replaced by k white marbles. Let

$$\theta = \frac{k}{U_n + R_n + W_n} ,$$

a constant. Let π be the probability of E_1. Show that

$$P_n = \pi - (1 - u_1)(\pi - P_1) \frac{(1 - \theta)^{n-1}}{1 - u(1 - \theta)^{n-1}} , \qquad (52)$$

and show that for fixed $n > 1$, with equal values of θ and P_1, P_n is an increasing function of u_1.

---

[12] The theory and a brief description of the experimental result is given in D. L. LaBerge, A Model with Neutral Elements. In R. R. Bush and W. K. Estes (eds.), *Studies in Mathematical Learning Theory* (Stanford: Stanford University Press, 1959, 53–64). The experiment is described fully in D. L. LaBerge, The effect of preliminary trials on rate of conditioning in a simple prediction situation (*J. Exp. Psych.*, 1959, **57**, pp. 20–24).

CHAPTER TWO

Learning: Gradual   or   All-or-None

The previous chapter contrasted learning as replacement with learning as accumulation. For some simple experiments, the replacement model seemed closer to the facts. The issue was not decided, but a further analysis of the replacement theory will now be made.

Three forms of the replacement theory will be discussed. The first is closest to the theory described in the previous chapter; it shall be referred to as the *linear model*. This model supposes that on each trial the probability of the correct response is increased, directly following the replacement-theory equations.

A second form, which shall be referred to as the *Hullian model*, supposes that on each trial the *strength* of the correct response is increased, following the replacement-theory equations. However, the response strength is not equivalent to probability. We will assume that there is a threshold. At the time of test, if the strength of the correct response is above the threshold, it is made; or (in a choice experiment), if the correct response is momentarily the strongest response, it is made.

The third form is the *all-or-none model;* the assumption here is that on each trial the subject either learns completely, so that the probability of a correct response goes to one, or learns nothing, so that the probability of response remains the same.

Any theory has many forms depending on the experiment to which it is applied. For the present, let us consider an experiment with the following properties:

1. Every trial has the same effect on performance as any other; that is, all trials are intended to train for the same response, give the same information, have the same reward or reinforcer, etc.
2. Given enough trials, performance will stabilize at an endless string of correct responses; the asymptote of performance is perfection.

3. There is some initial probability of a correct response, called g, that does not depend upon specific previous training, but results from using a forced-choice test.

ASSUMPTIONS OF THE MODELS

Linear Model

The linear model deals directly with the probability of a correct response on trial n, P_n and assumes that all subjects in an ideal experiment have the same probability of correct response on trial n, and that the successive responses are statistically independent.

Use the linear difference equation

$$P_{n+1} = (1 - \theta)P_n + \theta. \tag{1}$$

The initial probability of trial 1 is here presumed to depend only on the structure of the situation; that is,

$$P_1 = g,$$

and as shown in Chapter 1,

$$P_n = 1 - (1 - g)(1 - \theta)^{n-1}. \tag{2}$$

Mean errors to solution. The outcomes of trials 1, 2, ... are represented by random variables. Give value 1 to an error and value 0 to a correct response, constructing the index variable,[1] X_n:

$$X_n = \begin{vmatrix} 1 & \text{if an error occurs on trial } n, \\ 0 & \text{if a correct response occurs on trial } n, \end{vmatrix}$$

$$P_n = P(X_n = 0). \tag{3}$$

Now the total number of errors in a given sequence would be the sum of X_n. Let T be a random variable, the total errors, where

$$T = \sum_{n=1}^{\infty} X_n. \tag{4}$$

By a simple rule of expectations, arising from the fact that addition over a set can be performed in any order,

$$E(T) = \sum_{n=1}^{\infty} E(X_n). \tag{5}$$

---

[1] An index variable takes value 1 if a certain logical condition is true, and 0 if it is false. It is convenient for expressing logical conditions numerically.

Since X_n takes only one of two values, 0 or 1, with probabilities P_n and $1 - P_n$,

$$E(X_n) = 0(P_n) + 1(1 - P_n) = 1 - P_n.$$

Therefore

$$E(T) = \sum_{n=1}^{\infty}(1 - P_n), \tag{6}$$

and from Eq. (2),

$$E(T) = \sum_{n=1}^{\infty}(1 - g)(1 - \theta)^{n-1}.$$

This geometric series is easily summed (see p. 6):

$$E(T) = (1 - g)[1 + (1 - \theta) + (1 - \theta)^2 + \cdots],$$

$$E(T) = \frac{(1 - g)}{\theta}. \tag{7}$$

Equation (7) is a formula for the total number of errors, depending upon the parameters, and Eq. (2) tells us how they will be distributed over trials.

Variability. It is also possible, by more complicated methods, to get an estimate of variability between subjects. This is very important in comparing the linear with the all-or-none model, because the linear model predicts less variance than the all-or-none when the means are equated.

In the simple linear model, we assume that the X_n are mutually independent. Therefore, since T is the sum of a sequence of random variables, X_n, the variance of T is the sum of the variances of the X_n.

Each X_n has variance

$$\text{Var}(X_n) = P_n(1 - P_n). \tag{8}$$

Recall that the variance is the expectation of the squared deviation from the mean. On a proportion P_n of the cases, $X_n = 0$; hence the deviation from the mean is $1 - P_n$. On the remaining $1 - P_n$ of the cases, the $X_n = 1$ deviation is P_n. By definition, then,

$$\text{Var}(X_n) = P_n(1 - P_n)^2 + (1 - P_n)P_n^2$$
$$= P_n(1 - P_n)(1 - P_n + P_n),$$

which leads to Eq. (8). This is the variance of the binomial distribution, Npq, when $N = 1$ and $p = P_n$.

Now, since the X_n are independent,

$$\text{Var}(T) = \sum_{n=1}^{\infty} \text{Var}(X_n)$$

$$= \sum_{n=1}^{\infty} P_n(1 - P_n).$$

Substituting Eq. (2), we find that

$$\text{Var}(T) = \sum_{n=1}^{\infty} [1 - (1 - g)(1 - \theta)^{n-1}](1 - g)(1 - \theta)^{n-1}$$

$$= (1 - g)\left[\sum_{n=1}^{\infty}(1 - \theta)^{n-1} - (1 - g)\sum_{n=1}^{\infty}(1 - \theta)^{2n-2}\right]. \qquad (9)$$

We now use the general form with parameters α and β of the result obtained as Eq. (9) above. That is,

$$\sum_{n=1}^{\infty} \beta(1 - \alpha)^{n-1} = \beta/\alpha. \qquad (10)$$

Now define $(1 - \theta)^2 = a$; Eq. (9) becomes

$$\text{Var}(T) = \sum_{n=1}^{\infty}(1 - g)(1 - \theta)^{n-1} - \sum_{n=1}^{\infty}(1 - g)^2 a^{n-1}, \qquad (11)$$

whence, by application of Eq. (10),

$$\text{Var}(T) = \frac{1 - g}{\theta} - \frac{(1 - g)^2}{1 - (1 - \theta)^2}. \qquad (12)$$

Along with the learning curve, Eq. (2), the mean number of total errors, Eq. (7), and the variance of the total error score, Eq. (12), have now been calculated.

The importance of having three different statistics is this: Any one theoretical statistic can be brought into line with the data, if the theory is at all reasonable, by proper choice of parameters like g and θ. However, it may not be possible to get several quite different theoretical statistics all to agree with their factual counterparts, using a single set of parameters, and this gives a test of theory. For example, suppose that in fitting a learning curve and mean errors, the estimates chosen are $\hat{\theta} = 0.20$, $\hat{g} = 0.50$; but those parameters predict a variance of total errors that is only one-fifth of that obtained in the data. This would be a strong indication that another theory with more variance would be needed. Since the linear model can be disproved, it can be tested experimentally.

Hullian Model

The Hullian model is a linear model with a threshold. There is a response strength s_n increasing each trial according to the linear model, and also a threshold t_n, and the probability of response is the probability that s_n is greater than t_n. This theory takes several forms, but the simplest for our purpose assumes that the threshold t_n has a normal distribution. The probability of response on a few trials is shown diagrammatically in Fig. 2.1.

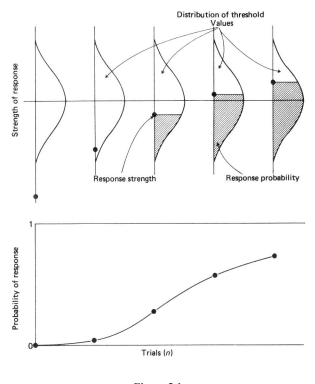

Figure 2.1

This theory requires two more parameters, namely, the mean threshold μ and the standard deviation σ of the normal distribution of thresholds. According to this theory,

$$P_n = P(s_n > t_n), \tag{13}$$

where t_n is from the normal distribution.

The simplest model of the theory has but a single value of θ, g, μ, and σ applying to all subjects. In more complicated versions of the theory, there traditionally is some recourse to individual differences between subjects and items, in both learning rates (θ) and thresholds (t).

An alternative theory of choice behavior does not use a threshold as described here. Instead, it says that the response strengths are variable, and when several responses compete, the one that is momentarily strongest is the one made. First, note that the theory behaves much the same with variable response strength as with variable threshold; in fact, both may be variable, just so they have normal distributions. Figure 2.2 shows diagrams of the theory with variable response strength. The probability of a response is written as the integral of a normal distribution from threshold t to ∞. If both threshold and response strength are variable, the probability depends on the integral from 0 to ∞ of the difference between strength and threshold, $s - t$.

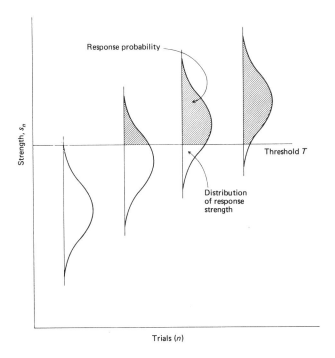

Figure 2.2

The Hullian model is relatively difficult to use in calculations if you are working with the raw data. Therefore it is common practice to first transform the response probabilities into normal-deviate or z-score form. Instead of the probability of response, P_n, use the standard normal deviate z_n defined by the integral equation

$$\int_{-\infty}^{z_n} e^{-x^2/2}\, dx = P_n.$$

Graphically, begin with a unit normal distribution, having mean zero and standard deviation one. Then for each P_n, find the value of z_n such that the area under the curve, up to and including z_n, is just P_n.

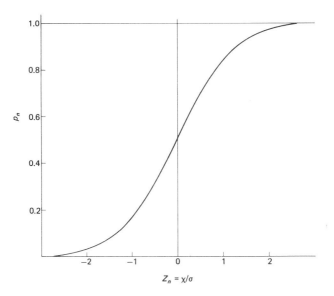

Figure 2.3

Each value of z_n obtained in this way can be interpreted as the difference between the mean value of s_n and the mean value of t_n. The unit is σ, the standard deviation of the difference $s - t$. Assume that σ and the mean threshold $\bar{t}$ are constant. Also assume that the mean response strength $\bar{s}_n$ increases over trials according to the linear model,

$$\bar{s}_n = a - (a - \bar{s}_1)(1 - \theta)^{n-1},$$

where a is the asymptotic value of the mean response strength after long training, and $\bar{s}_1$ is the mean response strength of the first trial. Then since $z_n = \bar{s}_n - \bar{t}$,

$$z_n = (a - \bar{t}) - (a - \bar{s}_1)(1 - \theta)^{n-1}. \tag{14}$$

If performance is to become perfect, $a - \bar{t}$ must be quite large, of the order of 3 or more, so as to allow P_n to get close to 1.0. Of course, since the tail of the normal distribution extends indefinitely, one cannot with this model have $P_n = 1.0$.

With this method it is fairly simple to calculate P_n on any trial. However, now suppose that it is necessary to calculate the total errors made in mastering a problem (up to $P_n = 0.99$, for example). For these trials, z_n can easily be computed, and it would be a simple matter to sum values of z_n over trials, or conversely any simple function of z_n. Therefore, total z-scores could be calculated over all trials. However, this sum would bear no clear relationship to the total errors made, for there would have to be summed, not z, but P.

Why bother to calculate total errors? It is not, of course, strictly necessary to calculate any particular summary statistic of the data, but both practical and theoretical considerations point imperatively to the advantages of a single, summary number that somehow characterizes over-all success on the problem. (Total successes in N trials, mean errors per trial, etc., are easily calculated if total errors are known.)

From the threshold model it is convenient to calculate the whole learning curve, but it is not at all convenient to calculate other, perhaps simple, summary statistics.

Only a few years ago this meant that quantitative investigations of the theory were extremely difficult. With modern computer applications, this is no longer so. One can estimate $(a - \bar{s}_1)$, $(a - \bar{t})$ and θ by trial-and-error techniques; try a value of each, compute the whole theoretical learning curve, and compare it with an obtained curve; then change one of the parameters a little, perhaps θ, and compute a new learning curve. Notice whether this gives a closer fit. If so, continue in that direction. This process is, of course, extremely laborious, but a high-speed electronic computer does each step so rapidly that it has time, in a few minutes, to search the whole space of possibilities and arrive at parameter estimates. These estimates of the parameters can be taken as summaries, that is, as containing the main information in the learning curve according to the threshold theory.

Estimating parameters by a computer search is quite a different matter from the mathematical method of deriving a simple formula as an estimator. The computer method yields no simplifications or mathematical insights, but it does produce acceptable numerical values of parameters, and accomplishes this with a minimum of labor and thought. Models which otherwise might be intractable are rendered usable by computer calculations. The main limitation of computer methods now available is that they are purely numerical, and hence require that all variables and parameters be given numerical values before computation can begin. Mathematical methods, in contrast, are attempts to simplify and gain mathematical insights, and yield estimation schemes and predictions only incidentally. When the mathematical approach is successful it may give the theorist understanding of functional relationships between parameters and statistics, as well as numerical values.

All-or-None Model

In the simple all-or-none model, the problem is in one of two states; at first, unlearned (state U) and later learned (state L). The transition from U to L occurs all in one trial.

The probability of a correct response in state U is g. In general, terminal performance may be imperfect, but consider the simple case in which the probability of a correct response in state L is 1.0.

In the experiments talked about, every trial gives the subject the same opportunity to learn. In the other models this led to an assumption that the learning rate θ is the same for all trials. In all-or-none theory, it is the *probability* of learning that is constant on all trials. Formally, let c_n be the probability of going from state U on trial n to state L on trial $n + 1$; more briefly,

$$c_n = P(L_{n+1} \mid U_n). \tag{15}$$

The assumption that all trials are alike is now made:

$$c_n = c, \qquad \text{a constant.}$$

This experiment can be visualized as a miniature board game. A biased coin is tossed every trial. The player starts in state U, and every time the coin comes up tails, he must remain in U for another trial. When the coin first comes up heads, the problem moves to state L, and stays there.

Learning curve and mean errors to solution. A number of probabilities can easily be calculated. For example, what is the probability that the problem is in U_5? *Answer:* It is in state U on trial 1, and must fail to leave by 2, 3, 4, and 5; that is, it must fail four times to leave. This is the probability of four consecutive tails. The probability of a head (i.e., of learning) is c, so the probability of four consecutive tails is $(1 - c)^4$.

What is the probability that learning occurs on trial n? *Answer:* It must fail to occur $n - 1$ times, then occur the nth time. This has the probability of $n - 1$ tails followed by a head, or $(1 - c)^{n-1}c$.

The probability of a correct response can be written

$$P_n = gP(U_n) + P(L_n) \tag{16}$$

on the grounds that if the problem is in state U, then the response is correct with probability g; if the problem is in state L, the response is certainly correct.

It has been shown that $P(U_5) = (1 - c)^4$. This is easily generalized, by the same argument, to the formula

$$P(U_n) = (1 - c)^{n-1}. \tag{17}$$

Since there are only two states, $P(L_n) = 1 - P(U_n)$. Hence, using Eq. (17) inserted into Eq. (16), we have

$$P_n = g(1 - c)^{n-1} + 1 - (1 - c)^{n-1}$$
$$= 1 - (1 - g)(1 - c)^{n-1}. \tag{18}$$

Notice that Eq. (18) is exactly the same as Eq. (2), which means that the learning curve for the linear model and for the simple all-or-none model are alike. Therefore the argument leading to Eq. (7) applies equally well to the all-or-none model, and in the all-or-none model,

$$E(T) = \frac{(1 - g)}{c}. \tag{19}$$

Variance of total errors.   In calculating the variance of T for the linear model, we assumed that the X_n on successive trials were mutually independent, because all subjects have the same P_n. In the all-or-none model, the X_n are highly dependent, because successive values of X_n may all be zero for a given problem that has been learned, while being thickly studded with 1's (errors) for another problem still in state U.

Several approaches are possible. For instance, use the fact that the variance of the sum of two random variables, x and y, is given by

$$\text{Var } (x + y) = \text{Var } (x) + \text{Var } (y) + 2r_{xy}\sigma_x\sigma_y.$$

From this formula, if the variances of the x_n and their intercorrelations could be calculated, it might be possible to compute the sum of the total.

However, such indirect approaches are not necessary with the all-or-none model. Another way to obtain the variance of T is to calculate the distribution of T, that is, $P(T = k)$ for all possible k. Then the variance is given by

$$\text{Var } (T) = E(T^2) - E^2(T)$$
$$= \sum_{n=1}^{\infty} k^2 P(T = k) - \left[\sum_{n=1}^{\infty} kP(T = k) \right]^2. \tag{20}$$

This formula requires the expression for $P(T = k)$, which is derived piecemeal in an entirely elementary fashion. Though much more elegant developments are possible, the line of thinking illustrated here is often heuristic for finding solutions to such problems. First, what is the probability of zero errors,

$P(T = 0)$? The problem is learned without error only if a correct guess is made on trial 1, with probability g, and then the problem is learned before any errors are made. For convenience, let l_n be the probability that the item first enters the learned state at the end of trial n. For example, l_1 is the probability that the item was learned at the end of trial 1. Then

$$P(T = 0) = gl_1 + g^2l_2 + g^3l_3 + \cdots + g^nl_n + \cdots, \qquad (21)$$

an infinite series. For with probability l_n, the subject had to make n successive correct guesses before learning, and this is a distinct possible way to make zero errors for each n.

Earlier, the probability of learning on trial n was derived as

$$l_n = (1 - c)^{n-1}c. \qquad (22)$$

Therefore, if we insert this into Eq. (21),

$$P(T = 0) = gc[1 + g(1 - c) + g^2(1 - c)^2 + \cdots].$$

Solving the geometric series, we have

$$P(T = 0) = \frac{gc}{1 - g(1 - c)}. \qquad (23)$$

In general, a subject can make k (>0) errors by learning at the end of k trials, but guessing wrong every trial before that; or by learning at the end of $k + 1$ trials, making one correct and k wrong guesses during that interval, etc. The probability of learning at the end of $k + i$ trials is l_{k+i}. The probability of making exactly k errors during the $k + i$ guesses is given by the binomial distribution

$$P(T = k \mid \text{Learn at trial } k + i) = \binom{k + i}{k} g^i(1 - g)^k.$$

The unconditional probability is

$$P(T = k) = \sum_{i=0}^{\infty} \binom{k + i}{k} g^i(1 - g)^k l_{k+i}. \qquad (24)$$

Substituting for l_{k+i} its value from Eq. (22), we obtain

$$P(T = k) = \sum_{i=0}^{\infty} \binom{k + i}{k} g^i(1 - g)^k(1 - c)^{k+i-1}c. \qquad (25)$$

Factor out all the terms that do not involve i from the summation sign, and

$$P(T = k) = (1 - g)^k(1 - c)^{k-1}c \sum_{i=0}^{\infty} \binom{k + i}{k} [g(1 - c)]^i. \qquad (26)$$

Now, the following sum is to be used:

$$\sum_{i=0}^{\infty} \binom{k+i}{k} a^i = \frac{1}{(1-a)^{k+1}},$$

whence, substituting $g(1-c)$ for a, and substituting the result in Eq. (26),

$$P(T = k) = \left[\frac{(1-g)c}{[1-g(1-c)]^2}\right]\left[\frac{(1-g)(1-c)}{1-g+cg}\right]^{k-1}. \tag{27}$$

This is a bulky expression, and it is helpful to simplify its form. Multiplying out, we have

$$P(T = k) = \left[\frac{c-cg}{(1-g+cg)^2}\right]\left(\frac{1-g-c+cg}{1-g+cg}\right)^{k-1}.$$

Now notice that the fraction

$$r = \frac{c}{(1-g+cg)} \tag{28}$$

can be introduced, and the above equation becomes

$$P(T = k) = \left(\frac{1-g}{1-g+cg}\right)r(1-r)^{k-1}.$$

This resembles a geometric distribution; if summed from $k = 1$ to ∞,

$$\sum_{k=1}^{\infty} P(T = k) = \frac{1-g}{1-g+gc}\sum_{k=1}^{\infty}r(1-r)^{k-1},$$

and since $\sum r(1-r)^{k-1}$ equals unity,

$$\sum_{k=1}^{\infty} P(T = k) = \frac{1-g}{1-g+cg}.$$

The probabilities add to one as any probability distribution must when the probability of $T = 0$ [from Eq. (23)] is added.

Let the probability of zero errors be called ρ (rho). Then the distribution derived for total errors is

$$P(T = k) = \begin{vmatrix} \rho & (k = 0), \\ (1-\rho)r(1-r)^{k-1} & (k > 0). \end{vmatrix} \tag{29}$$

This distribution, having a special value at zero and the remaining values arranged as a geometric series, will here be called an "almost geometric" distribution. Equation (29) is a convenient form for deductions.

It is now simple to compute the mean and variance of total errors from the all-or-none theory. The mean is, by definition,

$$E(T) = \sum_{k=0}^{\infty} kP(T = k) = \sum_{k=0}^{\infty} k(1 - \rho)r(1 - r)^{k-1}$$

$$= (1 - \rho)r \sum_{k=0}^{\infty} k(1 - r)^{k-1}.$$

The summation is $1/r^2$, whence

$$E(T) = (1 - \rho)/r.$$

Substituting Eq. (28) for r and Eq. (23) for ρ, we find that

$$E(T) = \frac{\dfrac{1 - g}{1 - g + gc}}{\dfrac{c}{1 - g + gc}} = \frac{1 - g}{c},$$

in agreement with Eq. (19). The variance is the expectation of the squared values of T, each expressed as a deviation from the mean. In practice, it is often a sensible first step to calculate the expectation of T^2, which is called the second raw moment.

It is now possible to compute

$$E(T^2) = \sum_{k=0}^{\infty} k^2 P(T = k) = \sum_{k=1}^{\infty} k^2 (1 - \rho)r(1 - r)^{k-1}$$

$$= (1 - \rho)r \sum_{k=1}^{\infty} k^2 (1 - r)^{k-1}, \tag{30}$$

$$\sum_{k=1}^{\infty} k^2 (1 - r)^{k-1} = \frac{2 - r}{r^3}.$$

Substituting this into Eq. (30), we find that

$$E(T^2) = \frac{(1 - \rho)(2 - r)}{r^2}.$$

Now the variance of T is given by

$$\text{Var}(T) = E(T^2) - [E(T)]^2$$

$$= \frac{(1 - \rho)(2 - r)}{r^2} - \frac{(1 - \rho)^2}{r^2}$$

$$= \frac{(1 - \rho)(1 + \rho - r)}{r^2}.$$

This is in sharp contrast with the variance predicted by the linear model for reasonable values of the parameters. Consider, for example, $g = \frac{1}{2}$ and a learning rate, $\theta = c = 0.25$. Both the linear and the all-or-none models agree that $E(T) = (1 - g)/c = (1 - g)/\theta = 0.50/0.25 = 2.0$. However, the variance is very different. From the linear model, Eq. (12),

$$\text{Var}\,(T) = 2.00 - \frac{0.25}{1.00 - (0.75)^2} = 1.43.$$

Hence the standard deviation is S.D. $= 1.20$.

According to the all-or-none model,

$$\text{Var}\,(T) = \frac{(0.80)(0.80)}{0.16} = 4.0$$

and the standard deviation is S.D. $= 2.0$. The all-or-none model predicts much more variability than the linear model.

TESTS OF THE THREE MODELS

Now, having available a comparable mathematical form for three theories— the threshold, the linear, and the all-or-none model—it is possible to consider efficient tests to decide which is correct for a given set of data. Three different experimental tacks have been taken, and it is our purpose now to decide precisely what the experiments mean. The three experiments are Estes' miniature experiment, Rock's substitution experiment, and the close quantitative analysis of a simple experiment.

Estes' Miniature Experiments[2]

In 1960 W. K. Estes, following Rock's work, reported a series of studies which appear to demonstrate all-or-none learning in a singularly simple and direct way.

A list of paired-associates is given once in training (a "reinforced" or *R*-trial) and then tested twice with a rest in between. The experimental procedure is schematized as *R-T-T*.

In his analysis of the data, Estes pits two theories against each other; the linear model and the all-or-none model. Both models assume that learning occurs only on the *R* trial, and that some forgetting may occur during the interval between the *T* trials. In the main experiments (Estes, Hopkins, and Crothers)[3] a list of eight paired-associate items were used

---

[2] See W. K. Estes, Learning theory and the new "mental chemistry," *Psych. Rev.* 1960, V. 67, 207–223.

[3] W. K. Estes, B. L. Hopkins, and E. J. Crothers, All-or-none conservation effects in the learning and retention of paired associates. *J. Exp. Psych.*, 1960, V. 60, 329–339.

Each stimulus was composed of three consonants (a *CCC* trigram), and the responses were the numerals 1–8. On an *R* trial, stimulus and response were exposed together for four seconds, as *XTR–5*. On a *T* trial, just the stimulus was exposed, and the subjects were to supply the response. One set of items was given in the order *R-T-T*, another set in the order *R-T-R-T*.

Since each item was tested twice, the possible strings of responses (1 being "wrong," 0 being correct) were 1 1, 1 0, 0 1, and 0 0. The relative frequencies of these four outcomes are to decide between the linear and the all-or-none models.

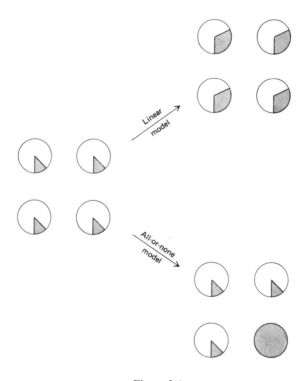

Figure 2.4

In Fig. 2.4 the situation is schematized for four items. They can be thought of as four different items learned by one subject, or as one of the paired associates learned by four different subjects. On the left are four circles, representing four items that have not been studied. In the linear model, the probability of correct response for each item is

$$P_1 = g,$$

and g is taken as 0.125, since there were eight responses. The value of P_1 is g in the all-or-none model also, since all the items start in state U.

Suppose that the learning rate (θ or c) equals 0.25. Then after one reinforced trial, the probability of correct response will increase to

$$P_2 = (1 - 0.25)P_1 + 0.25 = 0.344.$$

In the linear model, this increase applies to all four items. In Fig. 2-4 the upper arrow is the linear model, and the circles representing the items after one study trial are all the same.

In the all-or-none model, the probability of a correct response either goes to 1.0 or stays at 0.25, the learning having probability 0.125. In the schematic drawing, the lower arrow is the all-or-none model; one item has been learned (darkened circle), and three have been unaffected. The average probability of correct response is

$$\overline{P_2} = \frac{1.0 + 0.125 + 0.125 + 0.125}{4} = 0.344,$$

the same as for the linear model, but none of the single items has probability 0.344 of being correct.

To distinguish experimentally between the two theories, one need merely test each item twice. If the linear model is correct, all items should have equal probabilities of the correct response on the second test, regardless of the response on the first test. If learning is all-or-none, correct responses on the second test should come mainly on items that were correct on the first test. If an item was incorrect on the first test, it remained in state U in spite of the learning trial, and therefore the probability of correct response for such an item should be at chance.

The results of one experiment using 48 subjects on an eight-item list, a total of 384 cases, is shown in Fig. 2.5. The data shown are for R-T-T items, with no training trial between the two tests. The crucial sequence is failure on the first test and success on the second. By the all-or-none theory these should be rare, and the product of guessing on test 2 only. Notice that the probability of being correct on test 2, given error on test 1, is only 0.09 (the bolder line through Fig. 2.5) less than the elementary chance probability of $\frac{1}{8} = 0.125$.

Clearly, the results in Fig. 2.5 are in agreement with the all-or-none theory, and sharply disagree with the linear model.[4]

---

[4] The version of the linear model used by Estes has exactly the same parameters for all items and all subjects. A generalized linear model could fit the data much better.

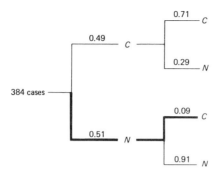

Figure 2.5

The all-or-none model assumes that there are just two states an item can be in; unlearned (U) or learned (L). If in state L, the item is answered correctly, whereas if in state U, it is only guessed. Estes' experiments seem to show that these paired-associates items are either answered correctly both times, or are guessed, and take no intermediate value of P. The linear model, at the other extreme, supposes that all items are alike at one intermediate value of P. Estes' experiments show that this is quite wrong for simple paired associates.

The other assumption of the all-or-none model is that the probability of learning; that is, of transition from U to L, is independent of how long the item may have been in U. That is, successive training trials do not push the item near the threshold and increase its probability of crossing over. The *R-T-T* experiment, by its nature, says nothing about this assumption since there is only one training trial.

The threshold model, discussed above, agrees in general with Estes' results, as was pointed out by Underwood and Keppel.[5] Consider a threshold theory in which the standard deviation of response strength is small. Then, after a suitable number of trials, an item will cross the threshold and shift from almost-zero to almost-perfect performance. In such a model, most items will be in one of the two states of performance, and only a few will be so near the threshold that they show intermediate levels of performance.

It is possible to design miniature experiments to test the assumption of the all-or-none model; the probability of learning remains constant as long as the subject does not learn. However, such experiments require a number of training (R) trials, and this means that the miniature experiment must grow back in the direction of a full-sized study. That path is not followed in this chapter.

---

[5] B. J. Underwood, and G. Keppel, One-trial learning? *J. Verbal Learning and Verbal Behavior*, 1962, V. 1, 1–13.

Replacement Experiments

Rock,[6] drawing upon the theoretical resources of classical association theory of human learning and the criticisms from Gestalt theory, formulated the question of whether repetition has any role in the formation of associations. By this question he meant to ask whether associations increase gradually in strength as they are repeated, or whether they are formed all-or-none. His general idea was that the subject, faced with a verbal-learning item, may try to form some mnemonic device, association, or strategy for remembering. If an effort results in a successful device the item is learned; otherwise it is forgotten, and the subject begins over.

Rock concentrated not on the question of two (or more) levels of performance, but on the idea that successive trials might accumulate response strength that is below the threshold, or "latent." His control group simply learned a list of paired associates in a standard way. The list was shown in a training trial (R), and then there was a test (T); then a second R exposure and T test, etc., to mastery. Rock put the S-R pairs on flash cards, and similarly the test stimuli. Thus on a trial the subject would first be taken through the deck of training cards, then through the randomly shuffled deck of test cards having the same stimuli but no responses.

The experimental group was not permitted to accumulate any partial associative strength. Whenever an experimental subject made an error on an item, that item was removed from the list and replaced by a new one, and the subject was now trained on a new item on the next trial. The only way an experimental subject could master an item was to remember it on the first and all succeeding tests. If it was ever once missed, it was dropped from the experiment and replaced by a new item.

According to the all-or-none theory, dropping unlearned items makes no difference if all items have the same parameters. If an item is not remembered, it must be in state U. If it is then replaced by a new item (also in state U), no change in performance is expected. Hence, by the all-or-none model, both experimental and control groups should perform equally well.

The linear model predicts a major difference. The learning curve for the control items, presented over and over, is given by Eq. (2). For an experimental item to be learned, however, it must be mastered without any errors. The initial guessing trial, included in Eq. (2), was omitted in Rock's experiment. Thus, the probability of learning an item is

$$P(\text{mastery with no errors}) = P(X_2 = 0)P(X_3 = 0) \cdots P(X_n = 0).$$

This can be calculated through by hand. Using rather generous parameter

[6] I. Rock, The role of repetition in associative learning. *Amer. J. Psych.*, 1957, V. 70, 186–193.

values of $\theta = 0.25$, $g = 0.50$, the result is that the probability of learning such an item without error is 0.182.[7]

Now, each item in the experimental group is either learned without error (probability 0.182) or replaced by a new item. This procedure enforces that learning is, in this sense, "all-or-none." Assuming that each new item is just as difficult as the one it replaced, the errors made on a given item and all its replacements can be added, up to the item that is passed. There is of course one error per replacement. The probability of zero replacements is 0.182; of one replacement, $(1.0 - 0.182)(0.182)$; in general, the probability of N replacements is

$$P(N \text{ errors}) = 0.182(1.0 - 0.182)^N,$$

a geometric distribution. The mean errors (replacements) are

$$E(N) = \frac{1.0 - 0.182}{0.182} = \frac{0.818}{0.182} = 4.50.$$

This is far from the expected value for the control group, given by a modification of Eq. (7). Notice that Eq. (7) has an initial guess trial included, but the Rock experiment does not. Therefore the expected number of errors by the linear model for the control group is

$$E(T) = \frac{1 - g}{\theta} - (1 - g). \tag{31}$$

With the given parameters, this is

$$E(T) = \frac{0.50}{0.25} - 0.50 = 1.50.$$

With these parameters, the linear model predicts that the control subjects will average 1.50 errors, whereas the experimental subjects, trying to overcome replacement, will make an average of 4.50 errors per item in the list. This striking difference should easily be detected in an experiment, and contrasts with the prediction of no difference from the all-or-none theory.

The main result from Rock's original experiment is more favorable to the all-or-none theory than the linear model. Using a list of letter-number paired associates, Rock found a mean of 1.49 errors per item for the control group, and 1.43 for the experimental. The all-or-none model predicts that

---

[7] Again, the above calculation assumes that all items and subjects have the same parameters and are independent.

the two will be the same, whereas the linear model predicts that the experimental group should make a mean of near 4.5. In a second experiment, using nonsense-syllable pairs in a list of eight items, Rock found a mean of 3.34 errors per item in the control group and 3.65 errors per item for the experimental group—again, close to one another.

Because of its surprising outcome, this experiment has been subjected to searching criticism, (Postman,[8] Underwood and Keppel,[9] et al.). The worst difficulty is item selection. In training the experimental group, the experimenter removes any failed items and replaces them at random from the reserve pool. Suppose the items vary in difficulty. Each subject fails the most difficult items, and receives in replacement (on the average) a mixture of difficult, medium, and easy items. On the average, his list will become easier and easier, as illustrated in the following example.

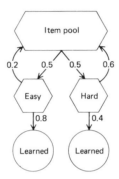

Figure 2.6

Suppose an infinitely long list made up half of easy (E) and half of hard (H) items is constructed. Easy items are mastered (without any errors) with probability 0.8, and hard items with probability 0.4. Consider an item taken at random from the first list. The probability that it is hard is

$$P(H) = \tfrac{1}{2}.$$

The probability that it will be replaced, given that it is hard, is 0.6, the probability that it will not be learned without error. If an item is easy, the probability that it will be replaced is only 0.2.

[8] L. Postman, One-trial learning. In C. N. Cofer & B. S. Musgrave (Eds.) *Verbal behavior and learning.* New York: McGraw-Hill, 1963.
[9] *Op. cit.*

Each item begins in the *item pool*—it is either easy or hard. In either case it may either be learned or be returned to the item pool. What is the probability that an item is easy, given that it is eventually learned?

$$P(\text{easy and learned}) = \frac{P(\text{easy and learned})}{P(\text{learned})}$$

$$= \frac{0.4}{1 - 0.4} = 0.67.$$

The final list should on the average contain two-thirds easy items. Compare this with the control list which has 0.50 easy items. See the diagram in Fig. 2.6.

Due to the possibility of item selection, Rock's experiment does not completely decide the issue, because selection may partly counteract effects of partial or gradual learning. However, the quantitative difference between the expectations of the two theories is very large, probably too large to be explained by the amount of difference in difficulty found to date among such materials. The question is not resolved, however, mainly because no one has calculated the actual advantage accruing to a subject through item selection, and no one has determined whether this can actually account for the coincidence of total performance of Rock's control and experimental groups.

There is some difficulty in predicting the outcome of Rock's experiment from the threshold model, because of the difficulty in specifying all of the parameters; learning rate, height of the threshold, and variability. However, it is possible to gain an approximate idea of how the threshold model behaves in a Rock replacement experiment.

First, it is known that some errors are made on most items. Therefore, the initial response strength is below threshold. Now imagine that the standard deviation of response strength is very small. The result is a model like that shown in Fig. 2.7. Since an error is always made on the first trial or two, this model will never make any headway in the Rock replacement experiment. Such a model clearly cannot explain Rock's results.

Therefore an explanation of Rock's result must be sought from a model with a wider standard deviation of response strengths. The kind of learning curve obtained from such a model is illustrated in Fig. 2.1. As has been mentioned by earlier writers, especially Spence,[10] this model produces an *S*-shaped learning curve. This, however, is precisely what makes Rock's replacement experiment difficult to do well, because a low probability of a correct response on early trials gives the subject a high probability of a new item, and he finds himself locked at the low level.

---

[10] K. W. Spence, Behavior Theory and Learning. Englewood Cliffs, N.J.: Prentice-Hall, 1960. See p. 116.

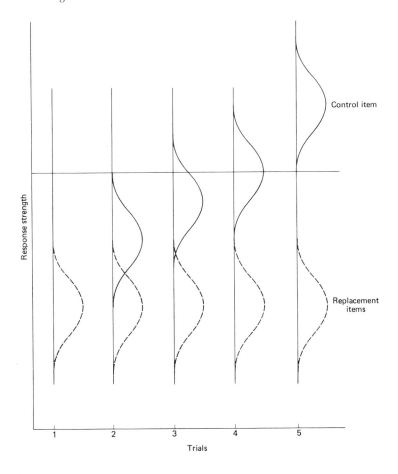

Response strength

Trials

Control item

Replacement items

Figure 2.7

The line of explanation actually put forward in defense of the threshold theory is now in two parts. First, it is noted (as in Estes' miniature experiment) that an individual item shows an *S*-shaped course, jumping from ineffective to nearly perfect performance. This agrees either with the all-or-none or the threshold concepts. Second, the ability of subjects to handle Rock's replacement task means that a sizable fraction of items will be mastered in one trial. The all-or-none theory says that the fraction is c, the overall learning rate. Defenders of the threshold theory must now say that the items, or else the subjects, differ widely in their rates of learning or in their thresholds, and the easy items cross the threshold almost at once.

The issue now becomes almost philosophical. Suppose that the proportion of items passing the threshold on each trial is a constant, c. This agrees perfectly with the all-or-none theory, in which some random device is supposed to control learning. However, the same result agrees perfectly with a threshold theory in which the same proportion of items happens to cross the threshold on each trial. One might then imagine that either genetic and social characteristics of the people, or a linguistic structure embedding the items, caused this distribution of difficulties. Since, in the Estes and Rock experiments, the experimenters did not purposely make up the distribution of difficulties, but instead merely picked items from pools commonly used, it would be natural to employ a random-sampling model as an explanation for the distribution of difficulties; the distribution of some ability, or of some property of nonsense syllables, might be predicted from ideas of how the words and subjects are selected by the experimenter.

The distinction between the two theories, all-or-none vs. threshold with differences, is now reduced to the question of when the differences are produced—before the experiment or during the experiment.

Replacement experiments, like Rock's, are powerful tools for deciding whether learning is all-or-none or gradual. Their weakness is that they require a large pool of replacement items, and the nature of the experiment permits the subject to select easier items from the pool.

Analysis of Ordinary Learning Data

Bower[11] has reported a complete analysis of the all-or-none model as it relates to data from an ordinary learning experiment in which each item is tested and trained repeatedly until mastered to a strict criterion. The idealization is an infinitely long experiment, and the element of data is a string of errors and correct responses, terminating with an infinite sequence of correct responses. A part of the analysis was given earlier in this chapter, when the learning curve, distribution of total errors, and the mean and variance of that distribution were derived.

The model has two main properties; first, that performance in state U is a sequence of independent events, like tosses of a coin with bias g, and second, that the probability of transition from U to L is a constant c. In the experiments in question, the subject responds once before he can learn, characteristic of learning by anticipation. Typically, the subject is shown a stimulus, and a response is elicited. Then, the correct response is paired with the stimulus for a training session or *reinforcement*.

Bower's paper is in several sections, and an example from each section is given so as to give the flavor of the work. The discussion of total errors is found on pp. 50–54, where the distribution of total errors and its mean and variance were discussed. Total errors is insensitive to the details of how the subject performs in state U, and mainly depends upon the constant probability of transition from U to L.

[11] G. H. Bower, Application of a model to paired-associate learning, *Psychometrika* **26**, (1961) 255–280.

Bower's second section deals with sequential properties of the data. An example of the results is the autocross-product, defined as the mean number of times we find, in a sequence, two errors exactly k trials apart and called c_k:

$$c_k = E\left[\sum_{n=1}^{\infty} X_n X_{n+k}\right]. \tag{32}$$

Now,

$$P(X_1 = 1 \ \& \ X_{k+1} = 1) = (1 - c)^k(1 - g)^2.$$

To make an error on trial k, the subject must have failed to learn on his first k opportunities, an event with probability $(1 - c)^k$. In addition, he must guess wrong twice, on trials 1 and $k + 1$, an event having probability $(1 - g)^2$. Similarly,

$$P(X_2 = 1 \ \& \ X_{k+2} = 1) = (1 - c)^{k+1}(1 - g)^2$$

and, in general,

$$P(X_n = 1 \ \& \ X_{n+k} = 1) = (1 - c)^{k+n-1}(1 - g)^2. \tag{33}$$

Inserting this into Eq. (32), we obtain

$$c_k = \sum_{n=1}^{\infty} (1 - c)^{k+n-1}(1 - g)^2 \tag{34}$$

because the expectation of the sum is the sum of the probabilities. Now, factoring out common terms, we have

$$c_k = (1 - g)^2(1 - c)^k \sum_{n=1}^{\infty} (1 - c)^{n-1},$$

and the sum is equal to $1/c$. Therefore

$$c_k = \frac{(1 - g)^2}{c}(1 - c)^k \tag{35}$$

is the expected total number of pairs of errors k trials apart.

Bower reports the results of a calculation for $k = 1, 2,$ and 3, as compared with his data on a simple paired-associates learning. He also compares his result with that from the linear model.

In the linear model the probability of errors on trial n and $n + k$ is simply the product of $1 - P_n$ and $1 - P_{n+k}$; that is,

$$P(X_n = 1 \ \& \ X_{n+k} = 1) = (1 - P_n)(1 - P_{n+k})$$
$$= (1 - g)(1 - \theta)^{n-1}(1 - g)(1 - \theta)^{n+k-1}$$
$$= (1 - g)^2(1 - \theta)^k \cdot (1 - \theta)^{2n-2}.$$

To obtain the expectation, c_k, this is summed over n, giving

$$c_k = \frac{(1 - g)^2}{1 - (1 - \theta)^2} (1 - \theta)^k. \tag{36}$$

Equation (36) is of much the same form as Eq. (35), since θ corresponds to c, but differs in the denominator, which is large in the linear model, Eq. (36). Hence, for the same learning curve, the linear model predicts a lower value of this cross-product than the all-or-none theory. This difference between theories is related to the correlations between the X_n, which are independent according to the linear model, but highly correlated in the all-or-none model.

The two theories are compared in Fig. 2.8 with the data for fitted parameter values $g = 0.50$, $c = \theta = 0.25$.

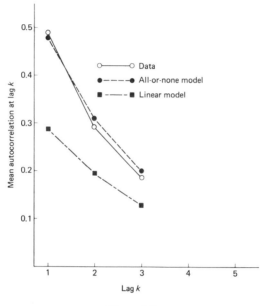

Figure 2.8

Bower also derives the distribution of the trial of last error. Ordinarily, this statistic is thought to be "unstable" because it depends upon a single occurrence, the last error, and is independent of everything else the subject does. For many models this statistic is rather complicated to derive, and the derivation for the simplest linear model (Bush and Sternberg,[12] Theorem 8) requires considerable skill in mathematics.

[12] R. R. Bush and S. Sternberg, A single-operator model. In R. R. Bush and W. K. Estes (Eds.), *Studies in Mathematical Learning Theory*. Stanford, Calif.: Stanford University Press, 1959, pp. 204–214.

The probability that the last error occurs on trial n is the probability of an error on trial n and no later errors. In the all-or-none model, the probability of an error on trial n is $(1 - c)^{n-1}(1 - g)$. The probability of no more errors, given an error on trial n, is called b, and is

$$b = c + (1 - c)gc + (1 - c)^2g^2c + \cdots$$

$$= \frac{c}{1 - (1 - c)g}. \qquad (37)$$

Therefore the probability that the last error occurs on trial n is

$$P(Y = n) = \frac{c(1 - g)(1 - c)^{n-1}}{1 - (1 - c)g} \qquad (38)$$

for $n > 1$. The probability that $Y = 0$ is, of course, the probability that there will be no errors in the whole experiment;

$$P(Y = 0) = gc + g(1 - c)gc + g(1 - c)^2g^2c + \cdots$$

$$= gb.$$

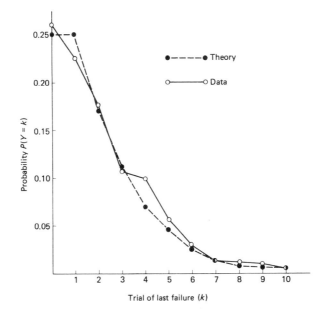

Figure 2.9

Therefore

$$P(Y = 0) = \frac{gc}{1 - (1 - c)g}.$$

(39)

Notice that Eqs. (38) and (39) constitute an "almost-geometric" distribution. Some illustrative data are given in Fig. 2.9.

Bower's experiments, and many replications and extensions made in his laboratory and at Indiana University in the past few years, verify that the all-or-none model closely fits the data from certain kinds of experiments. Investigations are currently in progress in several laboratories examining situations in which learning is not an all-or-none process. We will not take up these more complex cases in this book, primarily because the work is still of a preliminary nature, without clearly defined theoretical focus. For the present, we rest with the observation that in many details, the all-or-none model is not only easier to work with mathematically, but is also much more accurate than the linear model.

The linear model with a threshold is more difficult to evaluate, because it is mathematically almost intractable; hence, it is difficult to compare exactly with experimental results. However, the threshold model will not handle the Rock replacement experiment unless it postulates a broad spectrum of differences in difficulty.

ANALYSIS IN TERMS OF COMPLETE SEQUENCES

There is an important difference between the analysis given in this chapter and those of Chapter 1. In Chapter 1 we depended completely on the learning curve to draw conclusions about the nature of the learning process. The learning curve presents one kind of summary of the learning process—the average proportion of correct responses per trial. In this chapter we have been led to consider different properties of data, such as the variance of the number of errors per sequence, and the conditional probability of a correct response given an error on a preceding test. The direction of the analysis is toward a more detailed investigation of the learning data. We are led in this direction because different theories lead to similar or identical forms of the learning curve, and therefore the learning curve does not allow us to choose which theory is closer to the truth.

The student may wonder just how detailed an analysis is possible. The answer is that just as much detail can be put into the analysis as is permitted by the method of recording data. Data have been considered in the form of correct responses and errors. It would be possible to consider different kinds of errors—for example, to distinguish between omissions and cases where the subject made a wrong response. Or, it would be possible to measure the time taken to respond, in addition to recording which response was given. Then in the analysis of data, it would be possible to consider such properties as the number of omissions per sequence, the average time taken on trials with correct responses and wrong responses, and many other statistics.

It appears that a practical infinity of detail could be put into the analysis of data. Then it is important to consider how much detail *should* be put into the analysis. There is no single answer to this question, but a reasonable guideline is to consider data at whatever level of detail is necessary to permit an answer to the theoretical question that is at issue. If a question can be answered by finding out which of two situations produces faster learning, then there is no need to go beyond a gross summary of performance. However, if there is a question that requires a more precise examination of performance, it should be possible to examine the data in more detail. A closely related point is that details of data are often examined when theories which make predictions about those details are developed.

One advantage of using the all-or-none theory of learning is the relative ease of deriving predictions about data. Now, we will present a rather complete analysis of the all-or-none theory, partly because of empirical support for the theory just presented, and partly because the analysis illustrates some useful general concepts about the relationship between theories and data.

Purpose

To begin, a clear idea of the target of the theoretical work is necessary. The procedure of a learning experiment involves a number of trials, each with three events; (1) a stimulus is presented, (2) the subject performs some response, (3) the experimenter supplies some information to the subject. For each stimulus there is just one correct response, and the subject's task is to learn to give that correct response on each test. Ordinarily, all the stimuli are presented in some order, then the stimuli are presented again in a different order, with no set pattern in the orders. Therefore, very little information is lost if the experiment is summarized by listing the stimuli and stating what happened on each trial for each stimulus.

The Data and Logical Possibilities

Table 2.1 shows a raw data sheet for part of an experiment in paired-associate learning. Each subject worked on the task until he gave only correct responses five consecutive times through the list. In this summary, the exact response made was ignored if it was an error; any error was denoted as "1," and that of a correct response as "0."

Some general features of the data are easily seen. First, the data are highly variable. Second, the general trend of the data involves a reduction in the number of errors, and all items eventually meet the criterion.

Table 2.1 Data from three subjects in a paired associate learning experiment

Stimulus	Correct response	Trials																	
		1	2	3	4	5	6	7	8	9	10	11	12	13	14	15	16	17	18
Dome	*MUR*	0	0	0	0	0	0	0	0	0									
Gnat	*DIX*	0	1	0	0	0	0	0	0	0									
Napkin	*PEL*	0	1	0	0	0	0	0	0	0									
Sulphur	*MUR*	0	0	0	0	0	0	0	0	0									
Alley	*DIX*	1	0	0	0	0	0	0	0	0									
Beak	*PEL*	0	0	0	1	0	0	0	0	0									
Dome	*MUR*	1	1	0	0	0	0	0	0	0	0	0	0	0	0	0	0	0	0
Gnat	*DIX*	1	1	1	0	0	1	1	1	0	0	0	0	0	0	0	0	0	0
Napkin	*PEL*	0	1	0	0	0	0	0	0	0	0	0	0	0	0	0	0	0	0
Sulphur	*MUR*	0	0	0	0	0	0	0	0	0	0	0	0	0	0	0	0	0	0
Alley	*DIX*	0	1	0	0	0	0	0	0	0	1	1	0	1	0	0	0	0	0
Beak	*PEL*	1	0	0	0	1	1	1	0	0	1	1	0	0	0	0	0	0	0
Dome	*MUR*	0	0	0	0	0	0	0	0	0	0	0	0	0					
Gnat	*DIX*	0	0	0	0	0	0	0	0	0	0	0	0	0					
Napkin	*PEL*	1	0	1	0	0	1	1	0	0	0	0	0	0					
Sulphur	*MUR*	1	0	1	1	0	0	0	0	0	0	0	0	0					
Alley	*DIX*	1	1	0	0	1	0	0	0	0	0	0	0	0					
Beak	*PEL*	0	1	0	1	0	0	0	0	0	0	0	0	0					

Logical possibilities.   It is useful to consider a complete listing of the possible outcomes of the experiment. Each outcome is a series of errors and correct responses for a single item, and the set of all the possible outcomes is called the *outcome-space* of the experiment. For the experiment being considered, there are observable outcomes like

```
0 0 0 0 0
1 0 0 0 0 0
0 1 0 0 0 0 0
1 1 0 0 0 0 0
0 0 1 0 0 0 0 0
0 1 1 0 0 0 0 0
1 0 1 0 0 0 0 0
1 1 1 0 0 0 0 0
0 0 0 1 0 0 0 0 0
    .
    .
    .
```

While the observable outcome of each trial is either an error or a correct response, the theory gives a slightly more complicated picture of the situation. According to the all-or-none theory, each trial finds an item in either the learned or the unlearned state. This means that the outcome-space of the experiment can be considered from the point of view of theoretical states. Then the outcome-space of the experiment has sequences like

$$
\begin{array}{llllll}
U & L & L & L & L & \cdots \\
U & U & L & L & L & L & \cdots \\
U & U & U & L & L & L & L & \cdots \\
\end{array}
$$
$$
\begin{array}{l}
\cdot \\
\cdot \\
\cdot
\end{array}
$$

When the system goes to state L, all the responses are correct. As long as state U applies, either a correct response or an error is possible. Then it is convenient to distinguish between two states, which might be called U_G and U_E, indicating trials in state U when the subject guessed correctly and made an error. For simplicity of notation, these states will be called G and E, but it should be remembered that the difference between state G and state E is just the difference between being lucky and being unlucky in guessing. Then the outcome-space of the experiment in terms of theoretical sequences is

$$
\begin{array}{lllllll}
G & L & L & L & L & \cdots \\
E & L & L & L & L & \cdots \\
G & G & L & L & L & L & \cdots \\
G & E & L & L & L & L & \cdots \\
E & G & L & L & L & L & \cdots \\
E & E & L & L & L & L & \cdots \\
G & G & G & L & L & L & L & \cdots \\
G & G & E & L & L & L & L & \cdots \\
\end{array}
$$
$$
\begin{array}{l}
\cdot \\
\cdot \\
\cdot
\end{array}
$$

The theory assigns a probability to each possible sequence in the outcome-space. For example,

$$
\begin{aligned}
P(G\ L\ L\ L\ \cdots) &= gc, \\
P(E\ L\ L\ L\ \cdots) &= (1 - g)c, \\
P(G\ G\ L\ L\ L\cdots) &= (1 - g)^2(1 - c)c,
\end{aligned}
\tag{40}
$$

Now recall that sequences of theoretical states are not observed directly, but rather sequences of correct responses and errors are observed. It is a general feature of theories that if it were possible to know the sequence of theoretical states, the sequences of observable responses would then be known. For example, if it were known that the sequence of theoretical states was *G E E G E G L L* · · · then the sequence in data would be 0 1 1 0 1 0 0 0 · · · However, from the observed sequence it is not possible to tell exactly what theoretical sequence occurred. This is because several different theoretical sequences would produce the same sequence of responses. For example, the observed sequence 0 1 1 0 1 0 0 0 · · · might be produced by any of the following theoretical sequences:

$$G \ E \ E \ G \ E \ L \ L \ L \cdots$$
$$G \ E \ E \ G \ E \ G \ L \ L \ L \cdots$$
$$G \ E \ E \ G \ E \ G \ G \ L \ L \ L \cdots$$
$$G \ E \ E \ G \ E \ G \ G \ G \ L \ L \ L \cdots$$
$$\cdot$$
$$\cdot$$
$$\cdot$$

Probability of a Sequence

The main purpose of the present discussion is to give a clear idea of the probability of a single, complete experimental outcome. For example, calculating the probability of an event like 0 1 1 0 1 0 0 0 · · · is desirable. The theory specifies the probability that each sequence of theoretical states will occur. The probability of a sequence of observations is the sum of probabilities of theoretical sequences that could produce the observed sequences. For example,

$$P(0 \ 1 \ 1 \ 0 \ 1 \ 0 \ 0 \ 0 \cdots) = P(G \ E \ E \ G \ E \ L \ L \ L \cdots)$$
$$+ \ P(G \ E \ E \ G \ E \ G \ L \ L \ L \cdots)$$
$$+ \ P(G \ E \ E \ G \ E \ G \ G \ L \ L \ L \cdots) + \cdots$$
$$= g^2(1 - g)^3(1 - c)^4c + g^3(1 - g)^3(1 - c)^5c + g^4(1 - g)^3(1 - c)^6c + \cdots$$
$$= g^2(1 - g)^3(1 - c)^4c(1 + (1 - c)g + (1 - c)^2g^2 + \cdots)$$
$$= g^2(1 - g)^3(1 - c)^4c\left(\frac{1}{1 - (1 - c)g}\right). \tag{41}$$

The illustration shows that it is possible to calculate the probability of any sequence that can result in the experiment. With a very short experiment, it is appropriate to use these exact calculations in comparing the theory with the experimental results. For example, in Estes' *R-T-T* experiment, the possible theoretical sequences are

$$
\begin{array}{cc}
L & L \\
G & G \\
G & E \\
E & G \\
E & E
\end{array}
$$

and the probabilities are

$$
\begin{aligned}
P(L\ L) &= c, \\
P(G\ G) &= (1 - c)g^2, \\
P(G\ E) &= (1 - c)g(1 - g), \\
P(E\ G) &= (1 - c)(1 - g)g, \\
P(E\ E) &= (1 - c)(1 - g)^2.
\end{aligned}
$$

The outcome-space of observed sequences is

$$
\begin{array}{cc}
0 & 0 \\
0 & 1 \\
1 & 0 \\
1 & 1,
\end{array}
$$

$$
\begin{aligned}
P(0\ 0) &= P(L\ L) + P(G\ G) = c + (1 - c)g^2, \\
P(0\ 1) &= P(G\ E) = (1 - c)g(1 - g), \\
P(1\ 0) &= P(E\ G) = (1 - c)(1 - g)g, \\
P(1\ 1) &= P(E\ E) = (1 - c)(1 - g)^2.
\end{aligned}
$$

In applying the theory to Estes' data, the assumption is made that g is equal to 0.125, one over the number of responses; c will have to be estimated. A convenient estimate comes from the proportion of correct responses on the first trial:

$$
P(X_1 = 0) = P(0\ 0) + P(0\ 1) = c + (1 - c)g
$$

$$
\hat{c} = \frac{P(X_1 = 0) - g}{1 - g}.
$$

Since the obtained proportion of correct responses on the first test was 0.49,

$$
\hat{c} = \frac{0.490 - 0.125}{1 - 0.125} = 0.42.
$$

When the estimate of c and the assumed value of g are substituted,

$$
\begin{aligned}
P(0\ 0) &= 0.42 + (0.58)(0.125)^2 = 0.43, \\
P(0\ 1) &= (0.58)(0.125)(0.875) = 0.06, \\
P(1\ 0) &= 0.06, \\
P(1\ 1) &= (0.58)(0.875)^2 = 0.45.
\end{aligned}
$$

The obtained proportions of these sequences were 0.35, 0.14, 0.05, and 0.46. As noted earlier, there appears to have been forgetting between the two tests, and this factor is not included in the theory.

Bower's experiment and summary statistics. Now consider a longer experiment like Bower's, or one similar to that which gave the data in Table 2.1. There are a great number of different sequences that can occur. Therefore it would be extremely impractical to try to compare the empirical proportions of all the sequences with their theoretical probabilities. Instead, *summary properties* of the data are considered and then compared with predictions from the theory.

One such summary property is the learning curve. In fact, each point of the learning curve is a summary statistic in the sense that the statistic represents the combined probability of a set of sequences. The empirical learning curve is obtained by counting the number of errors per trial as in Table 2.2. In calculating the value for the learning curve at trial n, the relevant question about each sequence is whether there is an error or correct response at trial n, regardless of what happened before or after trial n.

Table 2.2 Data for the learning curve

Trials (n):	1	2	3	4	5	6	7	8	9	10	11	12	13	14	15	16	17	18
	0	0	0	0	0	0	0	0	0									
	0	1	0	0	0	0	0	0	0									
	0	1	0	0	0	0	0	0	0									
	0	0	0	0	0	0	0	0	0									
	1	0	0	0	0	0	0	0	0									
	0	0	0	1	0	0	0	0	0									
	1	1	0	0	0	0	0	0	0	0	0	0	0	0	0	0	0	0
	1	1	1	0	0	1	1	1	0	0	0	0	0	0	0	0	0	0
	0	1	0	0	0	0	0	0	0	0	0	0	0	0	0	0	0	0
	0	0	0	0	0	0	0	0	0	0	0	0	0	0	0	0	0	0
	0	1	0	0	0	0	0	0	0	1	1	0	1	0	0	0	0	0
	1	0	0	0	1	1	1	0	0	1	1	0	0	0	0	0	0	0
	0	0	0	0	0	0	0	0	0	0	0	0						
	0	0	0	0	0	0	0	0	0	0	0	0						
	1	0	1	0	0	1	1	0	0	0	0	0						
	1	0	1	1	0	0	0	0	0	0	0	0						
	1	1	0	0	1	0	0	0	0	0	0	0						
	0	1	0	1	0	0	0	0	0	0	0	0						
$\sum X_n$	7	8	3	3	2	3	3	1	0	2	2	0	1	0	0	0	0	0

In calculating the theoretical learning curve, the sequential properties of the data are similarly ignored. The learning curve is the function $P(X_n = 1)$, and this is the probability of a large set of sequences. For example, the probability of an error on trial 1 is

$$
\begin{aligned}
P(X_1 = 1) = \ &P(1\ 0\ 0\ 0\ \cdots) \\
+ &P(1\ 1\ 0\ 0\ 0\ \cdots) \\
+ &P(1\ 0\ 1\ 0\ 0\ 0\ \cdots) \\
+ &P(1\ 1\ 1\ 0\ 0\ 0\ \cdots) \\
+ &P(1\ 0\ 0\ 1\ 0\ 0\ 0\ \cdots) \\
+ &\cdots
\end{aligned}
\tag{42}
$$

and the probability of an error on trial 3 is

$$
\begin{aligned}
P(X_3 = 1) = \ &P(0\ 0\ 1\ 0\ 0\ 0\ \cdots) \\
+ &P(1\ 0\ 1\ 0\ 0\ 0\ \cdots) \\
+ &P(0\ 1\ 1\ 0\ 0\ 0\ \cdots) \\
+ &P(1\ 1\ 1\ 0\ 0\ 0\ \cdots) \\
+ &P(0\ 0\ 1\ 1\ 0\ 0\ 0\ \cdots) \\
+ &P(1\ 0\ 1\ 1\ 0\ 0\ 0\ \cdots) \\
+ &\cdots
\end{aligned}
\tag{43}
$$

Sets of sequences like those partially listed in Eqs. (42) and (43) are called *cylinder sets* of the outcome-space of the experiment. In geometry, a cylinder is a set of points, all with some common property. (In the simplest case, the points are all on a circle and therefore they all satisfy the equation $x^2 + y^2 = a$.) The shared property determines what a cross section of the cylinder looks like. In the outcome-space of an experiment, each point is a particular sequence of responses. A cylinder set is just a set of sequences, all with some common property. For example, the property $(X_3 = 1)$ specifies a cylinder set; the set contains all outcome-sequences that have an error on trial 3. The property that specifies the set is called the *cross section* of the cylinder set.[13]

A clear idea of the probability of some summary event like $(X_3 = 1)$ is desirable. Each outcome-sequence represents a set of theoretical sequences. For example, the sequence $(0\ 0\ 1\ 0\ 0\ 0\ \cdots)$ corresponds to the set

$$
\begin{aligned}
&(G\ G\ E\ L\ L\ L\ \cdots) \cup (G\ G\ E\ G\ L\ L\ L\ \cdots) \\
\cup\ &(G\ G\ E\ G\ G\ L\ L\ L\ \cdots) \cup (G\ G\ E\ G\ G\ G\ L\ L\ L\ \cdots) \cup \cdots,
\end{aligned}
$$

where $\cup$ denotes the union of sets. The probability of a single sequence of responses is the sum of several theoretical probabilities, as was seen in Eq.

---

[13] W. K. Estes and P. Suppes, Foundations of linear models. In R. R. Bush and W. K. Estes (Eds.), *Studies in Mathematical Learning Theory*, 1959.

Table 2.3 Data for trial of last error and total errors per item

Trials																		Trial of last error	Total errors
1	2	3	4	5	6	7	8	9	10	11	12	13	14	15	16	17	18		
0	0	0	0	0	0	0	0	0										0	0
0	1	0	0	0	0	0	0	0										2	1
0	1	0	0	0	0	0	0	0										2	1
0	0	0	0	0	0	0	0	0										0	0
1	0	0	0	0	0	0	0	0										1	1
0	0	0	1	0	0	0	0	0										4	1
1	1	0	0	0	0	0	0	0	0	0	0	0	0	0	0	0	0	2	2
1	1	1	0	0	1	1	1	0	0	0	0	0	0	0	0	0	0	8	6
0	1	0	0	0	0	0	0	0	0	0	0	0	0	0	0	0	0	2	1
0	0	0	0	0	0	0	0	0	0	0	0	0	0	0	0	0	0	0	0
0	1	0	0	0	0	0	0	0	1	1	0	1	0	0	0	0	0	13	4
1	0	0	0	1	1	1	0	0	1	1	0	0	0	0	0	0	0	11	6
0	0	0	0	0	0	0	0	0	0	0	0							0	0
0	0	0	0	0	0	0	0	0	0	0	0							0	0
1	0	1	0	0	1	1	0	0	0	0	0							7	4
1	0	1	1	0	0	0	0	0	0	0	0							4	3
1	1	0	0	1	0	0	0	0	0	0	0							5	3
0	1	0	1	0	0	0	0	0	0	0	0							4	2

(41).   Thus a summary event like $(X_3 = 1)$ is a set of these outcome-sequences, and the probability of a summary event is the sum of probabilities of the different sequences in that set, as shown in Eqs. (42) and (43).

Of course, the learning curve is just one kind of summary. For many purposes, it is useful to combine the data in different ways. In the discussion of Bower's analysis, the distribution of a summary statistic Y, the trial of the last error was presented. Table 2.3 shows the data from Table 2.1 with this summary statistic given for each sequence in the next-to-last column. Notice that with the trial of last error, as with the learning curve, different sequences are being combined according to a common property. For example, the sixth, sixteenth, and eighteenth sequences all have the last error on trial 4, though they are all different sequences. The property $(Y = k)$ can be used to specify a set of sequences in the outcome-space, just as can the property $(X_n = 1)$. For example, the set specified by $(Y = 3)$ is

$$(0\ 0\ 1\ 0\ 0\ 0\ \cdots)$$
$$\cup\ (0\ 1\ 1\ 0\ 0\ 0\ \cdots)$$
$$\cup\ (1\ 0\ 1\ 0\ 0\ 0\ \cdots)$$
$$\cup\ (1\ 1\ 1\ 0\ 0\ 0\ \cdots).$$

Then the probability of the event $(Y = 3)$ is

$$P(Y = 3) = P(0\ 0\ 1\ 0\ 0\ 0\ \cdots) + P(0\ 1\ 1\ 0\ 0\ 0\ \cdots)$$
$$+ P(1\ 0\ 1\ 0\ 0\ 0\ \cdots) + P(1\ 1\ 1\ 0\ 0\ 0\ \cdots)$$

$$= (1 - c)^2 g^2 (1 - g)\left(\frac{c}{1 - (1 - c)g}\right)$$

$$+ 2(1 - c)^2 g(1 - g)^2 \left(\frac{c}{1 - (1 - c)g}\right) \tag{44}$$

$$+ (1 - c)^2 (1 - g)^3 \left(\frac{c}{1 - (1 - c)g}\right)$$

$$= (1 - c)^2 (1 - g)\left(\frac{c}{1 - (1 - c)g}\right),$$

which agrees with Eq. (38).

Still another partition of the data is represented by another summary property, the number of total errors in a sequence, T. To form the set based on the property $(T = j)$, simply count the number of errors and ignore the trial numbers on which they occurred. For example, the seventh and the last sequences in Table 2.3 both have the property $(T = 2)$ and so they are both members of the set specified by the property $(T = 2)$. A partial listing of the sequences in this set is

$$(1\ 1\ 0\ 0\ 0\ \cdots)$$
$$\cup\ (1\ 0\ 1\ 0\ 0\ 0\ \cdots)$$
$$\cup\ (0\ 1\ 1\ 0\ 0\ 0\ \cdots)$$
$$\cup\ (1\ 0\ 0\ 1\ 0\ 0\ 0\ \cdots)$$
$$\cup\ (0\ 1\ 0\ 1\ 0\ 0\ 0\ \cdots)$$
$$\cup\ (0\ 0\ 1\ 1\ 0\ 0\ 0\ \cdots)$$
$$\cup\ (1\ 0\ 0\ 0\ 1\ 0\ 0\ 0\ \cdots)$$
$$\vdots$$

For some purposes it is useful to partition the data in more complicated ways. The all-or-none theory being considered says that there are no changes in performance prior to the occurrence of learning. This leads us to the idea that if only the trials before the last error were looked at, then only items that had not yet been learned would be observed, and there would be no changes in performance over trials. On any trial, only those sequences that have at least one error after trial n are of interest. It is easy to find the probability of this event. Using Eq. (38), we find that

$$P(Y > n) = \sum_{j=n+1}^{\infty} P(Y = j) = \frac{(1 - g)}{1 - (1 - c)g}(1 - c)^n. \qquad (45)$$

In Table 2.4, the illustrative data are given with a line drawn starting with the trial of the last error. Then on any trial, interest is on all the sequences that still have data for that trial in Table 2.4. The number of these sequences in the data is given for each trial in the bottom row of the table. These frequencies correspond to the set of theoretical probabilities given as Eq. (45).

Table 2.4 Data for precriterion performance, counting trials before last error forward from trial 1

	1	2	3	4	5	6	7	8	9	10	11	12
	—											
	0	—										
	0	—										
	—											
	—											
	0	0	0	—								
	1	—										
	1	1	1	0	0	1	1	—				
	0	—										
	—											
	0	1	0	0	0	0	0	0	0	1	1	0	—
	1	0	0	0	1	1	1	0	0	1	—	
	—											
	—											
	1	0	1	0	0	1	—					
	1	0	1	—								
	1	1	0	0	—							
	0	1	0	—								
Errors	6	4	3	0	1	3	2	0	0	2	1	0
Cases	12	8	8	4	4	4	3	2	2	2	1	1

In calculating the proportion of errors on a trial before criterion, the sequences in a subset of the set where $Y > n$ are counted. In Table 2.4, there are 12 sequences with an error later than trial 1, and six of these sequences have an error on trial 1. There are four sequences with an error on trial 2 and a later error, and there are eight sequences that have an error after trial 2. The conditional proportions of errors before the last error are 0.50, 0.50, 0.375, 0.00, etc.

The theoretical quantities corresponding to these conditional proportions are conditional probabilities,

$$P(X_n = 1 \mid Y > n) = \frac{P(X_n = 1 \cap Y > n)}{P(Y > n)}. \tag{46}$$

It is known that

$$P(X_n = 1) = (1 - c)^{n-1}(1 - g),$$

and Eq. (37) shows that the probability of no more errors after an error on trial n is a constant:

$$b = \frac{c}{(1 - (1 - c)g)}.$$

Therefore the probability needed for the numerator in Eq. (46) is

$$\begin{aligned}
P(X_n = 1 \cap Y > n) &= P(X_n = 1)P(Y > n \mid X_n = 1) \\
&= (1 - b)P(X_n = 1) \\
&= \frac{(1 - c)(1 - g)}{1 - (1 - c)g}(1 - c)^{n-1}(1 - g). \tag{47}
\end{aligned}$$

By substituting in Eq. (46), we find that

$$P(X_n = 1 \mid Y > n) = 1 - g, \tag{48}$$

which is the probability of an error occurring as a result of guessing. In the experiment by Bower described earlier, performance before the last error was tabulated and presented, and was in good agreement with the prediction given in Eq. (48).

CONCLUSIONS

In this chapter we have reviewed the experimental controversy about all-or-none learning, specified three models (linear, threshold, and all-or-none), worked out some of the consequences of each, and tried to show how the experimental data bear precisely upon the hypotheses. Finally, concentrating on the all-or-none model, we have shown some elementary methods of derivation.

Notice that it is not possible to make very detailed derivations from any of these theories without simplifying assumptions. The simplest form of each theory has been used for purposes of showing how the mathematical methods may be introduced and exploited. For this reason, the experimental data are not presented or analyzed in complete detail, for such an analysis would require picking not the simplest, but the most appropriate and accurate model of each type.

However, the accuracy of the all-or-none models, and their superiority to the linear model in explaining crucial experiments, may begin to emerge from the discussion. Many readers would prefer that we stop and argue this point at length, or at least not go further until the superiority of one or the other theory has been established.

A definite decision cannot be arrived at in practice. There are many more linear models and versions of the linear model to try, and a number of them will probably fit the data very well. There are several ways to increase the intrinsic variability of a linear model, and some of these methods do not greatly increase the complexity. The possibilities of the threshold model have barely been touched. In fact, in later chapters many applications of both the continuous-response strength and the threshold ideas shall be found along with variations of all-or-none models that closely resemble the other models here.

So far as the facts require, all three theories may be pursued, and that would be the prudent approach except for the effort involved on the part of both the writer and the reader. In order to show other things about learning theory, it is practical to choose one of the three theories as a main vehicle. Of the three, the all-or-none theory is the most interesting, and we think it is the one most deserving of future work. The next chapter discusses various psychological theories of why learning might be all-or-none, and how we may distinguish between the theories discussed so far.

EXERCISES

1. In the Hullian model, suppose that $s_1 = 0.0$, $a = 10.0$, and $\theta = 0.2$. Calculate values of $\bar{s}_n$ for trials 2 through 12. Then consider four cases: (a) $\bar{i} = 1.0$, $\sigma = 3.0$; (b) $\bar{i} = 4.0$, $\sigma = 3.0$; (c) $\bar{i} = 1.0$, $\sigma = 1.0$; (d) $\bar{i} = 4.0$, $\sigma = 1.0$. Obtain values of z_n for the 12 trials using each case, and then plot learning curves of p_n.

2. Working from the results of Exercise 1, obtain rough estimates of the mean numbers of errors and variance of total errors for the four cases of the model.

3. Calculate the mean errors and standard deviation of errors per sequence using the all-or-none model and the linear model using the following parameter values: (a) $g = 0.10$, $c = \theta = 0.30$; (b) $g = 0.10$, $c = \theta = 0.10$.

4. An infinitely long list has 0.25 easy, 0.50 medium, and 0.25 hard items. The probability of mastery in one trial is for easy items, 0.90; for medium items, 0.40; for hard items, 0.10. Calculate the mean proportions of the final list that will be easy, medium, and hard. (*Ans.* 0.50, 0.44, 0.06).

5. Imagine a research project in which items mastered in experiment 1 are then used as the item pool for experiment 2; items mastered in experiment 2 are used as the item pool for experiment 3, etc. Use Exercise 4 as experiment 1. Putting the proportions of items that survive experiment 1 into experiment 2,

$$\frac{0.450}{0.632}, \frac{0.176}{0.632}, \frac{0.006}{0.632} = 0.71, 0.28, 0.01.$$

Prove this, and then obtain a general expression for the three proportions after N experiments.

6. Assume that learning is all-or-none and let W be the trial on which learning occurs. Assume that $c = 0.20$, and $P(W = 1) = c$. Calculate

a) $P(W = n)$ for $n = 2, 3, 4, 5$,
b) $P(W > n)$ for $n = 5, 10, 20$,
c) $P(3 \le W \le 5)$,
d) $P(W = n + 1 \mid W > n)$,
e) $P(W = n + 2 \mid W > n)$,
f) $P(W = n + j \mid W > n)$.

7. For the Bower all-or-none model, find the probability of at least one error on trials 3 through 5.

8. Define a random variable $V_n = nX_n$—that is, an error weighted by the trial on which it occurs. Find the expectation of V_n according to the Bower all-or-none model.

9. In Estes' miniature experiment, some items were given the R-T-T sequence and others had an R-T-R-T sequence. List the possible sequences of theoretical states for the R-T-R-T items, and give their probabilities in terms of c and g. Show what set of theoretical sequences corresponds to each possible sequence of responses in the data, and give the theoretical probability of each outcome-sequence as a function of c and g. The obtained proportions were $0.35, 0.05$, and 0.32 for the sequences $(0\ 0)$, $(0\ 1)$, $(1\ 0)$, and $(1\ 1)$. Let $g = 0.125$, estimate c, and calculate theoretical probabilities.

10. Consider an experiment with just five trials. Assume that learning is all-or-none and that every sequence is either in state E or state G on trial 1. How many different sequences of theoretical states are possible? How many different observable outcome-sequences are there?

11. For the five-trial experiment of Exercise 10, enumerate the sets of outcome-sequences specified by the following properties:

a) $(X_2 = 1 \cap X_5 = 1)$,
b) $(T = 3)$,
c) $(Y = 2)$,
d) $(X_3 = 1 \cap Y > 3)$,
e) $(X_3 = 0 \cap Y > 3)$.

12. Give the probabilities of events given as (a), (b), and (c) in Exercise 11, and give the probability $P(X_3 = 1 \mid Y > 3)$, all as functions of c and g in the all-or-none theory.

13. Table 2.5 shows the data from Table 2.1 arranged for a different tabulation of precriterion performance than the one considered before. Here, the sequences are lined up with the trial before the last error given number 1, and going back to the first trial. Then for each sequence, the response farthest to the left is the response on trial 1, and the real trial number on the right is $Y - 1$, where Y is the trial of last error for that sequence. A sequence contributes a case to the tabulation for trial k if the last error occurred after trial k, and the conditional probability that is calculated from the theory is $\sum_{m=1}^{\infty} P(X_m = 1, Y = m + k)/\sum_{j=k+1}^{\infty} P(Y = j)$, which can be denoted $P(X_{Y-k} = 1 \mid Y > k)$. Show that for the all-or-none theory given in the text, this conditional probability equals $1 - g$.

Table 2.5 Data for precriterion performance, counting trials backward from the trial preceding the last error

	Trials before last error											
	12	11	10	9	8	7	6	5	4	3	2	1
											—	0
											—	0
									—	0	0	0
											—	1
					—	1	1	1	0	0	1	1
											—	0
	0	1	0	0	0	0	0	0	0	1	1	0
		—	1	0	0	0	1	1	1	0	0	1
						—	1	0	1	0	0	1
									—	1	0	1
								—	1	1	0	0
									—	0	1	0
Errors	0	1	1	0	0	1	3	2	3	3	3	5
Cases	1	1	2	2	2	3	4	4	5	8	8	12

14. Make a table corresponding to Table 2.4, but where the last error is included in the tabulation for each sequence. This corresponds to a slightly different theoretical function from that given in Eq. (48). Show that

$$P(X_n = 1 \mid Y \geq n) = 1 - (1 - c)g.$$

CHAPTER THREE

Selection of Hypotheses

Why should learning be all-or-none? The oldest explanation, as offered by K. S. Lashley[1] in the 1930's, is that when a subject is in a learning experiment, he tries one cue or hypothesis after another. When one hypothesis does not work, he discards it and adopts another. In this way, the subject continues trying one strategy after another until he hits one that satisfies him. For an uncertain number of trials he goes from one wrong hypothesis to another. Suddenly, without any previous gradual improvement, he hits upon the correct hypothesis, and at once begins to perform correctly. Therefore his performance reflects "all-or-none learning."

This chapter pursues this line of argument in several ways. First, the simplest form of the theory is presented, the "one-hypothesis-at-a-time" model, and many of the statistics of all-or-none learning are derived from this model.

To specify a model within the theory of selection of hypotheses it is necessary to specify the set, H, of hypotheses; that is, the probability that a response based on each hypothesis h will be correct, and a statement of how the subject is believed to sample and use hypotheses.

MODEL OF CONCEPT FORMATION

A typical simple concept-formation experiment uses a deck of cards. On each card is a stimulus pattern which may be one of two colors, two shapes, two sizes, etc. A typical card might have one large red triangle, or two small blue circles, etc. On each trial the subject is shown such a card and asked to classify it into one of two categories, say, A versus B. After his response, the subject is told the correct classification, which follows a simple rule such as "red is A, blue is B." This kind of experiment was originally intended as an

---

[1] K. S. Lashley, *Brain mechanisms and behavior*. Chicago: University of Chicago Press, 1928.

analogue of the process whereby a child or a foreigner learns the meaning of a word by experience. He may call a certain animal "cat," and if wrong will be corrected and told that the correct response is "dog." When the learner can reliably use the word "cat" only for cats, he might be said to have formed the concept. Research on this experimental procedure no longer depends upon the validity of the analogy with concept formation, and the procedure is often called "concept identification."

The possible hypotheses in such a problem can be grouped into three classes: correct (C), wrong (W), and irrelevant (I). The correct hypothesis is red—A, blue—B. A wrong hypothesis in this experiment is the reversal of a correct one: red—B, blue—A. The unfortunate subject who chooses this hypothesis is never right. Most other hypotheses, like "circle—A, triangle—B" are irrelevant, and will lead to correct and wrong responses at random with probability 0.5.

One Hypothesis at a Time

The one-hypothesis-at-a-time model says that the subject on the first trial chooses one h from H. If it is in C, he makes a correct response and keeps the hypothesis. If it is in W, he certainly makes an error and then returns his h to H, preparing to take a new random h for trial 2. If the h he selects is in I, then it may lead either to a correct answer or a wrong one. If the answer given is correct, the subject keeps the h, for at this time he does not know whether it is in C or I. If the response based on the irrelevant hypothesis is wrong, then the subject returns it to H and resamples on trial 2.

It may seem absurd to suppose that the subject would return an h to H, sampling with replacement, when he has just been shown that it is not correct. However, remember that to do otherwise the subject must remember the particular h's he has tried. The simple one-h-at-a-time model, analyzed here, contains the assumption that the subject has no effective short-term memory for h's that have been tried and found wrong.

unlikely.

Markov states. A stochastic process is a set of states and a set of probabilities of passing from one state to another. A Markov process is a special class of stochastic process in which the probability of transition from state i to state j is independent of the past history of the system—for example, this probability does not depend on how long the system has been in state i, where it was before, or how long since it has been in state j. In a Markov chain, the transition probabilities are constant over time.

The learning models growing from the all-or-none concept all attempt to specify states of the learner, possibly "underlying" states, which along with their transition probabilities will constitute a Markov chain.

The subject can, on a given item, be in any of four states: he may have a correct hypothesis (state C), he may have a wrong strategy (state W), or he may have an irrelevant strategy and make either a correct response (state

S) or an error (state *E*). The probabilities of transition from one state to another are as follows. From state *C*, the subject always makes a correct response, hence always stays. From states *E* and *W* the subject always makes an error, and then goes to one of the four states with the probabilities (1) *c* for state *C*, (2) *w* for state *W*, (3) $p(1 - c - w)$ for state *S*, and (4) $i(1 - p)$ for state *E*. Note that $c + w + i = 1$. These represent the sampling probabilities of the three kinds of hypotheses, *C*, *W*, and *I*, and the assumption that when an irrelevant strategy is chosen, the probability it is correct on the next trial is *p*. From state *S*, the subject will not change his hypothesis, but it may be either correct or wrong on the next trial, with the probabilities *p* and $1 - p$. The transition matrix is shown in Eq. (1).

$$
\text{From state} \quad
\begin{array}{c}
C \\ S \\ E \\ W
\end{array}
\begin{array}{c}
\overset{\displaystyle \text{To state}}{\overset{\displaystyle C \quad\; S \qquad E \qquad W}{\left[
\begin{array}{cccc}
1 & 0 & 0 & 0 \\
0 & p & 1 - p & 0 \\
c & ip & i(1 - p) & w \\
c & ip & i(1 - p) & w
\end{array}
\right]}}
\end{array}
\tag{1}
$$

States *E* and *W* have the same exit probabilities, since both lead to the same resampling process. They can therefore be lumped into one state of a reduced Markov chain, the following three-state chain:

$$
\begin{array}{c}
C \\ S \\ R
\end{array}
\overset{\displaystyle C \quad S \qquad\quad R}{\left[
\begin{array}{ccc}
1 & 0 & 0 \\
0 & p & 1 - p \\
c & ip & 1 - c - ip
\end{array}
\right]}.
\tag{2}
$$

In the above matrix, the transition from *R* to *R* should be written $w + i(1 - p)$. However, since *c*, *w*, and *i* are the probabilities of choosing correct, wrong, and irrelevant hypotheses, and (in this model) there are no others,

$$
c + w + i = 1
\tag{3}
$$

from which

$$
w + i(1 - p) = (w + i) - ip = 1 - c - ip.
$$

Written this way, the model has only three unknown parameters, *c*, *i*, and *p*.

Notice further that states *C* and *S* lead to correct responses, state *R* to errors. To get from *S* to the absorbing state *C*, the subject must make an error. Therefore, all correct responses in *S* are followed by at least one error, while all correct responses in *C* come after the last error. By looking at any sequence of correct and wrong responses, the state of the subject on each trial can be determined at once.

$$1 \; 1 \; 1 \; 0 \; 1 \; 0 \; 0 \; 1 \; 0 \; 1 \; 0 \; 0 \; 0 \; 0 \; \cdots$$
$$R \; R \; S \; R \; S \; S \; R \; S \; R \; C \; C \; C$$

Every error is in state R, and every success before the last error is state S.

A model of this sort can be analyzed easily by consideration of the special role of errors. Every error, when it occurs, signifies that the subject is back at his starting point, resampling from the original pool H.

Errors as recurrent events. The theory of recurrent events deals with the next occurrence of an event. Suppose that an error occurs on some trial n. Then let $f_{k,n}$ be the probability that the next error occurs k trials later:

$$f_{k,n} = P(\text{error on } n + k \text{ and correct on } n + k - 1 \cdots \mid \text{error on } n).$$

An error is a *recurrent event* if $f_{k,n}$ is a constant independent of n. In this case, whenever an error occurs, the probability that the next one occurs k trials later is f_k. An error can be a recurrent event only if every error resets the learner to the same condition. The theory of recurrent events simplifies analysis because, instead of worrying about the distribution of all possible later errors, it deals with the occurrence of the next error.

In the simple strategy-selection theory, the probability of an error immediately after an error is

$$f_1 = w + i(1 - p) = 1 - c - ip. \tag{4}$$

The probability of an error after one correct is the probability of transition from R to S and back to R; namely, $ip(1 - p)$. Any greater values of k arise because the subject stays in state S for more trials; in general, for $k > 1$,

$$f_k = (ip)p^{k-2}(1 - p) = i(1 - p)p^{k-1}. \tag{5}$$

This does not give rise to a proper probability function, because

$$\sum_{k=1}^{\infty} f_k = 1 - c - ip + i(1 - p)\sum_{k=2}^{\infty} p^{k-1}$$
$$= 1 - c - ip + i(1 - p)[p(1 - p)]$$
$$= 1 - c. \tag{6}$$

This total is conventionally called f, and it is the probability that the recurrent event, the error, will ever recur. With probability $1 - f$, (in this model equal to c), the next error never arrives. In the usual terminology, errors are *uncertain recurrent events.*

A general *theorem* is as follows: If E is an uncertain recurrent event, and T is the total number of times E occurs, then

$$P(T = k) = f^k(1 - f).\tag{7}$$

The proof is very simple. Clearly, $1 - f$ is the probability of zero errors. Then f is the probability that an error occurs. If an error occurs, it returns the system to its initial state so that the probability of no more errors is again $1 - f$.

Statistics of simple learning. The distribution of total errors, in the simple strategy-selection theory, is

$$P(T = k) = (1 - c)^k c.\tag{8}$$

Hence

$$E(T) = \frac{1 - c}{c},\tag{9}$$

$$\text{Var}\,(T) = \frac{1 - c}{c^2},\tag{10}$$

and this is an all-or-none model.

Notice that total errors do not depend upon p or i, but only on c, the probability of sampling a correct strategy. This suggests, as will be seen later, that the best estimate of c is based on total errors.

The distribution of successes up to the first error is given by Eq. (5), the distribution f. Notice that it does not add up to unity, because there may be no first error.

When an attempt is made to calculate the learning curve, the mathematics becomes somewhat complicated (see Restle[2]). The wrong strategies W produce some peculiar effects. If the assumption is made that W is empty and all noncorrect strategies have the same probability p of leading to a correct response, then fairly simple equations can be derived.

On each trial the probability that the subject learns, that is, the probability that he makes an error and then chooses a correct hypothesis upon resampling, is $(1 - p)c = qc$. Therefore the probability that the subject is in an unlearned state at trial k is simply

$$P(\text{unlearned at } k) = (1 - qc)^{k-1}.\tag{11}$$

The probability of an error at trial k is the probability that the item is

[2] F. Restle, The selection of strategies in cue learning. *Psych. Rev.*, 1962, **69**, 329–343.

unlearned times $1 - p$. That is,

$$P(\text{error at trial } n) = q(1 - qc)^{n-1}. \tag{12}$$

This is the learning curve.

The trial of last error is calculated by noticing that for the trial of last error to be at trial n, there must be an error on that trial and then no more errors. The probability of an error on trial n is given by Eq. (12), and the probability of no more errors is c. Therefore

$$P(\text{last error on trial } n) = cq(1 - qc)^{n-1}. \tag{13}$$

Since this is a geometric distribution with parameter qc, its mean and variance are easily calculated.

For many purposes we are mainly interested in the rate of learning, which corresponds to the parameter c. Given a set of data, Eq. (9) can be used to estimate c. Let $\bar{T}$ be the mean total errors in the data, and set up the estimation equation parallel to Eq. (9),

$$\bar{T} = \frac{(1 - \hat{c})}{\hat{c}},$$

whence

$$\hat{c} = \frac{1}{(1 + \bar{T})}. \tag{14}$$

Equation (14) can fit the data only if they come from a simple learning situation, and if training is sufficiently extended so that all errors that will happen are observed. Parameters estimated in other ways may be dealt with in the discussions to follow.

Tests of the Model

In a simple problem, c is the probability of choosing a relevant cue. Suppose that a problem has color, form, size, position, and number cues available, along with some set I of irrelevant cues, source unknown. If form is the correct answer (triangle—A, circle—B), then the probability c should equal the probability of choosing the form dimension and the correct assignment of responses (A to triangle, not vice versa).

The probability of choosing form depends upon the potency or weight of the form cues, here called w_F, relative to the total weight of all other cues available, w_H. Thus if form is correct,

$$c = \frac{w_F}{w_H}. \tag{15}$$

If two of the dimensions are correct, say, form and color, then

$$c = \frac{w_F + w_C}{w_{II}}. \tag{16}$$

The above formula assumes that form and color cues are mutually exclusive, so that the subject may choose one or the other but not some "common element."

Notice that the above theory gives c as a function of cue weights, and says that c is the relative weight of the correct one. This means that the learning rate is not a free parameter or a function of the individual subject, but instead is a parameter of the experimental situation. This may seem absurd, at first; clearly a rat and a man will not do equally well on the same problem, for example, on a fine size discrimination. According to the present theory, however, size cues have relatively great weight for the college student, and relatively small weight, perhaps zero, for the rat in the same situation. More exactly, of course, it is not the cues but the hypotheses that must be weighted.

Additivity of cues experiments. Clearly, to test a theory that makes learning depend on cue weights, one should vary the cue weights experimentally and see whether the data agree with the theory. However, many theories predict that concept formation or discrimination will proceed more quickly when the relevant stimuli are made stronger and more distinctive, that is, when the relevant cue is increased in weight. Similarly, it is obvious that the removal of distracting and competing irrelevant cues should make learning more rapid. A result in the correct general direction would merely be an example of what is called "additivity of cues" in the experimental literature.

Fortunately, an experiment exists in which true additivity of cues, in the sense of Eq. (16), can be tested. The experiment consists of measuring the learning rate of three problems, with cue A relevant and cue B irrelevant, with cue B relevant and cue A irrelevant, and with cue B and cue A relevant and redundant. If the theory is correct, the weight of relevant cues in the third problem should equal the sum of the weights of relevant cues in the first two problems, provided cues A and B are not interrelated.

An experimental example is Trabasso's[3] study of concept learning. Line drawings of flowers were prepared, each consisting of a flower and three leaves: two on one side of the stalk and one on the other. Irrelevant dimensions were type of flower, number of leaves on left, and serration of the leaves. The standard relevant dimension was the angle of leaves to the stem, and, in addition, either the stem or the flower might be colored either red or green.

[3] T. R. Trabasso, Stimulus emphasis and all-or-none learning in concept identification. *J. Exp. Psych.*, 1963, **65**, 398–406.

One group of subjects learned the angle problem when colors were painted on the angle with $\hat{c} = 0.067$. This means that

$$\frac{w_A}{w_A + w_{IRRELEVANT}} = 0.067,$$

where w_I is the weight of all the irrelevant dimensions put together. From the above equation,

$$w_A = 0.072w_I.$$

Another group of subjects solved a problem in which the color at the angle was relevant (for example, red led to response A, green to B), and the angle of the leaf to the stem was not varied. These subjects learned with an estimated $c = 0.190$, whence

$$\frac{w_C}{w_C + w_I} = 0.190, \qquad w_C = 0.235w_I.$$

In the additivity-of-cues condition, angle and color varied together, and subjects could solve the problem using either cue. The model predicts that

$$c_{A+C} = \frac{w_A + w_C}{w_A + w_C + w_I} = \frac{0.072 + 0.235}{1 + 0.072 + 0.235}$$

$$= 0.234.$$

This was the prediction for the learning rate of the two-cue subjects; the observed value of c, for the group having two cues, was 0.225. Thus the theory not only predicted that the two-cue group would learn faster than either one-cue group, but made an accurate quantitative prediction, in error by only 0.009.

Notice that the predicted performance on the two-cue problem was only a little better than on the strong color cue alone: 0.235 versus 0.190. It is characteristic of this theory that when a weak cue (with small w) is added to a strong cue, the difference in performance is relatively slight. This is, of course, quite sensible, but it does mean that experimenters will not always find their two-cue group doing better than both one-cue groups in the observed data.

A second form of "additivity of cues" measures the effect of adding irrelevant cues. One group, from Trabasso's experiment, had the angle as the relevant cue as above, and the angle was colored, but the color was irrelevant. This procedure adds color to the standard set of irrelevant cues, so that c becomes

$$c = \frac{w_A}{w_A + w_C + w_I}$$

which, with the estimated values from above, is

$$\hat{c} = \frac{0.072}{1 + 0.072 + 0.235} = 0.055.$$

The observed estimate of c for this problem was 0.055. The prediction is perfect to three decimal places.

Notice that in this experiment, addition of an irrelevant cue has the effect of slowing down learning, reducing c. Since adding a relevant cue speeds up learning, and adding an irrelevant cue slows it down, the theoretical predictions are verified in both directions. Thus it appears reasonable that c depends upon the ratio of relevant to total cues. What is more important, of course, is that the predictions are quantitatively accurate in these experiments. In further support of the theory, Trabasso has shown that the rate of learning can be greatly increased either by holding fixed all aspects of the stimulus except the relevant cue, or by increasing the magnitude of the relevant stimulus difference.

What is learned? Suppose that subjects have mastered the problem with both color and angle relevant. Then, the experimenter switches to colorless cards with the same angle dimension, and tests subjects on their mastery of the angle problem.

A simple association theory might suppose that some habit strength had built up to both stimulus dimensions, and partial success could be attained using the angle alone. In fact, with sufficient overtraining, the angle itself might pick up enough habit strength to support performance alone, in which case the transfer would be perfect.

The one-hypothesis-at-a-time model makes quite a different prediction. When the subject has mastered the color + angle problem, this means he has chosen an hypothesis based on either the color or the angle cue. Having chosen either cue he will make all correct responses, hence will not resample, and will not pick up the second cue. At the end of original learning, some subjects have adopted the angle cue and will transfer perfectly to the problem without color. Other subjects have adopted the color cue. When put on the colorless test problem, they will have no basis for response and will be in the state of subjects first trying the angle problem.

This leads to a theory of all-or-none transfer. When the set of relevant dimensions is constricted by removing some, the group of subjects will divide into two parts—some performing without error, the remainder looking exactly like control subjects with no learning. To the extent that performance improves overall with practice (probably through elimination of some entirely inappropriate hypotheses), the experiment must be performed with appropriately prepared control groups.

All-or-none transfer in concept formation was first shown by Trabasso.[4] Performance of his transfer groups was predicted by assuming, for each statistic, that the data consisted of a fraction π of perfect performers, and $1 - \pi$ of subjects just like the control group. Thus, for example, suppose that for the control group the distribution of total errors is called $\{t_k\}$ for $k = 0, 1, \ldots$ Then for the experimental group, the probability of zero errors is $\pi + (1 - \pi)t_0$, and for any k greater than zero, the probability of k errors in transfer is $(1 - \pi)t_k$. Exactly the same probability holds for the trial of last error, the learning curve, etc. As may be imagined, it is not difficult to estimate the new parameter π.

There is, however, a theory of the parameter π. Consider, again, the group of subjects (the third in the additivity-of-cues experiment) which had both angle and color relevant. According to the estimates made, they had angle cues with weight $w_A = 0.072w_I$ and color cues with weight $w_C = 0.235w_I$. At the end of the experiment, they were using one cue or the other, and the conditional probability that it was the angle cue is

$$P(A \mid A \text{ or } C) = \frac{w_A}{w_A + w_C} = \frac{0.072}{0.307} = 0.234.$$

This is the predicted value of π for subjects shifted to the angle problem. In fact, 5 of the 20 subjects learned without error; that is, the estimated proportion of subjects with zero errors is 0.250. The learning rate for subjects learning this problem, angle without any color, is 0.034. Therefore, the probability of zero errors is

$$P(\text{zero errors}) = \hat{\pi} + (1 - \hat{\pi})t_0$$
$$0.250 = \hat{\pi} + (1 - \hat{\pi})(0.034),$$

whence

$$\hat{\pi} = \frac{0.216}{0.966} = 0.224.$$

With only 20 cases in this particular group, the estimate is not very stable. Certainly, however, it agrees very closely with the predicted value of 0.234.

Furthermore, the remainder of the distribution of total errors was predicted accurately by the model.[5]

---

[4] T. R. Trabasso (cited above).

[5] The data are not presented here, because Trabasso stopped training while a substantial fraction of subjects had not yet learned. He was able to calculate the distribution of total errors taking account of the fact that the distribution would pile up at the upper end where training was terminated, but the result was not simple.

More recent experiments, making a more exact study of transfer of training, have recently been reported by Bower and Trabasso.[6]   These authors begin, as in the Trabasso experiments above, by teaching subjects a two-cue problem; that is, a problem with two redundant correct cues. Then, as a test, they first give the subject a sequence of trials with one cue present and the other absent. The same subjects were then tested with the second cue present and the first absent. This experiment determines whether a subject can use neither cue, either one and not the other, or both.

The simple one-cue-at-a-time model says that every subject who learns the original problem will know either one cue or the other, but not both. The reason is simple; when, during original learning, the subject first hits on either a color or size cue, he begins to respond correctly, never resamples, and has no chance to pick the other relevant cue. To solve the problem he must have at least one dimension, and it is not possible to have more than one.

It should come as no great surprise that in the experiments performed, a substantial fraction of the subjects knew both of the relevant dimensions. How was this managed by the subjects? One possibility might be that the subjects sample more than one cue at a time. However, previous experiments have established fairly well that (a) learning is all-or-none in these experiments, and (b) the rate of learning, c, corresponds to the proportion of correct strategies. How can these facts be reconciled with the idea of sampling more than one cue at a time?

Random Sample of Hypotheses

The basic idea of the random-sample-of-hypotheses model of the theory of hypothesis selection is this; when the subject samples, he takes a random sample of the hypotheses in H. Usually, on some future trial, these several cues will lead to different responses. The subject at that time must choose between subsets of his sample, and he does so on a simple probability basis. After such a choice, any time he is correct in his response he can eliminate those hypotheses he threw away, and has a chance of narrowing down to just the correct hypotheses. However, at each decision the subject may make a wrong choice of hypotheses. Suppose that when he chooses one subset of hypotheses, the subject puts aside the other and cannot recover it. Then when he makes an error, he has lost the correct hypothesis in a wrong subset, and the only hypotheses he has left are wrong or irrelevant. If so, then the subject must resample, taking a new set of hypotheses, and begin the problem over.

Errors as recurrent events. In this model, every error is an occasion for the subject to resample from his pool of hypotheses. This means that each error resets the subject to his initial state, and this in turn means that, theoretically, an error is a *recurrent event* in the sense defined at the beginning of the chapter.

---

[6] G. H. Bower and T. R. Trabasso, Concept identification. In R. C. Atkinson (Ed.) *Studies in mathematical psychology*. Stanford, 1964.

A recurrent event is characterized by its distribution f_i, the probability that an error will be followed by $i - 1$ correct responses and then an error. Consider a simple special model to fix ideas and display the process. A problem has 4 hypotheses: 1 correct, 1 wrong, and the other 2 irrelevant. The 2 irrelevant hypotheses are correct with $p = 0.6$ or wrong with probability $1 - p = 0.4$. The subject takes a random sample of 2 hypotheses whenever he samples.

There are six possible samples of the hypotheses C, W, I_1, and I_2:

Sample	Contents	Probability of an error (f_1)
ω_1	C, W	0.5
ω_2	C, I_1	0.2
ω_3	C, I_2	0.2
ω_4	W, I_1	0.7
ω_5	W, I_2	0.7
ω_6	I_1, I_2	0.4

In a random sample, each has the same probability, $\frac{1}{6}$. Now let us consider f_1, the probability of an error immediately after resampling. If the subject takes sample ω_1, then his two hypotheses at once conflict, and he must choose between them in his first response. If he chooses C, he will never make an error, and if he chooses W, he makes an error at once. Let f_1 (sample 1) be the probability of an error right away (a value of f_1) given the subject chooses sample 1. Then

$$f_1(\omega_1) = 0.5.$$

In samples ω_2 and ω_3, the subject has one correct and one irrelevant hypothesis. If the irrelevant hypothesis happens to agree with the correct response, $p = 0.6$, then he need not choose between them but does not make an error. If the irrelevant hypothesis disagrees with the correct one and points to the wrong response, $p = 0.4$; the subject must choose, and if he happens to choose the irrelevant hypothesis, he will make an error at once. Therefore

$$f_1(\omega_2) = f_1(\omega_3) = (0.4)(0.5) = 0.20.$$

In samples ω_4 and ω_5, the subject has a wrong and an irrelevant hypothesis. If the two agree (with probability $1 - p = 0.4$), then the subject certainly makes an error at once, and if they disagree, $p = 0.6$, he still has probability 0.5 of choosing the wrong hypothesis; thus, $0.4 + 0.6(0.5)$ is the probability, and

$$f_1(\omega_4) = f_1(\omega_5) = 0.7.$$

Finally, in sample ω_6, there is probability 0.4 of an error no matter which hypothesis is followed, since both are irrelevant. This is

$$f_1(\omega_6) = 0.4.$$

Giving each sample a probability of $\frac{1}{6}$, we find that

$$f_1 = \frac{0.50 + 2(0.20) + 2(0.70) + 0.40}{6} = 0.45. \tag{17}$$

Now to calculate f_2, again we go through sample by sample. Sample 1 cannot lead to f_2, because the C hypothesis never leads to an error, and the W always leads to an immediate error. In fact, notice that the only way an error can arise after a correct answer is when the subject has narrowed down to an irrelevant hypothesis. Obviously, he cannot be narrowed down to a correct or wrong hypothesis. If he had both an irrelevant and a wrong hypothesis they must have been confounded on the first trial, but then he would have made an immediate error. He might have had a correct and an irrelevant hypothesis confounded earlier, but at the trial on which the error is made he certainly has been forced to choose, and has chosen the irrelevant one.

This consideration allows a simplification of the study of the process. In sample ω_6 the subject certainly uses an irrelevant cue no matter what; the probability of the sequence, correct–wrong on two trials is $(0.6)(0.4)$, so

$$f_2(\omega_6) = (0.6)(0.4).$$

For samples 2–5, the probability is $\frac{1}{2}$ that the subject will choose the irrelevant one of the two hypotheses, and then $(0.6)(0.4)$ that it leads to the sequence of responses, correct–wrong. Thus

$$f_2(\omega_i) = 0.5(0.6)(0.4), \qquad i = 2, 3, 4, \text{ or } 5.$$

Totaling over the samples, each with probability $\frac{1}{6}$, we have

$$f_2 = 0.5(0.6)(0.4).$$

Notice that f_3 also requires that the subject ends up with an irrelevant hypothesis and that it gives the following sequence of responses: correct, correct, wrong, with joint probability $(0.6)(0.6)(0.4)$. In general, for $j > 1$,

$$f_j = 0.5(0.6)^{j-1}(0.4) \tag{18}$$

and this gives the whole distribution f_j. Summing, we find that

$$f = 0.45 + (0.5)(0.4)\sum_{j-2}^{\infty}(0.6)^{j-1}$$

$$= 0.45 + 0.20\frac{0.6}{0.4} = 0.75.$$

Surprisingly, this agrees in a simple way with the one-strategy-at-a-time model, as in Eqs. (4), (5), and (6) of this chapter. There is one correct, one wrong, and two irrelevant strategies; hence, let the proportions be

$$c = 0.25, \qquad w = 0.25, \qquad i = 0.50,$$

and recall that the probability of a correct response, based on an irrelevant cue, is $p = 0.60$. Then, by Eq. (4), we have

$$f_1 = w + i(1 - p) = 0.25 + 0.50(0.40) = 0.45,$$

and for $j \geq 1$, using Eq. (5), we find that

$$f_j = i(1 - p)p^{j-1} = 0.5(0.4)(0.6)^{j-1}$$

just as in Eqs. (17) and (18). Closer study of the numerical example reveals that if c, w, and i are the proportions of correct, wrong, and irrelevant hypotheses, then Eqs. (4) and (5) apply to the two-strategies-at-a-time model with 1 correct, 1 wrong, and 2 irrelevant hypotheses.

Similarity of random sample to one-h-at-a-time model. It has been shown (Restle[7]) that in any experiment having C correct, W wrong, and I irrelevant hypotheses that (1), if each is equally potent (2), if the probability of a correct response given an irrelevant hypothesis is p, and (3) if the subject after an error makes a random sample of size N (N being any whole number less than or equal to the total number of hypotheses), then the sequence of correct and wrong responses will be a system of recurrent events, where f_j is given by

$$f_1 = w + i(1 - p),$$
$$f_j = i(1 - p)^{j-1} \qquad \text{for } j > 1,$$

so that

$$f = 1 - c.$$

In these formulas,

$$w = W/(W + C + I), \qquad i = I/(W + C + I), \qquad c = C/(W + C + I).$$

This result is called the "indifference-to-sample-size" theorem.

Why is this of interest? Recall that experimental results on simple concept formation had shown that concept-learning data appear to be all-or-none, in good agreement with the simple one-hypothesis-at-a-time model. However, it is now apparent that the sequence of correct and wrong responses, which is all that could have been used to decide that learning was all-or-none, are statistically exactly the same in the random-sample-of-hypotheses model as in the one-at-a-time model. Therefore, using this

---

[7] F. Restle (cited above).

theoretical development, it is possible to believe that subjects are using a random sample of hypotheses rather than one at a time.

Recall that the experiments on additivity of cues seem to have shown that c, the rate of learning, is the proportion of correct hypotheses. This followed from the one-hypothesis-at-a-time model, for there c was the probability of choosing a correct hypothesis when sampling only one. However, in the random-sample-of-hypotheses model, $c = C/(C + W + I)$ is also the proportion of correct hypotheses. The theory that yielded additivity of both relevant and irrelevant cues, using the one-hypothesis-at-a-time model, makes exactly the same predictions from the random-sample-of-hypotheses model.

Finally, how about all-or-none transfer? Suppose that a subject has been taking random samples of hypotheses, and has mastered a problem (like the angle-plus-color problem of Trabasso's experiment) using either angle or color but not both. This could happen if the subject, in one of his random samples, chose the angle cue and not the color cue and then happened to make a series of correct decisions and narrow down to the angle hypothesis. When shifted to the test, he would perform perfectly on the angle problem. If he happened, instead, to choose the color and not the angle cue, he would have no basis for response on the test problem and would start over. If the subject happened to have both angle and color in his sample during learning, and by a sequence of correct decisions narrowed down, he would end up with both hypotheses. When transferred to the angle problem for a test, he would perform perfectly. Thus one would have all-or-none transfer.

Now remember the last of the experiments discussed, those done by Bower and Trabasso in which the subject was trained with two redundant correct hypotheses, then separately tested on each. Recall that a number of subjects could respond correctly to both color and size. The one-hypothesis-at-a-time model cannot do this, but the random-sample-of-hypotheses model obviously can end up with both correct hypotheses. This model, therefore, can handle all the main data discussed in this chapter.

The problem of estimating sample size. Consider a model experiment having two unitary correct hypotheses, C_1 and C_2, two corresponding wrong hypotheses, W_1 and W_2, and four irrelevant hypotheses, I_1 through I_4. Each hypothesis is equally likely to be chosen in a random sample, and the subject ends up centering on whatever correct hypotheses were finally found in his last sample.

Hypotheses:

C_1	W_1
C_2	W_2
I_1	I_3
I_2	I_4

Clearly, if the subject takes samples of size $s = 1$, the probability of solving on any sample is $\frac{2}{8} = 0.25$, and the probability of having both hypotheses in the sample is 0.

If the sample is of size 2, then there are $\binom{8}{2} = 28$ possible samples. Of these, 1 has both correct hypotheses, and that certainly leads to the solution if chosen. Of the total, 12 samples have one correct and one other hypothesis, and each of these has probability $\frac{1}{2}$ of solving the problem. That is, in each such sample, the subject at some time must choose between the correct and the other hypothesis, and he will solve the problem if he chooses the correct hypothesis. Thus the total probability of solving the problem is $[1 + 0.5(12)]/28$, which is 0.25. This agrees with the hypothesis that 2 of the 8 hypotheses are correct.

Furthermore, given that the problem is solved, the probability that both hypotheses are in the sample is given by

$$\frac{1}{[1 + 0.5(12)]} = \frac{1}{7}.$$

If the sample is of size 3, there are 6 samples having both correct hypotheses and one other, $2\binom{6}{2}$ samples having one correct hypothesis and two others, and then $\binom{6}{3}$ samples having no correct hypothesis, a total of $\binom{8}{3} = 56$ samples. With two correct and one other hypothesis, there is probability $\frac{2}{3}$ of solving the problem; with one correct and 2 others, the probability is $\frac{1}{3}$. Thus the total probability of solving the problem is

$$\frac{(\frac{2}{3})6 + (\frac{1}{3}) \cdot 2 \cdot \binom{6}{2}}{56} = \frac{(4 + 10)}{56} = 0.25$$

as before. The probability of having both correct strategies, given at least one, is

$$\frac{4}{4 + 10} = \frac{2}{7}.$$

In general, we find that if the sample is of size s, the probability of solving is constant at 0.25, and the probability of having both correct hypotheses, given that the problem is solved, is given by

$$P(\text{both correct} \mid \text{problem solved}) = \frac{s - 1}{7}.$$

The meaning of this answer is seen when it is realized that at least one correct hypothesis must be picked for the problem to be solved. The subject is known to narrow down to that hypothesis, and the question is whether he also narrows down on the other correct hypothesis. In the preceding example there are seven other strategies, and there are (in a sample of size s, with one hypothesis known to be correct) a total of $s - 1$ hypotheses not accounted for. The probability that the correct hypothesis is in the remaining part of the sample is, therefore, $(s - 1)/7$.

Now it is evident that if there are a total of H hypotheses, of which 2 are correct, and if the sample is of size s, the probability of having both correct hypotheses in the final sample is

$$P(\text{both correct}) = \frac{s - 1}{H - 1}. \tag{19}$$

Many equal hypotheses. The trouble with the above model is that it almost requires the assumption that all hypotheses have equal weight. Otherwise, one might question whether a sample of two very weak hypotheses was a sample of size 2, in the same sense as a sample of two very strong hypotheses. In experiments, of course, different dimensions may differ widely in weight. To handle this fact, one simple model says that there are many hypotheses available, each having an equal small weight. Then, an experimental dimension like "size" is associated with a whole set of hypotheses in H. To say that one dimension is more salient than another is to say that it corresponds to a set of hypotheses having more elements.

Bower and Trabasso[8] used a deck of concept-formation cards varying in form (F), circle or triangle; in the position of a dot above or below the figure (D); the color, red or blue; the number of lines within the figure, either one or two; and the position of an open gap in the side of the figure, either on the left or right.

The weight of the form and dot dimensions are called w_F and w_D; the other dimensions, all being irrelevant, are lumped into I, with measure w_I.

Now suppose that on each trial the subject takes a sample of size s. Of these, some number j are form hypotheses, k are dot hypotheses, and the remainder, $s - j - k$, are irrelevant. Suppose that the proportions or measures of dot hypotheses and of form hypotheses are

$$d = \frac{w_D}{w_D + w_F + w_I}, \qquad f = \frac{w_F}{w_D + w_F + w_I}.$$

Then the probability of exactly j form and k dot hypotheses is given by the

---

[8] G. H. Bower and T. R. Trabasso (cited above).

multinomial distribution:

$$P(j \text{ form and } k \text{ dot hypotheses}) = \binom{s}{j, k} f^j d^k (1 - f - d)^{s-j-k}, \quad (20)$$

where $\binom{s}{j, k}$ is the multinomial number $s!/j! \, k! \, (s - j - k)!$ Intuitively, it is the number of different ways one can take samples of j, k, and the remainder of s objects.

Now, the probability of solving the problem in this model when both form and dot hypotheses are correct is

$$P(\text{solve}) = \sum_j \sum_k P(\text{solve} \mid j, k) \cdot P(\text{sample with } j + k \text{ relevant})$$

$$= \sum_j \sum_k \frac{j + k}{s} P(j \text{ form and } k \text{ dot hypotheses}),$$

where the last term is as in Eq. (20). However, the last expression is just $(1/s)$ times the mean of $j + k$, which in the multinomial is just equal to the sample size times the probabilities of the two events. That is,

$$P(\text{solve}) = \frac{1}{s} [E(\text{number of form}) + E(\text{number of dot hypotheses})]$$

$$= \frac{1}{s} (sf + sd) = f + d. \quad (21)$$

Thus the probability of solving the two-cue problem is just the sum of the probabilities of solving either of the two one-cue problems, and the additivity-of-cues theorem holds for this theory.

Now, if the subject takes a sample of size s and happens to solve the problem (i.e., narrows down to the correct hypotheses within his sample), what is the probability that he has only form, only dot, or both kinds of hypotheses in his final sample? The probability that the final set contains only form and no dot hypotheses is

$$P_f = \frac{P(\text{solution \& } j > 0 \text{ \& } k = 0)}{P(\text{solution})}. \quad (22)$$

The numerator is the sum of the probability in Eq. (20), over all values of j from 1 to s, with $k = 0$. Thus

$$P(\text{solution \& } j > 0 \text{ \& } k = 0) = \sum_{j=1}^{s} \frac{j}{s} \binom{s}{j} f^j (1 - f - d)^{s-j}.$$

This is like the sum of a binomial distribution, except that the two probabilities f and $1 - f - d$ do not add to unity. Multiply and divide by

$(1 - d)^s = (1 - d)^j(1 - d)^{s-j}$. This becomes

$P(\text{solution \& } j > 0 \text{ and } k = 0)$

$$= \frac{(1 - d)^s}{s} \sum_{j=1}^{s} j\binom{s}{j}\left(\frac{f}{1 - d}\right)^j\left(\frac{1 - f - d}{1 - d}\right)^{s-j},$$

and the summation is just the mean of the binomial distribution, equal to $sf/(1 - d)$. Hence

$$P(\text{solution \& } j > 0 \text{ \& } k = 0) = \frac{(1 - d)^{s-1}}{s} sf$$

$$= f(1 - d)^{s-1},$$

whence by Eqs. (22) and (21),

$$P_f = \frac{f(1 - d)^{s-1}}{f + d} \tag{23}$$

is the conditional probability that the final solution contains only form hypotheses. By the same argument, the probability that it contains only dot elements is

$$P_d = \frac{d(1 - f)^{s-1}}{f + d}, \tag{24}$$

whence the probability that it contains both kinds of hypotheses is

$$P_{f+d} = 1 - P_f - P_d$$

$$= 1 - \frac{f(1 - d)^{s-1} + d(1 - f)^{s-1}}{f + d}. \tag{25}$$

These results give the probability of the two single hypotheses and the joint hypotheses as a function of the two single-cue learning rates, f and d, along with one more parameter, the size of sample s.

Bower and Trabasso[9] had 45 subjects learn the form problem with dot irrelevant, and estimated $\hat{f} = 0.094$. Another group of 45 subjects learned dot with form irrelevant, and had $\hat{d} = 0.164$. A third group of 90 subjects had both form and dot relevant and redundant, and had an estimated $\hat{c} = 0.239$. In this case the combined cues should theoretically equal $f + d$; notice that the observed c at 0.239 is close to $\hat{f} + \hat{d} = 0.258$.

The subjects trained on $F + D$ were then tested in two series of trials to see whether they could respond correctly to trials with form varied and dots missing, and whether they could respond with dots varied and forms

---

[9] Cited above.

eliminated as a cue. It turned out that subjects fell into one of three categories; D subjects could do the dot test but not the form, F subjects could do the form but not the dot, and $F + D$ subjects could do both.

If $s = 1$, that is, if the subject samples only one hypothesis at a time, he cannot have both hypotheses. Then, the number of $F + D$ subjects should be 0, and the remainder should be divided f/d, that is, 0.094/0.164 between form and dot performance. In the data, though, 31(= 0.348) had the form hypothesis only, 45(= 0.505) had the dot hypothesis only, and 13(= 0.146) had both dimensions.

The nearest integer value to handle these data is $s = 2$. If $s = 2$, then Eqs. (23), (24), and (25) predict the proportions of subjects knowing d, f, and both; the total number of responses of the 89 subjects tested are shown in Table 3.1.

Table 3.1 **Number of subjects knowing dot only, form only, and both dimensions; observed and predicted with sample size = 2**

Hypotheses known	Observed	Predicted
Dot only	45	51.4
Form only	31	27.3
Both dot and form	13	10.4

The predicted and observed values in Table 3.1 are in good enough agreement—a stringent statistical test (chi square with 1 degree of freedom) revealed no significant discrepancy. Obviously, this is not a verification of the theory in any detail, since there was no way of knowing the sample size s in advance. It is interesting that the data are well fit by a value as reasonable as 2 in this experiment. What is now needed is an independent measurement of s.

STIMULUS SELECTION IN MEMORIZING

If subjects select cues in concept identification, it is possible they will also select cues when learning paired associates. In most such lists, the stimuli are complex and it is difficult to tease apart dimensions, hypotheses, or cues that might be used. An experiment by Underwood, Ham, and Ekstrand[10] illustrates the main empirical attack on this problem. Their experiment uses two lists, the word list and the nonsense list. There are seven items in each list; in the *word-color list*, each item is a common three-letter word, like

---

[10] B. J. Underwood, M. Ham, and B. Ekstrand, Cue selection in paired-associate learning. *J. Exp. Psych.*, 1962, **64**, 405–409.

GAS, in a different colored rectangle. In the *nonsense-color list*, there is a trigram like *DWK* or *DHX* in a colored rectangle.

Subjects who learn the word-color list are divided into two subgroups, half tested on words with no color, the other half tested on the original colored rectangles with no words. Subjects trained on the nonsense-color list were likewise divided into two subgroups, half tested on the nonsense syllables without color, the other half on the colors alone.

The subjects using words and colors transferred well to words and not so well to color. Subjects trained with nonsense trigrams and colors did very poorly on the trigrams alone, and very well on colors.

When the subjects with word + color training were tested on color alone, they made about 0.55 correct responses. The subjects trained on nonsense syllables + color, when tested on color alone, were correct 0.79 of the time. The experience of the two groups with color was exactly the same, so that the difference cannot be attributed to any difference in opportunity to learn. The words cannot be said to dominate the color more than do the nonsense syllables, so there is no difference in how easy the colors are to perceive.[11] The only conclusion left is that the subjects *select* parts or aspects of the stimulus presented, and when they select one part they neglect others. When words are available, subjects use them and tend not to learn much about the colors, whereas when only nonsense trigrams are available, the subjects do not use them, hence use the colors more.

This observation sets the stage for a mathematical theory of paired-associates memorizing. The stimulus-selection shown above appears, in principle, to be very like that found in the Trabasso-Bower experiments on concept identification. Paired-associates learning is on the surface quite different from concept identification, and usually is thought of as a form of "simple associative learning." The discussion to follow will pursue the idea that paired-associates learning is, in a way, closely akin to concept identification.

A Simple Cue-Selection Model

Suppose that a process like that of concept identification occurs during paired-associates learning, in that subjects choose among hypotheses or cues. Also, for the moment, consider the one-cue-at-a-time model. In the word-color list, a given word was always associated with a particular color, and the subject knew this fact from the instructions. Therefore, the color and the distinctive properties of the word are redundant relevant cues upon which correct responses can be based. Let the weights of these cues be C and W, for color and word. Then during learning the subject has chosen a single

---

[11] A fault in this argument is that the nonsense-color list was more difficult to learn; hence subjects had more trials on it than on the word-color list.

cue from one set or the other, and upon test, the probability that the cue was a color cue is

$$P(\text{respond to color}) = \frac{C}{C + W} .$$

From the original learning data, and also some supplementary data collected on learning with single stimuli, a rough estimate of the learning rates can be calculated. For the three kinds of stimuli, some reasonable estimates are[12]

$$C = 0.34I, \qquad W = 0.36I, \qquad T = 0.20I,$$

where I is the common set of unknown irrelevant cues.

The probability of choosing color, hence transferring to color cues when only they are available, is different in the two contexts. When trigrams are learned with colors,

$$P(\text{correct on color test}) = \frac{C}{C + T} = 0.34/0.54 = 0.63.$$

respond to colour given
       colour and trigram ···

In contrast, when words are learned with colors,

$$P(\text{correct on color test}) = \frac{C}{C + W} = 0.34/0.70 = 0.48.$$

respond to colour given colour
                   & word ···

Thus, according to this theory, more subjects will learn the color cue when it is paired with trigrams than when it is paired with words. Consequently, this theory correctly predicts one of the main findings. This, in turn, supports the idea that paired associates, at least with compound stimuli, are learned by a process that involves selection of stimulus aspects, and that this selection has at least some of the properties of simple concept identification.[13,14]

Nonindependence of the Codes in a List

A single paired associate learned in isolation would be very easy, but a long list is difficult. One possible reason for the difficulty is interference between the items, but a length-difficulty relationship appears even when the items are selected to be relatively easy to discriminate.

---

[12] The estimates are taken merely from published summary statistics, but should be sufficiently close for the purposes of this argument.

[13] The important finding of all-or-none learning in both paired-associates learning and in concept formation would suggest that both are underlain by the same process. Our suggestion differs from that of Atkinson, Bower, and Crothers in *Introduction to Mathematical Learning Theory* (Wiley, 1964) who treat concept identification and paired-associates learning as mathematically similar but psychologically quite separate.

[14] C. T. James, and J. G. Greeno, Stimulus selection at different stages of paired-associate learning. *J. exp. Psych.*, 1967, **74**, 75–83.

To be learned, according to a current concept of paired-associates learning, the stimulus-response pair must be encoded into a form suitable for storage. The actual medium of storage may be neural or chemical, or may be thought of as the formation of a kind of mnemonic device or image to help in memorizing. Once coded and stored, the item remains in storage until the stimulus is again presented for test. At that time the stimulus is again encoded, and the subject must engage in a process of search in an attempt to retrieve the old engram, from which the response, learned earlier, can be reconstructed.

If an item is learned, according to this theory, its code can be retrieved when it is needed. A simple "conditioning" theory might say that the association is formed; hence the stimulus gives rise "automatically" to this response. However, paired-associates learning is not simple conditioning, for it involves the simultaneous mastery of many items.

It is true that for the subject to know the responses to all stimuli in the list, he must use unique aspects. of the stimuli. In addition, however, he must be able to recover the codes, and generate responses, at a relatively high rate (at most, about 4 sec per item) and must be able to generate the correct response and no other when the stimuli are thrown at him without warning and in random order. If a subject has a completely disconnected and disjointed list of mnemonic codes, he might be able to handle a few items, but this technique might well be expected to be inefficient as the basis for skilled, effortless responding.

These considerations suggest that paired-associates learning will not be efficient if the subject selects a code separately for each item in the list. A difficult list may in fact be first learned by a collection of separate and individual codes, but the subject will be able to perform easily and rapidly only if he can transcend this item-by-item structure and integrate the parts of his code. This integration, in turn, delineates the possibility that the subject may develop complex, higher-order structures enabling him to learn a list of paired associates.

One difficulty with all-or-none learning theories is that they give no account of the effects of overtraining. It is well known that performance improves after the subject has reached criterion, and that even a few trials of overtraining have a large beneficial effect upon later retention, change the pattern of transfer-of-training, and permit rapid and confident responding. In simple all-or-none learning, the subject has done all his learning as soon as he begins the criterion performance; hence he can hardly show any gain from overtraining. In contrast, a response-strength model (as discussed in Chapter 2) can say that criterion is reached when the items are relatively near the threshold, and that overtraining pushes the response strength far above the threshold. However, the response-strength theory cannot account easily for the all-or-none learning data.

One possible solution to this theoretical dilemma is through the theory of selection of hypotheses. This theory, as seen above, can give rise to all-or-none learning data, and a reasonable interpretation is that learning is the selection of an adequate and retrievable mnemonic code.

At criterion, the subject probably has a number of disparate mnemonic codes, and is under considerable strain to recall the responses in limited time. In order to stabilize his learning, the subject might attempt to integrate his separate mnemonic codes into a more integrated general strategy. He might make the same kind of stimulus selection in every item, or he might establish mnemonics all using a single principle of association, etc.

These questions are not purely speculative. Instead, they turn attention to any specific changes in performance that may be associated with over training, whereas the response-strength theory merely led to an expectation of "more and better" association. If, as in the strategy-selection theory, it is once accepted that the subject can resample, refine, and reorganize his codes during over-training, then the specific nature of these over-learning effects can be studied.

Some Effects of Overlearning

James and Greeno[15] found that overtraining is the occasion for subjects to pick up neglected cues. The experiment used compound stimuli with a word and a meaningless consonant–vowel–consonant (CVC) trigram. Each compound stimulus was paired with one of eight digit responses.

Three groups were run. Group U (undertrained) worked on the list with compound stimuli until they had a trial with at least four correct responses. Group C (criterion) worked until they had a trial with all eight responses correct. Group O (overlearned) worked until they had a trial with all eight responses correct, and then ten additional overtraining trials were given. After work on the first list was finished, a transfer list was presented where the stimuli were the stimulus components from the first list, and the response to each component was the one that had been paired with the compound containing that component in the first list. The transfer list was presented for several trials; in one running of the experiment all subjects had the transfer list for five trials, in another running each subject had the second list until two perfect trials were given.

Interest was centered in the amount of transfer to word components and to nonsense components in each of the three groups. This was measured by calculating the proportion of items in each condition for which there were no errors during the transfer trials. Averaging the results of two experiments, the proportions of perfect items with word stimuli were 0.32, 0.62, and 0.71 in the three groups, and the proportions of perfect items with nonsense stimuli were 0.08, 0.09, and 0.35.

---

[15] Cited above.

This means that when undertrained (only up to $\frac{4}{8}$ correct) subjects did relatively well on the transfer to word stimuli (0.32 correct) and not well at all to the trigrams (0.08). When the subjects had reached criterion of $\frac{8}{8}$, they were quite good with word stimuli (0.62) and still very poor on trigrams (0.09). In fact, at this point there was almost no apparent learning of nonsense trigrams. After overlearning, performance on word stimuli improved slightly (to 0.76), but performance on the nonsense stimuli was substantially better than in Group $C(0.35)$. Apparently, responses to the nonsense stimuli were either learned very early (for 0.08 were known before the subject reached $\frac{4}{8}$ correct on the original list) or very late during overtraining.

It appears that the subjects began the experiment by sampling cues from both words and nonsense syllables. During this time, a few responses were learned to nonsense syllables. Subjects soon adopted an overall strategy of using only the words. Since the words could easily be distinguished from the CVC's, this overall strategy could be applied to all items.

Finally, after the whole list was learned, the subjects apparently could shift their whole strategy again and begin seeking supplementary cues from the nonsense syllables. It seems plausible that college students, during overtraining, would forsee the possibility that they would be tested on the CVC's. Another possibility is that the subjects, having mastered the task in an efficient way, simply were interested in those parts of the stimuli they had been ignoring. At the very beginning of the experiment, subjects attended to complete stimuli before they learned that they could simplify their task by attending only to word components. For a simple model, we assume that on the first trial of the experiment the probability of learning an item is a, and the probability of a correct response on the first test is g for items that were not learned on the first study trial. By the beginning of the second study trial, most subjects must have noticed that the words were available and easier to use as stimuli than the CVC nonsense syllables. For a modest simplification, we assume that this shift of strategies occurred by the second trial for all subjects and applied to all items. Then, after the first trial, the learning probability is a higher constant, c, and the probability of correct responses on unlearned items equals p. The idea, then, is that learning is all-or-none, but the parameters on trial 1 differ from those after trial 1.

To illustrate the effect of the complication, the distribution of total errors per item, T, is derived. In order to have zero errors, an item must be learned on the first study trial, or guessed on the first test and then learned without errors:

$$P(T = 0) = a + (1 - a)g\left(\frac{c}{1 - p + pc}\right). \qquad (26)$$

Following any error on a trial after the first trial, there is a constant probability $c/(1 - p + pc)$ that there will be no more errors. The probability of at least one more error is therefore $1 - [c/(1 - p + pc)] = (1 - p)(1 - c)/(1 - p + pc)$. Now, for $k \geq 1$,

$$
\begin{aligned}
P(T = k) &= (1 - a)\left\{ g\left[\frac{(1 - p)(1 - c)}{1 - p + pc}\right]^{k} \right. \\
&\quad \left. + (1 - g)\left[\frac{(1 - p)(1 - c)}{1 - p + pc}\right]^{k-1} \right\} \cdot \frac{c}{1 - p + pc} \\
&= \frac{(1 - a)c}{1 - p + pc}\left[\frac{g(1 - p)(1 - c)}{1 - p + pc} + 1 - g\right]\left[\frac{(1 - p)(1 - c)}{1 - p + pc}\right]^{k-1} \\
&= \frac{(1 - a)c}{1 - p + pc}\left[1 - \frac{gc}{1 - p + pc}\right]\left[\frac{(1 - p)(1 - c)}{1 - p + pc}\right]^{k-1}. \quad (27)
\end{aligned}
$$

Figure 3.1 shows the obtained distribution of total errors per item during acquisition for the overtrained group, where practice was continued long enough to determine the number of errors on each item before learning occurred. The solid theoretical curve is calculated from a simple all-or-none theory assuming constant parameters across all trials. The dashed curve, which fits much better, was calculated using Eq. (27). It seems reasonable to

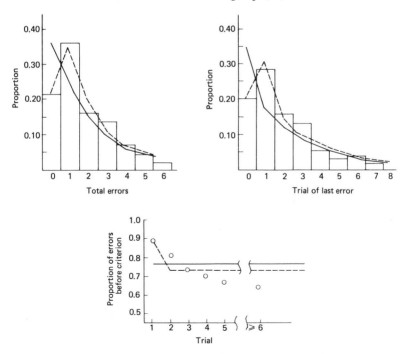

Figure 3.1

conclude, then, that items were learned in an all-or-none manner, but that on the first trial the probability of learning was lower, because subjects had yet to adopt an efficient strategy of selective attention to simplify their task.

Hypothesis Selection Theory of Paired-Associates Learning

Suppose that each item in a list can be coded in several different ways. For example, the subject might attend to any part of a stimulus, or he might try to remember the item using any of several mnemonic tricks involving associations he already knows. Thus the item corresponds to a set of possible codes.

Of the complete set of codes, some will permit the subject to remember the correct answer on later tests and others will either be forgotten or will not discriminate among the items. The assumption here is that on each study trial the subject samples one of the codes and stores it in his memory. If the subject samples one of the "good" codes, he will remember the item on later tests, and the item is learned. If the subject samples one of the inadequate codes, he may remember the item for a short time, but eventually the code will fail to provide the correct response.

According to the theory, the probability of learning on each study trial is c, the probability of sampling a code that will support retention. If an item has not been learned, there is a probability h that its code still supports retention in a temporary way. Then if g is the probability of a correct guess, the probability of a correct response for unlearned items is

$$p = h + (1 - h)g.$$

There are two parameters to estimate, p and c, and we are mainly interested in c. The parameters are easily estimated using the mean number of errors and the mean trial of last error. If subjects have a study trial on all items before they are tested, then

$$P(T = j) = \left(\frac{(1 - c)q}{q + pc}\right)^j \frac{c}{q + pc},$$

$$E(T) = \frac{(1 - c)q}{c}. \tag{28}$$

The distribution of the trial of last error is

$$P(L = k) = \begin{cases} (1 - c)^k \left(\dfrac{qc}{q + pc}\right) & \text{for } k \geq 1, \\[2ex] \dfrac{c}{q + pc} & \text{for } k = 0, \end{cases} \tag{29}$$

$$E(L) = \frac{(1 - c)q}{c(q + pc)}. \tag{30}$$

Combining Eqs. (28) and (30),

$$\frac{E(T)}{E(L)} = q + pc,$$

$$\hat{c} = \frac{E(T)}{E(L)[E(T) + 1]}. \qquad (31)$$

The actual situation is somewhat simplified by saying that all the codes for a given item can be divided into two dichotomous categories; those that will support retention, the set C, and those that will not, I. Then the set of codes for a stimulus will be called $S = C \cup I$.

Let the magnitude or probability of any set be described in general by a measure function[16] m; in the present application, $m(X)$ is the sum of the weights of all elements of X. Therefore the probability of choosing a correct code, when resampling on an item, is

$$c = m(C)/m(S).$$

Now consider an item in which the stimulus is made up of two quite separate parts, such as a nonsense trigram and a word. Let S_T be the total set of cues of the trigram, with subset C_T that lead to retention, and similarly, assume that C_w and S_w are the correct subset and the total set of codes for a word. The two learning rates, proportions of correct codes, are

$$c_T = m(C_T)/m(S_T)$$

and

$$c_W = m(C_W)/m(S_W).$$

When a compound is made up of a trigram and a word, as in the James and Greeno experiment, the new total set of codes should be $S_{T\&W} = S_T \cup S_W$, the union of the two sets, and similarly $C_{T\&W} = C_T \cup C_W$. Therefore

$$c_{T\&W} = m(C_{T\&W})/m(S_{T\&W}). \qquad (32)$$

---

[16] The measure function gives a general concept of magnitude or probability. The number of elements in a set is a measure of that set, but is empirically correct only when all elements are equally potent. Different elements can be assigned weights, and the measure of a set can be the sum of the weights of its elements. This is a satisfactory structure, assuming there are a finite number of weights, or at most a countable number, and that all sums are well behaved. However, a general formulation is the measure function m. Three axioms characterize such a function: $M1$: $m(\varnothing) = 0$; $M2$: for all sets X, $m(X) \geq 0$; $M3$: if X and Y are disjoint, then $m(X \cup Y) = m(X) + m(Y)$. A fourth axiom is often appended to ensure additivity of infinite unions of sets.

The following rule of set theory is the key to the implications of Eq. (32):

$$m(X \cup Y) = m(X) + m(Y) - m(X \cap Y).$$

Therefore

$$m(C_{T\&W}) = m(C_T) + m(C_W) - m(C_T \cap C_W). \tag{33}$$

There are several arrangements of the codes for a word and a trigram that might be obtained. The left side of Fig. 3.2 shows the general case. The center panel, labeled B, pictures the possibility that the inadequate codes are produced entirely by inattention or failures to process items successfully for memory. All items have the same set of inadequate codes, I, but each stimulus component has a unique set of codes that can be used to remember it. In this case,

$$\frac{c_W}{1 - c_W} = \frac{m(C_W)}{m(I_W)}, \qquad \frac{c_T}{1 - c_T} = \frac{m(C_T)}{m(I_T)}.$$

Since $m(I_T) = m(I_W) = m(I)$,

$$\frac{c_{T\&W}}{1 - c_{T\&W}} = \frac{m(C_W) + m(C_T)}{m(I)}$$

$$= \frac{c_T}{1 - c_T} + \frac{c_W}{1 - c_W}.$$

Then

$$c_{T\&W} = \frac{c_T + c_W - 2c_Tc_W}{1 - c_Tc_W}. \tag{34}$$

According to this assumption, compounding will always facilitate learning, and $c_{T\&W}$ will be larger than either c_W or c_T. (The student is asked to prove this assertion in Exercise 12.)

A second possibility is that the adequate codes of the word are disjoint from the adequate codes of the trigram, and the inadequate codes of the word are also disjoint from the inadequate codes of the trigram.

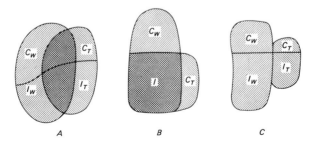

Figure 3.2

Consider the simple case of this theory in which the complete sets of codes for the two components have equal measure. Then

$$m(C_W \cup C_T) = m(C_W) + m(C_T),$$
$$m(S_W \cup S_T) = 2m(S_W).$$

This gives the result

$$c_{W\&T} = \frac{c_W + c_T}{2} ; \tag{35}$$

the learning rate for the compound is the average of the learning rates of the components.

In the concept-identification experiments discussed earlier, it was assumed that each dimension could be relevant or irrelevant; when two cues were both relevant and redundant, they also shared the same irrelevant dimensions. In applying the same theory to paired-associates learning, it should be apparent that each item may bring forth its own irrelevant codes as well as its own correct codes. If this happens, then the "additivity-of-cues" experiment, carried out in this case by providing compound stimuli, may not lead to faster learning, and may instead lead to slower learning than could be managed by subjects using only the best element of the stimulus. An extreme illustration is easily conceived—if, for example, the highly learnable word were embedded on a large card among 24 nonsense syllables, such extremely complex cards might well be less effective as stimuli than a single three-letter word. The explanation would then have to be that the complex card brings forth many wrong codes, or (in the terminology suitable to the concept-identification experiments) many irrelevant cues. In this theory it is the proportion of correct codes or cues, not their absolute number, that controls the rate of learning.

Systematic Selection of Types of Codes

In a recent study, Harrington[17] used word–trigram compound stimuli. In his experimental lists, a word–trigram or a trigram–word compound was used as a stimulus, and the response was a numeral. In the experimental list one of the components of each item, either word or trigram, was colored yellow for emphasis. In the control condition, no emphasis was used.

After a subject learned the list he was tested on both the word and the trigram components. For a given original compound he might get the word, the trigram, or both correct.

The overall effects of emphasis are first noticed. Table 3.2 shows that words were remembered best when emphasized, next best when neutral, and

[17] Harrington, A. L., Effects of component emphasis on stimulus selection in paired-associate learning. *J. Exp. Psych.*, 1969, **79**, 412–418.

Table 3.2 Test performance on component stimuli as a function of emphasis

Component tested	Word emphasized	Control	Trigram emphasized
Word	0.68	0.50	0.34
Trigram	0.05	0.13	0.22

worst when the trigram is emphasized. The converse relationship holds with trigrams.

This experiment also showed a competition between cues, in that subjects tended to do better in tests on words when they did not know the trigram, and vice versa. The facts are shown in Table 3.3. Each entry is a conditional probability; for example, P(correct on word | correct on trigram) and P(correct on word | incorrect on trigram.) In this experiment, notice that there were a substantial number of instances in which the subject knew the response to both stimulus components.

The main question about this experiment is, however, whether the subjects randomly chose codes for the items as they came up, choosing the word and the trigram randomly and independently, or whether they instead systematically chose one kind of code, e.g., all words or all trigrams.

In this experiment there were two systematic strategies available to the subjects: (1) they could choose the word for each item, regardless of which component was emphasized, or (2) they could choose the emphasized component for each item, regardless of whether it was a word or a trigram.

Using either strategy, subjects would know the word components that were emphasized. Therefore much information should not be expected from the items with emphasized words, and in fact subjects knew only five percent of the trigram components from those items. However, the items with emphasized trigrams were informative, since subjects using strategy 1 would choose the word components of these items and subjects using strategy 2 would choose the trigrams.

A further narrowing of the data was also carried out. If a subject knew both the word and the trigram, or knew neither, his data could not help us

Table 3.3 Test performance on one component stimulus as a function of success on the other

Component tested	Other component correct	Other component wrong
Word	0.30	0.54
Trigram	0.08	0.19

tell whether he learned two items the same way. Those items with trigrams emphasized, and where the subject knew one component (word or trigram) and not the other are the ones to be examined. There were 19 subjects who knew one component and not the other for exactly two items, 8 subjects who knew one component and not the other for three items, and 1 subject who knew all four of the relevant items.

Consider the implications of purely random, independent sampling. Suppose that there is some probability w that the subject will choose the word when he learns either the word or the trigram, and with probability $1 - w$ that he will know only the trigram. Now suppose such a subject knows one component each of two items. The probability that he learns the word component of both is w^2; the probability that he learns the trigram component of both is $(1 - w)^2$; and the probability that he learns the word component of one and the trigram component of the other is $2w(1 - w)$. Table 3.4 shows these predictions for the observed value of w, 0.57, along with the observed relative frequencies of subjects. Observed values are significantly discrepant (0.01 level) from predicted values. The direction of the difference is that subjects tended strongly either to know all the words and miss the trigrams, or to know all the trigrams and miss the words. Very rarely did they know one word and one trigram. Clearly, Harrington's subjects seem to have developed an overall strategy either to concentrate on words or to concentrate on trigrams.

Table 3.4 Predicted and obtained proportions of subjects

	Predicted from independent selection	Obtained
Know only words	0.30	0.54
Know some of each	0.56	0.18
Know only trigrams	0.13	0.29

SUMMARY

This chapter has shown how both simple concept formation and certain problems in paired-associate learning can be analyzed using a theory of hypothesis or cue selection. This theory says that the probability of learning is the joint probability that the subject resamples and hits a satisfactory hypothesis, cue, or code. This gives a theory of the rate of learning that applies both to concept formation and some work in paired associates.

The theory asserts that learning is fast when the proportion of correct elements is high, and therefore it leads to an experiment in additivity of cues.

A second major implication of the theory is all-or-none transfer. If two or more cues are relevant and redundant, the subject learns the problem, and when he is tested on one or the other component, he may know either component or both. If he uses one cue at a time, he will know at most one component. If he uses more than one hypothesis or cue in his sample, he may happen to hit more than one of the redundant relevant cues and then will be able to respond correctly to both.

Paired-associates learning uses somewhat less well-defined stimuli than concept formation, in that one is less sure what aspects of the stimulus are cues to the subject. When the subject is processing a whole list of stimuli, each of which is made of two components—a word and a trigram—he tends to learn the words first, then pick up the trigrams after the words are learned (James and Greeno). If this tendency is broken up by mixing up the arrangement of words and trigrams, the subjects apparently have a tendency to learn all the words or all the trigrams, rather than a random assortment of the two.

Apparently, then, a process of selection of hypotheses, cues, or codes takes place in both of these learning situations. Very simple models of the process can be constructed and tested, and the agreement with data is quite good. However, it must be remembered that the model of the experiment is a simplification, and the random resampling scheme may not be as simple as would be imagined. The particular codes and cues of particular stimuli are not well known, and overall calculations merely reflect simplifying assumptions as in Fig. 3.2. There is much to explore about the stimulus properties effective in paired-associates learning.

Furthermore, the simple one-element-at-a-time sampling scheme, though sometimes fairly close, is not usually the correct theory of learning. Instead, subjects sample several components or cues at a time, and may develop overall strategies of selection. It will be interesting to pick apart the various processes and complications by experiment. The theoretical contribution of the mathematical theory of cue selection is, first, to formulate and refine the experimental problems, and, second, to give a manageable and coherent theory of how the several processes go together.

EXERCISES

1. Using the assumption that W is empty [as was assumed in deriving Eqs. (11), (12), and (13)], derive expressions for $P(X_n = 1 \mid Y > n)$ and $P(X_n = 1 \mid Y \geq n)$, where $X_n = 1$ denotes an error on trial n, and Y denotes the trial of last error. Comment on the differences between these results and the corresponding results for the all-or-none model of Chapter 2.

2. Suppose that in a concept identification experiment, there are N possible hypotheses, with equal sampling probabilities. The subject selects one at random and uses it until (or if) he makes an error. Then he eliminates that hypothesis from the pool of hypotheses, selects one from the remaining hypotheses, and uses it until (or if) he makes an error, at which time he eliminates the second hypothesis and selects another. Find the distribution of the number of errors prior to solution, assuming that just one of the N hypotheses is correct.

3. Suppose that following an error, instead of sampling from the total set of hypotheses, the subject samples from that subset which is consistent with the information given to the subject on that trial. Assume the same focussing process following correct responses as in the text, and assume that H contains many hypotheses, possibly of different weights. Calculate the recurrence probabilities of an error, and give the transition matrix for the case where samples are of size $s = 1$.

4. Using the assumptions of Problem 3, give a state space and transition matrix for the case where samples are of size $s = 2$. [*Hint:* a state in this system on trial n is a triple $\langle S, U, R \rangle$, where S describes the set of hypotheses that the subject has in his sample on trial n, U is the hypothesis used by the subject to respond on trial n, and R is the response: correct or error.]

5. In a set of stimuli for concept identification, consider two cues A and B, where $w_A = 2$, $w_B = 3$. Let w_I denote the summed weights of all other cues, and $w_I = 9$. Calculate theoretical probabilities of solution, c, for the following problems.

i) A is relevant, and B and all other cues are irrelevant.
ii) A is relevant, B is absent, and all other cues are irrelevant.
iii) A is irrelevant, B is relevant, and all other cues are irrelevant.
iv) A is absent, B is relevant, and all other cues are irrelevant.
v) A and B are relevant and redundant, and all other cues are irrelevant.
vi) A and B are irrelevant, and all other cues are irrelevant.

6. In testing additivity of cues by the method described on pp. 88–90, data from two groups are used to estimate parameters and these are used to calculate predictions for the remaining groups. A better test uses all the data to estimate the needed parameters. The best technique uses all the data to minimize some goodness-of-fit criterion (see Chapter 9), but this often requires computer methods. Let $\bar{T}_1, \ldots, \bar{T}_5$ denote the mean errors obtained in situations (i), $\ldots$, (v) of Problem 5, and using Eq. (14), show that estimates of w_A/w_I and w_B/w_I are the solutions of the following simultaneous linear equations.

$$4\left(\frac{\hat{w}_A}{w_I}\right) = \left[\frac{1}{\bar{T}_1} + \bar{T}_3 - 1\right]\left(\frac{\hat{w}_B}{w_I}\right) + \frac{1}{\bar{T}_1} + \frac{1}{\bar{T}_2} + \frac{1}{\bar{T}_5} - 1,$$

$$4\left(\frac{\hat{w}_B}{w_I}\right) = \left[\bar{T}_1 + \frac{1}{\bar{T}_3} - 1\right]\left(\frac{\hat{w}_A}{w_I}\right) + \frac{1}{\bar{T}_3} + \frac{1}{\bar{T}_4} + \frac{1}{\bar{T}_5} - 1.$$

Also find estimates of these parameters using all the data if an experiment includes (a) only conditions (i), (iii), and (v), and (b) only conditions (ii), (iv), and (v).

7. Calculate predicted numbers of subjects knowing dot only, form only, and both dimensions for Trabasso and Bower's experiment assuming that $s = 3$. Carry out chi-square tests using the data of Table 3.1 against your predictions and the predictions obtained by Trabasso and Bower.

8. In the text, the subject's sample size s is assumed to be an integer. This is reasonable, but variations from one trial to another or among subjects might produce a situation better approximated by allowing s to take noninteger values. Show that an estimate of s can be obtained as

$$\hat{s} = \frac{\log P_d + \log (f + d) - \log d}{2 \log (1 - f)} + \frac{\log P_f + \log (f + d) - \log f}{2 \log (1 - d)}.$$

Calculate this estimate of s from Trabasso and Bower's data, and use it to obtain predictions for the data of Table 3.1.

✓ **9.** Consider the assumptions of p.108 in more detail.[18] Let L be the learned state, as before; let H be the state of an unlearned item that is remembered in a temporary way; and let G and E be the states of items that are unlearned and not in temporary memory that are guessed correctly and incorrectly, respectively. Give the transition matrix for the model, calculate the learning curve, and verify Eqs. (28) through (30).

✓ **10.** McFadden and Greeno[19] used the hypothesis selection theory of verbal learning to interpret results obtained when two different tests of retention were used. Subjects studied CVC trigrams. Then Group 1 received two completion tests where they saw the first two letters of each trigram and were asked to recall. For Group 1, $P_1(X_1 = 0) = 0.17$, $P_1(X_2 = 0 \mid X_1 = 1) = 0.06$, and $P_1(X_2 = 0 \mid X_1 = 0) = 0.66$. The near-chance value of $P_1(X_2 = 0 \mid X_1 = 1)$ is consistent with the idea that learning was all-or-none. (Recall Estes' *RTT* experiment described in Chapter 2.) Group 2 received a two-choice recognition test; they saw the first two letters of each trigram and two alternatives for the third letter. For Group 2, $P_2(X_1 = 0) = 0.70$. Group 3 received a completion test followed by a two-choice recognition test. For Group 3, $P_3(X_1 = 0) = 0.17$, $P_3(X_2 = 0 \mid X_1 = 1) = 0.58$, and $P_3(X_2 = 0 \mid X_1 = 0) = 0.88$.

First, apply the simple all-or-none model of Chapter 2, using $P_1(X_1 = 0)$ to estimate c, and assume guessing values of $g_r = 0.05$ for the completion tests of recall and $g_t = 0.50$ for the two-choice tests of recognition. Comment on the discrepancies involving $P_2(X_1 = 0)$ and $P_3(X_2 = 0 \mid X_1 = 1)$.

Next, apply the following assumptions. There is a set of codes S for each item. A subset C_t is adequate for retaining an item well enough to know the answer on a two-choice test given first, and a subset $C_r \subset C_t$ is adequate to retain an item well enough to recall its third member on a completion test given first. Finally, assume that a fixed proportion of codes f are lost between the first and second tests. Use $P_1(X_1 = 0)$, $P_1(X_2 = 0 \mid X_1 = 0)$, and $P_2(X_1 = 0)$ to estimate $c_r = m(C_r)/m(S)$, f, and $c_t = m(C_t)/m(S)$. Then calculate theoretical values of $P_3(X_1 = 0)$, $P_3(X_2 = 0 \mid X_1 = 1)$, and $P_3(X_2 = 0 \mid X_1 = 0)$. (*Partial ans.:* $c_r = 0.126$, $c_t = 0.40$, $f = 0.133$.) How could the forgetting assumption be modified to give better quantitative agreement with the data? Would the needed modification be psychologically reasonable?

---

[18] A detailed statistical analysis of these assumptions is given by J. G. Greeno, Paired-associate learning with short-term retention: mathematical analysis and data regarding identification of parameters. *J. Math. Psych.*, 1967, **4**, 430–472.

[19] McFadden, D. and J. G. Greeno, Evidence of different degrees of learning based on different tests of retention. *J. Verb. Learn. Verb. Behav.*, 1968, **7**, 452–457.

11. *Transfer of paired-associate training.* Greeno and Scandura[20] trained subjects on paired-associates using stimuli related by verbal concepts. (For example, "wheel," "barrel," and "doughnut" are all members of the concept category "round.") After training, new stimuli were presented from the concept categories, and values of a transfer parameter π were estimated. Two kinds of words were used, some called high-dominance words for which the connection with the concept was obvious, and others called low-dominance words for which the connection with the concept was subtle. Training for each concept involved either one, two, or four words that were either high or low dominance, with all the words from a a concept set paired with the same response. Transfer was tested either with a high- or low-dominance word from the same concept set, paired with the same response.

Assume that within the set of adequate codes C for each item, there is a subset A that allows the subject to recognize the item's concept membership and thereby acquire the concept. Assume that there is a fixed probability $a = m(A)/m(C)$ of acquiring the concept each time an item is learned in training, and that a has two values, a_H for high-dominance items and a_L for low-dominance items. Finally, assume that if a concept was acquired in training, there is a probability b that a new item presented in the transfer test will be recognized, thereby producing transfer to the new item; b also takes two values, b_H and b_L for high- and low-dominance items.

Greeno and Scandura estimated parameter values of $\hat{a}_H = 0.387$, $\hat{a}_L = 0.147$, $\hat{b}_H = 1.00$, $\hat{b}_L = 0.600$. There were 12 conditions: one, two, or four training items of high or low dominance, and a high- or low-dominance item given in transfer. Find the expression relating the parameters to values of π in the 12 conditions, and calculate theoretical values of π. Estimates of π obtained from the separate conditions are given in Table 3.5. [*Note:* these estimates are based on only 24 cases per cell, and hence are quite unreliable.]

Table 3.5 Estimates of π Obtained from Separate Conditions

Number of training items	High High	High Low	Low High	Low High Low	← Training dominance ← Transfer dominance
1	0.33	0.43	0	0	
2	0.86	0.28	0.19	0.14	
4	0.67	0.52	0.57	0.47	

12. Given Eq. (30), prove that $c_{T\&W} > c_W$ whenever $c_T > 0$

13. Suppose that to solve a problem a subject must accomplish two things. The two stages occur sequentially, and each is an all-or-none process. The first stage occurs with probability a following an error, and the second stage occurs with probability b following errors that occur after the first stage has been completed (including the error on which the first stage is accomplished). If T_1 and T_2 equal the

[20] Greeno, J. G. and J. M. Scandura, All-or-none transfer based on verbally mediated concepts. *J. Math. Psych.*, 1966, **3**, 388–411. The article presents the results described here, as well as evidence that transfer occurred in an all-or-none fashion.

number of errors in each stage, we have

$$P(T_1 = i) = (1 - a)^i a, \qquad P(T_2 = j) = (1 - b)^j b; \qquad i, j = 0, 1, \ldots.$$

Show that the distribution of errors is

$$P(T = k) = ab \left[\frac{(1 - a)^k - (1 - b)^k}{b - a} \right],$$

and that the mean of T is

$$E(T) = \frac{1 - a}{a} + \frac{1 - b}{b}.$$

CHAPTER FOUR

Adaptation Level

This chapter deals with a single general idea which cuts across many different topics in perception, and is particularly *psychological* in nature, as contrasted with more physiological or physical theories of perception. The idea is that of perceptual relativity.

Consider a perceptual demonstration, shown in Fig. 4.1. The subject is asked to judge which line segment is longer, and he chooses segment *ab*. However, physical measurement shows that segment *cd* is longer. In one sense, the subject's perception is "incorrect." Although he gives a false report about the physical stimuli, in another sense his report is correct. Because of the sizes of the squares, segment *ab* really appears to be longer.

Figure 4.1

One approach to the theory of perception starts with the idea that a percept of some object corresponds to the pattern of energy transmitted from that object to the receptor organs. This "physical" approach leads to the detailed description and analysis of the physical stimuli present, and this is all to the good. However, this theory can lead to some erroneous predictions. For example, in Fig. 4.1, the retinal image produced by segment *ab* is smaller than that produced by segment *cd*. These errors are corrected only by special psychological factors like "illusions," "bias," etc. From a physical point of view, perception is either correct or incorrect, and the psychology of perception is mainly a chronicle of errors.

In contrast, the theory of perceptual relativity states that perception of any stimulus depends on the overall pattern or flux of energy received by the observer. In other words, perception is intrinsically relative. Most physical

119

measurements are designed to be constant independent of the situation in which the measurement occurs.   Therefore there is a general difference between physical and perceptual measurements, and the various "illusions" are manifestations of this basic difference.   Perception will reflect physical measurement whenever the perceptual situation is held constant.   If perceptions are all relative to a constant background, then they will be directly related to absolute measurements.   However, as soon as the background changes, the perceptions will be sensitive to these changes whereas physical measurements will not.

If this idea is correct, there is a basic difference between physics and perception with regard to the treatment of a complex field.   Physical measurements of parts of a field are all independent; if a patch of gray paper reflects 30% of incident light, then this measurement is independent of what other reflections are nearby, or the intensity of the incident light.   A physical analysis of a field of various grays would proceed by scanning the field and measuring reflectances, or total light reflected, at each point of the field.

The perceptual analysis of the field holds that the brightness of any part of the field does not exist as a determinate number, except relative to other parts of the field.

Suppose that perceived brightness of a part of the field depends upon reflectances all over the field.   The observer will scan the field, and not take in all the light energy equally and at once.   This means that some of the input is "stored" temporarily, yet has its effect on the brightness of other parts of the field.   The implication is that not only *present*, but also *past* inputs may affect brightness, and perception is relative not only to present but past events.

This introduction indicates that the "field" to be considered, from the present point of view, should be as inclusive as possible, encompassing all possible influences, however widely they may be separated from the focal (judged) stimulus in space and time.

ADAPTATION LEVEL

A general theory of perceptual relativity seems extremely complicated, because the judgment of any particular focal stimulus depends upon its comparison with all other parts of the field.   Of course, the perceived magnitudes of other parts of the field, in turn, depend upon their relationships to all other parts including the focal stimulus.

A simplified description of this situation, put forward by Helson,[1] states that the perceived value of any focal stimulus is the physical magnitude of that stimulus divided by the adaptation level at that point.   The adaptation

---

[1] H. Helson, *Adaptation-Level Theory*. New York: Harper and Row, 1964.

level is a weighted average of the physical magnitudes of all stimuli in the total field, each weighted according to its psychological proximity or relevance to perception of the focal stimulus.

Any physical object has many attributes or properties, such as height, width, brightness, color, and texture. Any of these can be measured physically, and judgments related to the physical measurements can be made. If an observer is asked to make judgments of a single specified kind, for example, brightness or length, then the physical magnitude denotes the physical measurement of that dimension, and the judged magnitude of the stimulus is the judgment of that dimension. The basic assumption of the present theory is that J, the judged magnitude of a stimulus of physical magnitude S, is given by the formula

$$J = S/A, \tag{1}$$

where A is the adaptation level. The value of A represents a kind of standard or reference with which single stimuli are compared. Since S is the physical magnitude of a stimulus, it has units of physical measurement, for example, centimeters. Since A is an average of physical magnitudes, its units are the same physical measurement. Thus J is a pure number without physical units.

Because the judgment of a stimulus depends on A, a given physical stimulus will not always have the same appearance or judgment. If the adaptation level A can be changed, judgment of the stimulus will also change.

According to this idea, all factors in the perceptual field, including the past, are combined to form the adaptation level A. The theoretical formula used by Helson is the weighted geometric mean of the physical magnitudes of all the effective stimuli,

$$A = [S_1^{w_1} S_2^{w_2} \cdots S_N^{w_N}]^{1/(w_1 + w_2 + \cdots + w_N)}. \tag{2}$$

Taking logarithms, as is usual in manipulating this theory,

$$\log A = \left[\sum_{i=1}^{N} w_i \log S_i \right] \bigg/ \sum_{i=1}^{N} w_i. \tag{3}$$

Equation (3) is usually applied in a simpler form, classifying various sources of stimulation. A typical experiment may use test stimuli S of varying magnitudes, and certain aspects of the background B may be varied systematically. Other features of the background remain constant K; these include the size and illumination of the room, the size of the screen on which visual stimuli are projected, and other features. Consider a subject judging a stimulus of magnitude S, with the variable aspects of the background having magnitude B, and the constant factors having magnitude K. Then A will depend upon the stimulus itself, the background, and the constant factors as follows:

$$\log A = \frac{s \log S + b \log B + k \log K}{s + b + k}.$$

In this case, the judgment is

$$J = \frac{S}{A},$$

$$\log J = \log S - \log A$$

$$= \left(1 - \frac{s}{s + b + k}\right) \log S - \frac{b}{s + b + k} \log B$$

$$- \frac{k}{s + b + k} \log K.$$

To simplify the notation, we let $s' = s/(s + b + k)$, and so forth. Then

$$s' + b' + k' = 1,$$

and

$$\log J = (1 - s') \log S - b' \log B - k' \log K,$$

or, taking antilogs of both sides,

$$J = S^{1-s'}B^{-b'}K^{-k'}. \tag{4}$$

When a second stimulus in the field is varied, the "background" stimulus with magnitude B, this changes judgments about the focal stimulus. If S is held constant, Eq. (4) states that J is a power function of B, and the power is negative; increasing the physical value of the background *decreases* the judgment of the stimulus. This is a simple contrast effect, and will be analyzed in more experimental detail later.

Experimental Illustration: A Relative-Size Illusion

In our laboratories at Indiana University,[2] quite a number of subjects judged the length of lines having squares, of various sizes, appended as in Fig. 4.2.

On each trial, the subject was to judge the length of the line between the squares, and report his judgment by pushing one of six buttons. The size of the visual arc subtended by a stimulus is equal to the measure of the angle made by straight lines from the viewing point to the ends of the stimulus line. The lines subtended visual angles of 12, 16, 20, 24, and 28 min. The sides of the squares subtended visual angles of 8, 12, 16, 20, 24, and 28 min.

---

[2] F. Restle and C. T. Merryman, An adaptation-level theory account of a relative-size illusion. *Psychon. Sci.*, 1968, **12**, 229–230.

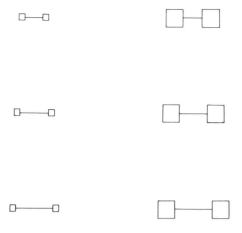

Figure 4.2

Combining each line length with each square size gave a total of 5 × 6 = 30 presentations, which were shown seven times to each of 50 subjects. Responses to the last four trials will be reported; there were a few less than 200 judgments per point due to occasional failures to respond.

Figure 4.3 shows the raw data, in the form of mean judgment as a function of the length of the line and the size of the square. Of course, *J*

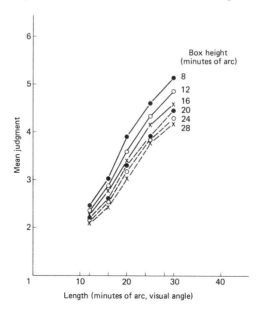

Figure 4.3

increases with the length of line S and decreases with the size of the background figure, the box, B. Now the question arises whether this configuration of data is in agreement with the quantitative formula given above. By Eq. (4),

$$J = S^{1-s'} B^{-b'} K^{-k'}$$

and

$$\log J = (1 - s') \log S - b' \log B - k' \log K.$$

In the data, S and B are the independent variables, whereas s' and b' are the unknown parameters. The last term is just a constant, and so long as the value of the constant frame of reference K is not known, the last term can be treated as a constant C:

$$\log J = (1 - s') \log S - b' \log B + C. \tag{5}$$

A simple procedure, satisfactory for the present, is to transform S and B into logarithms, and also transform the mean judgments J into logarithms, and plot $\log J$ as a function of $\log S$ (averaged over $\log B$) and then as a function of $\log B$, averaged over $\log S$.

These logarithmic plots are shown in Fig. 4.4. Notice first that straight lines give an excellent fit to the data points, suggesting that to a good

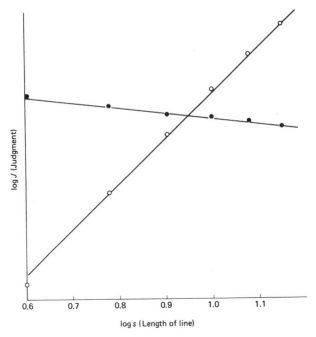

Figure 4.4

approximation, $\log J$ is a linear function both of $\log S$ and of $\log B$. This agrees with the general formulation of Eq. (5). Furthermore, the values of the parameters are reasonable; notice that self adaptation, the effect of the line on itself, is summarized by s', where $s' = 0.054$. The effect of the boxes is weighted by b', estimated at 0.108.

In this way a complete quantitative measurement of the illusion is given—now information is available not only as to how great the illusion is, but also exactly how its magnitude depends upon the sizes of the squares used.

A measure of illusion can be computed from the parameter b'. Intuitively, the amount of the illusion is calculated by varying the box size and asking how great an effect it will have on the apparent or judged length of the line. One might increase the box size by a given amount, thereby making the line look smaller, and then ask by how much the line must be increased to regain its original apparent length.

Suppose that S_1 and B_1 are the magnitudes of a stimulus and background where the subject gives J_{11} as the judged magnitude of the stimulus. By Eq. (4),

$$J_{11} = S_1^{1-s'} B_1^{-b'} K^{-k'}.$$

Now suppose that the box size is increased (or decreased) to B_2. The new judgment would be

$$J_{12} = S_1^{1-s'} B_2^{-b'} K^{-k'} = J_{11} \left(\frac{B_2}{B_1} \right)^{-b'}.$$

Note that if $B_2 > B_1$, then $J_{12} < J_{11}$ and if $B_2 < B_1$, then $J_{12} > J_{11}$, because b' is positive.

Now suppose that the line length is changed from S_1 to S_2, with the box size left at B_2. In this situation the judgment of line length will be

$$J_{22} = S_2^{1-s'} B_2^{-b'} K^{-k'} = J_{11} \left(\frac{S_2}{S_1} \right)^{1-s'} \left(\frac{B_2}{B_1} \right)^{-b'}.$$

If S_2 and B_2 are chosen so that $J_{22} = J_{11}$, then

$$\left(\frac{S_2}{S_1} \right)^{1-s'} \left(\frac{B_2}{B_1} \right)^{-b'} = 1$$

$$\frac{S_2}{S_1} = \left(\frac{B_2}{B_1} \right)^{b'/(1-s')}. \tag{6}$$

Equation (6) gives the ratio change in stimulus magnitude that just compensates a ratio change in background magnitude. For example, in the experiment using line lengths and box sizes, box sizes from 8 to 28 units were used, a ratio of 3.5. What increase in line length would compensate for this amount of change in box size? Using Eq. (6) and the estimated parameter values,

$$\frac{S_2}{S_1} = (3.5)^{0.108/0.946} = (3.5)^{0.114} = 1.154.$$

Illusions are often measured by presenting a stimulus with magnitude S_1 and background magnitude B_1 as a standard. A number of comparison stimuli are presented with a second background, B_2. The experimenters' task is to determine the magnitude of a stimulus in the second background that is judged equal to the first stimulus in its background. A number of psychophysical methods can be used. One is the method of constant stimuli, where several stimuli are presented and the subject says "greater," "less," or "equal" for each comparison stimulus. Another method is the method of limits, where comparison stimuli are presented in ascending or descending order until the subject judges one to be "equal." A third method is that of adjustment, where the subject changes the magnitude of the comparison stimulus until it appears equal to the magnitude of the standard. It is customary to describe an illusion as the proportional difference between physical stimulus magnitudes that are judged equal in the two backgrounds.

Let I be the amount of illusion, and let S_2 be the magnitude of a stimulus judged equal to the standard. Then

$$I = \frac{S_2 - S_1}{S_1} = \frac{S_2}{S_1} - 1. \tag{7}$$

The data reported here were obtained using the method of single stimuli, where each combination of a stimulus and a background is presented alone, and the subject makes a judgment—in the present case, a rating scale was used. In the laboratory, this method of single stimuli is relatively simple for observers and experimenters, yet (by use of adaptation-level theory) it gives the same kind of information obtained from the more laborious methods of constant stimuli, limits, or adjustment. The measurement of illusion is obtained from Eq. (7), substituting for S_2/S_1 using Eq. (6). For example, when the backgrounds have a ratio of 14:4, the estimated parameters give the result

$$I = \frac{S_2}{S_1} - 1 = \left(\frac{B_2}{B_1}\right)^{b'/(1-s')} - 1$$

$$= \left(\tfrac{14}{4}\right)^{0.114} - 1 = 0.154,$$

somewhat more than a 15% illusion.

Note that the calculation of proportional illusion does not refer explicitly to judgments *J*. In this calculation, one measures how judgments vary when line-length *S* is varied, and then sees how the same judgments vary when box-size *B* is varied. A relatively small change in *S* compensates for a relatively large change in *B*.

COMPARISON OF TWO STIMULI

In some experiments subjects are called upon to compare two stimulus objects, a standard with magnitude S_1 and a comparison with magnitude S_2. Subjects may be asked to judge which is greater, or they may adjust one until it appears equal to the other. These methods certainly reduce the complexity of the judgment required of the subject, and for that reason can be used to study the perception of animals and young children. Instead of a numerical judgment, the subject merely makes some sort of binary choice. The methods of comparison are more complicated, however, in that the display must include two stimuli, and the subject often looks or attends back and forth from one stimulus to the other. The data yield a *point of subjective equality*, PSE, which is that magnitude of the comparison stimulus S_2 which appears equal to S_1.

If the standard and comparison stimuli have different adaptation levels, A_1 and A_2, then using Eq. (1) separately for each stimulus,

$$J_1 = \frac{S_1}{A_1}, \qquad J_2 = \frac{S_2}{A_2}. \tag{8}$$

At the point of subjective equality (PSE), S_2 is judged equal to S_1:

$$J_1 = J_2. \tag{9}$$

Any differences in physical measurements, S_1 and S_2, can be attributed to differences in the adaptation levels. From Eq. (8), we find that

$$\frac{S_1}{A_1} = \frac{S_2}{A_2},$$

whence

$$S_2 = S_1\left(\frac{A_2}{A_1}\right), \tag{10}$$

and differences between S_1 and S_2 reflect differences in the adaptation level.

A line appears shorter when larger boxes are put at the end of it according to the method of single stimuli. Presumably, if subjects compare the length of two lines, one with larger and one with smaller boxes, they would want a slightly longer line to go with the larger boxes to arrive at the PSE. Note that Fig. 4.5 shows two equal lines; the one in the larger box appears to be shorter. The constant factors that appear in the formulas for both adaptation levels do not affect the value of A_2/A_1. Therefore, when the PSE is measured directly in an experiment, stimuli in the distant past and stimuli not particularly manipulated in the experiment can be ignored as having no effect on the main experimental measurements.

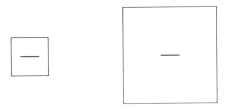

Figure 4.5

Künnapas on Frame Size

In his laboratories at the University of Stockholm, T. M. Künnapas[3] used the method of constant stimuli to study how the length of a line was affected by the size of an enclosing square background. He used a large blue field in which were displayed two white squares. The constant square was 70 × 70 mm, and the variable square was one of the following: 90 × 90, 120 × 120, 160 × 160, or 210 × 210. In the center of the constant 70 × 70 mm square was a line 50-mm long. In the center of the variable square was a line of variable length (variation in steps of 1 mm). On each trial the subject stated whether the variable line was longer or shorter than the constant 50-mm line.

From these judgments one can interpolate to find, to a close approximation, the length of a line in a given variable square that looks as long as the 50-mm line in the 70 × 70 mm frame, the point of subjective equality, PSE. According to Eq. (8), A_1 of the 50-mm line and A_2 of the variable line are weighted geometric means of the factors involved. However, there are different adaptation levels at the two lines, because of the different sizes of squares.

The important factors in the field are the lines themselves (self adaptation), the squares around them, here called the background factor B, and an agglomeration of constant factors K.

Let $S_1 = 50$ mm, $B_1 = 70$ mm (the linear dimensions of the square), S_2 be the PSE, and B_2 be the variable height of the square around the variable line.

---

[3] T. Künnapas, Influence of frame size on apparent length of line. *J. Exp. Psych.*, 1955, **50**, 168–170.

For a first study of the situation, consider two bold simplifying assumptions:

1. The standard stimulus and its background are functionally separated from the comparison stimulus and its background, so that only the constant factor K is shared.
2. The self-adaptation parameter s' and the box parameter b' are the same as in the experiments discussed above, namely, $s' = 0.054$ and $b' = 0.108$.

These assumptions are no doubt incorrect in detail, but might be close enough to give a first approximation to the data. By using Eq. (8),

$$S_2 = S_1\left(\frac{A_2}{A_1}\right),$$

where

$$A_1 = (50^s 70^b K^k)^{1/(s+b+k)}$$

and

$$A_2 = (S_2^s B_2^b K^k)^{1/(s+b+k)}.$$

Using Eq. (10), we find that

$$\frac{S_2}{50} = \left[\left(\frac{S_2}{50}\right)^s \left(\frac{B_2}{70}\right)^b\right]^{1/(s+b+k)},$$

and

$$\left(\frac{S_2}{50}\right)^{(b+k)/(s+b+k)} = \left(\frac{B_2}{70}\right)^{b/(s+b+k)}.$$

Then taking the $[(b + k)/(s + b + k)]$ root of each side,

$$\frac{S_2}{50} = \left(\frac{B_2}{70}\right)^{b/(b+k)}, \qquad S_2 = 50\left(\frac{B_2}{70}\right)^{b/(b+k)}, \tag{11}$$

which is the formula for calculating quantitative predictions. From the earlier experiment, $b' = 0.108$ and $s' = 0.054$, so $b'/1 - s' = 0.114$. Recall that $b' = b/(s + b + k)$ and $s' = s/(s + b + k)$, so that

$$b'/(1 - s') = b/(b + k) = 0.114.$$

Expressing Eq. (11) in terms of logarithms, we have

$$\log S_2 = a + 0.114 \log B_2, \tag{12}$$

which says that the PSE should increase as the square around the variable line becomes larger, and that the relationship should be linear on a log-log plot with slope 0.114.

In Fig. 4.6 the PSE, or length of line that appears equal to the 50-mm standard line, is plotted against the length of the square surrounding the variable line S_2. The relationship of log PSE to log B_2 is linear, but its slope is only 0.095 instead of the predicted 0.114.

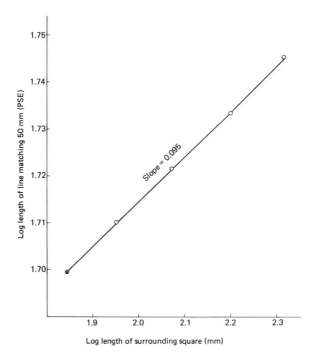

Figure 4.6

Since there were many differences between the two experiments, particularly in spatial arrangement of the figures, we cannot determine exactly what produced the 17% diminution in the estimated weight of the illusion-producing factor.

It is instructive, however, to consider precisely what factors may reduce illusions in a study of comparative judgment. Since both the squares and the lines are in the same field, even though separated somewhat, they may interact. That is, the adaptation level of the 50-mm line S_1 may be affected slightly by the size of the square B_2 surrounding the other line. Suppose there is some such "interaction" parameter i, so that

$$A_1 = (50^s 70^b B_2^i K^k)^{1/(s+b+i+k)}$$

and, conversely,

$$A_2 = (S_2^s B_2^b 70^i K^k)^{1/(s+b+i+k)}$$

assuming that the 70-mm square also has an effect on the adaptation level for the comparison stimulus. Then,

$$\frac{S_2}{50} = \left[\left(\frac{S_2}{50}\right)^s \left(\frac{B_2}{70}\right)^b \left(\frac{70}{B_2}\right)^i \right]^{1/(s+b+i+k)}$$

$$= \left[\left(\frac{S_2}{50}\right)^s \left(\frac{B_2}{70}\right)^{b-i} \right]^{1/(s+b+i+k)}$$

or

$$S_2 = 50 \left(\frac{B_2}{70}\right)^{(b-i)/(b+i+k)}, \tag{13}$$

a new calculating formula. Notice that this is precisely the same as Eq. (11) except that the exponent is now reduced by the interaction parameter i.

Assuming that the values of s, b, and k carry over from the earlier calculations,

$$\frac{b}{b+k} = 0.114 = \frac{1}{1+(k/b)}.$$

Then solve for k/b:

$$(0.114)(1+k/b) = 1, \qquad k/b = 8.77.$$

The exponent in Eq. (13) is

$$\frac{b-i}{b+i+k} = \frac{1-(i/b)}{1+(i/b)+(k/b)} = \frac{1-(i/b)}{9.77+(i/b)}.$$

The slope for Künnepas' data is about 0.095:

$$0.095 = \frac{1-(i/b)}{9.77+(i/b)}, \qquad 0.928 + 0.095\frac{i}{b} = 1 - \frac{i}{b},$$

$$i/b = 0.084.$$

This would mean that the interaction parameter is about one-twelfth of the effect of the boxes.

The analysis of interaction between subfields presented here has necessarily dealt with available data. It is certainly invalid to combine data from experiments run in Bloomington, Indiana, and Stockholm, Sweden, using different stimulus materials. The calculations above merely illustrate the relevant principles. However, precise measurements of the interaction between subfields can be made, based upon comparisons within a single experimental situation. The appropriate experiment has not yet been performed.

Rock and Ebenholtz on Relative Determination of Size

Following up the Künnapas experiment, Rock and Ebenholtz[4] performed a series of experiments in an attempt to demonstrate a very strong form of the theory of relative determination of size. In its extreme form, this theory states that the apparent size of any object in the visual field depends upon its relationship to its immediate surround. For example, suppose that a given visual object subtends a retinal angle of 2°. The object may appear small or large depending upon its immediate visual surroundings. This theory is an attempt to explain size constancy (the eye's ability to respond to the physical size of an object when it is either near or far) even though the retinal angle, that is, the information available at the eye, varies widely with the distance of the object. Large objects, either near or far, must have some common property different from small objects, either near or far. This property may be size relative to the framework consisting of other objects that are equally far away. A large object takes up much of its framework, whereas a small object takes up little of its framework, so the eye can ascertain object size by the ratio of object to framework.

The experiments discussed above, especially the Künnapas study, seem to set severe limits to the relative-size hypothesis. Recall that the size of a line decreased only slightly as the size of the surrounding field was increased; a power function with parameter 0.095 signifies a weak relationship. Clearly, the size of the line in Künnapas' experiment was controlled mainly by factors other than the immediate surrounding square.

The usual explanation of apparent size uses the notion of "unconscious inference." The theory of unconscious inference supposes that the apparent size of an object is based on two sets of cues: retinal size and distance. Suppose the observer knows that an object is at distance d. If h is the physical height of the object and the height of its retinal image is i, then

$$i = r\frac{h}{d},$$

where r is a constant.

The theory of unconscious inference assumes that the observer can use the height of the retinal image and a judgment about distance (obtained from cues such as convergence of the eyes and disparity between the images in the two retinas) to obtain a judgment of object height, presumably using

---

[4] I. Rock and S. Ebenholtz, The relational determination of perceived size. *Psych. Rev.*, 1959, **66**, 387–401.

the formula

$$h = \left(\frac{1}{r}\right)\left(\frac{i}{d}\right).$$

This theory has the difficulty that cues to distance may depend upon the sizes of objects, and especially gradients of the size of particles and grain in the field (Gibson[5]). The observer must use retinal image size, along with retinal disparity, convergence, and whatever other cues exist, to estimate distance. He then uses distance to estimate object size. If the calculated size is anomalous, he must recalculate distance. There is no assurance that such a process of calculations occurs, or, even if it did occur, that veridical judgments would result.

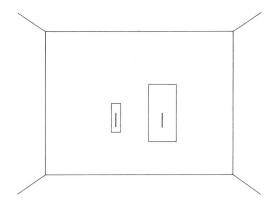

Figure 4.7

Rock and Ebenholtz hypothesize that an inclusive surrounding frame-work has a great effect on the objects within it (Fig. 4.7), and the effect of objects on the framework is relatively slight. The usual experiment includes a general framework, such as the room surrounding the objects. Therefore, Rock and Ebenholtz elected to show faintly luminous figures in a dark room. In this situation there is no effective larger framework, and the experimenter's manipulated frameworks can have a larger effect, as may be seen in Fig. 4.8.

The observer sat in a darkened room with a luminous target on either side of him. His task was to match one line with the other. Both lines were equally far from him and, under the experimental conditions, were surrounded by frames of unequal size. The instructions were to make a true

---

[5] J. J. Gibson, *The Perception of the Visual World.* Boston: Houghton Mifflin, 1950.

Figure 4.8

match of size, which was not necessarily dependent on the size of the framework.

Several experimental variables were manipulated in these studies. For example, some matches were made with ordinary binocular vision, and some with one eye and an artificial pupil, which made it very difficult to judge distance at all. This experiment attempted to get to the heart of the theory of unconscious inference by manipulating knowledge of distance. A second experiment varied the order of presentation of conditions and studied the series effect. Another study compared the effects of different ratios of sizes of frames, from 2:1 to 8:1. Finally, the two stimuli were actually presented at different distances and with different frame sizes.

These experiments, done one after another, do not lead to calculation of a single parameter or function, but instead permit *use* of the adaptation-level theory to interpret a collection of data on apparent size.

Experiment I. Binocular vs. monocular vision. In Experiment I, the standard line was 3 in. long in a 2 × 4 in. frame. The variable line was within a 6 × 12 in. frame. The two objects were both 5 ft away from the observer in opposite directions. In one condition the observer looked with both eyes (binocular viewing), and in the other condition he looked with only one eye and an artificial pupil, so that distance judgments were almost impossible.

The factors in this situation are the two lines, of length S_1 and S_2, the two frames of height B_1 and B_2, and any constant factors that may exist, including, of course, the traces of past trials.

According to Rock and Ebenholtz, the main innovation in their experiment was the absence of any visible background of constant size, common to both fields. This in turn should greatly reduce the weight of the constant factor k in all calculations. Since the visual background was obliterated, we begin by assuming that $k = 0$. As we will see in a moment, judgments were not controlled completely by the frames. However, it is possible that the constant background had no effect, and the observed data can be explained by considering only the effects of the stimuli and backgrounds.

If $k = 0$, then $b' + s' = 1$, or $b' = 1 - s'$. From Eq. (6) we find that

$$S_2 = S_1 \left(\frac{B_2}{B_1}\right)^{b'/1-s'},$$

and when $k = 0$, this is simply

$$S_2 = S_1\left(\frac{B_2}{B_1}\right);$$

or, in another form,

$$\frac{S_2}{B_2} = \frac{S_1}{B_1},$$

which is, of course, pure ratio determination of apparent size. The apparent size of the stimulus is controlled by its background.

The data did not show this sort of pure ratio determination, so there must have been some constant background cues. This does not contradict the authors, who say that the luminous lines and boxes were all that could be seen. The "constant" factor is not visual in the simple sense, but instead is in memory—the subject accumulates a general memory of previous stimuli, and each judgment is influenced by the memory of previous trials, weighted by their recency. This "series" factor was not constant, of course, for each trial produced a change in the remembered set. However, the stimuli were shown in random order, so the short-term fluctuations of the series factor were uncorrelated with the stimulus present. Therefore, the average series factor was the same for all the stimuli, and it shall be treated as a constant.

In the Rock-Ebenholtz experiment allowing binocular regard, S_1 was 3.0 in. within a 2×4 in. frame. For simplicity, since all frames were twice as high as they were wide, the height of the frame shall be used as its measurement. Thus $B_1 = 4$. In this experiment, $B_2 = 12$, for the variable line was within a 6×12 rectangle. On the average, observers set S_2 at 6.0 in. as their PSE. From Eq. (6), we find that

$$S_2 = S_1\left(\frac{B_2}{B_1}\right)^{b'/(b'+k')}$$

Inserting the given values, we have

$$6.0 = 3\left(\tfrac{12}{4}\right)^{b'/(b'+k')},$$

whence

$$2.0 = 3^{b'/(b'+k')},$$

and, using logarithms,

$$b'/(b' + k') = \frac{\log 2}{\log 3} = 0.63.$$

In the earlier experiments on judgments of length, s' was about one-half as great as b'. As an approximation we assume that the same relationship holds in this situation (also see Exercise 5);

$$\frac{b'}{b' + k'} = \frac{b'}{b' + (1 - s' - b')} = \frac{b'}{1 - \frac{1}{2}b'} = 0.63,$$

$$b' = 0.63 - 0.315b' = \frac{0.63}{1.315} = 0.48.$$

Then

$$s' = \tfrac{1}{2}b' = 0.24, \qquad k' = 1 - s' - b' = 0.28.$$

According to this calculation, in the darkened room with no constant visual framework, the weight of the constant term has dropped to 0.28 from a value of about 0.84 in Künnapas' experiments.

Now, what should be expected when the subject is forced to use monocular regard and an artificial pupil, hence having essentially no cues to distance? A simple approach would be to say that the visual field has been impoverished, so nonvisual factors, such as the series or memory term, should be relatively larger. However, notice that the line itself and its surrounding frame are exactly the same as they were with binocular regard—what is missing is any sense of the location or distance of the display. It appears that the line and box are all on a plane, but it is quite unclear that different displays, on different trials, are all at the same distance. Therefore, what is removed with the binocular cues is information as to the comparability of displays shown on different trials. If it becomes more difficult to compare displays on different trials, the series effect should be reduced, thereby reducing k'.

When subjects were allowed only monocular regard, with dimensions as above, they set S_2 at 6.7 as their mean PSE.

Recalculating exactly as above, $b'/(b' + k') = 0.73$, whence

$$b' = 0.54, \qquad s' = 0.27, \qquad k' = 0.19.$$

The value of k' was reduced from 0.28 in the binocular case. The fact that the constant factor k' is reduced when the subject switches to monocular viewing indicates that the observer has lost some of his ability to compare stimuli on different trials.

Experiment II. Effect of ratio of frame sizes. One problem that bothered Rock and Ebenholtz was that as they increased the ratio of the sizes of the two frames, the effect of the frames seemed to diminish. As they put it, "... as the transposition of dimensions increases, the ratio of the variable setting to the size of the standard increases."

They arrived at this conclusion from the results of an experiment using several ratios of the two frames. The various frame sizes, the length of the standard line, and the observed matches are shown in Table 4.1.

Table 4.1

| | Ratio of frames | | | |
	2:1	3:1	5:1	8:1
Standard	4.0	3.0	3.0	1.8
Mean observed PSE	6.4	6.7	6.6	6.2
C	0.800	0.744	0.440	0.430

Rock and Ebenholtz's expectations may be reconstructed as follows. The "effect" of frame size is measured as S_2/S_1. The factor producing the effect is the ratio of frame sizes, B_2/B_1. If the effect is relatively the same for all frame sizes, then

$$C = \frac{S_2/S_1}{B_2/B_1}$$

should be a constant for various values of B_2/B_1. In Table 4.1 it is apparent that C is less for greater ratios of frame sizes. Does this mean that the frame effect fades when the frames are very different?

According to the adaptation-level theory, using the parameter estimated for binocular viewing above,

$$S_2 = S_1\left(\frac{B_2}{B_1}\right)^{0.62}.$$

Substituting in the formula for C, we have

$$C = \frac{(S_2/S_1)}{(B_2/B_1)} = \frac{(B_2/B_1)^{0.62}}{(B_2/B_1)} = (B_2/B_1)^{-0.38},$$

which is the theoretical prediction. These predictions are shown along with the data points given in Fig. 4.9. The close correspondence shows that the apparent "fading" of the effect when the frames are very different fits the general theory of relational determination of perceived size.

This case illustrates a general principle regarding the use of mathematical models. Rock and Ebenholz's analysis was based on an *ad hoc* index, the "relative effect" C. While the value of C provides a reasonable measure of the effect of frame size, it is not related in any well-defined way to assumptions about the judgment process. The advantage of the adaptation-level analysis is that the measurement of experimental effects is carried out in relation to a set of assumptions about how judgments are made. The measurements give quantities that are properties of the judgment process—in this case, the weights of various stimulus factors. Because the assumptions of the theory are stated rather precisely, it is possible to derive theorems that

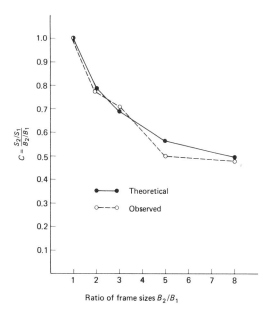

Figure 4.9

show which quantities should be constant across experimental conditions, and if a quantity is not constant, how the quantity should vary. In the case of the effect of frame size, the theory yields an accurate prediction, and the experimental result justifies greater confidence in the validity of the measurements obtained using the theory.

Lightness Constancy

If an observer looks at a piece of construction paper, he can judge whether it is white, gray, or black; in fact, he can judge its grayness accurately. However, to be seen the paper must be illuminated, and the eye merely receives the total light reaching the retina. The eye has no direct way of registering light absorbed by the paper, or of knowing what light would be reflected to the eye if the paper were illuminated differently.

The luminosity or amount of light reaching the eye from a diffuse gray surface depends on illumination and reflectance;

$$S = IR,$$

where S is the luminosity in apparent foot candles, I is the incident illumination, and R is proportional reflection. The eye receives only S, yet to perceive the lightness of the object the observer must see R, the reflectance of the surface.

The problem takes a more concrete form from consideration of the experimental arrangement. The apparatus is a box divided so as to have two viewing chambers. In each chamber is a color-mixing wheel with a disk made of sections of black ($R = 0.03$) and white ($R = 0.80$) paper. See Fig. 4.10 for a ground plan of the apparatus.

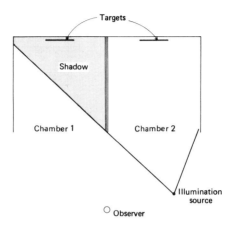

Figure 4.10

Chamber 1 is relatively dark or "shadowed"; Chamber 2 is more highly illuminated. The experimenter sets the color wheel in Chamber 1 at some reflectance by adjusting the white and black segments of paper. This experimental setting may be called

$$S_1 = I_1 R_1.$$

The observer now inspects the display and is free to adjust the reflectance of the color wheel in Chamber 2 until it appears to match the left-hand wheel. The new setting, measured in terms of the amount of light reaching the eye, is

$$S_2 = I_2 R_2.$$

The subject might make his adjustment so that $S_2 = S_1$, matching the luminosity. Of course, since the intensity I_2 is much greater than I_1, this subject must set R_2 very much lower than R_1. He would match white paper in a shadow by choosing black paper in the light. Such behavior might be expected from a simple theory that perception depends directly upon the energy falling on the eye.

Another simple response the subject might make is to match the objects, that is, adjust S_2 until it represents the same object as the one in the dark.

The object quality is reflectance R, whence this subject would match

$$R_2 = R_1,$$

the "constancy" response. Since I_2 is so much greater than I_1, this subject is receiving much more energy from the bright disk than from the darker disk, but calls them equal. As it stands, this hypothesis is mysterious because it does not tell how the subject *can* set R_2 equal to R_1.

Figure 4.11 shows an arrangement of the apparatus in which the subject *cannot* display constancy and will in fact respond to the amount of light S. The apparatus uses a "reduction screen" designed so that the subject can see only the surface of the disk through the screen. The image falling on the eye from the two sides of the figure is precisely the same when $S_2 = S_1$, and the subject cannot in any way discriminate a white object in a shadow from a compensated black object in bright light.

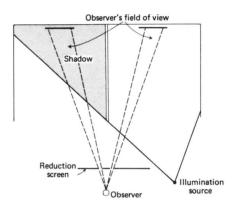

Figure 4.11

If a subject is to display constancy and match reflectances, he needs some information regarding the illuminations or the reflectances. The two variables are perfectly confounded in S and must be separated. If the subject can see other objects and surfaces besides the color wheel in the same illumination as the color wheel, then he has some basis for separating illumination from reflectance. The difference is shown in Fig. 4.12, a sketch of the approximate appearance of the apparatus from the point of view of an observer.

The possible effect of background and other objects must not be overestimated, however. At least in a simple field consisting only of surfaces, the subject can record the amount of light from each area, but does not thereby gain direct information about illumination and reflectance. It still remains possible that all surfaces are dark and the illumination is high, or that all

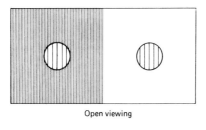

Open viewing

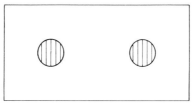

With reduction screen

Figure 4.12

surfaces are light and the illumination is lower. However, if the observer is limited to visual information and cannot inspect the illuminating lights, use a light-meter, or take an object out of the field and put it in some known illumination, then the information separating reflectance and illumination is in the form of relative luminances of parts of the visual field.

The theory of unconscious inference can be used to predict the setting made in a lightness-constancy experiment as follows:

1. Determine or guess whether the subject is trying to match R or S. Assume, for the present, that he is matching R.

2. From the values of S in the dark field, including the color wheel and other parts of the field, calculate the reflectances given the illumination.

3. Imagine that the subject, for example, guesses the illumination. He can then deduce the reflectances.

4. From the (guessed) illumination and S, he can calculate the reflectance R, using the formula

$$R = \frac{S}{I}.$$

This theory of unconscious inference is unsatisfactory because the subject actually has no definite information regarding the illumination I, and there is no way of knowing how he guesses I. Within the range available, the subject might make any estimate of I. This may not be too serious if the relative illuminations in the two fields can somehow be compared. For example, if the subject has corresponding points (a common background of single reflectance, for example) and makes measurements of S, then he may be able to solve definitely for the ratio of illuminations. Given that

$$\frac{S_2}{S_1} = k_S \qquad \text{and} \qquad R_2 = R_1$$

for some particular pair of areas, then, since $S = RI$,

$$\frac{I_B}{I_D} = k_S.$$

This in turn would be sufficient to compare and match reflectances in the two different illuminations.

If the judgments are all relational, then a subject might still be able to make veridical matches of reflectance of two test objects by relating them to corresponding parts of the two fields, given that the two corresponding parts have the same reflectance. But how, in a situation like this, could the subject know that certain points in the two fields have the same reflectance? If he can tell that two background areas have the same reflectance, presumably he can use the same method to decide whether the two disks are the same. Therefore, the theory of unconscious inference cannot really explain constancy without begging the question.

Adaptation level and brightness constancy. Suppose that the subject develops an adaptation level for the dark side of the apparatus, and that the disk can then be judged relative to its adaptation level. This judgment is based on the ratio

$$J_1 = \frac{S_1}{A_1}.$$

To judge that the disk on the bright side is equal to the disk on the dark side, in effect, is to give the same judgment to both. Now suppose that an adaptation level A_2 develops on the bright side of the apparatus. The judgment on that side, for a given luminance of the second disk S_2, is

$$J_2 = \frac{S_2}{A_2}.$$

This hypothesis implies that judgments of brightness depend upon all properties of the two visual fields, not just on certain locations that correspond. The subject is not instructed to match the reflectance R or the luminance S, but instead is instructed to make judgments based upon S/A. If A is affected mainly by the local environment of the judged disk, and if the judged disk and its environment have the same illumination, then changes in illumination will have little effect on judgment, since they will affect both S and A equally. This should produce constancy. On the other hand, if A depends heavily upon areas not in the same illumination as S, the luminance S may be changed without changing A, and the behavior will not show brightness constancy.

In an important experiment on lightness constancy, Helson[6] used two disks, one in a shadowed chamber and the other in a bright chamber. The shadowed disk was set by the experimenter at five levels of reflectance from 0.130 to 0.800. The bright chamber was always illuminated at 16.15 foot candles; in different observations, the shadowed illumination was 0.879, 0.388, and 0.009 foot candles. The reflectivity of the background of the apparatus could be varied. In this experiment, both bright and shadowed sides had backgrounds of the same reflectance, which could be white (0.800), gray (0.410), or black (0.130). This produced a total of $5 \times 3 \times 3 = 45$ different measurements of the reflectance of the brightly illuminated disk chosen by the subject to match the shadowed disk.

Helson found that reflectance of the shadowed disk, its illumination, and the reflectance of the two backgrounds, all affected adjustments of the brightly illuminated disk. His data give all the illuminations and reflectances. Hence one can calculate adaptation levels directly once it is learned how much weight each part of the field should have. One method is to estimate these weights from the data, then see if the adaptation-level theory can reproduce the data in detail.

The data of this experiment turn out to need a more general form of the adaptation-level theory than the one used for the earlier analysis in this chapter. For the darker compartment, assume that

$$A_1 = (S_1^{s_1} B_1^{b_1} K^k)^{1/(s_1+b_1+k)}.$$

And for the brighter compartment, assume that

$$A_2 = (S_2^{s_2} B_2^{b_2} K^k)^{1/(s_2+b_2+k)}.$$

Since

$$J_1 = \frac{S_1}{A_1} \quad \text{and} \quad J_2 = \frac{S_2}{A_2},$$

when $J_1 = J_2$, then

$$(S_1^{b_1+k} B_1^{-b_1} K^{-k})^{1/(s_1+b_1+k)} = (S_2^{b_2+k} B_2^{-b_2} K^{-k})^{1/(s_2+b_2+k)},$$

---

[6] H. Helson, Some factors and implications of color constancy. *J. Opt. Soc. Amer.*, 1943, **33**, 555–567.

whence

$$S_2^{b_2+k/(s_2+b_2+k)} = (S_1^{b_1+k}B_1^{-b_1}K^{-k})^{1/(s_1+b_1+k)}(B_2^{b_2}K^k)^{1/(s_2+b_2+k)}.$$

Let the ratio of total weights be

$$\frac{s_2 + b_2 + k}{s_1 + b_1 + k} = \rho,$$

and then

$$S_2 = S_1^{\rho((b_1+k)/(b_2+k))}B_1^{(-b_1\rho)/(b_2+k)}B_2^{(b_2)/(b_2+k)}K^{k(1-\rho)/(b_2+k)}.$$

Now, for abbreviation, let

$$\alpha = \rho\,\frac{b_1 + k}{b_2 + k}, \qquad \beta = \frac{-b_1\rho}{b_2 + k}, \qquad \gamma = \frac{b_2}{b_2 + k},$$

and

$$G = K^{k(1-\rho)/(b_2+k)}. \tag{14}$$

Then

$$S_2 = S_1^\alpha B_1^\beta B_2^\gamma G.$$

Helson did not vary the luminances S_1, B_1, and B_2 directly, but instead varied the reflectance of the disk in the dark (R_1), the illumination of the dark side (I_1), and the reflectance of the background of both sides of the field (R_B). Since calculations must work with these independent variables, we use the simple physical law which states that the luminance of a surface is illuminance times reflectance:

$$S_1 = R_1 I_1, \qquad B_1 = R_B I_1,$$
$$S_2 = R_2 k, \qquad B_2 = R_B k,$$

where k is the constant illuminance of the brighter field, 16.15 foot candles. Substituting in Eq. (14), we find that

$$R_2 k = (R_1 I_1)^\alpha (R_B I_1)^\beta (R_B k)^\gamma G = R_1^\alpha I_1^{\alpha+\beta} R_B^{\beta+\gamma} G k^\gamma \tag{15}$$

gives the formula in terms of the independent variables R_1, I_1, and R_B.

One way to estimate the weights of various parts of the figure from Helson's data is by using the method of least squares. A predicted value is calculated for each experimental point, based on the (unknown) parameter values. The sum of the squared discrepancies between observed and predicted points is minimized with respect to the parameters; this selects values of the parameters that minimize the sum of squares, and these values are the least-square estimates. (See Chapter 9.)

Actually, using the adaptation-level theory as written, it would be quite difficult to minimize squared deviations in the raw judgments, but it is relatively easy to minimize them when logarithms are taken, resulting in a linear system.

Let x, y, and z stand for the three experimental variables: x for log R_1, y for log I_1, and z for log R_B. Let s stand for the chosen value of S_2. The weights of these three factors will be given independent parameters for purposes of estimation, a, b, and c: $a = \alpha$, $b = \alpha + \beta$, and $c = \beta + \gamma$.

The predicted value of s, called s^*, is

$$s^* = ax + by + cz + g, \tag{16}$$

where g is the logarithm of Gk^γ. The sum of the squared deviations between observed choices of s and predictions s^* is written

$$
\begin{aligned}
\sum (s - s^*)^2 &= \sum (s - ax - by - cz - g)^2 \\
&= \sum s^2 + a^2 \sum x^2 + b^2 \sum y^2 + c^2 \sum z^2 + \sum g^2 \\
&\quad - 2a \sum sx - 2b \sum sy - 2c \sum sz - 2g \sum s \\
&\quad + 2ab \sum xy + 2ac \sum xz + 2ag \sum x + 2bc \sum yz \\
&\quad + 2bg \sum y + 2cg \sum z.
\end{aligned}
$$

To find the values of a, b, c, and g that minimize this sum of squares, we differentiate with respect to each of the parameters and set each derivative equal to zero. For example,

$$\frac{\partial}{\partial a} \sum (s - s^*)^2 = 2a \sum x^2 - 2 \sum sx + 2b \sum xy + 2c \sum xz + 2g \sum x.$$

When this operation is carried out with respect to each of the parameters a, b, c, and g, and the results are all set equal to zero, we obtain the four linear equations

$$
\begin{aligned}
a \sum x^2 + b \sum xy + c \sum xz + g \sum x &= \sum xs, \\
a \sum xy + b \sum y^2 + c \sum yz + g \sum y &= \sum ys, \\
a \sum xz + b \sum yz + c \sum z^2 + g \sum z &= \sum zs, \\
a \sum x + b \sum y + c \sum z + g &= \sum s.
\end{aligned}
\tag{17}
$$

The sums on the right-hand side of Eq. (17) are computed solely from independent, experimentally-manipulated variables as combined over the 45 experimental conditions; hence they are constants so far as calculation is concerned. The result is a system of four linear equations with four unknowns, having a unique solution provided that the square matrix of sums on the left-hand side is nonsingular, that is, provided that the system of values of the independent variables does not contain any linear dependencies. This condition may be tested by numerical calculation before the experiment is performed, and is a useful way of determining whether the desired parameters can be recovered from the experiment.

The result of the calculation is that all three factors serve to increase S_D and have the following weights:

a) Weight of reflectance of shadowed disk, $R_1 = 0.720$.
b) Weight of illumination of shadow, $I_1 = 0.310$.
c) Weight of reflectance of background, $R_B = 0.232$.

It is reasonable to ask how completely this theory can account for the detailed data. According to Eq. (15), the adjusted brightness S_2 should be a logarithmic function of log R_1, log R_B, and log I_1, since these stand for the reflectance of the standard disk, the reflectance of the background, and the illumination of the darker field. A plot of log S_2 as a function of log R_1 and log R_B is shown in Fig. 4.13. Notice that straight lines fall very close to the

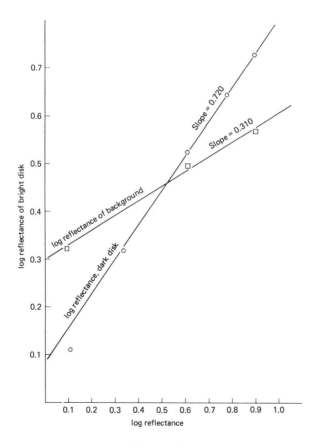

Figure 4.13

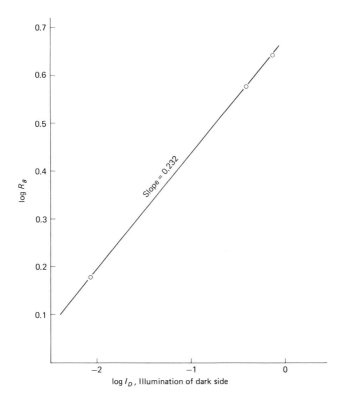

Figure 4.14

data points. A plot of log S_2 as a function of log I_1, the illumination of the dark standard side of the apparatus, is shown in Fig. 4.14. Again, a straight line accounts well for the three points. The accuracy of the theory is made more visible by calculating, for the 45 combinations of stimuli, a prediction concerning the setting subjects should make. These predictions can be converted into the raw experimental variable, namely, degrees of white paper on the disk. Some predictions and observed values are plotted in Fig. 4.15 and appear accurate. Most of the agreements are within 10° except at the white end, where discrimination may not be as good. No particular pattern of discrepancy can be seen in these results.

Interpretation of Parameters

The parameters a, b, and c are sufficient to give a good fit to the data. However, it is not obvious how they are to be interpreted, or what they tell us about how the subject samples the stimulus situation. Recall that

$$a = \alpha, \qquad b = \alpha + \beta, \qquad c = \beta + \gamma,$$

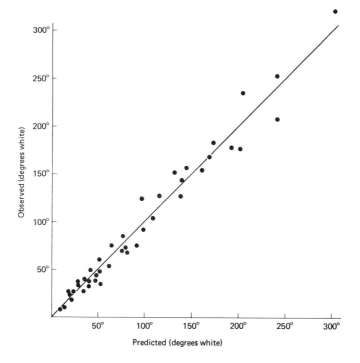

Figure 4.15

and that α is the weight of S_1, the luminance of the disk in the dark, β is the weight of the luminance of the background in the dark, and γ is the weight of the luminance of the background on the bright side of the apparatus. Using the estimated values,

$$\alpha = 0.720, \qquad \beta = -0.410, \qquad \gamma = 0.642,$$

whence

$$\alpha = \rho \, \frac{b_1 + k}{b_2 + k} = 0.720,$$

$$\beta = \frac{-b_1 \rho}{b_2 + k} = -0.410,$$

$$\gamma = \frac{b_2}{b_2 + k} = 0.642.$$

The model can be simplified to yield an approximation to the values estimated above. Let

$$b_1 = b_2 = b,$$

whence $\alpha = \rho$, approximately, let

$$\rho = 0.70.$$

Then, let

$$\frac{b}{b + k} = 0.60, \qquad \text{or} \qquad b = 1.50k$$

which approximately matches the observed value of γ. Then

$$\beta = -(0.60)(0.70) = -0.42.$$

The result of this analysis of brightness constancy can be summarized as follows:

1. The adaptation-level theory comprehends the form of the quantitative data and permits us to recover the weights of various parts of the field.

2. The study of logarithms of key values uses a simple linear model and makes it possible to weight the factors varied by the experimenter.

3. The backgrounds appear to have weights approximately 1.50 times greater than the constant factors. It is presumed that the constant factors in this experiment arise mainly from memory.

4. The brighter field, which is adjusted by the subject, receives only 0.70 as much weight as the darker field set by the experimenter. This ratio is ρ. Further investigation will be needed to determine whether the standard stimulus usually receives a higher weight than the comparison.

CATEGORY JUDGMENTS

In the experiments by Rock and Ebenholz, Künnapas, and Helson, the data consisted of magnitudes of stimuli judged to be equal to the magnitude of a standard. On each trial of these experiments, two stimuli were presented with different backgrounds, and the subject made a comparison. The basic perceptual ability of the subject used in these studies was that of judging when two stimuli seemed to have equal magnitude.

Certainly, people are able to make comparative judgments of the kind used in experiments that measure the PSE. However, people can also make judgments of magnitude when there is no obvious standard of comparison present. If you lift a box you may say, "This seems very light," or, "This is heavier than it looks." Responses of this kind involve the ability to judge the magnitude of a stimulus presented alone, and this ability is used in the method of single stimuli. The experiment on line lengths and box sizes described at the beginning of this chapter used the method of single stimuli, and judgments were made using a rating scale. Now an analysis of rating scale experiments will be given in some detail.

An experimenter specifies a set of response alternatives by naming a number of categories along some dimension. For example, if the subject is to judge the weights of some objects, the responses might be "very light," "light," "medium," "heavy," and "very heavy." We denote the responses $-N, \ldots, -1, 0, +1, \ldots, +N$, designating 0 as the middle category. On each trial a single stimulus is presented and the subject selects a category as his response. During the experiment, many stimuli are presented with different magnitudes. The subject must name each stimulus using one of the categories of the rating scale. The main theoretical problem regarding rating scale experiments is to explain how the subject classifies a set of stimuli according to categories along some dimension.

In the theory of adaptation level, all stimuli are judged relative to a standard that depends on a stimulus field. In the experiments using comparative judgments, most of the analyses dealt with influences of background stimuli that were present when the judgment was made. However, it was necessary to consider series effects in relation to some of those data—that is, the adaptation level for a judgment depended partly on the magnitudes of stimuli that the subject had seen on previous trials. In the theory of category judgments, the adaptation level is assumed to depend on the total set of stimuli used in the experiment.

Basic Assumptions

In the general theory of adaptation level, the judged magnitude of a stimulus with physical magnitude S is given by

$$J = \frac{S}{A},$$

where A is the adaptation level. In the theory of category scales given by Michels and Helson[7] it is assumed that the category of any stimulus depends on the ratio of that stimulus to the adaptation level. A stimulus with magnitude equal to the adaptation level is judged in the middle category C_0, and the remaining categories are located so that there are equal ratios between the stimuli that are classified in adjacent categories.

Let M_0 denote the magnitude of a stimulus equal to the adaptation level. Other stimuli with magnitudes near M_0 would probably be classified in category M_0, but stimuli with magnitude M_0 are in the "middle" of category C_0.

Suppose that M_1 is the middle stimulus magnitude in category C_1, and let r be the ratio of M_1 to the adaptation level, such that $r > 1$. That is,

$$r = M_1/A = M_1/M_0.$$

---

[7] W. C. Michels and H. Helson, A reformulation of the Fechner law in terms of adaptation-level applied to rating-scale data. *Amer. J. Psych.*, 1949, **62**, 355–368.

Then r is the ratio of stimulus magnitudes in adjacent categories, and it is assumed that r is a constant throughout the scale. Then a stimulus with magnitude M_2, if it is a ratio r above M_1, should be put in category C_2, and so on. In general, the upper part of the scale is as shown in Table 4.2.

Table 4.2 The upper part of a simple category scale

Category	0	+1	+2	+3	$\cdots$	+N
Typical stimulus	S_0	S_0r	S_0r^2	S_0r^3	$\cdots$	S_0r^N

The relationship between stimulus magnitudes and categories can be given in two ways. First, the midpoint of category C_i, i steps above A, depends on the adaptation level A and the ratio r according to

$$M_i = Ar^i. \tag{18}$$

To see this, note that

$$M_0 = A.$$

Then

$$M_1 = M_0r = Ar, \qquad M_2 = M_1r = Ar^2,$$

and so on. Equation (18) says that the stimulus is an exponential function of the category.

The inverse of Eq. (18) gives the category as a function of stimulus magnitude. Take the logarithm of each side of Eq. (18):

$$\log (M_i) = \log (A) + i \log (r).$$

Then, rearranging terms,

$$i = \frac{\log (M_i)}{\log (r)} - \frac{\log (A)}{\log (r)}. \tag{19}$$

The ratio r is assumed to be constant, and the adaptation level is approximately constant after the subject has become experienced in the experimental situation. Therefore, the category is approximately a logarithmic function of stimulus magnitude.

Similarly, below the adaptation level,

$$M_0/M_1 = r, \qquad M_{-1} = M_0r^{-1},$$

and, following the same argument as before, it follows that for any category $-j$,

$$M_{-j} = M_0r^{-j},$$

and, taking logarithms of both sides and rearranging, we have

$$-j = \frac{\log M_{-j} - \log M_0}{\log r}.$$

This, of course, is precisely the same as Eq. (19) showing that the relationship holds in both directions. In general, if A is the adaptation level, M_i is the physical magnitude of a midpoint, and i is the judgment or category assigned to M_i, then

$$i = \frac{\log M_i - \log A}{\log r} = a + b \log M_i, \tag{20}$$

where

$$a = -\frac{\log A}{\log r}, \qquad b = \frac{1}{\log r}.$$

Up to now, the ratio r has been unknown. According to the Michels-Helson theory, the subject considers the stimulus M_0 at adaptation level A, and realizes that his scale has N categories above and below that level. Then he fixes the category just below the adaptation level so that

$$M_0 - M_{-1} = \frac{1}{N} A,$$

whence

$$M_{-1} = A - \frac{A}{N}.$$

Working from Eq. (19), it follows that

$$-1 = \left[\frac{\log (A - A/N)/A}{\log r}\right] = \frac{\log (1 - 1/N)}{\log r};$$

$$\log r = \log \left[\frac{N}{(N-1)}\right],$$

$$r = \frac{N}{N-1}. \tag{21}$$

Since r is the one free parameter of Eq. (19), every judgment of any stimulus permits an estimate of the adaptation level. From Eq. (19)

$$\log A = \log (M_i) - i \log r. \tag{22}$$

For an example, we consider a scale with 11 categories. Since

$$11 = 2N + 1,$$
$$N = 5,$$

whence with the Michels-Helson assumption,

$$r = \frac{N}{(N-1)} = 1.25.$$

Now suppose that a stimulus having physical measurement $S = 20$ is presented, and the subject gives a judgment

$$i = -3.$$

Then

$$\log(A) = \log(20) - (-3)\log(1.25).$$

Using common logarithms, we have

$$\log(A) = 1.301 + 3(0.098) = 1.595;$$
$$A = 39.3.$$

Thus, A is estimated from a nonzero judgment of a stimulus below A. Obviously, if many measurements are taken, the various individual estimates of adaptation level will differ. However, if the data are consistent with the theory, it should take only a relatively few responses, using various stimuli, to give a reliable estimate of the adaptation level obtained by averaging the various estimated values.

Effect of Self Adaptation

According to adaptation-level theory, A is a function of numerous factors in the field including the object being judged. This means that the adaptation level shifts with each presentation of a stimulus, dropping when a small object is shown and rising when a large object is shown. This, in turn, tends to move the judgments toward 0—more accurately, it moves the center of the scale, the adaptation level, toward each stimulus.

Let A_i be the adaptation level when the stimulus value is S, and let A be an overall average adaptation level. Then, because of self-adaptation,

$$A_i = S^p A^{1-p}. \qquad (23)$$

The exponent p is the self-adaptation constant, the relative effect of S on the momentary adaptation level. The net effect of other factors in the situation is A, which is assumed to be constant. Then, instead of Eq. (19), the category

i is given by

$$i = \frac{\log [M_i/A_i]}{\log r}$$

$$= \frac{\log (M_i/M_i^p A^{1-p})}{\log r}$$

$$= \frac{\log (M_i^{1-p}/A^{1-p})}{\log r}$$

$$= \frac{(1 - p) \log (M_i/A)}{\log r}. \tag{24}$$

Equation (24) gives a formula for the judgment of M_i very much like Eq. (19), except for the introduction of the self-adaptation constant p. However, with this parameter existing and unknown, it becomes impossible to determine a in a purely logical fashion. We can no longer calculate the adaptation level from the judgment of any stimulus—such calculations are possible only given an estimate of the parameter p.

Both Eqs. (19) and (24) give the judgment as a linear function of the logarithm of the stimulus value. In Eq. (19) the slope depends only upon N, the number of categories in the scale, whereas in Eq. (24) the slope also depends upon self-adaptation.

As an example, Michels and Helson presented data collected by Miss F. Emerson, taken from judgments of lightness. Presented here are data taken from judgments of seven samples against a gray background of 20% reflectance. A nine-point category scale was used, ranging from very, very dark (-4) to very, very light ($+4$). The data are listed in Table 4.3.

The data are fit by estimating the coefficients of the linear equation

$$i = k_1 + k_2 \log M_i.$$

Table 4.3 Judgments of lightness

Stimulus value S in percent reflectance	Log S	Mean category judgment
5.4	0.70	-4.0
8.0	0.90	-2.7
16.9	1.23	-1.3
25.8	1.41	-0.3
38.4	1.58	0.8
47.5	1.68	1.3
74.5	1.87	3.0

Using the method of least squares, we obtain the estimates as

$$k_1 = -7.96, \qquad k_2 = 5.62,$$

which gives a straight line; this can be compared with the data given in Fig. 4.16.

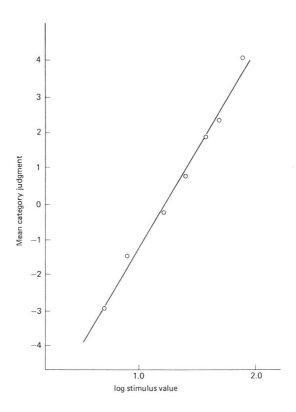

Figure 4.16

The estimates of k_1 and k_2 can be converted to estimates of the theoretical parameters, A and p. From Eq. (24), we have

$$i = \frac{-(1-p)\log A}{\log(N/N-1)} + \frac{1-p}{\log(N/N-1)} S \log(M_i). \qquad (25)$$

With a nine-point rating scale, $N = 4$. Then

$$k_2 = 5.62 = \frac{1-p}{\log 1.33},$$

$$k_1 = -7.96 = -k_2 \log(A),$$

whence

$$A = 26.3, \qquad p = 0.30.$$

These data, therefore, show a sizable degree of self-adaptation—that is, the slope of judgments vs. stimuli is flatter than predicted by Eq. (19).

Effect of the Range of Stimuli on the Normal Scale

The theory of the normal scale assumes that the range of stimuli is equally divided among the categories. However, as Michels and Helson have shown, some arrays of stimuli would not fit such a scale. The assumption of a "normal scale" implies that the value of r depends only on the number of categories, N. It can be shown that this result implies a specific range of stimuli.

First, notice that the stimulus values corresponding to judgment $J = -N$ and $J = +N$ can be calculated from Eq. (24). With stimuli ranging from $M_{\min}$ to $M_{\max}$, stimulus $M_{\min}$ will be assigned to category C_{-N} and $M_{\max}$ to C_{+N}. Hence

$$-N = (1 - p)\frac{\log (M_{\min}/A)}{-\log [(N - 1)/N]}, \tag{26}$$

or

$$N \log [(N - 1)/N] = (1 - p)[\log (M_{\min}) - \log (A)]. \tag{27}$$

Similarly,

$$-N \log [(N - 1)/N] = (1 - p)[\log (M_{\max}) - \log (A)]. \tag{28}$$

Subtracting Eq. (27) from (28), we find that

$$(1 - p)[\log (M_{\max}) - \log (M_{\min})] = -2N \log [(N - 1)/N], \tag{29}$$

whence

$$\frac{M_{\max}}{M_{\min}} = \left(\frac{N}{N - 1}\right)^{2N/(1-p)}. \tag{30}$$

Notice that Eq. (30) follows from the assumption that the subject fixes category -1 at $[(N - 1)/N]A$. The result implies that the subject can accomplish this division only if he is given an appropriate range of stimuli to divide. A few illustrative values of the appropriate range are given in Table 4.4, under the assumption that self-adaptation is negligible. In cases where self-adaptation cannot be ignored, the appropriate range of stimuli for a normal scale will be somewhat larger.

As an example, Michels and Helson present data on judgments of lifted weights. Their experiment used a judgment scale with nine categories; this

Table 4.4 Ratio of highest to lowest stimulus intensity appropriate for normal scale

Number of categories	Appropriate S_{max}/S_{min}
5	16.0
7	11.4
9	10.0
11	9.3

corresponds to an *appropriate* stimulus range of 10:1, as shown in Table 4.4. However, under different conditions, the *actual* stimulus ranges were 2:1, 4.5:1, and 4.5:1. When the data were fit using Eq. (29), the results gave values of $1 - p$ equal to 2.0, 1.5, and 1.1. These values are impossible if p is considered as the self-adaptation constant, unless it is possible for the presented stimulus to have negative weight.

Recall that the effect of self-adaptation is to move the judgments toward the center of the category scale. In the example above, the range of stimuli was smaller than it should have been to permit judgments in accordance with the normal scale. Thus the subject's judgments tended to be spread out more than should be expected according to the theory of the normal scale. This result is opposite in direction to that produced by self-adaptation. When equations are fitted without regard to this "spreading" caused by the small stimulus range, the effect appears as a negative value of the self-adaptation parameter, and $1 - p > 1$.

The point may be emphasized by reconsidering the brightness judgments analyzed above and given in Table 4.3. A nine-category scale was used— therefore a stimulus range of 10:1 would be optimal for judgments on the normal scale. The actual range of stimuli was $74.5/5.4 = 13.8$, which is somewhat larger than the optimal range. The estimate of p was equal to 0.30, indicating substantial self-adaptation. Actually, it is not certain whether the judgments really were influenced that much by self-adaptation. It is possible that the self-adaptation constant was really considerably lower than 0.30, but that the range of stimuli was too large to permit optimal judgments using the normal scale. The effect of having too great a range of stimuli would be a relative compression of the judgments, giving a smaller value of $1 - p$ than if the estimate of self-adaptation were not confounded with effects of the range.

Effect of Stimulus Frequencies and Stimulus Spacing

Michels and Helson stressed the importance of having an appropriate range of stimuli in order for the subject to be able to use the normal scale. It is also necessary to select an appropriate distribution of stimulus frequencies for the subject to be able to apply the normal scale. This is because the stimulus distribution determines the adaptation level, which anchors the zero point on the category scale. Then the subject classifies each stimulus according to its ratio with the adaptation level. Therefore, if the subject's responses are to fit properly with the stimulus range, as assumed in the calculations regarding the range of stimuli, the adaptation level has to be located properly within the range.

Recall that the adaptation level is the weighted geometric mean of the stimuli in a field. Assume that A, the "base-line" adaptation level, is the geometric mean of the stimulus values weighted by their respective frequencies. For this analysis, leave out the effect of the residual stimulus and the background in order to simplify the calculation. Let the stimulus magnitudes in the experiment be $S_1, S_2, \ldots, S_s$ in order of increasing magnitude; then

$$\log(A) = \sum_{i=1}^{s} P(S_i) \log(S_i). \tag{31}$$

The derivation proceeds like that leading to Eq. (29); since $S_s = M_{\max}$,

$$C(S_s) = N = (1 - p)\frac{\log S_s - \log A}{-\log(1 - 1/N)}$$

as in Eq. (28). Solving for $\log A$,

$$\log A = \frac{N \log(1 - 1/N)}{1 - p} + \log S_s. \tag{32}$$

Similarly, using the smallest stimulus magnitude S_1,

$$C(S_1) = -N = (1 - p)\frac{\log S_1 - \log A}{-\log(1 - 1/N)}$$

as in Eq. (26). Solving for $\log A$,

$$\log A = -\frac{N \log(1 - 1/N)}{1 - p} + \log S_1. \tag{33}$$

Adding Eqs. (32) and (33) eliminates the term containing N and p, and yields

$$2 \log A = \log S_1 + \log S_s.$$

Since A is the geometric mean of all stimuli on the average,

$$\sum_{i=1}^{s} P(S_i) \log(S_i) = \tfrac{1}{2}[\log(S_s) + \log(S_1)], \tag{34}$$

a result which restricts the stimulus distribution needed for the normal scale to apply. Equation (34) states that the weighted geometric mean should equal the geometric midpoint.

Equation (34) could be satisfied in various ways, though the usual equal frequencies of equally spaced stimuli will not be satisfactory. One stimulus distribution that will permit judgments using the normal scale is obtained if the stimuli are presented with equal frequency, but are equally spaced logarithmically, so that

$$S_i = b^{i-1}S_1. \tag{35}$$

The constant b will be greater than one, and will be selected so that Eq. (35) is satisfied:

$$\frac{M_{\max}}{M_{\min}} = \frac{b^{s-1}M_{\min}}{M_{\min}} = b^{s-1} = \left(\frac{N}{N-1}\right)^{2N/(1-p)}. \tag{36}$$

This will yield a set of stimuli ranging from $M_{\min}$ to $M_{\max}$ with equal spacing on a logarithmic scale. That is,

$$\log(S_i) = \log(S_1) + (i-1)\log(b). \tag{37}$$

If the S_i are presented with equal frequency, the probability of each stimulus is

$$P(S_i) = \frac{1}{s}.$$

Then

$$\sum_{i=1}^{s} P(S_i)\log(S_i) = \frac{1}{S}\sum_{i=1}^{s}\log(S_i)$$

$$= \log(S_1) + \frac{s-1}{2}\log(b). \tag{38}$$

From Eq. (36), taking logarithms,

$$\frac{s-1}{2}\log(b) = \tfrac{1}{2}[\log(S_s) - \log(S_1)].$$

When this result is combined with Eq. (38), the result is identical with Eq. (34).

The implications of this result are considerable. First, consider the normal experimental procedure of presenting equally spaced stimuli equally often. The upper panel of Fig. 4.17 shows an ideal spacing of equally frequent stimuli for an experiment with seven response categories, and assuming that self-adaptation, background, and residual effects are negligible. The lower panel of the figure shows an even spacing of stimuli using the same range.

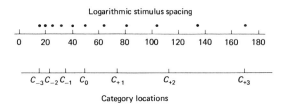

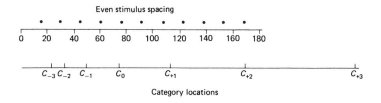

Figure 4.17

The category locations are those calculated using the assumption of the normal scale, with the adaptation level equal to the geometric mean of the stimulus values.

The important point about Fig. 4.17 is that the stimulus range is equal in both cases, and is equal to the range required to satisfy the normal scale assumptions. With the logarithmic spacing in the upper panel, the category locations are distributed appropriately across the stimulus scale. The subject could allocate stimuli to the normal scale categories quite easily. However, in the lower panel, considerable compression of the scale would have to occur at the high end for the stimuli to be judged by means of the normal scale categories.

The use of linear stimulus spacings may account for quite a number of experimental results in which the data contradict the prediction of a logarithmic relationship between stimulus values and category judgments. Figure 4.18 shows data presented by Stevens and Galanter[8] for judgments of the lengths of metal rods. The stimulus spacing was approximately even, though greater densities were used at the ends of the scale than in the middle. The data are markedly discrepant from the predicted linear function between category ratings and log stimulus values. However, this is not surprising when we consider the stimulus distribution in relation to the normal scale. Figure 4.18 gives the normal scale categories that are calculated with the adaptation

---

[8] S. S. Stevens and E. H. Galanter, Ratio scales and category scales for a dozen perceptual continua. *J. Exp. Psych.*, 1957, **54**, 377–411.

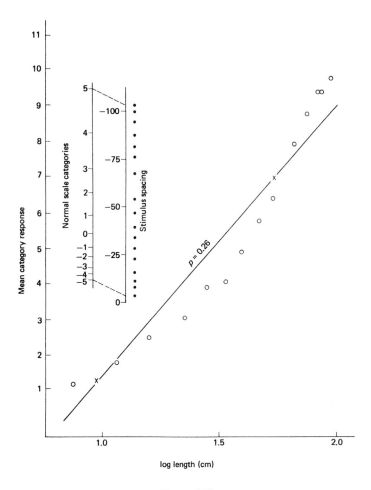

Figure 4.18

level equal to the geometric mean of the stimuli, and we can apply Eq. (38) assuming that self-adaptation and residual effects are negligible. The data show the kind of distortion that is to be expected; in order to fit the stimuli to the scale, the subject must use the lowest categories for a large number of stimuli, thus giving a decreased slope for the rating scale function. The results contrast with the data given in Fig. 4.16 for judgments of brightness. Note that in Emerson's experiment the spacing of the stimuli was approximately logarithmic, as required for the normal scale categories to be applied without distortion.

One especially striking comparison between logarithmic and linear stimulus spacing is found in data from judgments of duration of white noise,

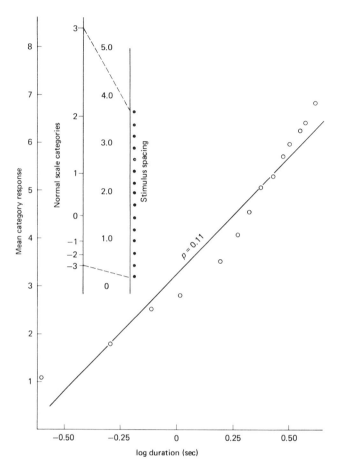

Figure 4.19

also presented by Stevens and Galanter. Figure 4.19 gives the results obtained when stimuli were spaced linearly, showing a marked discrepancy
from the expected logarithmic function, much like that shown in Fig. 4.18
for judgments of length. However, with stimuli in about the same range but
with a logarithmic spacing, the result shown in Fig. 4.20 was obtained. The
experiment also included a condition with most of the stimuli near the high
end of the range. This produced data even more out of line with the logarithmic function than those of Fig. 4.19.

When the stimulus distribution departs from that needed for a normal
scale, the judgments depart from the theoretical predictions in what seems
to be a meaningful pattern. The theory given above does not predict the form
of the discrepancies. Further investigations are needed to give an account

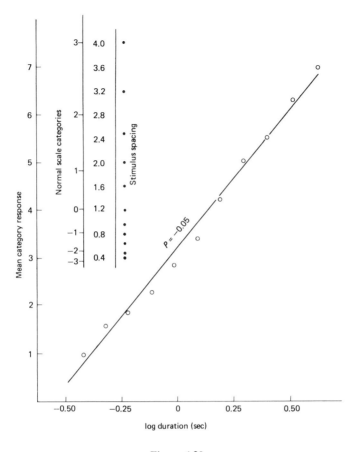

Figure 4.20

of how the subject adjusts his category scale when the stimulus range and frequencies do not allow him to use the categories in a natural way.

Experimental Study of Range and Frequency Effects

In a recent analysis, Parducci[9] showed that the range of stimulus magnitudes, and the relative frequencies with which various stimulus magnitudes are presented, affect category judgments. His idea is that the category boundaries used by the subject represent a compromise between two ideal systems of category judgment. One set of ideal boundaries, called "range thresholds," divides the range of stimuli into equal intervals of subjective stimulus

[9] A. Parducci, R. C. Calfee, Louise M. Marshall, and Linda P. Davidson, Context effects in judgment: adaptation level as a function of the mean, midpoint, and median of the stimuli. *J. Exp. Psych.*, 1960, **60**, 65–77.

quantity. The other set of ideal boundaries, called "frequency thresholds," divides the stimulus range into categories so that all category responses can be used equally often.

The "trace" of a category C is defined as the function giving the probability that a judgment equal to or greater than C is made to any stimulus magnitude S; that is, $P(J \geq C; S)$. Parducci defines a category threshold empirically; the lower threshold of category J is a value of the stimulus S that would be put in category J or above just half the time. That is, the lower threshold of category J is defined as the stimulus L_J that satisfies the equation

$$P(J \geq L_J) = \tfrac{1}{2}.$$

In practice, the value of L_J is often determined by interpolation. For convenience, experimenters often transform the proportions by an inverse normal curve transformation to work with z-scores, which often are approximately linear functions of the stimulus variable.

Table 4.5 Cumulative frequency of four category responses to each of six stimuli (Hypothetical data)

| | | \multicolumn{4}{c}{Judgmental categories J} | | | |
		1	2	3	4
Stimuli	s_1	0.80	0.95	1.00	1.00
	s_2	0.55	0.90	1.00	1.00
	s_3	0.30	0.75	0.90	1.00
	s_4	0.15	0.55	0.85	1.00
	s_5	0.05	0.20	0.60	1.00
	s_6	0	0.05	0.20	1.00

Table 4.5 gives hypothetical data from a four-category experiment involving six stimuli. In Fig. 4.21 the proportions have been transformed to z-scores, and graphed in a way that permits estimation of the empirical thresholds. Estimates of thresholds, as defined by Parducci, are taken from plots of standard scores against stimulus values, where the category responses compose the parameter.

The analysis uses hypothetical range and frequency thresholds. The most straightforward approach is to estimate the range thresholds. One method would be to merely divide the actual range of stimuli into $2N + 1$ equal intervals. Unfortunately, this would lead to a contradiction with the data. In Parducci's experiment, subjects tended to use the highest category infrequently as compared with the lowest category, even when top and bottom stimuli were presented equally often.

This discrepancy has several possible interpretations, but a reasonable one is that the subjective range extends somewhat beyond the highest stimulus

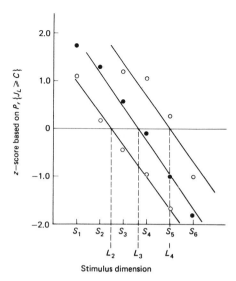

Figure 4.21

values. In a study of apparent size of squares, Parducci used stimuli ranging from 5.4 to 23.2 cm wide, and the estimated lower threshold of the highest category was a stimulus about 25.7 cm wide. Thus the locations of the range thresholds do not depend only on the range of stimuli, hence must be estimated from the data.

The frequency thresholds are simply those divisions that put an equal frequency of stimulus presentations in each category. If the subject could discriminate perfectly, and had perfectly sharp category boundaries, then these would be placed so as to put an equal frequency of presentations in each category.

The lowest category, $-N$, has its trace farthest to the left, and that of the highest category, $+N$, is farthest to the right. In calculating, Parducci assumes that the categories are otherwise the same.

The frequency of responses C or higher is given by

$$F(C) = \sum_S P(J > C \mid S)P(S).$$

The frequency of using just category C is given by

$$P(C) = F(C) - F(C + 1).$$

In a category scale from $-N$ to $+N$, having $2N + 1$ categories, the frequency threshold is set so as to make each of the above probabilities equal. That is,

$$P(C) = \frac{1}{2N + 1}.$$

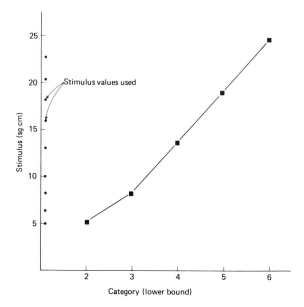

Figure 4.22

The problem of locating the frequency thresholds is solved, in practice, by choosing a trace function $P(J \geq C \mid S)$, then sliding it from the left toward the right until the area behind it is $1/N$: the stimulus value for which $P(J > 1 \mid S) = \frac{1}{2}$ is the threshold of the first category. The trace function is then slid to the right again until another $1/N$ has been left behind, etc. The trace function may be selected empirically from inspection of the data like those graphed in Fig. 4.21.

Parducci adopts the hypothesis that the observed threshold L_0 is the average value of the frequency threshold and the range threshold. That is,

$$L_0(C) = \tfrac{1}{2}L_F(C) + \tfrac{1}{2}L_R(C) \tag{39}$$

though the parameters, above set at $\frac{1}{2}$ and $\frac{1}{2}$, may in other experiments be replaced by different weightings of the range and frequency thresholds.

The data yield estimates of the $L_0(j)$, and the $L_F(j)$ are obtained from the stimulus frequencies and a judgment about the form of the category psychometric functions. As noted above, subjects do not seem to make use of the true range of stimuli. However, in a series of experiments with several different stimulus distributions in the same range, the range thresholds can be estimated from the results of one of the experiments and then applied to others. In Parducci's study of judgments of size, the estimated range thresholds were obtained from judgments of equally frequent stimuli. Using values of $L_F(j)$ obtained *a priori*, and obtained values of $L_0(j)$, the values of $L_R(j)$ were obtained by solving Eq. (39); that is,

$$L_R(j) = 2L_0(j) - L_F(j).$$

The results are plotted in Fig. 4.22.

The obtained estimates of the range thresholds were then applied to different distributions of stimulus frequency all having the same range: negatively skewed, positively skewed, normal, and U-shaped distributions, and distributions with high and low medians (but the same mean). Using a single function form for $P(J > j \mid S_i)$, Parducci calculated a set of frequency thresholds for each stimulus distribution.   Then these thresholds were averaged with the single set of range thresholds that were theoretically unaffected by the distribution of stimulus frequencies. The resulting averages are predictions of the empirical thresholds of categories; they were compared with the observed thresholds of categories obtained with the various distributions of stimuli. The results were extremely encouraging, at least with the reasonable distributions used by Parducci, using only trials after the subjects had had extensive experience with the distribution of stimuli. It is notable that the judgments involved predictions for a number of quite different stimulus distributions.   Two illustrative results, shown in Fig. 4.23, are predictions of mean judgments of both negatively and positively skewed distributions, and "normal" and "U-shaped" distributions.

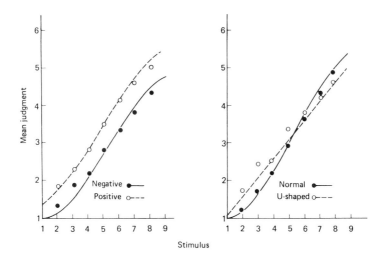

Figure 4.23

GENERAL REMARKS

This chapter has shown how the reported judgment of an object, in length or brightness (and presumably in other aspects) depends upon the object and its environment. The general position taken is that all perceptual judgments are completely relative; whenever judgments appear to be absolute, this is because many factors affect the frame of reference.

The theory of unconscious inference, introduced early in this chapter, can now be evaluated in contrast with the simple adaptation-level theory.

First, the adaptation-level formulas, which indicate that all factors in the field are averaged into a geometric mean and that the judgment depends upon the stimulus relative to that geometric mean, have been successful in accounting for the data. The formulas for unconscious inference, which appeal to physical relationships (such as luminance equals reflectance times illuminance) rather than to the geometric mean, seem to have been less able to handle details of data.

Second, the main experimental unknowns are the relative weights of each factor in the field. Since all the factors can be measured physically, the outcome of an experiment is a set of estimates of the weights. A theoretical analysis of an experimental situation must, therefore, include the job of rationalizing or predicting these weights.

The adaptation level must be defined with respect to a particular test stimulus and depends upon any of a number of other stimuli. The weight of a given stimulus with magnitude B_i on the adaptation level for judgment of a test stimulus may depend on the magnitude B_i, the propinquity of the two stimuli, and other more subtle factors. In terms used by Gestalt psychologists, the weight of any background stimulus in determining the adaptation level for the test stimulus should depend upon the degree to which the background stimuli and the test stimuli are organized into the same whole or organization.

A very subtle experiment on this problem has been done by Hochberg and Beck[10] who showed that a change in the subject's knowledge about a field could completely change the apparent brightness of a figure. A field was constructed of blocks strewn on a table top, illuminated mainly from above, and viewed through a reduction screen. The target was a trapezoidal erect card, of such a shape that it looked like a square lying down flat on the table. Since the square would be under strong illumination from above (a fact shown by shadows on other figures in the field), and its luminosity was moderate, it was judged to be quite dark (low reflectance). When the experimenter, without otherwise changing the visual array, waved a rod behind the trapezoid and thereby showed the subject that it was actually

---

[10] J. E. Hochberg and J. Beck, Apparent spatial arrangement and perceived brightness. *J. Exp. Psych.*, 1954, **47**, 263–266.

upright, it then appeared to have a much higher reflectance and was judged to be much whiter. This sort of experiment appears to demonstrate the basic idea of the theory of unconscious inference, and to unseat the frame-of-reference theory.

The weights of various factors in an adaptation level are dependent on the field situation. When judging the reflectance of a plane surface in overhead or other directional lighting, it is expected that the observer will give greatest weight to surfaces having the same orientation as the test surface. It is perhaps amazing that such judgments of orientation can be made so quickly, but the reader will notice that he can, by glancing about his room, rapidly pick out many surfaces parallel to one another, ignoring other surfaces.

Thus, in an experiment like Hochberg and Beck's, it is possible to change all the weights in the field, shifting from heavy weights on horizontal surfaces to heavy weights on vertical surfaces, by a relatively slight shift in the situation.

With some further refinement, it may be possible to establish a formal theory of adaptation level on a firm mathematical foundation. Then the measurements taken can be related to the real perceptual dependent variables, the various selections the perceptual system makes.

EXERCISES

1. Suppose that three experiments are conducted. One uses a constant box of size 1.0 on the left and varies the line length and box size on the right. Estimated parameter values are $s'_1 = 0.058$ and $b'_1 = 0.046$. The second experiment uses a constant box of size 1.0 on the right and varies the line length and box size on the left. Estimated parameters are $s'_2 = 0.056$ and $b'_2 = 0.067$. The third experiment varies line length and keeps the two boxes of equal (but varying) size. Assume that there is no interaction between the effects of the two backgrounds, and calculate predicted parameter values s'_3 and b'_3.

2. Let $B_1 = 8$ and $B_2 = 16$. Using the parameters estimated for the line-length and box-size experiment, calculate the percent of illusion. Also calculate the percent of illusion if $B_1 = 16$ and $B_2 = 24$.

3. Let r be the ratio of stimulus magnitudes S_2/S_1 that are judged equal when the standard stimulus has a background with magnitude B_1 and the comparison stimulus has a background with magnitude B_2. Let r_s be the ratio of stimulus magnitudes judged equal according to the method of single stimuli, and let r_c be the ratio of stimulus magnitudes judged equal in a method where two stimuli are presented together and compared directly. Show that

$$\frac{i}{b} = \frac{(1 - s')(\log r_s - \log r_c)}{b' \log r_c + (1 - s') \log r_s},$$

where b' and s' are the parameters estimated from the single-stimulus experiment.

4. Assume that $s' = 0.054$ and $b' = 0.108$, as in the experiment on line lengths and box sizes. Recall that there was a 15% illusion measured by the method of single stimuli. Calculate the percentage of illusion for a method of compared stimuli (a) where $i/b = 0.05$ and (b) where $i/b = 0.50$.

5. The calculations about the series effect in Rock and Ebenholz's Experiment I were carried out using the strong assumption that $s' = (\frac{1}{2})b'$. A much weaker assumption is sufficient to make the point. Assume that $s' = cb'$, $0 \leq c \leq (1 - b')/b'$. Show that

$$k' = \frac{2 \log 3 - \log S_2}{(1 - c) \log 3 + c \log S_2},$$

and show that k' is a decreasing function of S_2. Recall that with binocular vision, S_2 was 6.0, and with monocular vision, S_2 was 6.7. This shows that k' was less with monocular vision, and the only assumption is that s' and b' maintained a constant ratio in the two situations.

6. In the experiment by Emerson described in the text, judgments were obtained for the same stimuli shown against white, gray, and black backgrounds. The data for the gray backgrounds were given before. The data for the other two backgrounds were as follows:

Stimulus value	Mean judgment with white background (80% reflectance)	Mean judgment with black background (4% reflectance)
5.4	−5.5	−3.5
8.0	−3.7	−1.8
16.9	−2.2	−0.8
25.8	−1.2	0.2
38.4	−0.3	1.6
47.5	0.5	2.5
74.5	1.8	4.0

Assume that the value of p (and hence the slope of each function) is a constant independent of background, and equal to 0.30, as estimated for the gray background. Obtain estimates of A for the white and black backgrounds, using the means of the obtained judgments. Verify that the assumption of constant p is reasonable by drawing a graph of $J(S)$ against $\log X$ for all three backgrounds, comparing the above data with the appropriate theoretical functions.

7. Use the data in Table 4.5 to estimate category thresholds as they are defined by Parducci.

Table 4.6 P_{ij}, the probability that stimulus s_i is judged no greater than category c_j (Hypothetical data)

		Category j			
		1	2	3	4
	1	0.500	0.690	0.935	0.990
	2	0.420	0.555	0.790	0.905
Stimulus i	3	0.065	0.225	0.775	0.970
	4	0.310	0.380	0.540	0.655
	5	0.020	0.065	0.310	0.600

8. Using data from Table 4.6, draw a reasonable approximation to the function $P(R \geq J \mid S)$. Then estimate a set of frequency thresholds for four categories, assuming that the five stimuli are presented equally often. Using these frequency thresholds and the data, estimate a set of range thresholds. Now estimate frequency thresholds assuming that the stimulus frequencies are (a) 0.40, 0.20, 0.20, 0.10, and 0.10, and (b) 0.10, 0.10, 0.20, 0.20, 0.40.

CHAPTER FIVE

Detection and Discrimination

The main question of this chapter may be stated: What determines the limits of the sensory system? There are two alternative conceptualizations. The older theory, centering around the idea of a sensory threshold, holds that some stimuli are too weak to evoke any response; and if a stimulus, though present, is changed too slightly, the change may be too small to evoke any differential response. The focus of research in this area has been limited to the determination of thresholds—finding the weakest stimulus or the smallest change that can be noticed. The classical psychophysical methods for determining thresholds are still in constant use.

The alternative theory is based on the idea of an imperfect channel of communication. If a stimulus is received in a pure form, with nothing else happening, the subject is not very likely to miss it. However, if much other stimulation is arriving at the same time, the stimulus may be lost in the background of accompanying noise.

Noise, by definition, varies randomly, so that on some occasions when a signal is present it will be masked by the noise, and on other occasions when there is no signal the noise may produce a stimulus similar to those that occur when signals are presented. The problem of detection requires a decision as to whether or not the stimulus comes from the signal generator. Perfect performance is impossible because of the variability of the noise, and the best a person can do is to set some criterion that will allow him to make the correct decision on some maximum number of occasions.

A typical practical problem is hearing and understanding a friend's voice over the telephone. Sometimes the voice is too weak to be heard easily—the speaker may be talking too softly or he may be directing his voice away from his telephone mouthpiece. At other times, the listener receives plenty of sound, but the voice he is trying to understand arrives along with a great deal of static. In this case the problem is not that of detecting a weak stimulus but of extracting the stimulus from its background of noise.

172

It is reasonable to suppose that in some situations detection fails because the stimulation is not strong enough or because differences between stimuli are too small, whereas in other situations failures of detection occur because of accompanying noise. The theories of these two situations are similar in form, and at the usual level of analysis, they imply the same statistical structure of data in most experiments.

Method of Constant Stimuli

In order to determine whether a stimulus is noticeable or whether two stimuli are noticeably different, the experimenter must obtain appropriate responses from his subject. To eliminate the effects of expectations and misunderstandings, the task should be clearly defined. Then the situation is arranged and stimuli are presented in a way that makes it as easy as possible for the subject to answer whether he perceives a stimulus or whether he can discriminate between two stimuli.

For example, the method of constant stimuli can be used to measure how precisely a subject can discriminate between weights. One weight is selected as a standard, say, 100 g, and a series of comparison weights, 78, 90, 100, 112, 125 g are chosen. Each observation consists in some comparative judgment made by a subject picking up the standard and then a comparison weight. In some modalities, notably vision, it is possible to display the standard and comparison stimuli at the same time.

Several forms of judgment can be made, and the relation between them is a theoretical problem. For example, in some experiments, the comparison stimulus is either *stronger or the same*, and the subject makes a judgment $+$ or $=$. The question in this case is: How small an increment can be detected? This kind of judgment is always used in measurement of the "absolute threshold," that is, the weakest detectable stimulus.

A second judgment, which is the most commonly used, is *forced choice*. The observer must judge the comparison stimulus X to be either stronger or weaker than the standard S. This judgment is $+$ or $-$, and permits the experimenter to put comparison stimuli above and below the standard.

In a third judgment, the comparison stimulus may be judged stronger, equal, or weaker; this is a choice of $+$, $=$, or $-$. The set of stimuli judged to be equal are said to be in the subject's *interval of uncertainty*.

A fourth logical possibility is equal vs. unequal, where the comparison stimulus may be either weaker or stronger than the standard. This judgment is not liked by subjects and merely throws away information; hence it is rarely used.

In the first method, X is to be judged either stronger than S or the same; here the subject may be unclear as to how much difference he must notice to call the two different. The two stimuli cannot be perfectly identical, and the experimenter has ensured that X will not be smaller than S. Therefore, some subjects may feel that when in doubt they can safely say that X is larger. Other subjects may feel that two objects may look slightly different even when they are actually the same; hence, they are more likely to say that X and S are the same when small differences are perceived. These are differences in attitude, not in sensation or perception, but they may affect the measurement of discrimination.

A similar problem appears in the third method using judgments $-$, $=$, and $+$. Different observers may differ widely in their use of the middle category, not because they have more or less precise sense organs, but because they employ different criteria for reporting a weak and uncertain difference.

Most experimenters prefer the forced-choice judgment in which X must be called stronger or weaker than S, even if the two stimuli are (physically) equal.

Analysis of Forced-Choice Data

On each observation the subject calls X either stronger or weaker than S. Of course, S is a constant and there are several values of X. The first step is to calculate the proportion of times X is called stronger than S for each value of X. (Clearly, to obtain stable values, a large number of observations is needed for *each* comparison stimulus.)

Table 5.1 shows some illustrative data from an experiment in weight lifting. Using these same data we can plot X against p, illustrating what is often called the psychometric function. (See Fig. 5.1.) This graph gives a general and compact summary of the raw data. However, even more compactness is obtained by smoothing the data, and fitting a curve to the points. The data can often be fit by a normal ogive. Theories relating p to the normal ogive will be given below. For the present, consider that for stimulus magnitudes far below S, the subject will seldom, if ever, say "stronger." The probability of saying "stronger" will increase with stimulus magnitude, approaching or reaching one for stimulus magnitudes far above S. Any cumulative density function increases from zero to one as the variable increases. In the case of the normal density, the cumulative function is

$$N(x) = \int_{-\infty}^{x} f(y)\, dy, \tag{1}$$

where $f(y)$ is the normal density function, and $N(x)$ is assumed to equal p. Recall that

$$f(y) = \left(\frac{1}{\sqrt{2\pi}\sigma}\right) e^{-(y-\mu)^2/\sigma}, \tag{2}$$

where μ and σ are the parameters of the normal curve, the mean, and the standard deviation. To fit the normal ogive, it is necessary to estimate μ and σ.

Table 5.1 Proportion of response "heavier" in forced-choice experiment (from Woodworth and Schlosberg, p. 216)

Stimulus weight	P(heavier)	Stimulus weight	P(heavier)
82	0.00	100.5	0.56
83	0.01	101	0.58
84	0.00	102	0.61
85	0.01	103	0.67
		104	0.75
86	0.02	105	0.77
87	0.03		
88	0.03	106	0.83
89	0.04	107	0.83
90	0.06	108	0.88
		109	0.89
91	0.10	110	0.92
92	0.12		
93	0.13	111	0.95
94	0.20	112	0.94
95	0.19	113	0.95
		114	0.97
96	0.29	115	0.97
97	0.29		
98	0.38	116	0.97
99	0.44	117	0.98
99.5	0.50	118	0.98
100	0.53		

The most practical way to fit the curve is by use of probability paper. When the data of Fig. 5.1 are plotted on probability paper, the values usually fall near a straight line. The straight line may then be fitted by eye or by simple statistical methods, and transformed back to the original graph. See Fig. 5.2 in which the steps are illustrated. Probability paper has the x-axis spaced equally. The y-axis is spaced widely at values of p near 0 and 1, and closely packed near 0.50, so that a normal ogive would just be straightened out. This transformation of p is often called z, and values of z are given on the right side of Fig. 5.2.

Suppose that the plot of z against X is approximately linear, and the straight line is drawn. The point at which this line crosses $p = 0.50$, or $z = 0$, is an estimate of the median, hence of the mean, of the underlying normal distribution. The slope of the line estimates the standard deviation. From a normal-curve table it may be determined that when $z = -2.0$, $p = 0.0228$. And when $z = +2.0$, $p = 0.9778$. Recall that one unit of z equals σ. Hence the difference between the values of X that give rise to

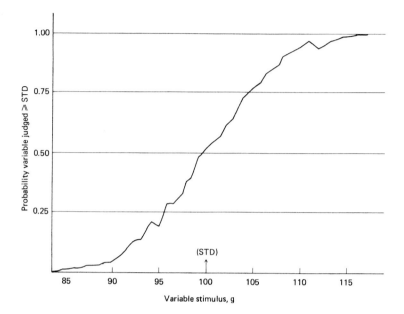

Figure 5.1

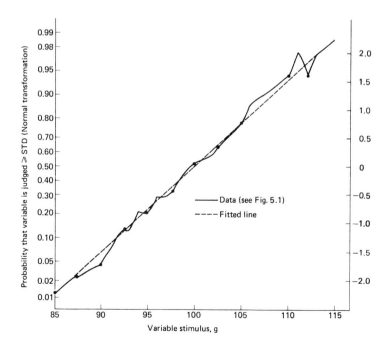

Figure 5.2

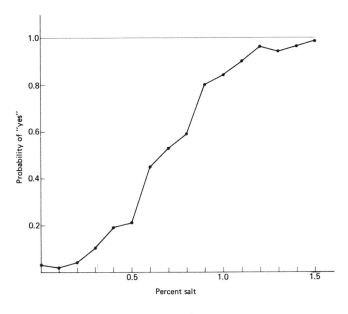

Figure 5.3

$p = 0.9772$ and $p = 0.0228$ is 4σ, and σ can thereby be estimated by dividing the difference between these X's by 4.

The preceding illustration has dealt with the measurement of a difference threshold—the sensitivity for detecting differences between two stimuli. When absolute thresholds are measured, the data are similar in appearance. Of course, the subject's response is different—he says "yes" or "no" on each trial, indicating whether or not he detected a stimulus. In the method of constant stimuli, the subject is presented with a number of stimuli, varying in intensity, and he reports on each trial whether or not he detected the stimulus. Thus a psychometric function is obtained which looks much like Fig. 5.1, except that the ordinate is the probability of the response "yes," and the abscissa is the intensity of the stimulus. A typical set of data are graphed in Fig. 5.3, and these data can be fit by a cumulative normal distribution in the same manner as that described for the difference-threshold data.

THEORY OF THE METHOD OF CONSTANT STIMULI

Two main perceptual theories can provide a basis for analyzing data of this kind. Following is the classical threshold idea of detection of weak stimuli (see Woodworth and Schlosberg[1]).

[1] R. S. Woodworth and H. Schlosberg, *Experimental Psychology*. New York: Holt, 1954, p. 193.

Threshold Theory of Detection of Weak Signals

It is assumed that there exists a minimum level of stimulation required to evoke a response. This level is the threshold, and the subject will respond "yes" if and only if the stimulus received is stronger than the threshold. Ideally, according to this theory, the psychometric function for a detection experiment should be a step function. The threshold would be fixed at some intensity L. The probability of "yes" would be zero for all stimuli below the threshold, and unity for all stimuli above (see Fig. 5.4). The results of experiments do not have such sharp corners, but the data do seem to be roughly in accord with the threshold idea. The results in Fig. 5.3 can be interpreted as a case of the threshold theory with the corners rounded off. The theory can assume that the threshold is not a fixed constant, or that a given stimulus does not always produce the same intensity of sensation, or that both the threshold and the sensation vary.

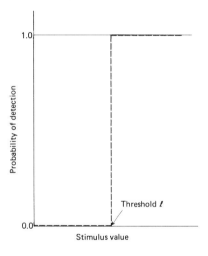

Figure 5.4

The classical theory includes an assumption that the momentary probability of saying "yes" is either unity or zero, depending on whether the momentary sensation intensity is above or below the momentary threshold. That is, let $l(t)$ be the threshold value at time t, and let $x(t)$ be the value of a sensory input at time t. Then the subject will say "yes" if and only if

$$x(t) \geq l(t).$$

A set of diagrams is shown in Fig. 5.5 which describes how the psychometric function would be generated by the theory of variable threshold and an

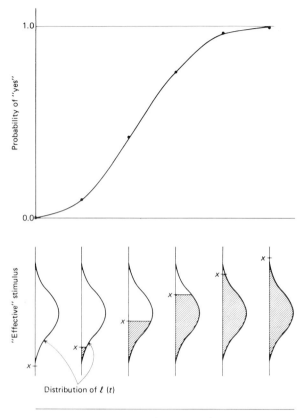

Figure 5.5

all-or-none response rule. The sensation produced by a stimulus is taken to be a simple function of the constant stimulus X, but the threshold, $l(t)$, varies in a normal distribution.

A very similar model results when the threshold is assumed to be fixed at L, but the sensory value of the comparison is a random variable, $x(t)$. See Fig. 5.6.

From a psychometric function it is not possible to decide between the two theories. In fact, one may imagine that $l(t)$ and $x(t)$ both vary randomly. Then the probability that the subject will say $X > L$ is just the probability that

$$x(t) - l(t) > 0.$$

If X and L are independent and normally distributed, then their difference

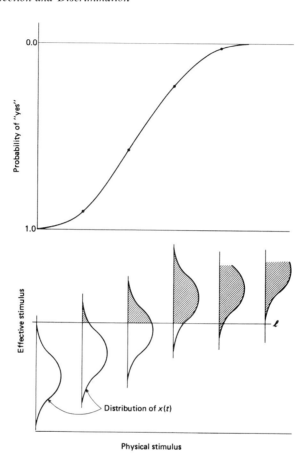

Figure 5.6

also has a normal distribution. Then $d(t_1)$, defined as

$$d(t_1) = x(t_1) - l(t_1),$$ (3)

is normally distributed with parameters

$$\mu_d = \mu_x - \mu_l, \qquad \sigma_d = \sqrt{(\sigma_x^2 + \sigma_l^2)}.$$ (4)

The generation of the psychometric function is shown in Fig. 5.7.

The assumption of a normal distribution may seem gratuitous, but actually it is quite reasonable. Suppose, for example, that at time t_0 the threshold $l(t_0)$ is a constant. However, in any instant the threshold value l may jump to other values. Suppose, for one theory, that the jump from any

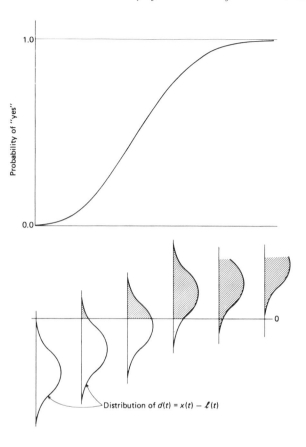

Figure 5.7

value l to any value $l + e$ can be given by the function $f(e)$. That is, the probability of a jump of given magnitude is a function only of the magnitude of the jump, not of the starting place l or the time of the jump t. The magnitude of the jump, e, may be either positive or negative.

Now suppose that several jumps take place, of magnitudes $e_1, e_2, \ldots, e_n$, in the time between t_0 and t_1, the time of judgment. Then the position of the trace of the standard, $l(t)$, is given by

$$l(t_1) = l(t_0) + e_1 + e_2 + \cdots + e_n. \tag{5}$$

If, for a simple restriction, $f(e)$ has a finite range, and if n is fairly large, it follows that $l(t_1)$ approaches a normal distribution. The reason is that under the restriction, $e_1, e_2, \ldots, e_n$ are independent random variables, and the sum of a number of independent random variables always approaches a normal distribution; the restrictions are extremely general and would be met by many reasonable psychological models.

Another advantage of the normal distribution is that it gives a simple mathematical form to the idea that both S and X vary. If both have normal distributions, then their difference is also normally distributed.

Extension of Threshold Theory to Discrimination Experiments

Now consider an experiment for measuring the difference threshold. Two stimuli are presented, and may be the same or different. Assume that the subject is required to give a response of "higher" or "lower" on every trial (the forced-choice procedure described earlier).

Again, it is useful to begin with an idealization. Suppose that each of the stimuli produces a unique sensation and that sensory magnitude is a monotonic function of physical magnitude. Then the subject should be able to respond "higher" with perfect accuracy whenever the second stimulus X is higher than the first, S. The ideal psychometric function will look like Fig. 5.8.

The ideal discrimination theory can be modified to allow for errors, as was the threshold theory described above. The theory was originally presented by Thurstone[2] and was called the Law of Comparative Judgment. Thurstone assumed that on repeated presentations, a stimulus produces a distribution of sensory effects. The standard stimulus has a distribution $s(t)$, and comparison X has distribution $x(t)$. It is assumed that the subject

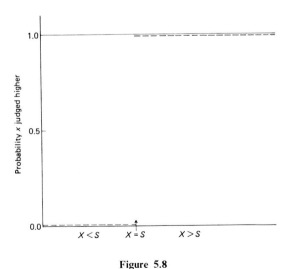

Figure 5.8

---

[2] L. L. Thurstone, A Law of Comparative Judgment. *Psych. Rev.*, 1927, **34**, 273–286.

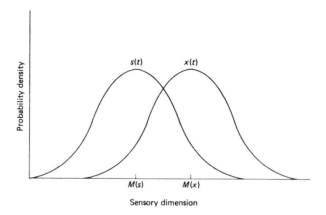

Figure 5.9

responds on the basis of the momentary values of $s(t)$ and $x(t)$, saying "higher" whenever $x(t) > s(t)$ and "lower" otherwise. The situation is described in Fig. 5.9. Then the probability of the response "higher" is a function of the distribution of the difference, $D = x(t) - s(t)$;

$$P(\text{"higher"}) = P[x(t) > s(t)] = P[x(t) - s(t) > 0].$$

Let $d(t)$ stand for the difference between $x(t)$ and $s(t)$, as before. Then $d(t)$ is distributed with variance equal to

$$\sigma_d^2 = \sigma_s^2 + \sigma_x^2 - 2r_{sx}\sigma_s\sigma_x,$$

and the subject responds "higher" if and only if $d(t) > 0$.

External Noise Theory of Detection

The above theory leads to the idea that if it were not for faults in the sensory system leading to the introduction of random variation of traces, performance would be perfect. However, the theory of detection of tones and other signals in auditory noise leads to a different theory, that of *detectability*.

Sometimes the signal to be detected is tangled inextricably with a source of external noise. In Fig. 5.10 is shown the wave form of a weak pure tone and a strong noise, and the resultant. No detector, including the human ear, can be sure from inspection of the resultant itself, whether or not it contains a signal. Yet the wave form contains all possible information available to the ear.

Performance usually can be improved if the wave form is put through a filter, eliminating variations that could not be caused by the signal. If pure noise is put through such a filter, there will be some energy in the region of the signal, and that energy will fluctuate up and down, depending upon the random fluctuations of the noise generator. When signal-plus-noise are put through the same filter, the resultant will also fluctuate up and down: it will increase when the noise component happens to be in phase with the signal, decrease when the noise component is out of phase with the signal, but the average will be higher than with noise alone.

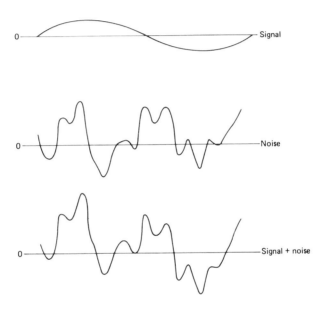

Figure 5.10

A Gaussian noise is defined as one which gives a normal distribution of the amplitude at any given point in the spectrum. If a signal is added at that point in the spectrum, the mean of the normal distribution is raised by a constant amount. See Fig. 5.11; the result is just like those of the threshold theories.

Imagine that the ear, as a very fine detector, observes a given amplitude. A decision must be made as to which source it came from; noise alone (N), or signal plus noise (SN). Such a particular amplitude is called y in Fig. 5.11. The likelihood of y, given N, is shown by the line called $l_N(y)$, and the likelihood of y given SN is shown as $l_{SN}(y)$. In this case, since y is fairly low, l_N is greater than l_{SN}.

There is a slight ambiguity in the discussion above, for the stimulus has been tacitly equated with amplitude. The complete wave form contains

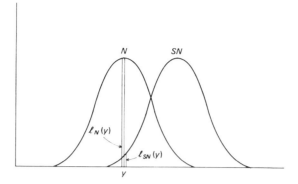

Figure 5.11

information in addition to the amplitude. However, within acoustical theory it is often possible to relate various physical properties of a stimulus to the corresponding statistical properties of a noise generator, so that the likelihood of a stimulus can be calculated, based on knowledge about the sources.

In a detection experiment, the subject's task is to report "yes" or "no" depending on whether he thinks there was a signal present on that trial. Assume that the subject knows the properties of the acoustical equipment and the probabilities of various outputs both when there is a signal present, and when there is nothing but noise. The subject listens to an auditory stimulus, y, in his earphones, and is able to make a judgment of how likely that stimulus would be on trials when there was no signal, and a judgment of how likely that stimulus would be on trials when there was a signal. Physically, these likelihoods are well defined, at least for auditory stimuli. If the subject can judge these likelihoods, $l_N(y)$ and $l_{SN}(y)$, his responses may be a function of the likelihood ratio,

$$\lambda(y) = \frac{l_{SN}(y)}{l_N(y)}. \tag{6}$$

The subject may make his judgment on the basis of any of several stimulus properties, and the above theoretical analysis uses the ratio of likelihoods. The analysis is appropriate if the subject bases his decision on a function of stimulus variables that is monotonic with the likelihood ratio. Although experiments on stimulus properties yield specific information regarding the sensory processes, the analysis in terms of likelihoods permits investigation of relationships between physical noise and decision processes; and the theory of the decision process can be developed even though knowledge about the sensory process is incomplete.

Consider the theory of signal detectability where the dimension of the stimulus has been translated to log likelihood ratios. A typical pair of distributions is shown in Fig. 5.12.

In detection experiments, a stimulus is presented from either the N or SN distribution on each trial. The subject's task is to decide which distribution "fathered" the stimulus—that is, whether the signal was or was not a part of the input he received.

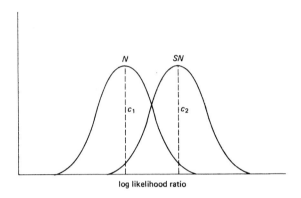

log likelihood ratio

Figure 5.12

Given that the subject's response depends on the log likelihood ratio (log λ) of the stimulus, the response should be "yes" when the value of log λ is very high, and "no" when log λ is very low. The assumption of the theory is that there is a criterion, c, set by the subject and depending on his expectancies and motives, and the subject responds "yes" if and only if log $\lambda > c$. If the criterion is set low, say at point c_1 in Fig. 5.12, then the subject will say "yes" on nearly all the SN trials, but he also will say "yes" on a sizable number of the N trials. If the criterion is set high, say at point c_2, then the subject is conservative and will say "yes" to very few of the N trials, but he will say "no" on a fair share of the SN trials.

The criterion plays a role analogous to the threshold in the classical theory. On SN trials, if the criterion has a single value, we can derive a theory exactly like the fixed-threshold, variable-sensation version of the threshold theory. (See Fig. 5.6 and the accompanying text.) The theory of signal detectability differs from the classical theory in three ways. First, stimulus variation is interpreted in terms of the likelihood ratio rather than directly in terms of intensity. This means that the theory of detectability can be applied to experiments in which the sources of stimulus variation are complex, or even where the physical situation is not completely understood or specified. Second, the theory of detectability uses an adjustable criterion, not a fixed threshold. This brings in choice and decision factors that undoubtedly influence behavior in detection experiments, but are not easily integrated with the notions of the threshold. Finally, the theory of detectability considers the variation present on trials when there is *no* signal, giving a detailed interpretation to false-alarm responses.

If a subject can alter his criterion, then his detection data do not bear a one-to-one correspondence between stimulus values and the probabilities of saying "yes." The probability that a subject will say "yes" to a given stimulus depends on the criterion he is using at the time. A typical curve, describing the probability of "yes" on SN trials depending on the criterion, is shown in Fig. 5.13. In the absence of an independent measure on the strictness of a subject's criterion, the function relating $P(\text{"yes"})$ to the strictness of a criterion must remain unknown. However, it is possible to go beyond the mere statement that the criterion affects the probability of "yes." The key to a more informative analysis is in the fact that a criterion determines not only a probability $P(\text{"yes"})$ on SN trials, but a corresponding probability $P(\text{"yes"})$ on N trials as well. Depending on the overlap of the distributions (Fig. 5.12), a given cutpoint determines two conditional probabilities of the "yes" response. Let $P(Y \mid SN)$ be the probability of "yes" on SN trials, and let $P(Y \mid N)$ be the probability of "yes" when there is no signal. [Note that $P(Y \mid N)$ is the probability of one of the errors that can occur.] A criterion determines a pair of coordinates in two-space, as illustrated in Fig. 5.14. The points in Fig. 5.14 can be related to the cutpoints indicated in Fig. 5.12. Criterion c_1 corresponds to a lax criterion. Much of

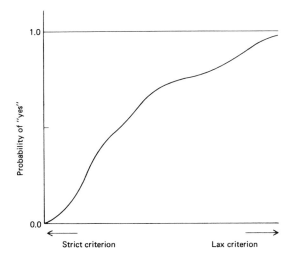

Figure 5.13

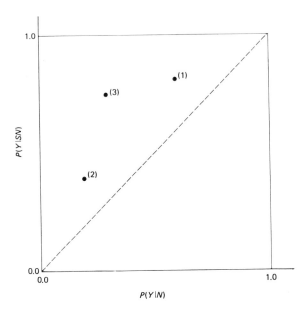

Figure 5.14

the area under both distributions is to the right of c_1. Therefore the probability of "yes" is relatively high both on SN and N trials, giving point 1 in Fig. 5.14. Criterion c_2 is strict, a relatively small portion of each of the distributions is to the right of c_2, and the probability of "yes" is relatively low on both SN and N trials, providing point 2. This variation in $P(Y \mid SN)$ and $P(Y \mid N)$ occurs for a single stimulus signal presented along with a single distribution of noise. The detectability of that stimulus is represented not by a single number, but by a curve, such as the one that would go through points 1, 2, and 3. Such a curve is called the receiver operating characteristic (ROC), or an "isosensitivity" function. The success of the subject in detecting the stimulus is measured by the degree to which each point $P(Y \mid SN)$ is greater than $P(Y \mid N)$—he says "yes" more often when there is a signal than when there is none. With good detection, the ROC is far above the dashed line in Fig. 5.14, and as the stimulus becomes harder to detect, the ROC will be closer and closer to the dashed chance line. If the ROC is on the chance line, then the subject's $P(Y \mid SN)$ and $P(Y \mid N)$ are equal, indicating that he is not discriminating between SN and N trials at all.

External Noise and Forced-Choice Experiments

In two-alternative forced-choice acoustical testing, the observer is presented with two intervals, well marked by lights. He knows that a tone will appear in exactly one of the two intervals, but there is a noise burst in both intervals.

The observer's response is "first" or "second," accordingly as he believes the tone to have been in the first or second interval.

The classical or internal-noise theory says that the input in each interval gives rise, on successive trials, to a distribution of intensities. On each trial the subject has two intensities, x_1 and x_2, from the two intervals. If x_1 is greater than x_2, he says "first," but if x_2 is greater, he says "second."

In signal detectability theory, the subject can entertain only two hypotheses:

H_1: SN, N (signal + noise followed by noise),

H_2: N, SN.

He observes a complex wave form, w, composed of two parts w_1 and w_2 in the two intervals. The probability (or likelihood) of w given hypothesis H_1 can be written

$$l_{H_1}(w) = l_{SN}(w_1)l_N(w_2),$$

where the expression $l_{H_1}(w)$ refers to the likelihood of wave form w based on the hypothesis H_1.[3]

Similarly, the likelihood of w based on hypothesis H_2 is

$$l_{H_2}(w) = l_N(w_1)l_{SN}(w_2).$$

Recall that w is the double wave form; its likelihood, on a given hypothesis, is just the product of the two parts given that the two-noise segments are independent.

The likelihood ratio λ is

$$\lambda = \frac{l_{H_1}(w)}{l_{H_2}(w)} = \frac{l_{SN}(w_1)}{l_N(w_1)} \bigg/ \frac{l_{SN}(w_2)}{l_N(w_2)}.$$

But notice that the two ratios on the right are themselves the likelihood ratios for the separate intervals. Taking logarithms and referring to the separate likelihood ratios in intervals 1 and 2 as λ_1 and λ_2,

$$\log \lambda = \log \lambda_1 - \log \lambda_2. \tag{7}$$

An experiment using noise gives rise to a multitude of possible wave forms w. Each w has a value of λ associated with it, so that randomizing the experiment will produce a distribution of λ (or $\log \lambda$). Since the two parts of the wave form, w_1 and w_2, consist of independent segments of noise in such experiments, it follows that λ_1 and λ_2 have independent distributions.

---

[3] The assumption that $l_H(w)$ is the product of simple likelihood elements presupposes that the subject evaluates the information in the two intervals independently.

With certain common kinds of noise, the distribution of amplitude in the relevant part of the spectrum, from one trial to another, is such that $\log \lambda_1$ has a normal distribution, as does $\log \lambda_2$. From Eq. (7) it follows that $\log \lambda$ has a normal distribution. In the usual experiment the subject is highly trained to expect that the two intervals will have the signal just half the time, and is aware that there is no differential payoff. If he adjusts to this training without bias, then he should set his criterion such that

$$c = 0.$$

Thus he should choose interval 1 only when he believes it is more likely that the signal is in the first interval; that is, when $\log \lambda_1$ is greater than $\log \lambda_2$, and $\log \lambda$ is greater than 0. The model is quite analogous to that from the classical case with internal noise, the subject choosing whichever interval or object showed the larger amplitude on that trial.

The assumption of classical internal-noise theory is that the subject samples from two distributions of discriminal processes, chooses the larger value, and that the result can be described as the difference between two normal distributions. In contrast, the assumption of external noise is that the subject has two hypotheses and calculates the likelihood of the given specific wave form from them, and then makes his choice by an optimal statistical decision. A powerful advantage of the external-noise decision-making theory is that it *generates* the normal distributions needed from physical properties of the noise.

WEBER'S LAW

After measuring how accurately a subject can discriminate loudness, weight, brightness, etc., experimenters often report the result in percentages; under optimal conditions, a subject can discriminate between two stimuli that differ in energy by, say, 5%. If this discriminable proportion is constant, then the necessary difference is proportional to the strengths of the two energies involved. Over a wide range of magnitudes, this constancy is usually found; it is called Weber's law.

Weber's law begins with the physical measurements S and X, for example, from the method of constant stimuli. Suppose that X_1 has been chosen such that

$$P(X_1 \text{ is seen as larger than } S) = 0.75,$$

so that X_1 is one just-noticeable difference above S or is just at threshold.

Then, Weber's law states that

$$\frac{\Delta S}{S} = \frac{(X_1 - S)}{S} = k. \tag{8}$$

A generalization would be to suppose that the same law would hold for more or less rigorous definitions of threshold. Suppose, for example, that a π-threshold is defined as a value of X, say X_π, such that

$$P(X_\pi \text{ is seen as larger than } S) = \pi.$$

Now, the π-generalization of Weber's law is

$$\frac{X_\pi - S}{S} = k(\pi), \tag{9}$$

where $k(\pi)$ is a constant, depending on π but independent of S. This implies that the psychometric function, whatever its shape, is the same at all values of S. For a more precise statement, we can take the logarithm of both sides of Eq. (9) and obtain

$$\log (X_\pi - S) = \log k(\pi) + \log S. \tag{10}$$

The psychometric function relates X_π to π, and since they are related monotonically in all theories, the function has an inverse relating π to X_π. According to Eq. (10), the relation between $X - S$ and π is composed of two parts: the logarithm of the arbitrary function $k(\pi)$, and the additive log S. Therefore, when the standard S is varied, the logarithmic psychometric function is changed only by addition of log S.

Weber's law holds in good approximation over a wide range of stimuli, but does not usually hold either for very weak or very strong stimuli. This phenomenon is illustrated in Fig. 5.15.

According to Eq. (8), if $\Delta S/S$ is plotted, the result should be constant, that is, a horizontal straight line. Note that the curve in Fig. 5.15 is higher at low values, and turns slightly higher at high illuminations, but is relatively flat at near 0.03 for most of the perceivable range. The discrepancies at the two ends are explained differently.

One theory says that S itself is irrelevant to the discrimination, which depends only on the difference $X - S$. Increasing S amounts to adding more and more irrelevance to the situation, and a corresponding amount of difference must also be added. However, these are vague terms and must be defined.

The experimenter measures a threshold at S by finding a value of X, say X_π, such that the subject distinguishes X_π from S a proportion π of the time. Assume that all along the scale σ_X is proportional to σ_S so that the variance of the difference is

$$\sigma_d^2 = \sigma_S^2 + a^2\sigma_S^2 - 2ra\sigma_S\sigma_S,$$

where $a = \sigma_X/\sigma_S$ is taken to be a constant. Then to be detectable with

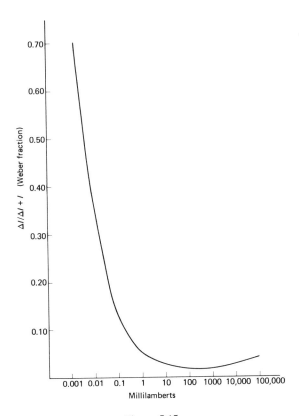

Figure 5.15

probability π, in the standard theory, the difference must be some constant proportion k of σ_d. That is,

$$\Delta S = k\sigma_d = k\sqrt{\sigma_S^2 + a^2\sigma_S^2 - 2ra\sigma_S^2} = K\sigma_S,$$

where K is the product of k and another constant involving a and r.

Consider the relationship between ΔS and S, laws of the type of the Weber fraction. Suppose that a given stimulus is divided into parts, and that each unit part gives rise to effects in the nervous system that describe a normal distribution with mean μ and standard deviation σ. A more intense stimulus can be constructed by adding more unit stimuli; in all simple cases, the number of unit stimuli is proportional to the intensity of the stimulus.

Now imagine that a stimulus has n units. If each unit is thought of as a random component with mean μ and variance σ^2, and if the various units vary independently, then the mean and variance of the stimulus will be given by

$$\mu_n = n\mu, \qquad \sigma_n^2 = n\sigma^2,$$

and the standard deviation of the stimulus will be $\sigma\sqrt{n}$. Since the number of unit stimuli is proportional to the physical intensity S of the stimulus,

$$\sigma_S = \beta\sqrt{S}. \tag{12}$$

This, combined with Eq. (11), yields

$$\Delta S = K\sigma_S = C\sqrt{S}, \tag{13}$$

and the Weber fraction is

$$\frac{\Delta S}{S} = \frac{C\sqrt{S}}{S} = \frac{C}{\sqrt{S}}. \tag{14}$$

This is obviously not a constant; on the contrary, the Weber fraction decreases with the square root of S, as shown in Fig. 5.15. This is sometimes called the Rose-DeVries law.

A slightly different formulation of this classical theory gives Weber's law. In this version, an increase of the intensity of the stimulus is represented by the addition of random variables, as above, when the variables are perfectly correlated. Then a stimulus with n components will be like a single stimulus multiplied by n, and

$$\mu_n = n\mu, \qquad \sigma_n^2 = n^2\sigma^2, \qquad \sigma_n = n\sigma.$$

With this hypothesis, σ increases as does μ, proportional to the number of components added; therefore ΔS, which is proportional to σ_S, is also proportional to S. This theory leads to Weber's law, for $\Delta S/S$ is constant.

How might the extra sensory factors, added by increasing the strength of the stimulus, all be correlated? One possibility is that the variability is provided by the subject; the stimulus is constant, but the subject lets through a variable amount from one trial to another. If all n parts of the stimulus present at a given moment are affected equally by variations in the subject's threshold, the variations are perfectly correlated.

Recall from Fig. 5.15 that the Weber fraction drops as intensity increases up to about 1 millilambert, then is approximately constant to at least 10,000, perhaps 100,000 millilamberts. This may reflect the following mechanism: at higher amounts of light, from 1 to 100,000 millilamberts, the variability in the system is contributed by the subject, operating in a coordinated way, so that all parts of the stimulus vary with perfect correlation. At very small amounts of light, below one millilambert, however, a significant proportion of the variation is produced by quantum variation of the light (since light is composed of quanta and cannot vary continuously), random absorption of quanta in the eyeball, and perhaps random fluctuations in firing of individual receptor cells. These molecular factors may act upon units of input energy, each unit being affected randomly and independently of the others.

The theory given here is a mere sketch—it does not do justice to the known structure of light, transmittance of the eye, size and density of photo-pigments, structure of the retinal nerves, complexity of subcortical and cortical visual systems; or the effects of wavelength, size, location, or duration of the target.

Another limitation of this theory is its lack of any mechanism for counting how many of the *n* possible events may have occurred.

INFORMATION THEORY

The methods above are used to analyze a subject's ability to discriminate between two stimuli. It is often interesting to study the discriminability of a whole set of stimuli. Total discriminability may not be quite the same thing as accuracy; partial discrimination of many stimuli may represent more accomplishment than excellent discrimination of only two. An example is given in Table 5.2. In Case 1, the judgments are correct 80% of the time, whereas in Case 2 they are correct only 70 or 75% of the time. Therefore it is natural to say that Case 1 shows greater accuracy. On the other hand, Case 2 shows more transmission of information; the subject is doing quite well with four categories. If the number of categories is increased, often the accuracy will then decrease, but the amount of information transmitted may increase.

Notice what would happen in Case 2 if the subject were only required to say whether a stimulus came from the pair *A*, *B* or the pair *C*, *D*. Then the proportion correct would increase from 0.70 or 0.75 to 0.85 or 0.90. This reflects the obvious fact that it is harder to perform consistently with a fine-grained classification than with a gross classification of the stimuli.

A second variable in the experimental situation is the frequency with which the different stimuli are presented. Suppose that one of the stimuli is presented on almost every trial, and the others are presented infrequently. The subject could take advantage of this fact by guessing the frequent

Table 5.2 Two hypothetical sets of discrimination data; contrasting accuracy with total discrimination

| | Case 1 Responses | | | Case 2 Responses | | | |
	A	*B*		*A*	*B*	*C*	*D*
A	0.8	0.2	*A*	0.75	0.15	0.10	0.00
B	0.2	0.8	*B*	0.15	0.70	0.15	0.00
			C	0.00	0.15	0.70	0.15
			D	0.00	0.10	0.15	0.75

stimulus when in doubt, and he would usually be correct. Then the proportion correct would be higher than if the stimuli had been presented equally often, but the higher proportion correct would reflect the sequence of stimuli, not better discrimination by the subject.

The two variables—the number of different stimuli and their relative frequencies—determine the degree to which the individual stimuli in the sequence are predictable in advance of observation. In the extreme case, if a sequence contains only one stimulus (presented with probability one) every single outcome is predictable and no observations need to be made. The larger the number of stimuli, the more uncertain the particular experimental outcome becomes as long as the various stimuli are approximately equally frequent.

It is important to analyze the predictability of stimuli if one wishes to measure a subject's ability to discriminate among them. Even given that stimuli are predictable, high performance does not necessarily indicate good discrimination.

The statistical theory of information[4] permits measurement of discrimination taking predictability into account. First, an index is used to describe the sequence of stimuli. This index is high if the sequence is unpredictable, and lower if the sequence is more predictable. Then discrimination can be measured relative to the unpredictability of the sequence.

Consider an experiment with N independent trials of a random process. At each trial, there are r possible outcomes, with probabilities $p_1, \ldots, p_r$. For example, if $N = 6$ and $r = 4$, then sequences like 3, 4, 2, 2, 4, 1 would result. A sequence in this order has probability

$$p_3 p_4 p_2 p_2 p_4 p_1 = (p_1)(p_2)^2(p_3)(p_4)^2,$$

The *improbability* of any event E, having probability $P(E)$, is defined as

$$\text{Improbability } (E) = \frac{1}{P(E)}.$$

The improbability of the sequence 3, 4, 2, 2, 4, 1 mentioned above is, therefore,

$$\frac{1}{p_1 p_2^2 p_3 p_4^2} = p_1^{-1} p_2^{-2} p_3^{-1} p_4^{-2}.$$

To generalize, let E be the joint occurrence of a sequence of elementary events having independent probabilities $p_1, p_2, \ldots, p_r$, the elementary events

---

[4] C. E. Shannon and W. Weaver, *The Mathematical Theory of Communication.* Urbana, Illinois: University of Illinois Press, 1949.

occurring with frequencies $N_1, N_2, \ldots, N_r$. The improbability of the sequence is

$$I(E) = p_1^{-N_1} p_2^{-N_2} \cdots p_r^{-N_r}.$$

Of course, any very long sequence is very improbable, but the average improbability per elementary event is of medium size. This is the Nth root of that product, the geometric mean, not the product of all the probabilities of elementary events. That is, if

$$N = N_1 + N_2 + \cdots + N_r$$

is the total number of elementary events in E, then the mean improbability per event is

$$\begin{aligned}
\bar{I}(E) &= [p_1^{-N_1} \cdots p_r^{-N_r}]^{1/N} \\
&= p_1^{-N_1/N} \cdots p_r^{-N_r/N}.
\end{aligned} \tag{18}$$

The reason for using the geometric mean is the following: If every event has the same probability p, then the mean improbability per event must certainly be $1/p$. If we ask what function F satisfies the formula

$$\bar{I}(E) = p^{-1} = F(p^{-N_1} p^{-N_2} \cdots p^{-N_r}) = F(p^{-N}),$$

the answer is, of course, that F is the Nth root. Hence, to act upon the improbability of an event of N elements, so as to obtain a consistent mean value, one must take the Nth root, obtaining Eq. (18).

Equation (18) gives the mean improbability for a finite sample of size N. Information is better defined as a property of the source of the events, the device or entity that generates the elementary events. If it is a simple probability machine, so that each of its alternatives has some constant probability, then $p_1, \ldots, p_r$ are the parameters of a multinomial distribution. As the number N of observations increases without bound, the ratio N_i/N will converge to p_i. Thus in the limit, as N increases,

$$I(\text{source}) = p_1^{-p_1} p_2^{-p_2} \cdots p_r^{-p_r}.$$

This formula contains the central concept of information theory. However, this quantity of improbability has no desirable simple mathematical properties, whereas its logarithm is particularly easy to analyze and use.

The amount of uncertainty in a combined system should, for any convenient theory, be the sum of the uncertainties in the part systems. The logarithm of improbability,

$$H = - \sum_{i=1}^{r} p_i \log p_i \tag{19}$$

has this additive property in several senses.

First, imagine that information can be attributed to individual events, so that H is the expected value of the uncertainty of the events. The uncertainty of event i is $f(p_i)$, and is presumed to depend only on the probability of that event. Now, suppose that events i and j are independent, so that

$$P(i, j) = p_i p_j.$$

Now, let the uncertainty of the joint event (i, j) be the sum of the uncertainties of events i and j. Then

$$f[P(i, j)] = f(p_i p_j) = f(p_i) + f(p_j).$$

This equation is satisfied by the function

$$f(p_i) = b \log p_i,$$

whence the average value for the distribution is

$$\bar{f} = b \sum_{i=1}^{r} p_i \log p_i.$$

If improbable events carry more information than probable ones, then b must be negative. Its value is determined by the choice of the base of the logarithms to be employed.

A further justification for the logarithmic formulation of Eq. (19) can be given by requiring a second rule of additivity. Suppose that two independent sets of events exist, having uncertainties H_1 and H_2, and these two sets are united into a single system. The uncertainty in this combined system should be the weighted average of H_1 and H_2, plus the additional uncertainty involved in choosing between the subsets.

Take two disjoint systems S_1 and S_2 having uncertainties H_1 and H_2, and make up a new system S^*. The set of categories of S^* is the union of the categories in S_1 and S_2, and there are no categories in common. The probability of an occurrence in any category of S^* is calculated as follows: there is a certain probability π_1 of going into the categories of system S_1, and once within it the probabilities are just as they were when S_1 was separate. With probability π_2, the system enters subsystem S_2, etc., as shown in Fig. 5.16.

Let H^* be the uncertainty of the combined system. Shannon's axiom states that H^* should be the weighted average of H_1 and H_2 (uncertainties in the part systems) plus the uncertainty of the initial choice between parts. That is,

$$H^* = \pi_1 H_1 + \pi_2 H_2 + H(\pi_1, \pi_2). \tag{20}$$

Now it will be shown that Eq. (19) is a measure that satisfies Shannon's axiom. A simple proof is to compute the mean improbability of the new

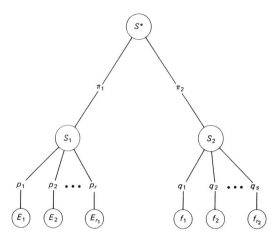

Figure 5.16

system. The ith elementary event in system S_1 originally had probability p_i. Since there is, in S^*, only a probability π_1 of going into system S_1, the new probability of the ith event is $\pi_1 p_i$. Similarly, the probability of the jth event in system S_2 was q_j, and is now $\pi_2 q_j$, since there is only probability π_2 of going into system S_2. Using the definition of mean improbability,

$$I(S^*) = (\pi_1 p_1)^{-\pi_1 p_1} \cdots (\pi_1 p_r)^{-\pi_1 p_r} (\pi_2 q_1)^{-\pi_2 q_1} \cdots (\pi_2 q_s)^{-\pi_2 q_s}$$

$$= \pi_1^{-\pi_1 \Sigma p_i} \cdot I_1^{\pi_1} \cdot \pi_2^{-\pi_2 \Sigma q_j} \cdot I_2^{\pi_2}$$

$$= \pi_1^{-\pi_1} \pi_2^{-\pi_2} I_1^{\pi_1} I_2^{\pi_2}.$$

Taking logarithms of both sides, we have

$$H^* = -\pi_1 \log \pi_1 - \pi_2 \log \pi_2 + \pi_1 H_1 + \pi_2 H_2,$$

which is the same as Eq. (20), since

$$H(\pi_1, \pi_2) = -\pi_1 \log \pi_1 - \pi_2 \log \pi_2$$

by definition.

Information Transmitted

The uncertainty measure given in Eq. (19) can be used as a base line for measuring the consistency of a subject's response in a psychophysical experiment. If H is low, stimuli are very predictable and even poor discrimination would result in rather good performance. But if H is high, stimuli are very unpredictable and good performance would indicate that the subject identified the stimuli successfully.

In an experiment there are s different stimuli and the subject classifies them into r categories. The results of the experiment yield a matrix in which each element N_{ij} is the number of occurrences of stimulus i classified in category j. The experimenter controls the number of presentations of each stimulus;

$$N_i = \sum_{j=1}^{r} N_{ij},$$

and the total number of trials is

$$N = \sum_{i=1}^{s} N_i = \sum_{i=1}^{s} \sum_{j=1}^{r} N_{ij}.$$

Consider experiments where the probability of each stimulus is a constant π_i and the presentation sequence is random—i.e., the choice of stimulus on trial n is independent of the rest of the sequence. The model is of an infinite experiment, so that when the elements of the matrix $[N_{ij}]$ are divided by N, the result is a matrix of probabilities. Let p_{ij} be the subject's probability of classifying stimulus i in category j; that is, $P(\text{category } j \mid \text{stimulus } i)$. Then the elements of the new matrix

$$\left\{ \frac{N_{ij}}{N} \right\} = \{\pi_i p_{ij}\}. \tag{21}$$

Also, of course, since the p's and π's are probabilities,

$$\sum_{j=1}^{r} \pi_i p_{ij} = \pi_i$$

and

$$\sum_{i=1}^{s} \sum_{j=1}^{r} \pi_i p_{ij} = 1.$$

The uncertainty of the total matrix is

$$H = \sum_{i=1}^{s} \sum_{j=1}^{r} -\pi_i p_{ij} \log (\pi_i p_{ij}). \tag{22}$$

Rearranging terms, we have

$$H = \sum_{i=1}^{s} -\pi_i \log \pi_i + \sum_{i=1}^{s} \pi_i \sum_{j=1}^{r} -p_{ij} \log p_{ij}.$$

For abbreviation, let

$$H(S) = \sum_{i=1}^{s} -\pi_i \log \pi_i,$$

$$H(R \mid S_i) = \sum_{j=1}^{r} -p_{ij} \log p_{ij}.$$

In this notation, Eq. (22) becomes

$$H = H(S) + \sum_{i=1}^{s} \pi_i H(R \mid S_i). \tag{23}$$

This shows that there is a minimum value for H, fixed by the probabilities of the stimuli. The extent to which H is greater than $H(S)$ depends on the average uncertainty in the responses to the individual stimuli.

At one extreme, suppose that the subject classifies every stimulus with perfect consistency. This means that for every stimulus S_i there is some value of p_{ij} equal to one, and the rest are equal to zero. But since

$$\log (1.0) = 0$$

and

$$\lim_{p \to 0} p \log p = 0,$$

it follows that for every stimulus,

$$H(R \mid S_i) = 0.$$

Therefore if each stimulus is always classified in the same way every time it appears,

$$H_{\min} = H(S). \tag{24}$$

Now consider the case of extreme inconsistency. Suppose that the subject uses the r categories with equal probabilities independently of the stimulus presented. Then for every i and j,

$$p_{ij} = 1/r.$$

Then for every stimulus,

$$H(R \mid S_i) = \sum_{j=1}^{r} -(1/r) \log (1/r) = -\log (1/r) = \log r.$$

The value, $\log r$, is the maximum of $H(R \mid S_i)$. When the responses are maximally uncertain,

$$H_{\max} = H(S) + \log r. \tag{25}$$

The consistency in the responses can be measured as the amount by which the uncertainty is kept below its maximum. That is,

$$I_C = H_{\max} - H = H(S) + \log r - H, \tag{26}$$

where H is calculated from the data according to Eq. (22). Clearly, the value

Table 5.3 Hypothetical values of p_{ij} and π_i

Stimulus (*i*)	Response (*j*)				
	1	2	3	4	π_i
1	0.80	0.20	0	0	0.10
2	0.425	0.50	0.075	0	0.40
3	0	0.10	0.60	0.30	0.30
4	0	0	0.20	0.50	0.20
$P(R_j)$	0.25	0.25	0.25	0.25	

of I_C will range from zero (when the responses are completely inconsistent) to log r (when the responses are completely consistent).

Consider the data of Table 5.3, an example of hypothetical data from an experiment with four stimuli and four responses. Using the stimulus probabilities there,

$$H(S) = \sum_{i=1}^{4} - \pi_i \log_2 \pi_i = 1.85.$$

Then the maximum uncertainty is

$$H_{\text{max}} = H(S) + \log_2 (4) = 3.85.$$

Calculating the uncertainty from the data, we find that

$$H = \sum_{i=1}^{4} \sum_{j=1}^{4} - \pi_i p_{ij} \log \pi_i p_{ij} = 2.97.$$

Then the amount of consistency in the responses is 0.88 bits.[5]

Note that Eq. (26) provides a measure of discrimination with the effect of stimulus predictability removed. Substitution using Eq. (23) gives

$$I_C = \log r - \sum_{i=1}^{s} \pi_i H(R \mid S_i)$$

$$= \log r - \sum_{i=1}^{s} \pi_i \sum_{j=1}^{r} - p_{ij} \log p_{ij}.$$

Thus I_C depends mainly on the conditional probabilities p_{ij}. The probabilities of the stimuli influence the value of I_C, but I_C can be very high or very low regardless of the predictability of stimuli.

---

[5] It is conventional to use logarithms with base 2. Then a system with n bits of uncertainty is equivalent to a system with 2^n equally probable outcomes.

The measure of consistency merely indicates how predictable the responses are on the average, given the stimuli. But the responses may be predictable for reasons that have nothing to do with the subject's ability to classify the stimuli. For example, there is no uncertainty in the system if the subject uses the same response for all the stimuli, and in general, the effect of any response bias will be to decrease the uncertainty by some amount. The data in Table 5.3 might result if a subject were constrained to use the four responses equally often. This seems likely in experiments in which the stimuli are equally probable, but subjects cannot always use all responses equally often. The measure of *information transmitted* takes account of the possibility of differing response probabilities.

Suppose that instead of responding with equal probabilities to all stimuli, a subject uses response j with probability p_j, but he responds without regard for the stimulus presented. Then the uncertainty in the data would be

Let

$$H_{\max} = H(S) + \sum_{i=1}^{s} \pi_i \sum_{j=1}^{r} -p_j \log p_j. \tag{27}$$

$$H(R) = \sum_{j=1}^{r} -p_j \log p_j; \tag{28}$$

then

$$H_{\max} = H(S) + H(R). \tag{29}$$

This will give the maximum value of H when both the marginal stimulus probabilities and the response probabilities are considered. Then the amount of information transmitted can be measured as the amount by which the uncertainty of the data is below $H_{\max}$. That is,

$$I_T = H_{\max} - H = H(S) + H(R) - H. \tag{30}$$

Some hypothetical data are listed in Table 5.4. The stimulus probabilities

Table 5.4 **Hypothetical data with unequal** $P(R_j)$

Stimulus (i)	R	esponse (j)			
	1	2	3	4	π_j
1	0.60	0.40	0	0	0.10
2	0.10	0.75	0.15	0	0.40
3	0	0.333	0.60	0.067	0.30
4	0	0.30	0.30	0.40	0.20
$P(R_j)$	0.10	0.50	0.30	0.10	

are the same as before, but the responses are biased (as would be expected if the subject knew about the stimulus probabilities). The uncertainty in these responses is

$$H(R) = \sum_{j=1}^{r} -p_j \log_2 p_j = 1.68 \text{ bits,}$$

and the uncertainty of the stimuli is 1.85 bits. The total uncertainty in the data is

$$H = \sum_{i=1}^{s} \sum_{j=1}^{r} -\pi_i p_{ij} \log \pi_i p_{ij} = 3.05.$$

Therefore the information transmitted is

$$I_T = H(S) + H(R) - H = 0.48 \text{ bits.}$$

Redundancy, Performance, and Channel Capacity

A system is said to be redundant when its uncertainty is less than the maximum possible. For example, consider a four-choice system. The maximum possible uncertainty of such a system is obtained when all four choices have probability 0.25, at which point the uncertainty is $H_{max} = 2$ bits.

One form of redundancy exists if the alternatives have different probabilities, such as 0.50, 0.30, 0.20, 0. This system has uncertainty $H = 1.48$ bits, and redundancy

$$H_{max} - H = 0.52 \text{ bits.}$$

Another form of redundancy exists if the successive occurrences are not independent, but are correlated. Then the uncertainty is based upon the conditional probabilities which are relatively near the extremes 1.0 and 0; hence there is low uncertainty.

In a psychophysical experiment using single stimuli, all cues given to the subject are sources of redundancy. If the sequence of stimuli is redundant, one might expect the performance of a subject to gain in consistency. This would not mean more information transmitted by the stimulus; since the input is redundant, the subject is being given less uncertainty to work with and there is less information to transmit. Information theory makes it possible to formulate certain general hypotheses. For example, as the redundancy of the input is varied, the information transmitted will remain the same; the subject becomes more accurate in his responses, but gains just the amount of redundancy put in by the experimenter.

Effort can be wasted in the attempt to construct theories at the level of uncertainty: a clear idea of the regularities in the underlying probabilities is necessary. For example, it is possible to arrange a very complicated sequence of stimuli, too long and confusing for the subject to learn, and then repeat it over and over. The stimulus sequence is entirely redundant and predictable, but the predictions are based on information the subject will probably not use. Information theory itself cannot distinguish between usable and unusable redundancy. Similarly, there are several ways the redundant series might affect responses, and quite different processes might be fitted to the same measurements of information. If an experimenter used only the information measure, which is an overall average, he might not notice that several competing theories are all possible explanations.

For a much more thorough and systematic discussion of information theory, and a richer view of its use in interpreting psychological data, see Garner.[6]

EXERCISES

1. Consider a detection experiment with distributions of log likelihood as shown in Fig. 5.12, and assume that the difference between the mean of the N and the SN distributions is one σ. (In the usual terminology, the mean difference divided by the standard deviation is called d'.) Choose three suitable criterion cuts and calculate both $P(Y \mid N)$ and $P(Y \mid SN)$. Plot the resulting values according to the diagram in Fig. 5.14.

2. In Eq. (7), λ_1 and λ_2 are, respectively, likelihood ratios for N and SN, provided the signal is in the second interval in the two-interval forced-choice experiment. Suppose that from an experiment using simple detection it was determined that d' is 2.0.

a) If $\sigma_{\lambda_1} = \sigma_{\lambda_2} = 1.0$, what is σ_λ?
b) What is the mean of λ relative to its standard deviation?
c) What is the predicted proportion of correct responses in an unbiased two-alternative forced-choice experiment, given the above?

3. According to the Rose-DeVries law, letting f be the Weber fraction $\Delta I/I$,

$$\log f = \log c - \tfrac{1}{2} \log I;$$

that is, the log of the Weber fraction should plot as a linear function of $\log I$, and the slope should be 0.5. Plot the data from Fig. 5.15 (up to 1 millilambert) in suitable form, and determine
a) whether the straight-line fit is reasonable,
b) whether the slope resembles 0.5,
c) what explanations could be offered for the discrepancies found.

4. *Fechnerian scaling:* Assume that Weber's law holds. Transform the magnitudes of stimuli by

$$\Psi(S) = \frac{1}{\log [1 + k(\pi)]} \log S.$$

Suppose that the distance between S_1 and S_2 is measured by determining the

---

[3] W. R. Garner, *Uncertainty and Structure as Psychological Concepts.* New York: Wiley, 1962.

π-threshold above S_1, $X_\pi(S_1)$, then the π-threshold above $X_\pi(S_1)$, repeating until S_2 is reached. Let $d_{12}(\pi)$ be the number of π-threshold units between S_1 and S_2, and show that

$$d_{12}(\pi) = \Psi(S_2) - \Psi(S_1).$$

5. Calculate the uncertainty, in bits, of the following multinomial distributions:

a) 0.50, 0.50

b) 0.25, 0.25, 0.25, 0.25

c) 0.25, 0.25, 0.15, 0.10, 0.20, 0.05.

6. Prove that with two alternatives, uncertainty is greatest if the alternatives have equal probabilities.

7. If there are s stimuli presented with equal probabilities, and the subject has r responses which he uses with equal overall frequency, what is the value of $H_{\max}(S, R)$?

8. Compare the two cases below with respect to (a) response uncertainty and (b) information transmitted.

	Case *i*						Case *ii*			
		Responses						Responses		
		1	2	3	4			1	2	3	4
Stimuli	1	$\frac{1}{8}$	$\frac{1}{8}$	0	0	Stimuli	1	$\frac{1}{8}$	$\frac{1}{8}$	0	0
	2	0	$\frac{1}{8}$	$\frac{1}{8}$	0		2	$\frac{1}{8}$	$\frac{1}{8}$	0	0
	3	0	$\frac{1}{8}$	$\frac{1}{8}$	0		3	$\frac{1}{8}$	$\frac{1}{8}$	0	0
	4	0	0	$\frac{1}{8}$	$\frac{1}{8}$		4	$\frac{1}{8}$	$\frac{1}{8}$	0	0

9. Calculate the information transmitted in the experiments described by the following matrices:

		Responses					Responses		
		1	2	3			1	2	3
	1	0.20	0.00	0.00		1	0.10	0.00	0.00
	2	0.10	0.10	0.00		2	0.05	0.05	0.00
Stimuli	3	0.03	0.14	0.03	Stimuli	3	0.06	0.28	0.06
	4	0.00	0.10	0.10		4	0.00	0.10	0.10
	5	0.00	0.00	0.20		5	0.00	0.00	0.20

(Note that the subject's responses to each stimulus are the same in both the matrices. The difference in information transmitted then results entirely from the different stimulus probabilities.)

10. Consider the data of Table 5.4. Suppose that, instead of responses 1, 2, 3, and 4, the alternatives were just "low" and "high." Also, assume that whenever the subject in Table 5.4 said "1" or "2," the two-response subject would say "low," and each time the four-response subject said "3" or "4," the two-response subject would say "high." Write out the matrix that would result, and calculate the information transmitted.

11. Equation (23) gives the uncertainty as the sum of two components: the uncertainty of the stimuli (which is considered as fixed) and the average of the response uncertainties associated with the various stimuli. The total uncertainty can also be viewed in another way, as an average of the subject's accuracy in using the various response categories. Define the following quantities (they are the Bayesian or posterior probabilities of the stimuli, given the responses):

$$q_{ji} = \frac{\pi_i p_{ij}}{\displaystyle\sum_{i=1}^{s} \pi_i p_{ij}} \, .$$

Then, for each response category j, define the conditional stimulus uncertainty

$$H(S \mid R_j) = \sum_{i=1}^{s} -q_{ji} \log q_{ji}.$$

Then show, analogous to Eq. (23), that

$$H = H(R) + \sum_{j=1}^{s} p_j H(S \mid R_j).$$

12. Using the definition of information transmitted and Eq. (23), show that

$$I_T = \sum_{j=1}^{r} \left\{ -p_j \log p_j + \sum_{i=1}^{s} \pi_i p_{ij} \log p_{ij} \right\}.$$

It would be reasonable to consider the quantity in brackets as the information transmitted by the jth response. Under what conditions will this equal zero?

13. Give an expression for information transmitted as the sum of quantities $I_T(i)$, where $I_T(i)$ can be considered as the information transmitted about the ith stimulus. What conditions will give $I_T(i) = 0$?

CHAPTER SIX

Theory of Choice and Preference

The separate theories of learning, perception, and motivation consider different factors leading to a response. Any complete quantitative theory in psychology must say how the various causal factors combine to produce the response, or, more exactly, the probability of each response. In recent years a variety of models have arisen and have been subjected to comparative analysis, so that it is possible to organize and compare various approaches to this general problem.

The problem, which was first formulated in Hull's *Principles of Behavior*,[1] is called the problem of behavior theory. Within current mathematical psychology it is usually called the theory of *choice*, as in Luce's *Individual Choice Behavior*[2] and Restle's *Psychology of Judgment and Choice*.[3] The scope of such a theory is wide; for example, Luce's theory can be applied to psychophysics, utility theory, and learning, treating these three disparate areas with the same theoretical apparatus.

Since the problem of choice theory is to specify the factors going into a response, the theory is not restricted to learning experiments, choices between gambles, or any other specific kind of experiment, and the theory of choice draws together information from a variety of laboratory situations.

One standard approach to the problem of choice is to say that motivational, experiential, and perceptual factors combine to yield a strength of a given response, and the process of responding involves some sort of comparison of these strengths. There are two main theories of how the strengths are compared. The next question is whether the factors in a response can correctly be summarized as a strength, or whether qualitative variations are

[1] C. L. Hull, *Principles of Behavior*. New York: Appleton-Century Crofts, 1943.

[2] R. D. Luce, *Individual Choice Behavior*. New York: Wiley, 1959.

[3] F. Restle, *Psychology of Judgment and Choice*. New York: Wiley, 1961.

also important and detectable. The experimental problems of comparing such theories are discussed in detail, and the several theories are then related to the problem of psychological measurement.

CLASSICAL STRENGTH THEORY

The basic assumption of the classical strength theory is that of two or more alternatives, the strongest will be chosen. Of course, if the strengths are fixed, then only the strongest will ever occur. Behavior is virtually never consistent in this way, so response strength must vary in some way.

In the most familiar form of this theory, due to Hull,[4] each alternative response R_i has some strength $_sE_{R_i}$, but there is a special oscillating factor $_sO_R$ subtracted from each response strength. The value of $_sO_R$ varies with an approximately normal distribution, with mean μ_0 and standard deviation σ_0. In this theory the momentary effective response strength X_i of the alternative R_i would have mean and standard deviation

$$\mu_i = {}_sE_{R_i} - \mu_0; \qquad \sigma_i = \sigma_0.$$

First suppose that the subject is choosing between two alternatives a and b. Let the strengths x_a and x_b be normally distributed with the same standard deviation σ, be independent, but have different means μ_a and μ_b. Suppose that the threshold is very low, so there is a response every trial. What is the probability of response a?

Figure 6.1 shows the two normal distributions for x_a and x_b. The probability of response a is the same as the probability that x_a is greater than x_b, which is to say that $x_a - x_b > 0$.

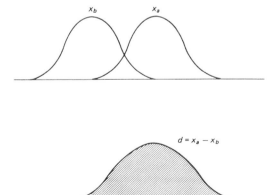

Figure 6.1

---

[4] Cited above.

The difference $x_a - x_b$ is normally distributed as shown in the lower panel of Fig. 6.1 with mean $\mu_a - \mu_b$ and variance $\sigma_a^2 + \sigma_b^2$. The probability of response a, shown as the shaded area, is the probability that the difference $x_a - x_b$ is positive.

Since x_a and x_b are assumed to be distributed normally, their difference also has the normal distribution. This exact preservation of the form of the distribution is a special property of normal variates; however, the statements made about the mean and variance of the distribution of differences hold for any random variables.

There is no need to assume that the strengths of the various responses all have the same standard deviation provided all are normally distributed. The reason is that the difference between any two independent normally distributed variables is itself normally distributed.

The moment-generating function of a normal distribution is $M(t) = e^{t\mu + 1/2 t^2 \sigma^2}$. The distribution of $x_a - x_b$ is the convolution of $f(x_a)$ with $f(-x_b)$, and $-x_b$ has a normal distribution with mean $-\mu_b$ and standard deviation σ_b.

The moment-generating function of a convolution is the product of the moment-generating functions of the two separate distributions. Therefore

$$M_{a+b}(t) = M_a(t)M_b(t)$$
$$= (e^{t\mu_a + 1/2 t^2 \sigma_a^2})(e^{t(-\mu_b) + 1/2 t^2 \sigma_b^2})$$
$$= e^{t(\mu_a - \mu_b) + 1/2 t_2 (\sigma_a^2 + \sigma_{b2})},$$

the moment-generating function of a normal distribution with mean $\mu_a - \mu_b$ and variance the sum of the variances.

The discussion above assumes that the choice is between two alternatives, but this theory may be extended to the analysis of more than two responses if they are presented only two at a time. Suppose that three objects all have the same σ but different values of μ. Given that $P(a, b)$—the probability of choosing a over b—is 0.70, and $P(b, c)$ is 0.60, what is the probability of choosing a over c, $P(a, c)$?

Because multiplication of all x_i by a constant leaves the probabilities the same, set $\sigma = 1$. Then the difference $\mu_a - \mu_b$ is found in the table of the normal distribution (the value of x/σ that corresponds to a choice probability of 0.70). The value is about 0.525. In the same way, the difference $\mu_b - \mu_c$ that gives rise to choice probability of 0.60 is found to be 0.253. The three distributions can now be located as in Fig. 6.2. Now the distance from $\mu_a - \mu_c$ must be $(\mu_a - \mu_b) + (\mu_b - \mu_c)$:

$$\mu_a - \mu_c = 0.525 + 0.253 = 0.778.$$

In the table of the normal curve, the probability that x_a is greater than x_c is

$$P(a, c) = 0.782$$

when $x/\sigma = 0.778$. If $P(a, b)$ and $P(b, c)$ are both greater than $\frac{1}{2}$, it follows that $P(a, c)$ will be greater than either of them provided the variances are all equal.

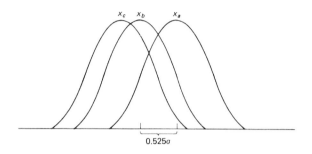

x_c x_b x_a

0.525σ

Figure 6.2

The classical theory works well when only two alternatives are available at a time, but presents more difficulty when there are three.

Assume that the strengths of the three responses are all normally distributed with variance σ^2. The probability that response a will be chosen is just the probability that x_a will be the largest of x_a, x_b, and x_c.

Let $F(w)$ be the probability that the variable x takes a value less than or equal to w. This function is called the cumulative distribution function (cdf) or sometimes just the distribution function. The normal cdf is shown in Fig. 6.3.

The density function $f(x)$ is the rate of change of F at x. If cases are dense at x, $F(x)$ will increase rapidly with x and if they are sparse, $F(x)$ will increase slowly. The density function is defined as

$$f(x) = \frac{dF(x)}{dx}. \tag{1}$$

By the basic theorem of calculus,

$$\int_v^w f(x)\, dx = F(w) - F(v).$$

That is, the probability of an observation between v and w, given by the probability that it is less than w and not less than v, $F(w) - F(v)$, is also calculated by integrating the density function from v to w.

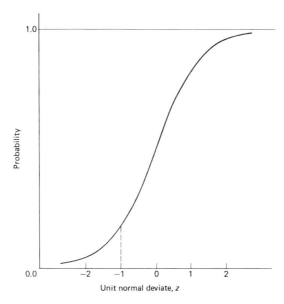

Figure 6.3

When x_a is the greatest of the three variables x_a, x_b, and x_c, the three variables can take on many configurations. The probability that x_b and x_c are both below some low number w is $[F_b(w)][F_c(w)]$. The density of x_a at w is $f(w)$; the density that it is also greatest is

$$f_a(w)[F_b(w)][F_c(w)], \tag{2}$$

and the probability that x_a is greatest is the integral of this density over the whole possible range of w from $-\infty$ to $+\infty$:

$$P(x_a \text{ is maximum}) = \int_{-\infty}^{\infty} f_a(x)[F_b(x)][F_c(x)]\,dx. \tag{3}$$

Equation (3) cannot be simplified in any very useful way, because the distribution function $F(x)$ cannot be written explicitly as elementary functions. In practice, this requires numerical calculations, which are not difficult using high-speed computers.

THEORY OF THE BEHAVIOR RATIO

The classical strength theory explains variability in choices by assuming that response strengths oscillate. An alternative is to assume that response strengths are constant, but there is variability in the process of choosing.

According to this idea, used in an early paper by Tolman,[5] the probability of each response is proportional to the strength of that response.

The theory of the behavior ratio was developed in a precise form by Luce.[6] First, let U be a set of possible choice alternatives. Let T be a finite subset of U, and suppose that a subject has an opportunity to choose from T. If x is one of the alternatives and an element of T, then $P_T(x)$ denotes the probability that x is chosen from T. Further, if S is a subset of T, then $P_T(S)$ denotes the probability that some element of S is chosen. The choice probabilities are assumed to obey the usual axioms of probability:

i) for $S \subset T$, $0 \leq P_T(S) \leq 1$,

ii) $P_T(T) = 1$,

iii) If $R, S \subset T$ and $R \cap S$ is empty, then $P_T(R \cup S) = P_T(R) + P_T(S)$.

Repeated application of Axiom *iii* implies the corollary

$$P_T(S) = \sum_{x \in S} P_T(x).$$

Axiom *iii* states that the probability of the union of two disjoint events is the sum of their probabilities, and the corollary says that the probability of any set of disjoint alternatives is computed by adding up the probabilities of the alternatives in the set. The last statement depends on the earlier restriction that T be a finite set.

Two special simplifications of notation are useful. When one of a pair of alternatives is chosen, that is, when $T = \{x, y\}$, then

$$P_{\{x,y\}}(x) \qquad \text{is written} \qquad P(x, y).$$

The notation $P(x, y)$, therefore, is shorthand for a two-choice task and the probability that x is chosen over y.

Finally, it is often simpler to write an expression if it is possible that an alternative might be compared with itself. For convenience, assume that

$$P(x, x) = \tfrac{1}{2}.$$

The Choice Axiom

Luce's theory was developed by consideration of the effects on choice of different sets of alternatives. Ordinary probability theory gives many theorems about the probabilities of various events (i.e., various subsets of T)

---

[5] E. C. Tolman, The determiners of behavior at a choice point. *Psych. Rev.*, 1938, Vol. 45, 1–41.

[6] Cited above.

in terms of one another for all the probabilities called P_T. However, if the set of alternatives is changed from T to another set, then, because there is a new universe, there must (at least formally) be a new probability measure. It is not possible, by ordinary probability theory, to draw a valid conclusion from one probability measure to another. The most familiar example is that of the soldier's meal. A young soldier might prefer ice cream to sausages until sauerkraut is added. Imagine that the first universe is

$$T_1 = \{\text{ice cream, sausages}\};$$

it may be that

$$P_{T_2}(\text{ice cream}) > P_{T_2}(\text{sausages}).$$

However, the second universe is

$$T_2 = \{\text{ice cream, sausages, sauerkraut}\}$$

and, possibly,

$$P_{T_2}(\text{sausages}) > P_{T_2}(\text{ice cream}).$$

The point here is not concerned with food interactions; it merely says that when the set of alternatives is changed, it is no longer logically possible to argue from one universe to another, because it is logically possible for such probabilities to be unrelated, reversed, or related in any other way. To state a relationship between different universes of choice alternatives, a psychological hypothesis is needed. Luce's approach was to choose an axiom that has many simple and desirable mathematical consequences. He used it as both an hypothesis and as an underlying assumption to set up theories in difficult or complicated situations. For these purposes the hypothesis should avoid unnecessary commitments to underlying theoretical structures, and (if possible) should be directly testable. Such an assumption would deserve to be classified as an axiom.

Luce's solution to this problem was to assume that the relative probabilities of any two alternatives would remain unchanged as other alternatives are introduced. Suppose, for example, that a person has probability 0.20 of choosing beefsteak and 0.30 of choosing chicken from a given menu. Now suppose that he learns that everything else on the menu is unavailable, so he must choose between just the two. The axiom implies that the probability of choosing beefsteak would be 0.40, and of chicken, 0.60. Why? Given that these are the only alternatives, by probability theory their probabilities must add to 1.00, and by the axiom they must maintain the same relative probabilities; thus

$$0.20:0.30::0.40:0.60.$$

Consider a chain of two-choice probabilities among the objects a, b, c,

d, and e, for instance:

$$P(a, b) = 0.70, \qquad P(b, c) = 0.60,$$
$$P(c, d) = 0.90, \qquad P(d, e) = 0.80. \tag{4}$$

This information, along with Luce's assumption, suffices to calculate the probabilities of all other pairs.

To find $P(a, c)$ as an example, note that

$$\frac{P(a, b)}{P(b, a)} = \frac{0.70}{0.30}.$$

The same ratio holds, if S contains both a and b, for

$$\frac{P_S(a)}{P_S(b)} = \frac{0.70}{0.30}.$$

For the same reason, if S contains both b and c,

$$\frac{P_S(b)}{P_S(c)} = \frac{0.60}{0.40}.$$

Therefore

$$(\tfrac{3}{7})P_S(a) = P_S(b), \tag{5}$$

$$(\tfrac{6}{4})P_S(c) = P_S(b). \tag{6}$$

Combining Eqs. (5) and (6), we have

$$(\tfrac{3}{7})P_S(a) = (\tfrac{6}{4})P_S(c),$$

whence

$$P_S(a) = (\tfrac{42}{12})P_S(c).$$

If the subject compares a and c, his probabilities $P(a, c)$ and $P(c, a)$ must have the ratio $42:12$, and

$$P(a, c) = \tfrac{42}{54} = 0.778.$$

If $S = \{a, b, c\}$, then

$$P_S(a) = 0.581, \qquad P_S(b) = 0.250, \qquad P_S(c) = 0.167$$

by the same principle.

The ratio $P(a, b)/P(b, a)$ cannot always be calculated if one alternative is absolutely dominated by some other. Consider the probabilities

$$P(a, b) = 0.70, \qquad P(b, c) = 0.60, \qquad P(c, d) = 1.00.$$

Notice that the ratio, in any set T, of $P_T(d)$ to $P_T(c)$ must be zero. Hence if $H = \{a, b, c, d\}$, then $P_H(d) = 0$, and furthermore, for any other alternative x,

$$P_H(x) = P_{H-(d)}(x).$$

This is easily derived by calculation, and simply represents the fact that since d is dominated by c, it therefore is dominated by anything else that c does not dominate. Its significance is this; for any pair $\{x, y\}$ of alternatives in T, if $P(x, y) = 1.00$, then y can be deleted from T and all probabilities remain the same.

All the considerations given above can be summarized aptly by Luce's Axiom 1. He puts the above assumption in the form most strategic for deductive purposes. In his form (assuming there are no deletable alternatives), a formula similar to the basic formula for conditional probability is put forward.

Axiom 1. Let T be a finite subset of U such that, for every $S \subset T$, P_S is defined. Then

i) If $P(x, y) \neq 0, 1$ for all $x, y \subset T$, then for

$$R \subset S \subset T, \qquad P_T(R) = P_S(R)P_T(S).$$

ii) If $P(x, y) = 0$ for some x, y in T, then for every $S \subset T$,

$$P_T(S) = P_{T-\{x\}}(S - \{x\}).$$

The basic formula of part (i) of the axiom is very similar to the formula of conditional probability; that is for $R \subset S \subset T$,

$$P(R \mid T) = P(R \mid S)P(S \mid T).$$

This situation can, in turn, be seen in the diagram of Fig. 6.4. The basic

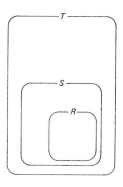

Figure 6.4

formula of conditional probability is

$$P(A \mid B) = P(A \cap B)/P(B).$$

The above formula is, therefore,

$$\frac{P(R \cap T)}{P(T)} = \left[\frac{P(R \cap S)}{P(S)}\right]\left[\frac{P(S \cap T)}{P(T)}\right].$$

However, when S is a subset of T, it follows that $P(S \cap T) = P(S)$. Simplification yields

$$\frac{P(R)}{P(T)} = \left[\frac{P(R)}{P(S)}\right]\left[\frac{P(S)}{P(T)}\right],$$

and this is obviously true.

The formula for conditional probability assumed a single probability measure applying to all formulas; that is, the assumption for the conditional probability is that the probabilities are all choices from the same set of alternatives. Then, for example, $P(R \mid S)$ is the probability that the choice is in the set R, *given* that it is in the set S, but $P(R \mid S)$ is not necessarily the probability of a choice within R when the subject is *constrained* to choose from within S.

Axiom 1 does refer to different constraints put on the chooser, therefore differs from mere conditional probability, and is a stronger assumption.

A variety of interesting and important theorems are proved by Luce,[7] but only one is shown here.

Existence of a v-Scale

Some readers, in doing the exercises above, will have hit upon an efficient way of solving the problem as follows. Assign some arbitrary value to alternative a, say, 1.00. By using Eq. (4) a is chosen over b 0.70 of the time, so $a/b = 0.7/0.3$, and b has the value $\frac{3}{7}$ or 0.429. Since $b/c = 0.6/0.4$, $c = (0.4/0.6)b$, or $0.667(0.429) = 0.286$.

The values of a and c are 1.000 and 0.286, so

$$P(a, c) = \frac{1.00}{(1.00 + 0.286)} = 0.778.$$

Furthermore, based on the choice set $\{a, b, c\}$, the probabilities are

$$P(a) = 1.000/(1.000 + 0.429 + 0.286)$$
$$= 1.000/1.715 = 0.581,$$
$$P(b) = 0.429/1.715 = 0.250,$$
$$P(c) = 1.286/1.715 = 0.167.$$

---

[7] Cited above.

The method is to assign numbers to the various alternatives, making the numbers proportional to the probabilities. Then the probability of any alternative in any set is its value divided by the sum of the values within the set. It is a theorem that this method can always be used, given that Luce's axiom holds.

First, note that if any of the alternatives is absolutely dominated by any other [if there exists an x, y such that $P(x, y) = 0$], then the dominated alternative can be eliminated. Anyway, it would get a value of zero. Therefore consider a finite set of alternatives T, none of which is eliminable. If Axiom 1 holds, then we have the following theorem.

Theorem. There exists a positive real-valued function v on T, which is unique up to multiplication by a positive constant, such that for every $S \subset T$,

$$P_S(x) = v(x) \Big/ \sum_{y \in S} v(y).$$

Proof. Define $v(x) = kP_T(x)$ for $k > 0$. Then from Axiom 1,

$$P_S(x) = \frac{P_T(x)}{P_T(S)} = kP_T(x) \Big/ \sum_{y \in S} kP_T(y)$$

$$= v(x) \Big/ \sum_{y \in S} v(y),$$

so the function v exists. To show uniqueness, suppose that v' is another such function. Then for any $x \in T$,

$$v(x) = kP_T(x) = [kv'(x)] \Big/ \sum_{y \in T} v'(y).$$

Now let

$$k' = k \Big/ \sum_{y \in T} v'(y),$$

which is, of course, a constant. It follows that

$$v(x) = k'v'(x),$$

and it is shown that any two value scales are related by multiplication by a positive constant. This concludes the proof.

Parenthetically, the reader should notice the strategy of this proof; first, a simple example of the function is introduced to establish existence. To establish uniqueness, another function satisfying the conditions is introduced, and then a strong relation between the two candidates is established.

COMPARISON BETWEEN THEORIES

The classical strength and the behavior-ratio theories have been compared in experiments where several alternatives are presented in pairs, and subjects make comparative judgments of preference. Each theory makes a clear prediction about the probabilities of choice among sets of three alternatives, say a, b, and c. In the classical strength theory, assume that all three alternatives have independent normal distributions of response strength with the same variance, σ^2. Then the difference between any two strengths is normal with variance $2\sigma^2$. The choice probabilities will be

$$P(a, b) = \Phi\left(\frac{\mu_a - \mu_b}{\sigma\sqrt{2}}\right),$$

$$P(b, c) = \Phi\left(\frac{\mu_b - \mu_c}{\sigma\sqrt{2}}\right),$$

$$P(a, c) = \Phi\left(\frac{\mu_a - \mu_c}{\sigma\sqrt{2}}\right).$$

The quantities in parentheses are called the z-scores corresponding to the probabilities. Clearly, for the classical strength theory,

$$z_{a,c} = z_{a,b} + z_{b,c}, \tag{7}$$

when equal variances are assumed.

In the behavior-ratio theory, a different relationship holds. First, it is true that if Luce's axiom holds, there is a scale v such that for any pair of alternatives a and b,

$$P(a, b) = \frac{v(a)}{v(a) + v(b)}.$$

But then

$$v(a)P(a, b) + v(b)P(a, b) = v(a);$$

hence

$$\frac{v(a)}{v(b)} = \frac{P(a, b)}{1 - P(a, b)} = \frac{P(a, b)}{P(b, a)}.$$

Of course, the same relationship holds when the alternatives are b and c, and also when the alternatives are a and c. But then

$$\frac{P(a, c)}{P(c, a)} = \frac{v(a)}{v(c)} = \left[\frac{v(a)}{v(b)}\right]\left[\frac{v(b)}{v(c)}\right].$$

Therefore

$$\frac{P(a, c)}{P(c, a)} = \frac{P(a, b)P(b, c)}{P(b, a)P(c, b)}. \tag{8}$$

Equation (8) is called the *product rule*. Burke and Zinnes and Hohle[8] applied Eqs. (7) and (8) to data from a paired-comparison experiment to see which theory agrees better with the data.

The difficulty is that the two equations lead to approximately the same predictions, despite their mathematical difference. For example, if $P(a, b) = 0.70$ and $P(b, c) = 0.60$. According to the classical theory, this implies that $P(a, c) = 0.782$; according to the ratio theory, $P(a, c)$ should be 0.778. A difference this small could hardly be detected in data. The similarity is a general one. Table 6.1, presented by Luce and Galanter[9], shows the value of $P(a, c)$ predicted by each theory for different combinations of $P(a, b)$ and $P(b, c)$. There does not seem to be any combination where the theories are different enough to permit a clear choice between the theories.

Table 6.1 Predicted values of $P(a, c)$

	Behavior-ratio theory $P(b, c)$					Classical strength theory $P(b, c)$			
	0.6	0.7	0.8	0.9		0.6	0.7	0.8	0.9
$P(a, b)$ 0.6	0.692	0.778	0.857	0.931	$P(a, b)$ 0.6	0.695	0.782	0.864	0.938
0.7		0.845	0.903	0.954	0.7		0.853	0.915	0.965
0.8			0.941	0.973	0.8			0.954	0.983
0.9				0.988	0.9				0.995

Recall that in the behavior-ratio theory, response strengths are treated as fixed quantities, but there is variability in the choice process. In the classical strength theory, the choice is considered to be determined strictly by the momentary response strengths, but response strengths are random variables. Thus the theories differ in the aspect of the process that is assumed to produce variability.

The usual form of the classical theory assumes normal distributions of response strengths, and leads to predictions that are practically indistinguishable from those of the ratio theory. If a slightly different assumption

[8] C. J. Burke and J. L. Zinnes, A paired comparison of pair comparisons. *J. Math. Psych.*, 1965, **2**, 53–76. R. H. Hohle, An empirical evaluation and comparison of two models for discriminability scales. *J. Math. Psych.*, 1966, **3**, 174–183.

[9] R. D. Luce and E. Galanter, Discrimination. In R. D. Luce, R. R. Bush, and E. Galanter (Eds.), *Handbook of Mathematical Psychology*, Vol. 1. New York: Wiley, 1963, pp. 191–244.

is made about the distribution of response strengths, the variable-strength theory is identical to the ratio theory.

If strengths are distributed normally, the difference between response strengths is also distributed normally with mean and variance

$$\mu_{b-a} = \mu_b - \mu_a, \qquad \sigma_{a-b}^2 = 2\sigma_a^2$$

when the distributions are independent with equal variance. For abbreviation, let

$$y = (x_b - x_a) - (\mu_b - \mu_a)$$

$$r = \mu_a - \mu_b,$$

$$k = 4\sigma_a^2,$$

whence

$$P(a, b) = P(x_a - x_b > 0) = \frac{1}{\sqrt{k\pi}} \int_{-\infty}^{r} e^{-y^2/k} \, dy.$$

In the normal theory, μ_a and μ_b are the "true values" of response strength for choosing a and b, and the distribution about them is produced by some process that results in variability. The probability of choice depends on the difference, $\mu_a - \mu_b$, and on k, a parameter of the process that produces variability.

Now consider another theory having true values $u(a)$ and $u(b)$ representing response strengths of choosing a and b, with difference

$$u(a) - u(b) = r,$$

and let

$$y = x_b - x_a + r.$$

Now let the difference $x_b - x_a$ be distributed so that for some $k > 0$,

$$f(y) = \frac{ke^{-ky}}{(1 + e^{-ky})^2}, \tag{9}$$

the logistic distribution. Notice that the distribution of differences depends on the value of r and a parameter k, as before. The choice probability is

$$P(a, b) = P(x_a > x_b) = P(y < r);$$

$$P(a, b) = \int_{-\infty}^{r} \left[\frac{ke^{-ky}}{1 + e^{-ky}} \right] dy = \frac{1}{1 + e^{-ky}} \bigg|_{-\infty}^{r}$$

$$= \frac{1}{1 + e^{-kr}}. \tag{10}$$

Equation (10) gives the probability of choosing *a* over *b* as a function of the difference between their true values using the logistic distribution.

Luce and Suppes[10] have shown that this will give identical predictions to those of the ratio theory. According to the simple choice theory,

$$P(a, b) = \frac{v(a)}{v(a) + v(b)} = \frac{1}{1 + v(b)/v(a)}. \tag{11}$$

Now, suppose that in place of $v(a)$ and $v(b)$ any linear function of their logarithms is used; that is, with some $\alpha > 0$

$$u(a) = \alpha \log [v(a)] + \beta,$$

and similarly for $u(b)$. Then

$$\log [v(a)] = \frac{1}{\alpha} [u(a) - \beta]; \qquad v(a) = e^{[u(a) - \beta]/\alpha},$$

$$v(b) = e^{[u(b) - \beta]/\alpha},$$

but then, substituting into Eq. (11),

$$P(a, b) = \frac{1}{1 + e^{[u(b) - \beta]/\alpha - [u(a) - \beta]/\alpha}}$$

$$= \frac{1}{1 + e^{[u(b) - u(a)]/\alpha}},$$

and since $[u(a) - u(b)]/\alpha = kr$,

$$P(a, b) = \frac{1}{1 + e^{-kr}}$$

in agreement with Eq. (10). The ratio model can be rewritten as equivalent to the "greater strength" model with a logistic distribution of strengths, *x*.

SIMILARITY OF ALTERNATIVES

The idealized theory of simple choice assumes that all alternatives are entirely discrete and disjoint. However, when a theory begins to involve complex choice situations, there are times when a choice is between two "bundles" or complexes of outcomes. Consider, for example, the decision of a major field in graduate school in psychology. One choice, clinical psychology, includes an opportunity to help people in need, the study of

---

[10] R. D. Luce and P. Suppes, Preference, utility, and subjective probability. In R. D. Luce, R. R. Bush, and E. Galanter (Eds.), *Handbook of Mathematical Psychology*, Vol. 3. New York: Wiley, 1965, pp. 249–410.

profound secrets of human nature, power, prestige, and perhaps a big income from private practice as a possibility, but requires a long and demanding study program, acquisition of many testing and therapeutic skills, and limited opportunity for high-level pure research in the future. Opposing this, experimental psychology offers an opportunity to work on well-formulated theoretical problems, to teach a variety of interesting scientific subjects, to help build a new science, and for the successful student, high prestige and intellectual standing. On the other side, there is a possibility of meaningless and arid studies on unimportant topics, a requirement of creative research with no idea where the creative spark comes from, and a relatively low ceiling on income. The choice (whether or not it is represented correctly here; and this representation must be close to the thinking of at least *some* graduate students) is certainly complex.

A theory of choice must propose, at least in a general way, how it intends to consider choices between complex alternatives. The general behavior-ratio theory will merely add up the valences of the elements of each alternative, producing a total valence for each, and then form the behavior ratio. This, however, leads to some surprising results.

Consider a choice between an apple and a candy bar. Imagine that at a certain point in the afternoon, a subject is offered a choice between the two, and suppose that the probability of choosing the apple is $P(a, b) = 0.80$. Now, under the same conditions, two new alternatives are offered. One is the apple plus a ten-dollar bill; the other is a candy bar plus a ten-dollar bill. Clearly, the money is much more valued than either the apple or the candy bar.

From the first choice,

$$0.80 = \frac{v(a)}{v(a) + v(b)}.$$

Call the ten-dollar bill d. Then in the second choice the probability of choosing the apple and money is

$$P(a \ \& \ d) = \frac{v(a) + v(d)}{v(a) + v(d) + v(b) + v(d)}$$

$$= \frac{v(a) + v(d)}{v(a) + v(b) + 2v(d)}.$$

If the person is appropriately money conscious, he will judge the ten-dollar bill as at least 100 times more desirable than the candy bar. As an approximation, let the value of the candy bar be 1.0, the value of the apple 4.0, and the value of the ten-dollar bill 100.0. Therefore

$$P(a \ \& \ d, b \ \& \ d) = \frac{104.0}{205.0} = 0.51.$$

The simple behavior-ratio theory suggests that a subject who would consistently choose the apple over the candy bar becomes almost random in his choice when ten dollars is added to each choice.

The simple behavior-ratio theory has failed to consider that most of the source of valence 104.0 to the apple plus money was not only the same in amount, but was *identical* to the source of most of the valence of 101.0 for the candy bar and money. Therefore the money should not enter into the decision at all, since as far as the money is concerned there is no choice to make.

According to Restle,[11] the choice between two complex and overlapping alternatives depends not at all on the common elements, but only on the differential elements.

Each alternative is considered to be a set of objects or outcomes, each with its own valence. Then when the subject chooses between sets A and B, the situation becomes like that shown in Fig. 6.5. The set actually contributing to the choice of A is $A - B$, the hashed area, and the set contributing to the choice of B is $B - A$, stippled. The intersection of the two sets, marked I, is left blank in the diagram and is assumed not to affect the response.

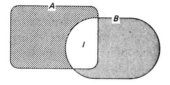

Figure 6.5

In the language of set theory, the union of the two differences $(A - B) + (B - A)$ is called the symmetric set difference. In this theory,

$$P(A, B) = \frac{v(A - B)}{v(A - B) + v(B - A)}, \tag{12}$$

where v is a measure function. Notice that $v(A)$ includes the intersection, and so does $v(B)$, so that

$$v(A) - v(B) = v(A - B) + v(I) - v(B - A) - v(I)$$
$$= v(A - B) - v(B - A).$$

---

[11] Cited above.

Now if $P(B, A)$ is the probability of choosing B over A,

$$P(A, B) - P(B, A) = \frac{v(A - B) - v(B - A)}{v(A - B) + v(B - A)}$$

$$= \frac{v(A) - v(B)}{v(A - B) + v(B - A)}, \tag{13}$$

the ratio of the difference in valence of the two objects divided by the value of the symmetric set difference.

In the ordinary behavior-ratio theory,

$$P(A, B) = \frac{v(A)}{v(A) + v(B)},$$

whence

$$P(A, B) - P(B, A) = \frac{v(A) - v(B)}{v(A) + v(B)}. \tag{14}$$

Equations (13) and (14) have the same numerator, the difference in valence of the two sets, but differ in the denominator. The Restle theory uses just the value of the symmetric set difference, whereas the usual behavior-ratio theory uses the sum of the valences of the two sets. These theories are the same if the sets A and B are disjoint, for then $A - B = A$ and $B - A = B$ by ordinary set algebra.

One difficulty with the behavior-ratio theory is that it gives no explanation of why people will always choose the larger of two amounts of money. Unless specific amounts of money have special significance (i.e., concepts like "fair wage" or "fair price"), a person will always choose the larger of the two offered amounts of money. This is most difficult for a simple behavior-ratio theory to handle, for it means that the value of, say, ten dollars is almost infinitely greater than that of five dollars. The only simple explanation is that value increases very rapidly with the amount of money, which is an unreasonable interpretation.

In the Restle theory it is assumed that money, by its nature, is without intrinsic value. Therefore any two ten-dollar bills are equal, not only in amount of valence, but in the very quality of valence. Therefore, if M and N are two amounts of money, N the larger, then M is a subset of N;

$$M \subset N.$$

This, of course, means that $M - N$ is the empty set Ø, whence

$$P(N, M) = \frac{v(N - M)}{v(N - M) + v(\emptyset)}.$$

The measure of O is 0, an axiom of set theory. Therefore

$$P(N, M) = 1.0.$$

This is true of any two amounts of money. However, similar consistency of choice cannot be expected of objects having intrinsic value. For example, consider a person choosing between a vacation in the California mountains and a vacation in Florida. The two vacations may have much in common, but they also have many qualitative differences. That is, both $C - F$ and $F - C$ have relatively many elements; if the two sets have comparable valence (i.e., if the two vacations are approximately equal in value) then the probabilities may be near one-half.

According to this theory, the effective valence of an alternative depends upon what it is compared with, for the effective valence will be limited to those aspects that are differential. An object is perceived and evaluated differently, depending upon what it is contrasted with. If the Restle theory is correct, there actually exists a fixed set of aspects for each object and a valence for that object, but only some of the aspects enter into a given choice, and the effective set differs depending upon the alternatives presented. In this sense, then, the valence of an alternative is not constant. However, it is easily seen that the considerations about similarity of alternatives, though they complicate the situation, do not conflict in a deep sense with the assumptions of the behavior-ratio theory.

An illustration of these ideas was provided in an experiment by Rumelhart and Greeno.[12] A set of nine alternatives was constructed, consisting of three political leaders (Lyndon Johnston, Harold Wilson, and Charles DeGaulle), three athletes (Johnny Unitas, Carl Yastrzemski, and A. J. Foyt), and three film stars (Brigitte Bardot, Elizabeth Taylor, and Sophia Loren). Paired-comparison choices of all 36 pairs of the nine alternatives were made by 234 subjects. The subjects were instructed to imagine that they could spend one hour with a person, discussing a topic that they chose. In each paired comparison, the subject reported his preference between two of the choice alternatives.

The list of alternatives has some aspects shared by all the members (well-known individuals). Let I be this set of elements shared by all the alternatives. The common aspects of set I will not appear in any of the comparisons made in the experiment. Hence they can be disregarded in further analysis.

Let A_1, A_2, A_3, B_1, . . . , C_3 denote the alternatives, the letter indicating the category. The intersection $A_i \cap B_j$ between elements of two categories

---

[12] D. L. Rumelhart and J. G. Greeno, *Choices between similar and dissimilar objects: an experimental test of the Luce and Restle choice models.* Paper read at Midwestern Psychological Association, Chicago, 1968.

is intended to be empty. When this is so,

$$P(A_i, B_j) = \frac{v(A_i)}{v(A_i) + (B_j)}$$

according to Restle's theory. This agrees with the Luce formulation, whence the probabilities must satisfy the ratio rule. Note, however, that this is true only for comparisons between alternatives of different categories, e.g., Charles DeGaulle and Sophia Loren. The estimated values of v for each alternative were estimated, and they are shown in Table 6.2.

Table 6.2 Estimated values of choice alternatives, $v(A_i)$

Lyndon Johnson	1.49
Harold Wilson	1.01
Charles DeGaulle	0.80
Johnny Unitas	0.46
Carl Yastrzemski	0.36
A. J. Foyt	0.51
Brigitte Bardot	0.47
Elizabeth Taylor	0.79
Sophia Loren	1.00*

* *Note:* This value was fixed at 1.0.

Since one alternative can be chosen as a unit, there are eight parameters estimated. From these it is possible to compute the predicted probabilities of choice between the 27 pairs of dissimilar alternatives. The predictions were compared with observed frequencies, as shown in Table 6.3. If the theory is exactly correct, the mean-squared discrepancy between observed and predicted frequencies should be distributed as chi square with 19 degrees of freedom. The test statistic took value 21.7, which is not significant ($p > 0.30$). In these data there is no evidence against the simple Luce model if the only choices considered are those between dissimilar alternatives.

According to the Restle model, the product rule should not be able to predict choices between similar alternatives, e.g., Charles DeGaulle and Lyndon Johnson. The overlapping aspects are, theoretically, not considered, and therefore the probability of the more favored choice should increase toward 1.0.

For example, suppose that A_1 has a value of 1.50 and A_2 a value of 0.80, and there is an overlap between the two values of 0.25. The simple behavior-ratio theory will yield

$$P(A_1, A_2) = \frac{1.50}{(1.50 + 0.80)} = 0.65.$$

Table 6.3 Predicted and obtained proportions of choice

		LJ HW CD	JU	CY	AF	BB	ET	SL
LJ	p_0		0.76	0.80	0.74	0.76	0.65	0.60
	o		0.75	0.78	0.76	0.74	0.68	0.61
HW	p_0		0.69	0.74	0.66	0.68	0.56	0.50
	o		0.70	0.74	0.68	0.67	0.52	0.52
CD	p_0		0.64	0.69	0.61	0.63	0.50	0.45
	o		0.62	0.67	0.59	0.60	0.52	0.51
JU	p_0					0.49	0.37	0.32
	o					0.53	0.37	0.26
CY	p_0					0.43	0.31	0.27
	o					0.41	0.31	0.26
AF	p_0					0.52	0.39	0.30
	o					0.57	0.39	0.30

Note: Entries are p_0 where p = predicted proportion, o = obtained proportion.

The Restle model will give

$$P(A_1, A_2) = \frac{(1.50 - 0.25)}{(1.50 - 0.25) + (0.80 - 0.25)}$$

$$= \frac{1.25}{1.80} = 0.69.$$

The first question is whether the comparisons within sets of similar alternatives will agree with the values of v estimated from comparisons of dissimilar ones, or whether the discrepancy predicted from Restle's set-theoretic approach will be found. The probabilities of choice within the similar sets, as predicted from the constant ratio rule and as observed in the data, are shown in Table 6.4. The alternatives are arranged so that the more preferred alternatives are above the less preferred, so that all predicted probabilities are greater than 0.5. The overlap theory leads to the prediction that the data frequencies will be higher than those calculated from the simple behavior-ratio theory, a result found in all but one case, and that case is very near 0.5.

The results of Table 6.4 clearly indicate the effect predicted. When combined with the results in Table 6.3, showing an excellent fit of Luce's behavior-ratio model with dissimilar alternatives, the result is promising.

Table 6.4 Observed proportions of choices within similar alternatives, and predictions from overall v-scale estimates

Predicted				Observed		
Politicians						
	HW	CD			HW	CD
LJ	0.60	0.65	LJ		0.68	0.70
HW	—	0.56	HW		—	0.59
Athletes						
	JU	CY			JU	CY
AF	0.53	0.59	AF		0.51*	0.67
JU	—	0.56	JU		—	0.75
Movie Stars						
	ET	BB			ET	BB
SL	0.56	0.68	SL		0.63	0.79
ET		0.63	ET			0.71

* The only exception to the prediction from similarity

The matter may be pursued further by estimating the values of the overlaps. Let p_{12} be the probability of choosing alternative 1 over 2; let v_1 and v_2 be the valences or measures of the alternatives; and let i be the valence of the overlap. Then from the set-theoretic formulation,

$$p_{12} = \frac{v_1 - i}{v_1 + v_2 - 2i}$$

whence, by simple algebra,

$$i = \frac{(v_1 + v)_2 p_{12} - v_1}{2p_{12} - 1}.$$

By application of this idea, within a general parameter-estimating program, estimates were made of the overlaps and are shown in Table 6.5. There is considerable variability in the size of these estimates, but they tend to average about half the value of the less valued of the two alternatives.

The natural next experimental step will be to manipulate the overlaps by using, not just complicated stimuli like famous persons, but actual bundles or combinations of various goods. By manipulating the actual contents of the alternatives, it should eventually be possible to make very strong tests of the theory, and at the same time to refine the theory of how simple choices are made.

Note that the similarity theory considers money a special kind of alternative. Since money has no intrinsic value (in an idealized economy),

Table 6.5 Values of $v(S_i \cap S_j)$ estimated from data

	LJ	HW	CD
LJ	1.49	0.58	0.27
HW		1.01	0.33
CD			0.80

	JU	CY	AF
JU	0.46	0.31	0.00
CY		0.36	0.22
AF			0.51

	BB	ET	SL
BB	0.47	0.26	0.29
ET		0.79	0.49
SL			1.00

if A is a larger amount of money than B, then the valued aspects of B are a subset of the valued aspects of A, and in a choice between the two, B will never be chosen. Therefore money should be perfectly "discriminable." Objects, especially if qualitatively different and therefore incommensurable, may have many unique valued aspects on both sides and be relatively indiscriminable in value. If this analysis is correct, as the preliminary results suggest, then the "price theory" is an inaccurate representation of economic choice, since objects behave differently in choice situations than do their prices.

THEORY OF MEASUREMENT

A second problem of the theory of choice is to measure the "underlying" values or utilities that a person has for alternative objects or situations. In this approach, choices are treated from the point of view of the information they provide about subjective feelings of liking or attraction for objects.

The theory of measurement deals with questions about the kind of information about theoretical quantities contained in the results of an experiment or test. In the basic method of paired comparisons, subjects make comparisons between pairs taken from a set of objects, and the goal of the investigation is the assignment of scale values representing the values or utilities of the objects for the subjects in the experiment.[13]

[13] Because of its legacy from classical liberal economics, this theory assumes that different people will have different utilities for the same object, but that utility remains relatively fixed for an individual, unless the measurement is of marginal utility.

The basic empirical relationship is defined on pairs of objects. The formal notation is *aRb*, and the intended interpretation is that object *a* is at least as attractive as object *b*. Using the basic relation *R*, two more relations can be defined:

$$aIb \text{ if and only if } (\textit{iff}) \ aRb \text{ and } bRa;$$

$$aPb \textit{ iff } aRb \text{ and not } bRa.$$

The intended interpretations of *I* and *P* are indifference and preference.

Weak Ordering

A relatively weak[14] relationship between the utilities and choices is specified if there is a function *u* that assigns a numerical utility value to every object in some set *A*, and the following rule holds: For all *a* and *b* in *A*,

$$aRb \textit{ iff } u(a) \geq u(b).$$

Then the set *A* will have the following properties:

i) For all $a, b \in A$, either *aRb* or *bRa* (or both).

Proof. Every object is associated with some numerical value by the function *u*, and therefore for every pair of objects *a*, *b*, either $u(a) \geq u(b)$, or $u(b) \geq u(a)$, or both.

ii) For all $a, b, c \in A$, if *aRb* and *bRc*, then *aRc*

Proof. From *aRb* and *bRc*, it is known that $u(a) \geq u(b)$ and $u(b) \geq u(c)$. But then $u(a) \geq u(c)$, hence *aRc*.

The two properties are called connectedness and transitivity; when they hold, the relation *R* is connected and transitive, and *R* is a *weak ordering* on the set *A*.

The following corollaries can be derived. For all $a, b, c \in A$,

1. exactly one of *aPb*, *aIb*, *bPa* holds.
2. *P* is transitive; if *aPb* and *bPc*, then *aPc*.
3. *I* is reflexive; *aIa*.
4. *I* is symmetric; if *aIb* then *bIa*.
5. *I* is transitive; If *aIb* and *bIc*, then *aIc*.
6. if *aPb* and *bIc*, then *aPc*; and if *aPb* and *aIc*, then *cPb*.

---

[14] Logically, a *strong* relationship implies *weaker* ones. If the effort is to obtain a theory without false assumptions, then the weaker the relationships are assumed, the better.

The first corollary follows directly from the property of connectedness. It is known that either aRb or bRa or both applies to any pair a, b. Therefore, there are three mutually exclusive possibilities: aRb and not bRa, or bRa and not aRb, or both aRb and bRa. But these are aPb, bPa, and aIb by definition.

The hypothesis of the second corollary is aPb and bPc. In other words, aRb and not bRa; bRc and not cRb. It is known that aRc, because R is transitive. Now suppose that cRa were true. Since aRb, cRb would occur by transitivity of R. But cRb is false by hypothesis. This implies that cRa is false, assuming it leads to a contradiction. Thus "aRc and not cRa" follows from the hypothesis. Since "aRc and not cRa" equals aPc, the theorem is proved. Proofs of corollaries 3 to 6 are left to the student as Exercise 10.

It is useful to consider the logical situation carefully. The assumption has two parts: that the function u exists, and that aRb *iff* $u(a) \geq u(b)$. The assumption that u exists seems innocent enough, but it does have important psychological implications.

In order for a well-defined utility function to exist, the values of all the objects must be commensurate. There is some question as to whether or not a person would be able to compare the values of all objects. For example, it might be very hard to compare the values of seeing a good play and eating a good dinner. Apart from the fact that these alternatives have different values depending on the momentary state of the subject involving hunger, fatigue, and other factors, it is possible that for some individuals, the alternatives of a good meal and a good play simply relate to different values and cannot be compared.

Of course, even if some objects cannot be compared in value, an experiment can still be carried out if the objects used in that experiment are comparable. If a set of objects is selected such as a collection of alternative meals, phonograph records, college courses, or some natural set, it is reasonable to suppose that the relative attractiveness of the objects corresponds to a set of scale values like those assumed when it is postulated that u exists. In that case, only the correspondence between the utilities and the judgments is problematic.

Suppose that a long list of paired comparisons includes three alternative meals a person likes about equally—say, sirloin steak, filet mignon, and broiled lobster. When the subject compares the sirloin and filet, suppose he chooses the filet. And when he compares sirloin and lobster, suppose he chooses sirloin. But when he compares lobster and the filet, suppose he chooses lobster. This could happen for any number of reasons. For example, just before comparing sirloin and lobster, the list of comparisons might include several very attractive sea-food dishes, so that the subject might be thinking about how much he liked sea food. But in any case, the data would show a failure of transitivity.

The question is what to conclude from the data. According to the assumptions, the relation of preference should be transitive. Since the data were not transitive, the function *u* may not be well defined. The reason might be that the attractiveness of an object depends on the situation at the moment, and that variation in the values of the objects are responsible for failures of transitivity.

The classical strength theory treats the value of the function *u* as the mean of a distribution. In that case, any single comparison involves a sample taken from a distribution. A large number of independent observations would be needed to obtain a reliable measurement of the relative attractiveness of any pair of alternatives.

Another possibility is that the value of each object is well defined, but that the values determine probabilities of choice, where probabilities are proportional to values. This interpretation is consistent with the behavior-ratio theory, and in this case also, it is apparent that a large number of independent observations are needed to obtain accurate measurements of the relative attractiveness of alternatives.

Define a relation of probabilistic preference,

$$aPb \text{ iff } P(a, b) > 0.50.$$

It should be kept in mind that the choice frequencies in an experiment only provide estimates of the true choice probabilities. For a paired-comparison experiment to decide about the existence of an ordinal utility function, it must provide enough data to decide for each pair of alternatives x and y whether $P(x, y) > 0.50$ or $P(x, y) < 0.50$ with reasonable confidence. This means that special care needs to be taken when sample proportions are near 0.50. A reasonable procedure would be to set some level of confidence in the conclusion about the true choice probabilities, and obtain sufficient data to meet that criterion or ignore those comparisons that failed to meet it. If measurements are taken with sufficient reliability, then the transitivity of P implies that if $P(a, b)$ and $P(b, c) > 0.50$, then $P(a, c) > 0.50$. This condition is called *weak stochastic transitivity*.

On the basis of the hypothesis of an ordinal utility function, paired-comparison data lead to conclusions about the utilities of a set of objects. Suppose that four objects a, b, c, and d are used in a paired-comparison experiment, and it is observed that cPb, bPd, and dPa result. This implies that

$$u(c) > u(b) > u(d) > u(a).$$

Any utility values can be assigned that are consistent with these inequalities. For example,

$$u(a) = 1, \quad u(b) = 3, \quad u(c) = 4, \quad u(d) = 2.$$

These values are unique up to monotonic transformations. For example, specify

$$u'(x) = \alpha u(x) + \beta u(x)^2 + \gamma$$

with α and β positive, or

$$u(a) = 1, \qquad u(b) = 3, \qquad u(c) = 100{,}000, \qquad u(d) = 2.$$

Then either u' or u'' would also give values consistent with the results. It may be sufficient for some purposes to have ordinal information about utilities, but clearly it would be preferable to have a stronger relationship between the utility scale and the preference data.

Higher-Order Scale

One way of strengthening the assumed relationship between utilities and preference judgments is to assume that differences between utilities are reflected in the data according to a quaternary relation D. The alternatives a, b, c, and d are related $abDcd$ if the amount by which a is preferred over b is greater than the amount by which c is preferred over d. Assuming that a utility function exists,

$$ab\,Dcd \ iff \ u(a) - u(b) \geq u(c) - u(d).$$

Some of the implied properties of the relation D include the following:

i) Strong connectivity of differences. For all a, b, c, and d, either $abDcd$ or $cdDab$. Clearly, if there is a well-defined numerical utility for each of the four objects, then $u(a) - u(b)$ will be greater than $u(c) - u(d)$, it will be smaller, or the two differences will be the same.

ii) Transitivity. If $abDcd$ and $cdDef$, then $abDef$. Again, the property follows directly from differences between numbers.

iii) If $abDcd$ then (a) $acDbd$ and (b) $dcDba$; (a) is called the *quadruple condition*, and (b) is called the *sign-preserving condition*. They both follow directly from inequalities on utility values:

$$if \ u(a) - u(b) \geq u(c) - u(d), \ then$$
$$u(a) - u(c) \geq u(b) - u(d) \ and$$
$$u(d) - u(c) \geq u(b) - u(a).$$

The following corollaries either follow directly or are implied by the properties given above:

1. Reflexivity: $abDab$.

2. Weak connectivity of differences: either $abDbb$ or $baDbb$.

234 Theory of Choice and Preference

3. If $a = b$ and $c = d$, then $ab\,Dcd$ and $cd\,Dab$.

Corollaries 1 to 3 are obvious. For Corollaries 4 to 6, define

$$aRb \text{ iff for all } x, ab\,Dxx.$$

4. aRb iff $u(a) \geq u(b)$. $ab\,Dxx$ means

$$u(a) - u(b) \geq u(x) - u(x) = 0.$$

But this applies *iff* $u(a) \geq u(b)$.

5. Transitivity of R: Suppose aRb and bRc. This implies that $ab\,Dbb$ and $bc\,Dbb$. By the quadruple condition, $bb\,Dcb$. Then, by transitivity $ab\,Dcb$. Applying the quadruple condition again, $ac\,Dbb$. Then by Corollary 3 and transitivity of D, it is possible to show $ac\,Dxx$ for any x. This proves that aRb and bRc implies aRc.

6. If aRb and bRc, then $ac\,Dbc$ and $ac\,Dab$. From aRb it follows that $ab\,Dcc$; then by the quadruple condition, $ac\,Dbc$. From bRc, $bc\,Daa$. The sign-preserving condition gives $aa\,Dcb$, and the quadruple condition gives $ac\,Dab$.

Coombs[15] has called a system involving an ordering on differences a *higher-ordered metric*. To test the implications of this metric requires a method of measuring the amount of preference, in addition to which alternative is preferred. It is possible to ask subjects to give direct judgments of the amounts of their preferences. Another method uses choice probabilities, and applies the relation D according to the rule

$$ab\,Dcd \text{ iff } P(a, b) \geq P(c, d).$$

Differences between probabilities usually require more observations than are needed for measuring single probabilities. Transitivity of differences provides an important way of testing the assumptions, but another implication is also interesting. As a direct result of Corollary 5,

if $P(a, b)$ and $P(b, c)$ are both greater than 0.50,
then $P(a, c) \geq P(a, b)$ and $P(a, c) \geq P(b, c)$.

This condition is called *strong stochastic transitivity*.

If a higher-ordered metric holds, the data from a preference experiment give more information about the utilities of the alternatives than if only ordinal utility can be assumed. Utility-scale values that are consistent with

---
[15] C. H. Coombs, *A theory of data.* New York: Wiley, 1964.

differences as measured in a preference experiment must meet the condition that

$$u(a) - u(b) \geq u(c) - u(d) \text{ iff } P(a, b) \geq P(c, d).$$

Such an assignment will be unique up to linear transformations. It is easy to see that once a set of utility scale values has been assigned, any linear function of those utility values will preserve the ordering of differences. Let

$$u'(x) = \alpha u(x) + \beta$$

with $\alpha > 0$. Then

$$u'(a) - u'(b) = \alpha[u(a) - u(b)]$$

and

$$u'(c) - u'(d) = \alpha[u(c) - u(d)].$$

Clearly,

$$u'(a) - u'(b) \geq u'(c) - u'(d) \text{ iff } u(a) - u(b) \geq u(c) - u(d),$$

as required. The proof that all assignments of utilities that preserve the ordering on differences are linear transformations of each other is more complicated. A proof is found in Suppes and Winet[16]—it depends upon having a large number of alternatives well spaced in utility.

IMPLICATIONS OF CHOICE THEORY FOR MEASUREMENT OF UTILITY

This last section presents some relationships between the theory of choice presented first, and the theory of utility measurement presented in the preceding section.

A classification of utility models has been given by Luce and Suppes.[17] A weak utility model is a set of assumptions that implies the existence of a utility function w and a choice rule such that

$$P(a, b) \geq 0.50 \text{ iff } w(a) \geq w(b).$$

A strong utility model is a set of assumptions that implies the existence of a utility function u, a cumulative distribution function ϕ, and a choice rule such that

$$\phi(0) = 0.50, \quad \text{and} \quad P(a, b) = \phi[u(a) - u(b)].$$

---

[16] P. Suppes and Muriel Winet, An axiomatization of utility based on the notion of utility differences. *Management Science*, 1955, Vol. 1, 259–270.

[17] Cited above.

Finally, a strict utility model is a set of assumptions that implies a utility function v and a choice rule such that

$$P(a, b) = \frac{v(a)}{v(a) + v(b)}.$$

It should be obvious that the classical strength theory is a strong utility model, and the behavior-ratio theory is a strict utility model. Some results will be presented involving Restle's generalization of the behavior-ratio theory, which takes into account similarities among alternatives.

Some examples in Rumelhart's data have shown that Restle's model is not a strict utility model for all sets of alternatives. An additional counter-example is presented here to illustrate a formal point. The following matrix gives hypothetical values of $v(S_i \cap S_j)$ for three alternatives.

	A	B	C
A	5	2	0
B		4	1
C			3

Calculating the choice probabilities from Restle's assumptions, it follows that

$$P(a, b) = 0.60, \qquad \frac{P(a, b)}{P(b, a)} = 1.5,$$

$$P(b, c) = 0.60, \qquad \frac{P(b, c)}{P(c, b)} = 1.5,$$

$$P(a, c) = 0.625, \qquad \frac{P(a, c)}{P(c, a)} = 1.67.$$

The probabilities do not satisfy the product rule; however, in this case the results are consistent with strong stochastic transitivity.

There is an interesting informal similarity between Restle's model and the classical strength theory. Suppose two alternatives are available, and both are improved by some common factor. For example, two car manufacturers might add identical safety features on next year's model without raising their prices. In Restle's model, this common increase in value would have no effect on the probability of choice between them. The same could be true in the classical strength theory. If the improvements merely moved each distribution of response strengths to the right without changing the variance, there would be no change in the choice probabilities. It seems reasonable to consider the conjecture that Restle's model is a strong utility model, which would imply that objects could be assigned utility values with the property of an interval scale.

Recall that one implication of the strong utility model is strong stochastic transitivity. The situation described in the example above is consistent with this implication. However, consider another set of hypothetical measures, such as those shown in Fig. 6.6.

	A	B	C
A	10	6	0
B		9	3
C			5

$$P(a, b) = 0.57, \qquad \frac{P(a, b)}{P(b, a)} = 1.33,$$

$$P(b, c) = 0.75, \qquad \frac{P(b, c)}{P(c, b)} = 3.0,$$

$$P(a, c) = 0.67, \qquad \frac{P(a, c)}{P(c, a)} = 2.0.$$

The results are inconsistent with both the product rule and strong stochastic transitivity.

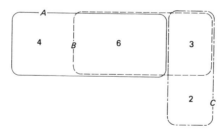

Figure 6.6

Restle's model is a weak utility model. Let the utility function on alternatives be

$$v(a) = m(A),$$

the measure of the set of a's aspects. From the model,

$$P(a, b) \geq 0.50 \text{ iff } m(A) - m(A \cap B) \geq m(B) - m(A \cap B),$$

whence

$$P(a, b) \geq 0.50 \text{ iff } v(a) \geq v(b).$$

On the basis of Restle's model, it is possible to assign utility-scale values that preserve the order of preference in a set of objects, but stronger scales depend upon special conditions.

Since Restle's model is a weak utility model, it implies that the data will satisfy weak stochastic transitivity. Actually, the model implies that a somewhat stronger relationship will be satisfied in the data. The relationship is called *moderate stochastic transitivity*, and is defined as follows: For any alternatives a, b, and c,

$$\text{if } P(a, b) \geq 0.50, \text{ and } P(b, c) \geq 0.50, \text{ then}$$
$$P(a, c) \geq \min [P(a, b), P(b, c)].$$

Note that this relationship is stronger than weak stochastic transitivity, which requires only that $P(a, c) \geq 0.50$. But it is weaker than strong stochastic transitivity, which requires that $P(a, c)$ must be greater than both $P(a, b)$ and $P(b, c)$.

For the proof that Restle's model implies moderate stochastic transitivity,[18] refer to Fig. 6.7. The three alternatives are divided into their seven disjoint subsets. Let v_i be the measure of the subset labeled i in the figure.

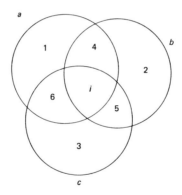

Figure 6.7

Assume that $P(a, b)$ and $P(b, c)$ are both greater than 0.50. The claim to be proved is that $P(a, c)$ is not smaller than both $P(a, b)$ and $P(b, c)$. From the assumption,

$$\frac{P(a, b)}{P(b, a)} = \frac{v_1 + v_6}{v_2 + v_5} \geq 1, \qquad \frac{P(b, c)}{P(c, b)} = \frac{v_2 + v_4}{v_3 + v_6} \geq 1.$$

When the expressions are cleared of fractions, two inequalities are obtained;

---

[18] The form of this proof was suggested by Alexander Pollatsek.

when these are added,

$$v_1 + v_2 + v_4 + v_6 \geq v_2 + v_3 + v_5 + v_6; \qquad v_1 + v_4 \geq v_3 + v_5. \quad (15)$$

This merely shows that $P(a, c)/P(c, a) \geq 1.0$, which follows from weak stochastic transitivity.

Now, however, assume that the conclusion to be proved is not true; that is, assume that $P(a, c)$ is smaller than both $P(a, b)$ and $P(b, c)$. This would imply

$$\frac{(Pa, c)}{P(c, a)} = \frac{v_1 + v_4}{v_3 + v_5} < \frac{v_1 + v_6}{v_2 + v_5}, \qquad \frac{v_1 + v_4}{v_3 + v_5} < \frac{v_2 + v_4}{v_3 + v_6}.$$

Clear these two inequalities of fractions, and add the resulting inequalities. The result is

$$(v_2 + v_3 + v_5 + v_6)(v_1 + v_4) < (v_1 + v_2 + v_4 + v_6)(v_3 + v_5).$$

A term equal to $(v_1 + v_4)(v_3 + v_5)$ can be subtracted from each side, leaving

$$(v_2 + v_6)(v_1 + v_4) < (v_2 + v_6)(v_3 + v_5), \qquad v_1 + v_4 < v_3 + v_5. \quad (16)$$

Equations (15) and (16) are contradictory, which shows that if $P(a, b)$ and $P(b, c)$ are assumed greater than 0.50, then it is contradictory to assume that $P(a, c)$ is smaller than both $P(a, b)$ and $P(b, c)$.

Restle's model is a strict utility model if all the overlaps between pairs of sets have equal measure. This can be seen from examining the product rule in the following form:

$$\frac{P(a, b)P(b, c)P(c, b)}{P(a, c)P(c, b)P(b, a)} = 1.$$

According to Restle's assumptions, this translates to

$$\frac{[m(A) - m(A \cap B)][m(B) - m(B \cap C)][m(C) - m(B \cap C)]}{[m(A) - m(A \cap C)][m(C) - m(B \cap C)][m(B) - m(A \cap B)]} = 1,$$

and if all the intersections have equal measures, the terms will cancel and the condition will be satisfied. For instance, each alternative may have (1) a set of aspects common to all alternatives, and (2) a unique set of differential aspects. For this reason it is possible for a "natural set" of objects, which obviously have common aspects, to follow a strict utility model, provided that within the definition they are all unique and dissimilar.

At the other extreme, it is possible to envisage a set of alternatives that are as similar to one another as possible. If set A has a greater measure than

B, then they are most similar when B is a subset of A. If the alternatives are called $A_1, A_2, \ldots, A_N$, and A_1 is preferred over A_2, A_2 over A_3, etc., and they are as similar as possible, then

$$A_N \subset A_{N-1} \subset \cdots \subset A_2 \subset A_1.$$

In this case, $P(A_1, A_2) = P(A_2, A_3) = \cdots = 1$, so that preferences are absolute. Such data permit a definite ordering of alternatives, but in themselves give no basis for comparing intervals, hence no basis for higher order, interval, or stronger scales. In Restle's discussion, the above condition is described as the problem of money, which is perfectly discriminable. The usual approach to this problem, following von Neumann and Morgenstern[19] has been to devise gambles involving both amounts of money and probabilities. The empirical problems of comparisons between gambles, and the theory by which they can be turned into measurements of utility, will not be covered in the present volume.

EXERCISES

1. Suppose that for three alternatives a, b, and c, we have $\mu_a = 5$, $\mu_b = 2$, $\mu_c = 3$, and $\sigma_0 = 2$. Calculate $P(a, b)$, $P(b, c)$, and $P(a, c)$ using the assumptions of the classical strength theory.

2. *Thurstonian scaling.* Let $\Phi(r; u, s)$ denote the probability of a value less than r for a variable whose distribution is normal with mean μ and standard deviation s. Recall that $z(p)$ is that value of r which satisfies

$$p = \Phi(r; 0, 1).$$

a) Show that classical strength theory implies that for any pair of alternatives i and j, $z[P(i, j)]$ is an estimate of $(\mu_i - \mu_j)/(\sqrt{2}\sigma_0)$, where σ_0 is the standard deviation of each individual distribution of response strength.

b) For a set of choice alternatives $1, 2, \ldots, N$, show that an estimate of μ_i is

$$\hat{\mu}_i = \frac{1}{N} \sum_{j=1}^{N} z[P(i, j)], \tag{17}$$

and that these estimates are on a scale with

$$\sum_{i=1}^{N} \mu_i = 0, \qquad \sqrt{2}\sigma_0 = 1. \tag{18}$$

3. Suppose that the results calculated in Problem 1 were obtained as data in an experiment. Calculate estimates of μ_a, μ_b, and μ_c using Eq. (17), and show that

---

[19] J. von Neumann and O. Morgenstern, *Theory of Games and Economic Behavior.* Princeton: Princeton University Press, 1944.

they are consistent with the assumptions of Problem 1 under the transformation of Eq. (18).

4. Let

$$y(i, j) = \log [P_S(i)/P_S(j)]$$

for any set of alternatives S. Find a procedure for calculating estimates of response strengths $v(i)$ in the behavior-ratio theory from paired-comparison data, and specify the scaling constraint that your procedure implies.

5. Apply the procedure found for Problem 4 to the values of $P(a, b)$, $P(b, c)$, and $P(a, c)$ calculated in Problem 1, and then calculate theoretical values of $P(a, b)$, $P(b, c)$, and $P(a, c)$ according to the behavior-ratio theory.

6. Let S_1 and S_2 denote disjoint sets of choice alternatives, and assume that we have complete information about choice probabilities within sets (e.g., paired-comparison data) so that we have scale values $\hat{\mu}_i$ for alternatives $i \in S_1$ and $\hat{\mu}_j$ for $j \in S_2$ according to classical strength theory or $\hat{v}_i$ for $i \in S_1$ and $\hat{v}_j$ for $j \in S_2$ according to behavior-ratio theory. Show that data for a single paired comparison between sets (that is, $P(h, k)$, $h \in S_1$, $k \in S_2$) is then sufficient to permit predictions for all choice probabilities $P(i, j)$ $i, j \in S_1 \cup S_2$ for the classical strength theory, and for all probabilities $P_R(i)$, $i \in R \subseteq S_1 \cup S_2$ for the behavior-ratio theory.

7. In 1960, Estes[20] collected preferences from student subjects regarding which of several famous persons they would most like to meet and talk with. The choice alternatives were Dwight Eisenhower (E), Winston Churchill (C), Dag Hamerskjold (H), and William Faulkner (F). The paired-comparison data were:

$$P(E, C) = 0.57, \qquad P(E, H) = 0.80, \qquad P(E, F) = 0.82,$$
$$P(C, H) = 0.76, \qquad P(C, F) = 0.80, \qquad P(H, F) = 0.60.$$

Estimate values of μ in the classical strength theory and of v in the behavior-ratio theory, and calculate theoretical probabilities for the experiment for both theories.

8. In the experiment cited in Problem 7, Estes also had subjects choose from sets of three alternatives: $R = \{E, C, H\}$ and $S = \{C, H, F\}$. The data were

$$P_R(E) = 0.51, \qquad P_R(C) = 0.36, \qquad P_R(H) = 0.13,$$
$$P_S(C) = 0.65, \qquad P_S(H) = 0.20, \qquad P_S(F) = 0.15.$$

a) Calculate theoretical probabilities for these situations using estimates of v obtained in Problem 7.

b) Devise estimates of $v(E)$, $v(C)$, $v(H)$, and $v(F)$ that use all the data from both situations, and calculate theoretical probabilities for the complete experiment using the resulting estimates.

9. The version of classical strength theory used in the text assumes independently distributed response strengths. Show that for the situation used by Rumelhart and Greeno, Restle's theory is indistinguishable from classical strength theory if

---

[20] Described by R. C. Atkinson, G. H. Bower, and E. J. Crothers, *An Introduction to Mathematical Learning Theory*. New York: Wiley, 1965, pp. 146–150.

independence is assumed for pairs of alternatives between subsets, but non-negative correlations are assumed for pairs of alternatives within sets.

10. Prove Corollaries 3 through 6, p. 231.

11. Using the data given in Tables 6.3 and 6.4, count the number of triples for which the paired-comparison data show violations of (a) strong stochastic transitivity, (b) moderate stochastic transitivity, and (c) weak stochastic transitivity. (There are 84 triples in all.) How many of each kind of violation involved at least one pair taken from a single subset?

12. Consider a single triple of alternatives (i, j, k) and a single set of paired-comparisons made by one subject. List the eight possible outcomes, and determine which ones violate transitivity. Next, calculate the probability of an intransitive outcome (a) if all three alternatives have equal strength, and (b) if the behavior-ratio theory is correct, and $v(i) = 12$, $v(j) = 11$, $v(k) = 10$.

13. Assume that response strengths for four alternatives h, i, j, k are known exactly and are $v(h) = 9$, $v(i) = 12$, $v(j) = 11$, $v(k) = 10$ in the behavior-ratio theory. Calculate the probability that data from a single subject will show (a) at least one intransitive triple, (b) two or three intransitive triples, (c) three intransitive triples. (There are four triples and 16 possible outcomes.)

14. Assume that Restle's theory holds, and for three alternatives we have $m(I) = 12$, $m(J) = 11$, $m(K) = 10$, with the intersections empty. Calculate the probability of a violation of strong stochastic transitivity (a) if $P(i, j)$ and $P(j, k)$ are estimated from an infinite number of observations, but $P(i, k)$ is estimated from 30 cases; (b) if $P(i, j)$ is estimated from 30 cases, but $P(i, k)$ and $P(j, k)$ are estimated from an infinite number of cases.

15. Repeat Problem 14, but generalize the result to any number of cases n instead of 30.

16. Repeat Problems 14 and 15, except assume that $m(I) = 20$, $m(J) = 15$, and $m(K) = 10$.

17. Repeat Problem 14, except assume that $m(I \cap J) = 8$, $m(J \cap K) = 4$, and $m(I \cap K) = 6$, and calculate probabilities of violating moderate stochastic transitivity.

CHAPTER SEVEN

Sentences, Sets, and Probabilities

Where do mathematical theories come from? A clear and logical presentation of a theory often deletes those historical and heuristic considerations that led the theorist to his formulation, so that to the reader the equations seem to have a life of their own.

In reality, most successful mathematical models in psychology arise from, or are connected with, the main stream of psychological theory, and mathematical theorists are sensitive to the various experimental outcomes that direct theoretical development.

To the student or newcomer to mathematical psychology, the connection between mathematical psychology and ordinary experimental work is apparent but unclear. How does one get from an experiment, described in a mixture of ordinary English and technical jargon, to a mathematical model? What choices are open? Can the same psychological theory lead to several different and conflicting mathematical models? Can the same mathematical model have several distinct theoretical interpretations, and if so, does this suggest that the theoretical interpretations are actually very much alike, though perhaps using different terminology?

Questions of this sort do not have a definite and general answer, except as the steps are filled in between ordinary sentences, such as those describing experiments, and formal mathematical structures.

The purpose of this chapter is to fill in this logical gap by beginning with the logic of simple sentences and building the necessary logical and mathematical structures to lead to a mathematical model in psychology. Much of the content appears in the main chapters of the book, but the account here is more systematic and complete, and follows the natural logical and mathematical flow of argument, rather than the structure arising from specific psychological applications.

This chapter will be of use to the student to the degree that he has begun raising philosophical questions, inquiring as to the meaning of response probabilities, questioning the mathematical formulations, seeking the full set of assumptions underlying a model, or troubling about why two probabilities can be multiplied. This chapter, which contains nothing but logic and mathematics, reveals that the above questions are actually questions of psychology, to be resolved by recourse to the psychological assumptions.

SENTENTIAL LOGIC

The study of logic begins with the simple formal theory of sentences. The theory is stated in abstract meaningless form, so as to ensure that no conclusion is reached invalidly, just because it seems true.

In this formal system, the usual interpretation is that each elementary variable refers to a sentence, like "Subject 15 made response 1 on trial 4." If such sentences are not taken apart, new sentences can be constructed, such as, from the above, "Subject 15 did *not* make response 1 on trial 4." If the first sentence is called "S," the second could be called "not-S." A new sentence can be introduced, "The green light was turned on for trial 4," symbolized by T. Then a new sentence can be constructed "S or T," saying "Subject 15 made response 1 on trial 4, *or* the green light was turned on for trial 4." The sentential logic deals with compound sentences of this sort. If one knows the truth value of the component sentences, then the truth value of compounds can be deduced merely from the *form* of the compound. This is the nature and purpose of this formal system.

So as to have more compact formulas, and also to help the reader employ purely formal methods, we introduce here a more mathematical notation for simple sentential logic. The connectives mentioned were *not*, *and*, *or*, and *if . . . then*. These will be written as follows:

$\overline{Y}$	means not Y,
$Y \mathbin{\&} D$	means Y and D,
$Y \vee D$	means Y or D,
$Y \rightarrow D$	means if Y then D.

By judicious use of parentheses, quite complex logical structures can be written.

The parts of a formal system include rules of formation, axioms, and rules of transformation. Given is a slight modification of those rules presented by Hilbert and Ackermann in *Mathematical Logic*.[1] The purpose of this presentation is to lead the reader to prove a number of theorems, and thereby capture both elementary technique and the flavor of a formal justification.

---

[1] D. Hilbert and W. Ackermann, *Principles of Mathematical Logic*. New York: Chelsea, 1950.

Rules of Formation

The letters X, Y, Z, etc., stand for sentential variables. The intended interpretation of X is a space in which any sentence can be inserted.

Rules of formation decide what is and what is not a well-formed formula (wff).

RULE 1. X is a wff, as are Y, Z, etc.

RULE 2.   Let **A** be any string of symbols. If **A** is a wff, then so are

a) (**A**) and
b) $\bar{\mathbf{A}}$,

and if **A** and **B** are wff's, then so are

c) **A & B**,
d) **A $\vee$ B**,
e) **A $\rightarrow$ B**.

All well-formed formulas can be shown to be so by application of the above rules. For example, the string of symbols

$$((X \& Y) \vee Z) \tag{1}$$

is a wff. X, Y, and Z are all wff's by Rule 1, hence so is $X \& Y$ by Rule 2(c); then $(X \& Y)$ is by Rule 2(a). Call this **A**, and then $A \vee Z$ is a wff by Rule 2(d); that is, $(X \& Y) \vee Z$ is a wff. By Rule 2(a), parentheses can be put around it, arriving at the formula $((X \& Y) \vee Z)$. Q.E.D.

Consider a nonformula, such as

$$((X \vee Y) \&). \tag{2}$$

Since, in the rules of formation, & appears only in Rule 2(c) between two wff's, it follows that) must be a wff for Eq. (2) to be one. However, notice that) is introduced only with a wff in Rule 2(a); hence it cannot stand alone as a wff. From this it is possible to see that the above statement is not a wff. The crucial logical point is that one cannot verify such a string of symbols to be well formed using the above rules.

Axioms

An axiom is a true primitive statement of the theory. In sentential logic, of course, the axioms are statements taken to be true merely because of their logical form. It is not the "truth" of the axioms, but their strategic value (their ability to generate a set of reasonable theorems of logic) that is essential.

A. $X \vee X \to X$

B. $X \to X \vee Y$

C. $X \vee Y \to Y \vee X$

D. $(X \to Y) \to ((Z \vee X) \to (Z \vee Y))$

In the proofs to be done, the above formulas will be used without any reference to their possible meanings, merely as first steps in the proofs. However, the symbol $\vee$ stands for inclusive or disjunctive "or," the ampersand & stands for "and," and the arrow $\to$ stands for "if . . . then" in what logicians call the "intended interpretation" of the calculus.

Defined Terms

Certain terms are defined with respect to others. In a proof, one can always replace a defined term by its definition or vice versa.

Definition. $X \to Y = \bar{X} \vee Y$.

This definition makes it clear that the arrow stands for what is called "material implication." That is, X implies Y in this sense if Y is true or if X is false. The implication itself is false only if X is true *and* Y is false, for the one restriction is "that true premises cannot imply false consequents." One need not worry about the sense of the implication, however, since the arrow can always be replaced by $\bar{X} \vee Y$.

Rules of Transformation

A system of logic has rules of transformation, telling what changes can be made in sentences.

α *Rule of substitution.* For a sentential variable (i.e., for a capital bold-face letter) any given sentential combination may be substituted, provided that the substitution is made wherever that sentential variable occurs.

β *Rule of implication* (*detachment*). From the two formulas **A** and **A** $\to$ **B**, the new formula **B** is obtained.

Derived Rules

The above material is all the equipment needed to construct the whole edifice of sentential logic. However, to make proofs easier, it helps to prove some rules of general use.

RULE 1. If **A** $\vee$ **A** is a theorem, then so is **A**.

Proof. By substitution of **A** for X in Axiom A, it follows that **A** $\vee$ **A** $\to$ **A**. By the rule of implication (β), **A** follows.

RULE 2. If **A** is a theorem and **B** is any other wff whatever, then **A** $\vee$ **B** is a theorem.

Proof. As above, but using Axiom B.

RULE 3 (Commutativety of *or*). If **A** ∨ **B** is a theorem, so is **B** ∨ **A**.

RULE 4 (Rule of implication). If **A** → **B** is a theorem and **C** any other wff whatever, then **C** ∨ **A** → **C** ∨ **B** is also a theorem.

Theorems

A theorem is any statement proved from the axioms. Of course, it is the set of true consequences of the theory, and in sentential logic, it is the set of all compound sentences that are logically true merely on the basis of the arrangement of their component sentences.

A proof of a theorem consists in a finite sequence of sentences, of which the first is an axiom. Every other sentence is either an axiom, or derivable by rules from sentences earlier in the sequence, and the last sentence is the theorem. A proof is written by giving a sequence of such sentences, and, with each step, a justification. The justification either names the axiom introduced, or gives the rule of transformation and names the sentences transformed.

Note that a proof, so described, is not a description of a process of reasoning, but a justification of the theorem. Some proofs are more elegant or interesting than others, especially in mathematics, but for entirely formal purposes, one proof is about as good as another provided it is valid. Anyone can check a proof merely by carefully ascertaining that each step of the proof does follow, as specified, either as an axiom or as a direct application of rules of the system as given above.

It is important to notice the distinction between proofs of theorems, which are perfectly formal, and the proof of a rule, as in the derivation of Rules 1–4. Rules are not sentences *within* sentential logic, but are statements *about* the logic. They exist, then, not in the language being studied [the *object language*, made up of sentences like $X \lor Y$ or $(Z \,\&\, \bar{Z}) \to Z$], but are stated in another language, called the *metalanguage.* The metalanguage used here is English, and more-or-less ordinary methods of communication are employed when proving or explaining rules. Sentences in the object language are subject to much more searching scrutiny and much more rigorous proof.

Theorem 1. $(X \to Y) \to [(Z \to X) \to (Z \to Y)]$.

Proof

1. $(X \to Y) \to [(Z \lor X) \to (Z \lor Y)]$ (Axiom D),
2. $(X \to Y) \to [(\bar{Z} \lor X) \to (\bar{Z} \lor Y)]$ (Substitute $\bar{Z}$ for Z, Rule A, in 1),
3. Theorem (Definition of →).

The following is a convenient rule of transformation.

RULE 5. If **A** → **B** and **B** → **C** are theorems, then **A** → **C** is also a theorem.

Proof. In Theorem 1, substitute **A** for Z, **B** for X, and **C** for Y, and then apply the rule of implication (Rule 4) twice.

The following series of theorems provide the basis for most elementary calculations in elementary logic.

Theorem 2. $\bar{X} \vee X$.

Proof

1. $X \to X \vee X$ (Substitute X for Y in Axiom B),
2. $X \vee X \to X$ (Axiom A),
3. $X \to X$ (Rule 5 applied to steps 1 and 2),
4. $\bar{X} \vee X$ (By definition of $\to$ put in step 4).

Theorem 3. $X \vee \bar{X}$.

Proof. From Theorem 2 by Rule 3.

Theorem 4. $X \to \bar{\bar{X}}$.

Proof

1. $X \vee \bar{X}$ (Theorem 3),
2. $\bar{X} \vee \bar{\bar{X}}$ (Substitute $\bar{X}$ for X in step 1),
3. $X \to \bar{\bar{X}}$ (Definition of $\to$ in step 2).

On the following two theorems, the reader should attempt the theorem himself before following the steps of proof given here.

Theorem 5. $\bar{\bar{X}} \to X$.

Proof

1. $\bar{X} \to \bar{\bar{\bar{X}}}$ (Substitute $\bar{X}$ for X in Theorem 4),
2. $X \vee \bar{X} \to X \vee \bar{\bar{\bar{X}}}$ (Rule 4),
3. $X \vee \bar{\bar{\bar{X}}}$ (Theorem 3 and Rule β),
4. $\bar{\bar{\bar{X}}} \vee X$ (Rule 3),
5. Theorem by definition of $\to$.

Theorem 6. $(X \to Y) \to (\bar{Y} \to \bar{X})$.

Proof

1. $Y \to \bar{\bar{Y}}$ (Theorem 4),
2. $\bar{X} \vee Y \to \bar{X} \vee \bar{\bar{Y}}$ (Rule 4),
3. $\bar{X} \vee \bar{\bar{Y}} \to \bar{\bar{Y}} \vee \bar{X}$ (Axiom C, substitutions),

4. $\bar{X} \vee Y \to \bar{\bar{Y}} \vee \bar{X}$ (Rule 5 applied to steps 2, 3),

5. Theorem by definition of $\to$.

It is now possible to derive an important but more complicated rule. Again, **A** and **B** refer to sentential expressions, complicated or simple. Let $\Phi(\mathbf{A})$ signify a new sentential expression within which the expression **A** can be found. An example would be $\mathbf{A} \vee X$, or for another example, $\mathbf{B} \to (\bar{\mathbf{A}} \vee \mathbf{C})$. Furthermore, if $\Phi(\mathbf{A}) = \mathbf{A} \vee \mathbf{C}$, then $\Phi(\mathbf{B}) = \mathbf{B} \vee \mathbf{C}$.

RULE 6. If $\mathbf{A} \to \mathbf{B}$ and $\mathbf{B} \to \mathbf{A}$ are theorems, then $\Phi(\mathbf{A}) \to \Phi(\mathbf{B})$ and $\Phi(\mathbf{B}) \to \Phi(\mathbf{A})$ are also theorems.

Proof. Each of the operations, negation, disjunction, and of course implication, can be applied to **A** and **B**. That is,

If $\mathbf{A} \to \mathbf{B}$ and $\mathbf{B} \to \mathbf{A}$, then

1. $\bar{\mathbf{A}} \to \bar{\mathbf{B}}$ and $\bar{\mathbf{B}} \to \bar{\mathbf{A}}$ (by substituting in Theorem 6)

2. $\mathbf{C} \vee \mathbf{A} \to \mathbf{C} \vee \mathbf{B}$ and $\mathbf{C} \vee \mathbf{B} \to \mathbf{C} \vee \mathbf{A}$ (Rule 4 on $\mathbf{A} \to \mathbf{B}$, etc.)

Now notice that every compound sentence $\Phi(\mathbf{A})$ can be built up from **A** by negation or disjunction, since every well-formed formula can be so constructed. The theorem holds with each step of construction, and therefore holds for any $\Phi(\mathbf{A})$ and $\Phi(\mathbf{B})$.

Definition of Conjunction

$$X \, \& \, Y = \overline{\bar{X} \vee \bar{Y}}.$$

From this definition follows one of the basic theorems of simple logic.

Theorem 7. $\overline{X \, \& \, Y} \to \bar{X} \vee \bar{Y}$.

Proof. (Left for the student. It is fairly difficult, and requires a large and tricky substitution.)

Theorem 8. $\bar{X} \vee \bar{Y} \to \overline{X \, \& \, Y}$.

Theorem 9. $\overline{X \vee Y} \to \bar{X} \, \& \, \bar{Y}$.

Theorem 10. $\bar{X} \, \& \, \bar{Y} \to \overline{X \vee Y}$.

Theorem 11. $X \, \& \, Y \to Y \, \& \, X$.

Theorem 12. $X \, \& \, Y \to X$.

Theorem 13. $X \, \& \, Y \to Y$.

All the above theorems have easy proofs.

Theorem 14. $X \vee (Y \vee Z) \to (Y \vee (X \vee Z))$.

[*Hint:* The proof of this theorem takes Hilbert and Ackerman 10 steps.]

Start:

1. $Z \to X \vee Z$ (From Axiom B and C, and Rule 5; that is, transposing the disjuncts $Z \vee X$ to $X \vee Z$.)

2. $Y \vee Z \to Y \vee (X \vee Z)$ (Rule 4; ... and keep building; the last step uses Rule 5.)

Theorem 15. $X \vee (Y \vee Z) \to (X \vee Y) \vee Z$.

Theorem 16. $(X \vee Y) \vee Z \to X \vee (Y \vee Z)$.

Theorem 17. $X \& (Y \& Z) \to (X \& Y) \& Z$

$\qquad\qquad (X \& Y) \& Z \to X \& (Y \& Z)$.

RULE 7. $\mathbf{B} \to (\mathbf{A} \to \mathbf{C})$ and $(\mathbf{A} \& \mathbf{B}) \to \mathbf{C}$ may be substituted for $\mathbf{A} \to (\mathbf{B} \to \mathbf{C})$.

Proof.   Merely substitute definitions of $\to$ and $\&$.

RULE 8. $\mathbf{A} \to \mathbf{B}$ may be substituted for $\mathbf{A} \to (\mathbf{A} \to \mathbf{B})$.

Proof. $(\mathbf{\bar{A}} \vee \mathbf{\bar{A}}) \vee \mathbf{B}$ or $\mathbf{\bar{A}} \vee \mathbf{B}$ may be substituted for $\mathbf{\bar{A}} \vee (\mathbf{\bar{A}} \vee \mathbf{B})$.

Theorem 18. $X \to (Y \to X \& Y)$.

Proof

1. $(\bar{X} \vee \bar{Y}) \vee \overline{\bar{X} \vee \bar{Y}}$ (Substitution in Theorem 3),

2. $\bar{X} \vee (\bar{Y} \vee \overline{\bar{X} \vee \bar{Y}})$ (Theorem 15 applied),

3. Theorem (Definitions of $\to$ and $\&$).

Theorem 19. $X \vee (Y \& Z) \to ((X \vee Y) \& (X \vee Z))$—The distributive law. The proof is difficult and fairly long.

Theorem 20. $(X \vee Y) \& (X \vee Z) \to X \vee (Y \& Z)$—The other distributive law.

THE PREDICATE CALCULUS

The system of sentential calculus discussed above, though a good introduction to the idea of logical proof, is not rich enough to give a good account of anything mathematical or scientific. For these more serious and applied purposes, it is necessary to analyze sentences into parts. In logic it is conventional to use a schematic analysis, rather than the more complete grammatical analysis now available from linguistics. Only simple declarative sentences are studied.

The statement, "Frank has gray hair," is written $G(f)$. Here G is the predicate, and f is the subject of the sentence. In sentential logic, $G(f)$ can be substituted for a sentential variable, *X*. An individual (or subject) variable, denoted by lower-case *x*, can take the place of the subject. This leads to the formula

$$G(x)$$

meaning, "*x* has gray hair." This, of course, is not a sentence. The variable *x* is said to be a "free" variable, and the formula $G(x)$ is said to be a "sentential function."

A sentence can be made from $G(x)$ by placing some noun, the subject of the sentence, in place of *x*. Thus $G(x)$ becomes a sentence when *f*, the name of an individual, is substituted for the variable *x*.

Example. Let $Y(n)$ be the sentential function. A certain subject says "yes" on trial *n* of a psychophysics experiment where *n* is a variable. Let $S(n)$ mean that a signal is presented on trial *n*. The two can be combined into the compound sentential function

$$Y(n) \ \& \ S(n)$$

which says that the subject said "yes," and there was a signal on trial *n*. However, this expression does not say what *n* is, and here *n* is acting as the subject of the sentence. Since the expression has a variable for its subject, it is a sentential function.

Sentential functions are neither true nor false, in the usual logical usage of true or false. For some values of the variable they may be true, for other values false. However, two sentential functions may be equivalent, as for example,

$$Y(n) \ \& \ S(n) \text{ is equivalent to } S(n) \ \& \ Y(n).$$

Quantifiers

Besides substituting constants for the variables, one can turn a sentential function into a sentence by quantifying the variables, either by a universal quantifier $\forall$ or by an existential quantifier $\exists$. The formula

$$(\forall n) \, Y(n)$$

is read "for all *n*, $Y(n)$," and

$$(\exists n) \, Y(n)$$

means "There exists an *n* such that $Y(n)$."

The quantifiers do not make perfect sense except within an *understood universe of discourse*. Consider the assertion that for every pair of numbers *a* and *b* there exists a number halfway between, $(a + b)/2$. As a quantified expression, this would be written,

$$(\forall a)(\forall b)(\exists c)[c = (a + b)/2].$$

Now, if a and b are 1 and 2, we still do not know whether the statement is true or false. If the universe of discourse includes all real or all rational numbers, then c exists and is equal to $1\frac{1}{2}$. However, suppose that the universe consists of whole numbers only. Now there is no such c within the universe, and the above statement is false. Hence the truth of a sentence may depend upon the universe of discourse.

The example above also illustrates that a predicate may contain several variables, called "arguments." The above predicate could be written $H(a, b, c)$, or $c = (a + b)/2$. Some of the more complex predicates in psychology arise in the theory of scaling. For example, $L(x, y)$ may mean that object x is judged greater than y. A more elaborate predicate, used in some scaling theories, is

$$J(x, y, z, u),$$

meaning that the subject judges that the difference between objects x and y is greater than the differences between z and u.

Though sentential functions are neither true nor false, they are well-formed formulas and appear within deductions. In a more extended logical calculus one must be able to work with mixtures of sentences and sentential functions.

Along with the rules and axioms of the sentential logic, the logic of predicates uses several new rules and axioms.

New Rules of Formation

$F(x)$, $F(x, y)$, etc., are well-formed formulas. In such expressions, terms inside the parentheses are lower-case letters, and refer to individual variables.

If $A(x)$ is a wff with x a free individual variable, then so are $(\forall x)A(x)$ and $(\exists x)A(x)$.

New Axioms

E. $(\forall x)F(x) \to F(y)$,
F. $F(y) \to (\exists x)F(x)$.

These axioms should be pondered—in particular, note that they permit both introducing and removing free variables.

New Rules of Transformation

γ_1. If A does not contain x, then from $A \to B(x)$ one obtains $A \to (\forall x)B(x)$—*the rule of generalization*.

γ_2. If A does not contain x, then from $B(x) \to A$ one obtains $(\exists x)B(x) \to A$—*the rule of instantiation*.

δ. One may replace all the free and bound variables of a formula by other variables, taking care only that any variable is replaced at each occurrence by the same new variable; that is, different variables are replaced by different variables—*the rule of substitution.*

Development begins with a rule and a few theorems.

γ'. From $\mathbf{A}(x)$ is obtained $(\forall x)\mathbf{A}(x)$.

Proof. If $\mathbf{A}(x)$ is a theorem, then so is $X \vee \mathbf{A}(x)$. For X, we substitute $\overline{X \vee \overline{X}}$, obtaining $\overline{X \vee \overline{X}} \vee \mathbf{A}(x)$, and by definition of $\rightarrow$

$$X \vee \overline{X} \rightarrow \mathbf{A}(x).$$

Now by Rule γ_1,

$$X \vee \overline{X} \rightarrow (\forall x)\mathbf{A}(x).$$

From Theorem 3, $X \vee \overline{X}$, and applying the rule of implication, we have

$$\forall x)\mathbf{A}(x).$$

Theorem 21. $(\forall x)[F(x) \vee \bar{F}(x)]$.

Proof

1. $X \vee \overline{X}$ (Theorem 3),
2. $F(x) \vee \bar{F}(x)$ (Substitution),
3. $(\forall x)[F(x) \vee \bar{F}(x)]$ (Rule γ').

[*Note:* Step two is interesting in that a sentential function is substituted for a sentential variable in the theorem.]

Theorem 22. $(\forall x)F(x) \rightarrow (\exists x)F(x)$.

Proof

1. $(\forall x)F(x) \rightarrow F(y)$ (Axiom E),
2. $F(y) \rightarrow (\exists x)F(x)$ (Axiom F),
3. Theorem (Rule 5).

Theorem 23. $(\forall x)[\mathbf{A} \vee F(x)] \rightarrow \mathbf{A} \vee (\forall x)F(x)$.

Proof

1. $(\forall y)(\mathbf{A} \vee F(y)) \rightarrow \mathbf{A} \vee F(x)$ (Axiom E, and rule of substitution),
2. $(\forall y)(\mathbf{A} \vee F(y)) \rightarrow \overline{\overline{\mathbf{A}}} \vee F(x)$ (Replacement of A by $\overline{\overline{A}}$),
3. $(\forall y)(\mathbf{A} \vee F(y)) \rightarrow (\bar{\mathbf{A}} \rightarrow F(x))$ (Definition of $\rightarrow$).
4. $[(\forall y)(\mathbf{A} \vee F(y)) \,\&\, \bar{\mathbf{A}} \rightarrow F(x)]$ (Rule 7)
5. $(\forall y)(\mathbf{A} \vee F(y)) \,\&\, \bar{\mathbf{A}} \rightarrow (\forall x)F(x)$ (Rule γ)
6. Using Rule 7 and Rule δ, this may be transformed back into the theorem formula.

Theorem 24. $(\forall x)(\mathbf{A} \to F(x)) \to (\mathbf{A} \to (\forall x)F(x))$.

Proof (An easy one, left for the student.)

The above theorems give the reader an introductory idea of the methods of using quantifiers. Some more general rules and properties of the system can be indicated informally here. The statements below, when incorporated formally into the theory, are derived rules.

First, consider any complex sentential function or sentence using only the symbols &, $\lor$, $^-$, and the universal and existential quantifiers. The contradictory of this formula is obtained by first replacing the universal quantifiers by existential quantifiers and conversely, then interchanging the signs & and $\lor$, and finally replacing the sentential and the predicate symbols by their negations.

Example. $(\forall x)(\exists y)[F(x) \lor G(y)]$ has the contradictory

$$(\exists x)(\forall y)[\bar{F}(y) \& \bar{G}(x)].$$

In words, the original sentence said that for every x there existed a y such that either $F(x)$ or $G(y)$. Its contradictory is that there exists at least one x such that, for every y, both $F(y)$ and $G(x)$ are false.

A related result is as follows: Any theorem in the form $\mathbf{A} \to \mathbf{B}$, where $\mathbf{A}$ and $\mathbf{B}$ contain only $\lor$, &, $^-$, and the quantifiers, entails another theorem produced by replacing every universal quantifier by an existential quantifier in the same variable and vice versa, by interchanging the signs & and $\lor$, and by reversing the direction of the implication.

The following example is sufficiently complicated to show that new and (slightly) surprising results may come from this method. The following is a theorem:

$$(\forall x)\mathbf{A}(x) \& (\exists y)(\mathbf{B}(y) \lor \bar{\mathbf{B}}(y)) \to (\exists x)\mathbf{A}(x).$$

The indicated changes lead to

$$(\forall x)\mathbf{A}(x) \to (\exists x)\mathbf{A}(x) \lor (\forall y)(\mathbf{B}(y) \& \bar{\mathbf{B}}(y)).$$

Here the segment after the "$\lor$" is self-contradictory, so the whole formula boils down to $(\forall x)\mathbf{A}(x) \to (\exists x)\mathbf{A}(x)$, a theorem.

Constants and Variables

In the study of mathematics, and especially in applied mathematical models, the student frequently encounters things called "constants" and things called "variables." For example, in learning theory it is common to refer to the learning rate as a constant, and to trials as a variable. From one experiment to another the learning rate certainly varies, and it may well vary from one subject to another and from one group to another within an experiment.

Meanwhile, the same trials $(1, 2, 3, \ldots)$ are used in all experiments. What, then, is meant by constant and variable?

Suppose that a predicate or compound predicate A has two arguments, x and y. This compound predicate is taken to be a succinct statement of the theory. For example, in the simplest linear learning model, the predicate is

$$P(n + 1) = P(n)(1 - \theta) + \theta,$$

and the two arguments have the names n and θ. Here P is the probability of a response on the trial indicated, n refers to trials, and θ is the learning rate.

To make the above equation into a theory, that is, to close the sentential function into a sentence, it is sufficient to quantify over n and θ. Obviously, the same equation is intended to apply to all trials, not just to one. The argument n is a "variable," as indicated by the fact that it is closed by a universal quantifier. In this context, to say that a symbol is a variable means that the theory remains true even if the value of this symbol varies, and this is the significance of the universal quantifier. The above equation does not hold for all possible learning rates, but for only one rate in a given application, so θ is covered by an existential quantifier.

Now there are two possible ways to write the sentence

$$(\exists\theta)(\forall n)[P(n + 1) = P(n)(1 - \theta) + \theta] \tag{3}$$

or

$$(\forall n)(\exists\theta)[P(n + 1) = P(n)(1 - \theta) + \theta]. \tag{4}$$

In Eq. (3), the expression begins with the existential quantifier. It would be read, "There exists a θ such for all $n \ldots$," indicating that a single value of θ suffices for all trials. Therefore it is natural to say that θ is a constant, independent of n. This is the correct formulation. In Eq. (4), the expression begins with the universal quantifier, and would be read, "For all n, there exists a θ such that $\ldots$" This is slightly ambiguous in ordinary English, but in logic is taken to mean that "For each n, there is a $\theta \ldots$," that is, that there may be a different θ for each n. This, of course, is not what the equation would usually mean, for this implies that the learning rate is a variable, in fact, a function of the trial number. Such an idea would, in ordinary mathematical style, be signified by putting a subscript on θ, writing the equation

$$(An)(\exists\theta_n)[P(n + 1) = P(n)(1 - \theta_n) + \theta_n], \tag{5}$$

which makes it more obvious that θ depends upon n.

In Eq. (5), both n and θ_n are variables, n being the independent variable, and θ_n the dependent variable. Formally n is under a universal quantifier, and θ is under a following existential quantifier.

For another example, consider the statement that IQ is a function of mental age (MA) and chronological age (CA). Using quantifiers, and noting that both chronological age and mental age are independent variables, a superficial theory says that

$$(\forall MA)(\forall CA)(\exists IQ)[IQ = MA/CA].$$

According to intelligence-test theory (disregarding errors of measurement), IQ is a constant over years, though it varies from one child to another. The truly independent variables are individuals (i) and chronological age (CA), and the proper formulation is

$$(\forall i)(\exists IQ)(\forall CA)(\exists MA)[IQ_i = MA_{i,CA}/CA],$$

in which the dependent variables are completely subscripted to show what independent variables they depend on.

This example shows that the choice and arrangement of quantifiers is not merely a formal logical trick, but often carries the essential meaning of a theoretical statement. The same formula, IQ = MA/CA, may either be a trivial definition of IQ as in the first case, or the statement of a strong and definite theory of constancy of relative ability, depending merely upon the arrangement of quantifiers.

The discussion of estimation of parameters in Chapter 9 brings up again the question of choice and arrangement of parameters, and shows that there are two sorts of parameters in experiments; those varied by the experimenter, which lie under a universal quantifier, and those under an existential quantifier coming before the universal quantifiers, in a situation here called "constant." In an experiment, those parameters called "constant" are the ones to be estimated.

Satisfaction and Sets

A sentential function is neither true nor false, not being a sentence. It may be a formal tautology, in which case the sentence made by appending the universal quantifier is true; or it may be contradiction, so that the sentence made by appending the existential quantifier is false. However, most of the sentential functions used in science are not of either extreme type—they yield true sentences for some possible cases, and false sentences for others. The function "A correct response was observed on trial n" is a typical example—in most experiments, correct responses are observed on some trials and not on others. Imagine a 10-trial experiment, and suppose that correct responses are found on trials 3, 4, 6, 8, and 9. Then the following sentences are true: $C(3)$, $C(4)$, $C(6)$, $C(8)$, and $C(9)$, whereas the following are false: $C(1)$, $C(2)$, $C(5)$, $C(7)$, and $C(10)$.

What relation does the number 3 have to the sentential function $C(n)$ in the above example? The relation is that if 3 is put in place of the variable, the sentence resulting is true. In this case, 3 *satisfies* the function $C(n)$.

Notice, now, that a sentential function divides the universe into the set of things that satisfy it and the others. A tautology is satisfied by all, a contradiction by none of the universe. It is natural to associate, with a sentential function or predicate, the *set* of things that satisfy it. Then $C(n)$ is satisfied by the set of numbers $\{3, 4, 6, 8, 9\}$.

Definition. An element a satisfies the sentential function $F(x)$ if and only if $F(a)$.

SET THEORY

With every set-theory predicate there is associated a set of things that satisfy the predicate. The set is defined as follows (Let bold-face letters stand for sets, italic letters for predicates):

The set **A** satisfies the predicate A if, for all x, x is an element of **A** if and only if $A(x)$.

It should be noted that a given predicate has a unique set associated with it, but a particular set may satisfy any of several predicates. For example, let $\mathbf{A} = \{1, 2, 3\}$, the set whose only elements are the numbers 1, 2, and 3. This set satisfies the predicate "is an integer less than or equal to 3," and also "is an integral factor of 6."

To simplify the theory it is useful to say that two predicates, A and B, are equivalent (though not identical) if they are satisfied by the same set.

A set is any arbitrary collection of things. The things may be objects, abstract entities like numbers, or anything else. A set of sets is often called a family, and other names for sets include "space," "collection," "range," and "domain." Certain sets have certain abstract conditions or properties of general interest, such as "group," "ring," "lattice," etc.

A set may be designated in three ways: by giving it a name like A, by listing its members inside braces, like $\{1, 2, 3\}$, or by designating a defining property, such as $\{x: x$ has gray hair$\}$, which is read, "The set of all things x such that x has gray hair."

Two sets are equal or identical provided they have exactly the same members. For example, when talking only about integers, the sets $\{x: 1 \leq x < 10\} = \{1, 2, 3, 4, 5, 6, 7, 8, 9\}$. Two listings of elements are equal even if the order of listing is different: for example, $\{1, 2\} = \{2, 1\}$.

One crucial distinction, especially needed in learning theory, is between members and subsets of a set. Consider the set $\{1, 2, 3\}$. Its members or elements are 1, 2, and 3. A subset is defined as a set all of whose members are also members of the parent set. Thus $\{1, 2\}$ is a subset of $\{1, 2, 3\}$. Also,

{1} is a subset of {1, 2, 3}, but 1 is not a subset—it is a member. We must distinguish between 1 and {1}. Here, 1 is a number and {1} is a set whose only member is the number 1.

This does not mean that a set cannot be the member of another set. A set is any collection of things; hence, one can form a set of sets. This sometimes gets a trifle complicated; for example, consider the set {1, {1}}. Here {1} is both a member and a subset. It is a member by virtue of being the second element in the set, and a subset by virtue of the fact that its only member, 1, is also the first member of the parent set. Fortunately there are no such sets in this book, but consideration of the possibilities may clarify the distinction between members and subsets.

A shorthand notation is commonly used in set theory; to say that a is a member of the set B, write $a \in B$. To say that set A is a subset of B, write $A \subset B$. The following logical formula defines the property of being a subset:

$$A \subset B \leftrightarrow (\forall x)(x \in A \rightarrow x \in B). \tag{6}$$

From this it is clearly seen that $A \subset B$ is not a set, but a sentence.

There are also several set-theoretic connections that permit new sets to be made from old; more exactly, these connections permit setting up the names of new sets by a formal calculation. The main connectives are union, complementation, and intersection. They are very close to the logical words *or*, *not*, and *and*.

The *union* of sets A and B, written $A \cup B$, is a set having all the members of A and all the members of B and no others. For example, if $A = \{1, 2, 3\}$ and $B = \{3, 5\}$, then $A \cup B = \{1, 2, 3, 5\}$. Note that although 3 appears in both A and B, it is written only once in $A \cup B$. This is an example of the rule that each element is written and counted only once in a set.

The connection between the set-theoretic connective of union, and the logical word *or*, is seen by writing the union of two sets described by properties. That is, let α and β be predicates, and define the sets

$$A = \{x \colon \alpha(x)\}, \qquad B = \{x \colon \beta(x)\}.$$

Then

$$A \cup B = \{x \colon \alpha(x) \vee \beta(x)\}, \tag{7}$$

where $\vee$ is the disjunction sign.

For example, restrict the discussion to integers from 1 to 10. Let A be the set of odd integers

$$A = \{x \colon x \text{ is odd}\},$$

and let B be the set of integers less than 5,

$$B = \{x \colon x \text{ is less than 5}\}.$$

Then

$$A \cup B = \{x\colon x \text{ is odd or less than } 5\}$$
$$= \{1, 2, 3, 4, 5, 7, 9\}.$$

The numbers 1, 2, 3, and 4 satisfy the condition because they are less than 5, whereas 5, 7, and 9 are included because they are odd. The numbers 1 and 3 are included in the set for both reasons.

Finally, notice that $A \cup B$ is a set, and its elements are drawn from the same universe as A and B.

The *intersection* of sets A and B, written $A \cap B$, is a set having those elements common to A and B and no others. For example, if $A = \{1, 2, 3\}$ and $B = \{3, 5\}$, then $A \cap B = \{3\}$.

The connection between the set-theoretic connective of intersection and the logical word *and* (&) is seen by writing the intersection of two sets described by properties. That is, if

$$A = \{x\colon \alpha(x)\}, \qquad B = \{x\colon \beta(x)\},$$

then

$$A \cap B = \{x\colon \alpha(x) \ \& \ \beta(x)\}. \tag{8}$$

Using the previous example where A stands for the set of odd integers from 1 to 10, and B stands for the numbers less than 5, then

$$A \cap B = \{x\colon x \text{ is odd } and \ x \text{ is less than } 5\} = \{1, 3\}.$$

The *complement* of a set A, written $\bar{A}$, is defined in terms of the universe of discourse, U. In set theory as in any other logical or mathematical argument, one must decide on the scope of study. The examples above use the integers from 1 to 10. In psychological applications the universe may be the set of responses, the set of stimulus situations, the set of cues, the set of people involved in a group discussion, the set of possible total outcomes of an experiment, etc. In every case a well-defined universe is needed for deductive analysis.

The complement, $\bar{A}$, is the set containing all elements of U except those in A. In the universe of integers 1–10, if A is the set of odd integers, then $\bar{A} = \{2, 4, 6, 8, 10\}$. In terms of the defining property,

$$\bar{A} = \{x\colon \bar{\alpha}(x)\}, \tag{9}$$

and complementation corresponds to the use of negation in logic.

Empty Set

Two sets are equal if and only if they have the same members. Now consider the following two sets:

$$A = \{3, 4\}, \qquad B = \{1, 6\}.$$

Obviously, $A \cap B$ has no members.

Now consider the set

$C = \{x: \text{Rat } x \text{ turns both right and left in a } T\text{-maze on trial } 1\}.$

However, in a *T*-maze it is impossible to turn both ways; therefore *C* also has no members. Since the sets $A \cap B$ and *C* have exactly the same members, they must be equal: $A \cap B = C$.

All sets that have no members are equal, or to put it another way, there is just one empty set. This unique set is given a particular name, and it is called Ø in this book.

The Algebra of Sets

The fact that set theory is based upon logic leads to many formulas, each coming from a theorem of logic, that permit and justify calculations. It is not necessary that the student receive here a complete presentation of the foundations of set theory, but some of the calculating formulas can easily be proved.

Theorem 25. $A \cup A \leftrightarrow A$.

Proof

1. $\alpha(x) \vee \alpha(x) \rightarrow \alpha(x)$ [$\alpha(x)$ for *X* in Axiom A],
2. $\alpha(x) \rightarrow \alpha(x) \vee \alpha(x)$ [$\alpha(x)$ for *X* and *Y* in Axiom B],
3. $\{x: \alpha(x) \vee \alpha(x)\} \leftrightarrow \{x: \alpha(x)\}$ (Rule 6),
4. $A \cup A \leftrightarrow A$.

Theorem 26. $A \cap A \leftrightarrow A$.

Proof.   It is relatively straightforward, in the sentential calculus, to prove the theorem $X \& X \leftrightarrow X$. Then as in the proof of 25, substitute $\alpha(x)$ for *X*, and then form the set formula

$$\{x: \alpha(x) \& \alpha(x)\} \leftrightarrow \{x: \alpha(x)\}$$

by Rule 6. From this the theorem follows by renaming the sets.

Theorem 27.   In any theorem of sentential calculus, replace each sentential variable by a corresponding set name, replace $\vee$ by $\cup$, replace & by $\cap$, and retain the bars, now changed in designation from negation to complementation. The resulting formula is a theorem of set theory.

Remark.   This general theorem says that every theorem of sentential logic is also a theorem of set theory, a fact that proves many theorems of set theory merely by copying over work done earlier in logic.

The door from ordinary scientific language to mathematics is open, and mathematical theories in psychology need not leave the firmer ground of "verbal" theory. Mathematical theories are not different in kind from other theories; they are characterized by strong logical structure and by energetic and fruitful application of the methods of deduction. In addition, mathematical models employ certain striking simplifications, intended to increase the simplicity and flexibility of the theory. A theory cannot ask acceptance merely by virtue of being mathematical—it must also be factual, and, for that matter, interesting in its own right. If it is mathematical, then it probably is relatively explicit and leads to quantitative predictions, and may have several other good (and bad) qualities. It is, however, at the basis, a theory like any other, stated in ordinary psychological language about those things and events, real and hypothetical, that are the ordinary subject of a psychologist's discourse.

MEASURES OF SETS

For many purposes, the size of a set is the number of elements in it. If there are infinitely many elements in a set, the concept of number of elements behaves strangely, and a new notion of magnitude is needed. Furthermore, and more relevant for our problems, it may be natural to give some elements more weight than others in calculating the measure of a set.

In concept identification an experimenter can imagine the sets of hypotheses subjects may use, and the measure of a set of hypotheses will correspond to the probability that the subject uses an element of that set. Different hypotheses have different weights, unless great pains are taken to equalize them, and calculations are far off unless account is taken of these weightings.

Consider the following true statements about the number of elements in finite sets:

$$n(X) \geq 0,$$
$$n(\emptyset) = 0,$$
$$n(X \cup Y) = n(X) + n(Y) \quad \text{if and only if} \quad X \cap Y = \emptyset.$$

These conditions give a concept of measurement of sets; and most important of these is the third assumption, that of additivity. The first rule is that no set can have a negative number of elements, and the second says that the empty set has 0 elements. These, along with the third assumption of additivity, characterize the magnitude of the set. A somewhat more abstract concept of magnitude includes, but is not limited to, the number of elements in the set. This is called a measure function. With the finite and discrete sets used in this book, there is nothing complicated about measure functions.

Definition. Let S be a set of sets such that if X and Y are elements of S, then so are $X \cap Y$, $X \cup Y$, and $\bar{X}$. Then the function m, taking elements of

S into the real numbers, is said to be a *measure function* if

1. $(\forall X)[m(X) \geq 0]$,
2. $m(0) = 0$,
3. If $X \cap Y = 0$, then $m(X \cup Y) = m(X) + m(Y)$.

Theorem 28. For any X and Y, $m(X \cup Y) = m(X) + m(Y) - m(X \cap Y)$.

Proof. $X \cup Y$ can be partitioned into three mutually exclusive subsets, $X \cap \bar{Y}$, $X \cap Y$, and $\bar{X} \cap Y$. See Fig. 7.1.

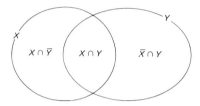

Figure 7.1

Therefore, by the third property of measure functions,

$$m(X \cup Y) = m(X \cap \bar{Y}) + m(X \cap Y) + m(\bar{X} \cap Y). \qquad (10)$$

Since, by elementary set algebra,

$$X = (X \cap Y) \cup (X \cap \bar{Y})$$

and

$$Y = (X \cap Y) \cup (\bar{X} \cap Y),$$

it follows that the right-hand side of Eq. (10) turns into $m(X) + m(Y) - m(X \cap Y)$, as was to be proved.

PROBABILITIES

The probability of an event is how likely it is to happen. Recall that above an event was described by a sentential function; for example, $C_3(\omega)$ was the sentential function, "all subjects were correct on trial 3 of sample ω." Some particular experimental outcomes satisfy $C_3(\omega)$, and they constitute a set C_3.

   An event is probable to the degree that it is satisfied by a large set from the sample space.

Equiprobable Measure

One simple theory is that every element of the sample space Ω is just as probable as any other. Then, calculation of the probability of any event is merely a problem in counting. Suppose that there are $n(C_3)$ elements of Ω in which all subjects are correct on trial 3, and $n(\Omega)$ total in the sample space. Then, assuming an equiprobable measure,

$$P(C_3) = \frac{n(C_3)}{n(\Omega)}. \tag{11}$$

This theory has many applications, but relatively few important and serious uses in psychology at present.

General Discrete Measure

Suppose that every element ω of the sample space Ω has some weight or likelihood, $w(\omega)$. Then, the probability of C_3 is

$$P(C_3) = \sum_{\omega \in C_3} w(\omega) \Big/ \sum_{\omega \in \Omega} w(\omega), \tag{12}$$

and the probability of an event is merely its relative weight. This formulation gives a clear definition of probability, but for many purposes does not give any way of calculating probabilities, except if somehow the weights w are known.

Models

Most of the present book has dealt with theoretical models from which it is possible to predict and calculate probabilities. Some models arise from the structure of the experiment, randomizations used by the experimenter, and general principles, and apply in general to many experiments. Other models are more specific to the experiment in question, and may include crucial psychological assumptions in their formulation.

The point of saying that probabilities arise from models is to emphasize that it is possible to have numerical values of probabilities, without knowing "what the probability is" in any fundamental philosophical sense. When a psychologist (or other scientist, for that matter) states that a certain probability is $P = 0.43$, and someone raises the challenge, "How do you know, what is your proof?" the usual correct answer is, "I don't know, for sure, but it is my hypothesis. If my hypothesis is wrong, I must trust to experiments to disprove it."

The importance of clear logical models is to ensure that hypotheses about probabilities are possible. This does not turn out to be as easy as it seems, for many theories may lead to probabilities greater than 1.0, or to negative probabilities, or to $P(A) = 0.2$, $P(B) = 0.3$, but $P(A \text{ or } B) = 0.7$. The interesting facts about probability theory are the restrictions imposed by the concept of probability—the events described may be chaotic, but the descriptions must be impeccably ordered, or else they become logically impossible.

Mathematically, a probability is a measure function, with the property that the probability of the universe U is given as unity. However, the actual functional use of probability theory is bound up in the notion of a conditional probability.

Conditional Probabilities

Given that a subject is correct on trial 3, what is the probability that he is also correct on trial 4? This asks for what is called a "conditional probability." Philosophically, the above statement is somewhat disturbing, for it is not obvious who is in a position to "give" that the subject is correct on trial 3. The word "given" clearly refers to some sort of hypothesis, but its position within the description of a probability is not at once obvious.

The reason is that the word "given," in such an expression, is not purely logical, but is a concept of probability theory. Equation (12) said that the probability of event C_3 was the sum of the weights of elements in C_3 divided by the sum of weights in the whole sample-space Ω. Now consider a subset of C_3. In the example, C_3 is the set of protocols in which there is a correct response on trial 3. Let C_{34} be the set with correct responses on both trial 3 and trial 4. Clearly, C_{34} is a subset of C_3, written $C_{34} \subset C_3$.

The conditional probability of being correct on trial 4 given a correct response on trial 3, is given by

$$P(C_{34} \mid C_3) = \sum_{C_{34}} w(\omega) \bigg/ \sum_{C_3} w(\omega).$$

A probability *given* C_3 entails a change in the sample space so that C_3, instead of Ω, is treated as the total set of possibilities.

What is the probability of A given B, $P(A \mid B)$? If B is to be the new "universe of discourse," then the only elements of A that are of interest are those that are also within B. Hence

$$P(A \mid B) = \sum_{A \cap B} w(\omega) \bigg/ \sum_{B} (\omega). \tag{13}$$

The notation of Eq. (13) is clear to readers who have used the concept of summation, but it is a bit bulky. If the measure of set A is written $m(A)$,

$$P(A \mid B) = \frac{m(A \cap B)}{m(B)}. \tag{14}$$

An "absolute" probability is simply a probability conditional on the universe, that is, conditional merely upon the experiment's being run.

Independence

In some experiments it is arranged, or strongly believed, that some events are not connected with one another. For example, different subjects may be run quite separately, and the experimenter may be sure there is no connection between the work of one subject and that of any other.

To say that event A is independent of B is to say that $P(A)$ is the same whether or not B has occurred. In one form,

$$P(A \mid B) = P(A). \tag{15}$$

From this follows two theorems.

Theorem 29. If A is independent of B, then

$$P(A \cap B) = P(A)P(B).$$

Proof. By hypothesis,

1. $P(A \mid B) = P(A)$,

2. $\dfrac{m(A \cap B)}{m(B)} = \dfrac{m(A)}{m(U)}$,

3. $m(A \cap B) = \dfrac{m(A)m(B)}{m(U)}$,

4. $P(A \cap B) = P(A)P(B)$.

Theorem 30. If A is independent of B, then B is independent of A.

Proof

1. $m(A \cap B) = \dfrac{m(A)m(B)}{m(U)}$ (Step 3 of the above proof),

2. $\dfrac{m(A \cap B)}{m(A)} = \dfrac{m(B)}{m(U)}$,

3. $P(B \mid A) = P(B)$,

which by definition gives the theorem.

The first of these theorems is of particular strategic importance in calculating probabilities, for it gives $P(A \cap B)$, merely on the basis of knowing $P(A)$ and $P(B)$. In the special case of independence however, the probabilities of intersections are known and are easily calculated.

For example, what is the probability, in a coin-tossing example, of throwing five consecutive heads when $P(\text{heads}) = p$? Everyone knows that the answer is p^5, but how is this simple answer to be justified? In coin-tossing experiments, it is always assumed that the several individual tosses are independent, whence the probability of the intersection of two heads is just the product of their probabilities, and P(heads on 1 and heads on 2 ... and heads on 5) $= P(H_1 \cap H_2 \cap H_3 \cap H_4 \cap H_5) = P(H_1) \cdot P(H_2) \cdots P(H_5)$; since the probabilities are all equal to p, the answer is p^5. With a solid logical underpinning, such simple questions receive complete answers. The apparent simplicity of the question was deceiving, for there were several "simplifying" assumptions bound up right in the question.

Mutually Exclusive Events and Partitions

Another special case of conditional probabilities has $P(A \mid B) = 0$, even though $P(A)$ is not 0. In this case, of course, $m(A \cap B) = 0$, and if the sets are discrete, $A \cap B$ is empty—there is no overlap between A and B.

It is often possible to see that two sets have no overlap, because of their definitions. Consider, for example, all the ways to throw five pennies and have three of them come up heads. Call this set A. Now consider all the ways four coins can come up heads, and call this set B. Clearly, $A \cap B = \emptyset$, since no particular throw of the coins can come up both with three and with four heads.

This is a typical example of mutually exclusive events. Sometimes it is possible and useful to contrive a set of sets with the following properties; all the sets are mutually exclusive of one another, and every element of the universe appears in a set. This division into mutually exclusive and exhaustive subsets is called a *partition*, and the subsets are called *cells*.

Theorem 31. If A and B are cells of a partition, then

$$P(A \cup B) = P(A) + P(B).$$

Proof. This is an axiom of probability.

Theorem 32. If $A_1, A_2, \ldots, A_N$ constitute a partition of the universe, then

$$\sum_{i=1}^{N} P(A_i) = 1.$$

The probability of the union of several cells of a partition is the sum of the probabilities of the cells, and the probability of the intersection of independent subsets is the product of the probabilities of the subsets. These two special cases permit relatively simple mathematical calculations. Therefore, when a complicated situation is to be analyzed, it is commonplace to attempt to identify independent events so that joint probabilities can be calculated, and then to divide the universe into a partition so that results can be added up.

Example. What is the probability of exactly two heads when three coins, all with $P(H) = p$, are tossed—a simple case of the binomial distribution?

The event of two heads comes about with any of the following sequences of three tosses: *HHT*, *HTH*, and *THH*. Consider *HHT*: its probability is $p \cdot p \cdot (1 - p)$, for the three events are independent. Hence the probability of their intersection, their joint probability, is the product of their separate probabilities. The same numerical probability, $p^2(1 - p)$, can be calculated for the other two sequences also. Since the three types of sequences are mutually exclusive, the probability of their union is the sum of their probabilities, and

$$P(\text{two heads of three tosses}) = 3p^2(1 - p).$$

COMPOUND SENTENTIAL FUNCTIONS

A variable is a labeled blank space in a sentence. In simple sentential functions there was only one variable name, x, by which it is signified that only one subject is to be used in the whole compound sentence. Now consider the compound sentential function

$$[F(x) \text{ and } G(y)].$$

The first obvious fact about satisfying such a sentence is that it requires two subjects, one to replace x and a different one to replace y. (Possibly, if x and y have the same range, the same object *might* be used for both variables, but it need not; and if $x = y$, it is only a coincidence.) A psychological example would be, $F(x)$ means that x is the stimulus shown, and $G(y)$ means that y is the response obtained in a given block of trials. Then $F(x)$ will be satisfied by a certain set of stimuli F, and $G(y)$ by a set of responses G. It is obvious that $[F(x) \text{ and } G(y)]$ is not satisfied by $F \cap G$, for since F is a set of stimuli and G a set of responses, $F \cap G$ is presumably empty. The compound sentence $[F(x) \text{ and } G(y)]$ is satisfied by a pair, $\langle s, r \rangle$, $F(s) \text{ and } G(r)$. The set of all pairs, the first element of which is taken from F and the second from G, is called the cartesian product $F \times G$.

Now consider the set satisfying the compound sentence, $[F(x) \text{ or } G(y)]$. Obviously, $F \times G$ satisfies this sentence and, in addition, any pair consisting of an element of F paired with something not in G, and any pair consisting of an element of G paired with something not in F. That is, the set satisfying $F(x) \text{ or } G(y)$ is

$$F \times G \cup F \times \bar{G} \cup \bar{F} \times G.$$

Note that since $F \times G$ is a set (of pairs of elements), it is perfectly possible to take the unions between such sets.

Example. Let n be a variable taking the values 1–10; let $C(n)$ mean that the subject makes a correct response on trial n; and let $A(n)$ mean that a type-A stimulus is shown on trial n. Let m be another variable taking values 1–10.

Suppose that C satisfies $C(n)$; that is, C is the set of trials on which correct responses are made, and A is the set of trials on which type-A stimuli are presented.

For example, suppose that $C = \{5, 8, 9, 10\}$ and $A = \{2, 4, 5, 8\}$. Now

a) Find the set that satisfies $C(n)$ *and* $A(n)$.
   Answer: $A \cap C = \{5, 8\}$.

b) Find the set that satisfies $A(n)$ *or not* $C(n)$.
   Answer: $A \cup \bar{C} = \{2, 4, 5, 8\} \cup \{1, 2, 3, 4, 6, 7\}$
   $= \{1, 2, 3, 4, 5, 6, 7, 8\}$.

c) Find the set that satisfies $C(n)$ *and* $A(m)$.
   Answer: $C \times A = \{\langle 5, 2\rangle, \langle 5, 4\rangle, \langle 5, 5\rangle, \langle 5, 8\rangle, \langle 8, 2\rangle, \langle 8, 4\rangle, \langle 8, 5\rangle,$
   $\langle 8, 8\rangle, \langle 9, 2\rangle, \langle 9, 4\rangle, \langle 9, 5\rangle, \langle 9, 8\rangle, \langle 10, 2\rangle, \langle 10, 4\rangle,$
   $\langle 10, 5\rangle, \langle 10, 8\rangle\}$.

d) Find the set that satisfies $C(n)$ *or* $A(m)$.
   Answer: Consideration reveals that this includes $C(n) \times U$ along with $U \times A(m)$. The first is the set of all pairs having $C(n)$, the second is the set of all pairs having $A(m)$. The union of these two sets satisfies $C(n)$ *or* $A(m)$.

These examples reveal the great difference between compounding $A(n)$ with $B(n)$, two atomic sentential functions with the same variable, and compounding $A(m)$ with $B(n)$, having two different variables. These differences make it clear why a logician cannot merely leave blanks in sentential functions, but must use variables.

Application: Sample Spaces

Consider an experiment with n subjects each tested t trials. Suppose, furthermore, that on each trial each subject can possibly display any of r different responses.

There are an astronomical number of possibilities in any real psychological experiment, which have to be lumped into relatively few broad categories, called "events." However, before combining possibilities into events it is useful to specify the set of logical possibilities.

Let S be the set of subjects, n in number; let T be the set of trials, t in number; and let R be the set of responses that can be made on any trial, being r in number.

Now consider the first subject. On trial 1 he can make any response in the set R. On the first two trials, his possibilities are the set $R \times R$, the cartesian product of R with itself. Therefore, on the set T of trials, the set of possible response protocols is

$$R \times R \times \cdots (t \text{ times}) \cdots \times R.$$

This, of course, displays the assumption that the set of responses R is the same every trial. If not, then the cartesian product of R with itself would be replaced by the cartesian product of the t separate sets of response possibilities, $R_1 \times R_2 \times \cdots \times R_t$.

An element of the above set is a possible response protocol or set of responses made by a single subject. Let the set of response protocols be called R^*. Now, each of the n subjects in the experiment can produce an element of R^*, a protocol. The set of possible total data sheets is the cartesian product of R^* with itself n times, that is,

$$\Omega = R^* \times R^* \times \cdots (n \text{ times}) \cdots \times R^*,$$

the set of possible outcomes of the experiment.

The sample space is the cartesian product of cartesian products. In terms easily recognized by an experimenter, Ω is the universe of all complete, detailed data sheets, where ω is an element of Ω.

A possible experimental event is, "All subjects were correct on trial 3." Clearly, this sentence as it stands is neither universally true nor universally false, when applied to the usual experiment. "All subjects were correct on trial 3 of outcome ω" is a sentential function with variable ω that could be written

$$C_3(\omega).$$

This sentential function, now, is satisfied by a certain subset of Ω, and that subset may be called C_3.

Thus an event is something that may or may not happen. One might say that $C_3(\omega)$ "happens" if an experiment is conducted; the outcome (data sheet) is ω_1, and $C_3(\omega_1)$.

Counting

The probability of a sentential function depends, first, on how many elements of the sample space satisfy the function. In physics, it is commonplace to assume that all elements of the sample space have the same probability, so that counting yields the answer. In psychology, counting may not suffice to yield the answer, but it is still necessary to be able to count instances.

Suppose that there are a elements in A, b elements in B, and i elements in the intersection $A \cap B$. Then the number of elements in various associated sets is as follows. Let $n(X)$ denote the number of elements in set X:

$$n(A \cup B) = a + b - i,$$
$$n(A \times B) = ab,$$
$$n[A \times A \times \cdots (r \text{ times}) \cdots \times A] = a^r.$$

Example. A pair of dice are thrown in craps. A failure is called at once if the first throw adds up to 2 (snake eyes), 3 (little Joe), or 12 (Boxcars). How many ways can an immediate failure occur?

A 2 can occur only if the two tosses are $\langle 1, 1 \rangle$. Thus the set S of throws yielding snake eyes is simply $\{\langle 1, 1 \rangle\}$. The set J, for little Joe, contains two elements; $J = \{\langle 1, 2 \rangle, \langle 2, 1 \rangle\}$. The set of boxcars again has only one element, $B = \{\langle 6, 6 \rangle\}$.

One can easily see that the set of failures, F, is

$$F = S \cup J \cup B.$$

Since none of the subsets S, J, or B has an intersection with one another,

$$n(F) = n(S) + n(J) + n(B)$$
$$= 1 + 2 + 1 = 4.$$

Consider a second example: a pair of dice are thrown, and a bet is made that both dice will have three or lower. Define the set $L = \{1, 2, 3\}$, the lower values. It is evident that the sentential function is satisfied by the set of pairs, $L \times L$. Since $n(L) = 3$, it follows that $n(L \times L) = 9$.

Example. A learning experiment is conducted in which each response is scored as correct, error, or omission. Thus the set of possibilities on a given trial is $P = \{c, e, o\}$. The set of possibilities in a four-trial experiment is $P \times P \times P \times P$. Therefore the number of possibilities, in four trials, is $3^4 = 81$. In an 8-trial experiment, there would be $3^8 = 6561$ possibilities.

Consider the number of sequences in which the subject is correct on the fourth trial. This sentential function, "Correct on trial 4," is satisfied by all of the elements of the set

$$P \times P \times P \times \{c\},$$

which has $3 \times 3 \times 3 \times 1 = 27$ members.

Exercise. In the four-trial experiment,

a) Sentential function is, "Subject fails, i.e., either omission or error, on the first two trials." How many sequences satisfy this function?
   Answer: This function is satisfied by the set $\{o, e\} \times \{o, e\} \times P \times P$. The number of sequences satisfying it is $2 \times 2 \times 3 \times 3 = 36$.

b) The subject is correct on trials 3 and 4. What set of sequences satisfies this, and how many elements in the set?

c) The subject is either correct on trials 2 and 3 or is correct on trials 2 and 4. What is the set of sequences satisfying this sentential function, and how many members does it have?

Notice that when dealing with a four-trial experiment, the elements of the universe consist of four-trial sequences of responses. A set of sequences is written as the cartesian product of four sets. This point is part of the foundation under the mathematical theory of learning.

Example. Calculating the number of elements in a set may become more complex when the set is described both by the formation of cartesian products and by the use of intersection, union, and complementation, as when the sentential function uses more than one variable (requiring use of the cartesian product) but then makes compound statements about the multivariable elements constructed.

Consider, for a simplest case, the statement that two tosses of a coin come out with the same result, both heads or both tails. The variables are X_1 and X_2, the outcomes of the two tosses. The statement, "both come up heads," is satisfied by the set having only one element $\{\langle H, H \rangle\}$, formed as the cartesian product of the set $\{H\}$ with itself, and the statement, "both come up tails," is satisfied by $\{\langle T, T \rangle\}$. The union of these two sets is $\{\langle H, H \rangle, \langle T, T \rangle\}$.

A more realistic case arises in the process of counting. Consider a four-trial experiment with two outcomes on each trial, correct (C) or wrong (W), so that the set of possibilities on a trial is

$$P = \{C, W\}.$$

Now consider the statement, "The subject makes three errors." It is satisfied by the set of sequences,

$$\{\langle C, W, W, W \rangle, \quad \langle W, C, W, W \rangle, \quad \langle W, W, C, W \rangle, \quad \langle W, W, W, C \rangle\}.$$

Permutations and Combinations

When objects are counted, they are counted in a particular order. The same objects might have been counted in a different order, in fact, in a number of different orders. How many? This is the question of the number of permutations.

Of k objects, any of the k can be placed first, any of the $k - 1$ remaining can be placed second, etc. Hence the number of permutations of k objects is

$$P_k = k(k - 1)(k - 2) \cdots 2 \cdot 1 = k!$$

or k-factorial.

This is the number of elements in the cartesian product of the sets S, $S - \{x_1\}$, $S - \{x_1\} - \{x_2\}$; that is,

$$P^* = S \times S - \{x_1\} \times S - \{x_1\} - \{x_2\} \times \cdots \times \cdots$$

where x_1 is the first element of the permutation, x_2 the second, etc. Since the sets have $k, k - 1, k - 2$, etc., elements in them, the numerical result holds.

Now consider all ordered sets of j of k objects, where j is less than k. For example, from five words, the problem is to form all ordered lists of three. The first on the list can be any of 5, the next any of the remaining 4, etc.; that is,

$$P_{j,k} = k(k-1)\cdots(k-j+1)$$

is the number of permutations of k things taken j at a time.

A numerical example will show another way of expressing this number. Consider all permutations of 4 things 2 at a time:

$$4 \cdot 3.$$

Now consider 4 things 3 at a time:

$$4 \cdot 3 \cdot 2,$$

and 4 things 4 at a time:

$$4 \cdot 3 \cdot 2 \cdot 1.$$

Now, the first of these, $4 \cdot 3$, can be expressed as $4 \cdot 3 \cdot 2 \cdot 1/2 \cdot 1 = 4!/2!$. The second is $4!/1!$ In general, the numerator is $(k-j)!$ in the examples above. Now look at 6 things taken 4 at a time: the number is $6 \cdot 5 \cdot 4 \cdot 3 = 6!/2! = k!/(k-j)!$

Combinations

Now consider a set S of k objects, and divide or partition it into two parts A and B. Now, how many sets A and B can be constructed such that A has exactly j elements, and A and B partition S, given that S has k elements.

There are several ways to determine the number of different combinations of k things taken j at a time. However, a useful insight is obtained if we begin by laying all k objects out in some permutation, then letting A be the first j of them. There are a total of $k!$ permutations of S, but this does not mean that there are $k!$ combinations of k things taken j at a time; the reason is that there are several different permutations of S that yield the same combinations A and B.

A particular permutation of S puts a particular order of the first j elements, constituting A, and a particular order the remaining $k-j$ elements, constituting B. The same set A can be permuted in any way, and there are $j!$ ways to make that permutation. For each permutation of A, there are $(k-j)!$ permutations of the $k-j$ elements of B. Therefore there are $j!\,(k-j)!$ different permutations of S, all of which give the same combination A, B.

The set of different permutations of S, all of which lead to the same A, B, are called an "equivalence class" of permutations. The total number of $k!$ permutations of S can be divided into a number of equivalence classes; since each equivalence class contains $j! (k - j)!$ permutations, it follows that the number of equivalence classes must be

$$_jC_k = k!/j! (k - j)!,$$

which is the number of different combinations of k things taken j at a time.

This number is also often written

$$\binom{k}{j}.$$

This is called the binomial number, because of its role in expansion of binomial numbers of the form

$$(a + b)^k = a^k + \binom{k}{1}a^{k-1}b + \binom{k}{2}a^{k-2}b^2 + \cdots + \binom{k}{j}a^k b^j + \cdots + b^n.$$

$$(16)$$

Here the binomial coefficients appear because the term with r a's and $n - r$ b's, can be constructed in different ways, and the number of ways is just the number of combinations of k things taken j at a time.

Because it appears in several forms and is useful in general, it is well to fix the general binomial formula given above. First, it permits an expansion of $(a + b)^k$ into many terms. Even more often it is useful in simplifying a complex expression, which may be arranged into the form of the right-hand part of Eq. (16).

SUMMARY

This chapter began with elementary logic of sentences, introduced sentential variables and quantifiers, brought in sets and related them to sentential functions, and then introduced measures on sets and probabilities on sentential functions. From this, it has become possible to give complete answers to some very simple questions of probability.

The point is to show that probability theory, sensibly applied, can make perfectly good logical sense. The statements of a probability model about a phenomenon do not *intrinsically* deviate from the ordinary logical formulation of the situation.

Since $m(A \cap B)$ cannot be deduced from $m(A)$ and $m(B)$, general probability theory is not very much use in making calculations. With the introduction of the concepts of independence and of partitions, it became possible to specify special models or situations that can conveniently be calculated.

CHAPTER EIGHT

Random Variables, Generating Functions, and Stochastic Processes

This chapter contains a brief presentation of mathematical topics commonly used in psychology. It is not intended that the reader learn these topics, unless he has some acquaintance with the concepts and methods of probability theory. However, the mathematical information needed by psychologists is often scattered, and is only part of the usual probability course in a mathematics department. Consequently, a summary of basic topics of special interest in psychology has been prepared here.

FOUNDATION CONCEPTS

Universe

The first task in framing any use of probability theory is to determine the set of logical possibilities. A logical possibility is best thought of as a complete outcome of an experimental session, as recorded on a data sheet.

In all experiments other than in social psychology, it is assumed that the subjects do not affect one another and are independent. Therefore the theory concerns an individual subject, and a *logical possibility* is one possible way that any individual's data sheet might appear.

Consider, for example, a subject who masters a list of paired-associate items. Suppose that in the experiment to be studied, the experimenter ignored the specific order of presentation of items within a trial, and scored each response as correct (0) or wrong (1). Then the data sheet might appear as follows:

Subject: John Brown

Item	Trial	1	2	3	4	5	6	7	8	9	10
GEX		1	1	0	0	0	0	1	0	0	0
VUH		0	1	0	0	0	0	0	0	0	0
ZOK		1	1	1	1	0	1	1	1	1	1
etc.											

Now suppose there are six items in the list, and ten trials of training are given. There are therefore 60 responses to be recorded, and any can be either a 0 or a 1. Thus the total number of logical possibilities is 2^{60}. Since $2^{10} = 1024$ is near 1000 or 10^3, this universe has approximately

$$10^{18} = 1,000,000,000,000,000,000$$

points in it.

A data sheet is a point or element of the universe, U. The universe has to be defined in such a way that every possible outcome is included. This is a question about how the experiment is organized and how the data are recorded, not about how the subjects behave in the situation.

In most experiments, individual subjects can usually be considered as independent elements in the universe. Some experiments can be given a simplified analysis by making smaller units the elements of the universe. For example, in some models of paired-associate learning, the experimental unit is a single subject-item sequence. It is assumed in this analysis that the several items learned by a subject are independent. While this assumption is almost certainly erroneous, the resulting analysis may be employed because individual differences and intercorrelations are not at issue, or because it provides a baseline from which to measure individual differences. Analyses may disregard important aspects of data in order to display other, more relevant facts more clearly and simply. Well-chosen simplifying assumptions have great importance and value in theoretical analysis.

The effect of simplifying assumptions is to yield a more powerful analysis of data. If an analysis assumes independence of items, then it has observations on many simple experimental units: the number of subjects times the length of list, instead of fewer, more complex entities, such as subjects. If the analysis assumes equality of parameters across subjects, then a single set of parameters can be estimated for the experiment; this leaves more information with which to evaluate the theory. Furthermore, there are often statistical tests that can detect serious errors in the simplifying assumptions.

Sampling distributions. In statistical work, the sampling distribution, that is, the probability of configurations of outcomes of whole samples of subjects may also be necessary. For example, suppose that each point in U, each particular data sheet, yields a certain total number of errors T. A group of 20 subjects will therefore give a mean $\bar{T}$. Suppose the sampling distribution of $\bar{T}$ is needed. This requires the probability of a point that is not a single subject's data sheet, but a bundle of data sheets for 20 subjects. If the 20 subjects are independent, the probability of any group of 20 subjects can (in principle) be calculated if the probabilities of individual subjects are available. A whole sample of 20 subjects, or more exactly that bundle of data sheets, is an element of a larger *sample space* Ω. If samples of size N are considered, then the logically-possible samples are all bundles of N individual data sheets.

Cartesian products. Let

$$A = \{a_1, a_2, \ldots, a_r\},$$
$$B = \{b_1, b_2, \ldots, b_s\}.$$

Then the set of ordered couples,

$$\{(a_1, b_1), (a_1, b_2), \ldots, (a_2, b_1), \ldots, (a_r, b_s)\},$$

is called the *cartesian product* of A and B, and is written $A \times B$.

A sample of two subjects can be any data sheet paired with any other data sheet. Therefore the set of samples of two is $U \times U$, the cartesian product of the universe with itself. The sample space of a group of N subjects is

$$\Omega_N = U \times U \times \cdots (N \text{ times}) \cdots \times U.$$

Relations and Functions

Let A and B be two sets. The cartesian product $A \times B$ contains *all possible* pairs. A *relation* would contain only some pairs. For example, let A and B be two sets of weights, and have the subject compare an element of A with an element of B on each trial. If the complete experiment is carried out, then the set of pairs tested is $A \times B$. If C is the relation "Is compared with," then all elements of A are compared with all elements of B, and relation C happens to include the whole cartesian product. Another relationship is "Is apparently heavier than," H. Presumably, only some elements of A are judged heavier than some elements of B. If all the pairs are singled out from $A \times B$ such that the element of A in the pair is judged heavier than the element of B, then that pair is an element of a new set of pairs, which is identified with the relation H.

Abstractly, then, a relation is a subset of the cartesian product of the sets involved. The idea can be generalized to cartesian products of several sets, so that some elements of $A \times B \times C$, where A, B, and C are sets, constitute a "ternary" relation.

A function is a special relation between two sets (or between several sets, called the domain, and one last set, the range) with the following restriction: To each element of the domain, there corresponds exactly one element of the range. Thus to say that b is a function of a is to say that if you pick the element a from the domain A, then you have uniquely determined which element b from the range B will go with it.

The relation H, heavier than, is not a function in general. If an element a from A is singled out, one would probably find that there are at least two elements in B, say, b_1 and b_2, and that a is heavier than either of them. That is,

$$(a, b_1) \qquad \text{and} \qquad (a, b_2)$$

are both elements of the relation H, and since there are two distinct elements, then B is not a function of A. However, suppose that A and B are finite sets, and the objects can be weighed with enough precision so that there are no ties. Then the relation "nearest in weight" is a function. For any $a_i \in A$, there is just one $b_j \in B$ which satisfies the relation, that is, which is nearer in weight to a_i than any other element of B. The difference between the two cases is shown in Fig. 8.1.

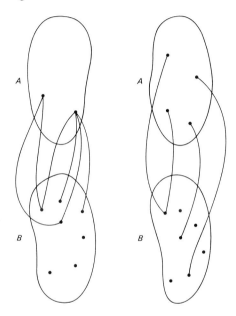

Figure 8.1

Let r_1 be the relation shown on the left in Fig. 8.1, and let r_2 be the relation shown on the right; r_2 makes B a function of A, but r_1 does not. Then we say that r_2 is a function with domain A and range B.

Note that r_2 makes B a function of A, but does not make A a function of B. However, by r_3, shown in Fig. 8.2, each b corresponds to just one a, and each a corresponds to just one b. That is, B is a function of A, and A is a function of B. Then r_3 is called a one-to-one function. Thus r_3 is a function with domain A and range B, and the inverse of r_3 is also a function.

Scientific theories are particularly concerned with numerical functions. For example, consider the sample-space U consisting of a subject's performance on six paired-associates items for ten trials. Let T be the total errors made on the items in those trials. Then there is a relation between u, an element of the universe U, and the set of integers from 0 to 60, here called I_{60}. Furthermore, this relation is a function, for if any particular data sheet

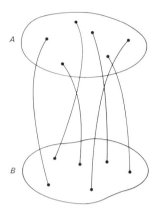

Figure 8.2

is considered u_0, there must be some one particular number of errors on that sheet, one element from I_{60}, and no other. Thus the number of errors is a *function* of the universe U. Obviously, there are many such functions: the number of errors on trial 1, the number of errors on item 3, the number of correct responses before the last error, the number of errors before the first success, etc. Almost anything of this sort that one can think of is a function of the universe U.

Random Variable

In general, a random variable is a function of the universe U. This book uses only simple numerical functions, such as the number of errors, the proportion of judgments above a number k, etc. The general theory of random variables is considerably more complex, because it delineates the relationship between different random variables, a problem which needs discussion only in very simple cases.

To every possible value of the random variable (i.e., to every element of the range) there corresponds some subset of the domain. Each element of the domain yields a particular value of the range, because the random variable is a function, but a given value may correspond to several different elements of U. In the previous example, using the data sheet from a paired-associates experiment, note that if a data sheet is singled out (element of U), then T, the total errors, can easily be determined; but if it is known that the sheet is to have, for example, exactly one error, this still leaves a set of 60 different elements of U, since that one error might be on any of ten trials of any of six items.

The probability that the random variable T takes a particular value k is defined as follows: Let U_k be that subset of the universe such that if u is an element of U_k, then $T(u) = k$; and if u is not an element of U_k, $T(u) \neq k$. Then the probability that $T = k$ is given by

$$P(T = k) = P(U_k). \tag{1}$$

The point of this remark is to show the connection between probabilities written on subsets of the universe, such as U_k, and probabilities regarding random variables.

To calculate the distribution of some random variable, that is, the probability that it takes the various possible values, it is only necessary to identify the subsets $U_0, U_1, \ldots$ of the universe corresponding to each value of T, and then calculate the probabilities of these subsets. Of course, if the function should happen to be continuous, the mathematical situation is considerably more complex because of the idealizations involved, but the general philosophy remains the same. All probabilities are ultimately probabilities on subsets of U; and the distribution of any random variable is induced from the basic probability space.

Some Simple Distributions

One very simple type of experiment yields the four basic distributions from which others are built. Imagine an experimenter tossing a coin for one or more trials. The coin comes up heads (H) or tails (T) and the probability of heads is p. The probability of heads p is the same every trial, no matter how long the experiment continues, or what may have happened on previous trials.

Bernoulli distribution. Consider a single toss, where a random variable is the number of heads on that toss. The universe consists of two logical possibilities, $\{H, T\} = U$. The random variable which is here called N takes value 1 if a head comes up, 0 if a tail comes up. It is therefore the function

$$N = \{(H, 1), (T, 0)\},$$

whence

$$P(N = 1) = P(H) = p, \qquad P(N = 0) = P(T) = 1 - p. \tag{2}$$

This is called the *Bernoulli distribution.* The above considerations apply to any event which may be considered to have a fixed probability p of occurring; the argument in no way depends upon the use of a coin or any other particular physical realization; a human or animal subject may yield a Bernoulli distribution on a given trial.

Binomial distribution. Consider a set of n tosses of the same coin, where a random variable N_n is the number of heads on all the tosses taken together. The universe U now consists of the 2^n possible arrangements of H and T

on the n tosses. For a simple example, if $n = 3$, then U is

$$
\begin{array}{ll}
H\ H\ H\} & U_3, \\[4pt]
\left.\begin{array}{l} H\ H\ T \\ H\ T\ H \\ T\ H\ H \end{array}\right\} & U_2, \\[12pt]
\left.\begin{array}{l} H\ T\ T \\ T\ H\ T \\ T\ T\ H \end{array}\right\} & U_1, \\[12pt]
T\ T\ T\} & U_0,
\end{array}
$$

consisting of $2^3 = 8$ elements.

Note that the list of elements of U can be partitioned into four subsets, the subsets having 0, 1, 2, and 3 heads.

Since the successive tosses of the coin are independent,

$$ P(H\ T\ H) = p(1 - p)p, $$

which is the product of the probabilities of the independent component tosses. Then, with a sample of size n, the probability of any particular element of U_k is

$$ P(u\colon u \text{ an element of } U_k) = p^k(1 - p)^{n-k}, $$

for any element of U_k has k heads and $n - k$ tails. Since all elements of U_k have the same probability, the total probability of the set U_k is just the above times the number of elements in U_k. This is the number of different ways one can arrange k heads on the n tosses, i.e., the number of distinct elements of U_k. This is

$$ \text{Number of elements of } U_k = \binom{n}{k} = \frac{n!}{k!\,(n-k)!}. \tag{3} $$

From this we can derive the *binomial distribution* directly:

$$ P(N_n = k) = \binom{n}{k} p^k (1 - p)^{n-k} \qquad (k = 1, \ldots, n). \tag{4} $$

Geometric distribution. Now suppose that the experimenter tosses the coin, not for a fixed number of trials, but only until the first head appears. The random variable of interest is now F, the trial of the first head. The universe U is now infinite, for it consists of the elements

$$
\begin{array}{l}
H \\
T\ H \\
T\ T\ H \\
T\ T\ T\ H \\
\cdots
\end{array}
$$

and so forth, with no end. In this case, however, as in the case of the Bernoulli distribution, there is only one element of U for each possible value of the random variable F; that is,

$$F[T \ T \cdots (k - 1 \text{ times}) \cdots T \ H] = k,$$

for an element with $k - 1$ consecutive T's followed by an H has its first H on trial k. Again, applying the basic assumption that the trials are independent, it follows that

$$P[T \ T \ T \cdots (k - 1 \text{ times}) \cdots T \ H] = (1 - p)^{k-1}p, \qquad k = 1, 2, \ldots$$

and because of the one-one correspondence,

$$P(F = k) = (1 - p)^{k-1}p \qquad (k = 1, 2, \ldots), \tag{5}$$

called the *geometric distribution*.

Another random variable, very closely related to the trial of the first head, is the trial of the last tail, understood to be zero if H occurs on the first toss. Call this random variable L and

$$P(L = k) = (1 - p)^k p \qquad (k = 0, 1, \ldots), \tag{6}$$

another version of the geometric distribution. In applying the geometric distribution, it is important to look closely at the index variable (k in the examples above) to see whether it ranges from 0 or from 1 to infinity.

Negative binomial or Pascal distribution. The same coin is being tossed, but now the experimenter stops the experiment when some particular number k of heads have been observed. The random variable is N_k, the trial on which the kth head is observed.

Consider the set U_N of sequences in which the kth head occurs on trial N. Each such sequence contains exactly k heads, hence $N - k$ tails. Thus each particular sequence has probability

$$P(u \colon u \text{ an element of } U_N) = p^k(1 - p)^{N-k}. \tag{7}$$

The last Nth element must be a head; the remaining $k - 1$ heads can be arranged over any of the $N - 1$ trials in any arrangement. The number of such arrangements is the binomial number

$$\binom{N - 1}{k - 1}.$$

Since every particular sequence with its kth head at trial N has the same probability, given in Eq. (7), the probability of the whole subset U_N is just the number of sequences times their probability, or

$$P(N_k = N) = \binom{N-1}{k-1} p^k (1-p)^{N-k} \qquad (N = 1, \ldots), \qquad (8)$$

the *negative binomial or Pascal distribution*.

This distribution resembles the binomial distribution, Eq. (4). However, considered in the binomial distribution is the probability of k heads in n tosses; k is the random variable, and n is a characteristic of the experimenter's plan. The random variable, the number of heads, ranges from 0 to n. In the negative binomial distribution, the probability of N trials to get exactly k heads is considered; N is the random variable, and k is part of the experimenter's plan. The random variable N ranges from 1 to infinity.

The difference in the binomial numbers comes about because, in the binomial distribution, it is not known where any of the heads may be on the n trials. In the case of the negative binomial, since trial N is the trial of the kth head, it is known there must be a head on trial N; hence there are only $k-1$ heads free to be distributed over $N-1$ trials.

These four distributions, the Bernoulli, binomial, geometric, and negative binomial, arise from four different questions that may be asked about a sequence of coin tosses or other simple, independent, two-alternative events that are independent and all have the same probability. It is true that in many psychological experiments, one event affects others. It may be relatively difficult to *produce* a sequence of independent events with constant probability, and the resulting procedures would not be particularly interesting. However, other psychological situations are somewhat more complicated to analyze than the Bernoulli trials, and the apparent complications may turn out (as seen in Chapter 2, especially) to be the result of a simple conjunction of two or more simple coin-tossing systems.

Moments

The mean of a set of data is calculated by adding up all the scores and dividing by the number of cases. A "score," in the present terminology, is a value of the random variable in question, say, T. If data is first grouped, putting together all cases having the same score, and then dividing each subgroup sum by the total number of cases, the same result as above is obtained. However, in this case the value of the random variable was taken, multiplied by the relative frequency of that value, and summed. Thus

$$M(T) = \sum_k f(T = k) \cdot k, \qquad (9)$$

where $f(T = k)$ is the relative frequency with which T takes on the value k in the experiment.

$M(T)$ depends upon the outcome of a particular experiment and the frequencies that happen to have been observed. Suppose that the relative frequencies f are replaced by the probabilities p. This produces the expectation of T, which is sometimes referred to as the "true mean." By definition,

$$E(T) = \sum_k p(T = k)k, \tag{10}$$

where $\sum_k$ means the sum of these probabilities over the range of values of T.

The relation between the mean $M(T)$ and the expectation $E(T)$ is relatively confusing. First, note that $M(T)$ arises from a particular set of data, is known (for a given experiment), and will vary from one experiment to another. It is a random variable. Unless the probability distribution itself in numerical values is known, $E(T)$ is not known as a numerical value. However, $E(T)$ is a number, not a random variable; $E(T)$ is often estimated by using $M(T)$, that is, by estimating the expectation using the observed mean. What is important, for the present, is not to confuse M and E.

$E(T)$ is called the "first moment" of the random variable T. Higher "raw moments" are given by

$$\mu^r = \sum_k P(T = k)k^r = E(T^r), \tag{11}$$

which is the rth raw moment. Thus the rth raw moment is the expectation of T^r.

For many statistical purposes, moments about the mean are used instead of raw moments. The rth moment about the point c is defined as

$$\mu_c^r = E[(T - c)^r]. \tag{12}$$

This is most often used in the case of central moments, in which $c = E(T)$. Then, of course, if $c = E(T)$,

$$\mu_c^1 = E(T - c) = \sum_k P(T = k)(k - c)$$
$$= E(T) - E(T) = 0. \tag{13}$$

The second central moment is called the variance:

$$\text{Var}(T) = E[(T - c)^2] = \sum_k P(T = k)(k - c)^2, \tag{14}$$

where c is the first moment.

The mean and variance have particular interest in statistics, because the conventional way of expressing the two parameters of a normal distribution is as μ and σ^2. These are equal to the first moment (expectation) and second central moment (variance) of the distribution. In other distributions, such as the geometric, negative, binomial, etc., the moments are relatively less important, though they have many uses and they tie into more advanced problem-solving methods.

COMPOUND PROCESSES

Psychological processes are sometimes thought to consist of sequences of parts. For example, reaction time may be the result of a sequence of elementary events, learning a complex problem may be a process of mastering a sequence of difficulties, and making a decision or judgment may consist of a sequence of steps.

Suppose that a reaction requires a subject to perform acts A, B, and C. Then if those acts are sequentially arranged, the total reaction time is the time used in A plus the time in B plus the time in C. The theoretical idea that parts are arranged in sequence leads to the mathematical idea that a random variable of the total process can be treated as the sum of random variables, one for each part.

Of course, the parts of a process can be arranged in many complicated ways. However, the idea of a simple sequential arrangement is clear. The subject cannot engage upon part B until A is performed, so the two stages are strongly related. However, the time spent in B, if it is variable, does not depend upon accidental variations in the time spent in A. This may not be a necessary property of a simple sequential arrangement, but it is a profound simplification of the problem. Thus for theoretical as well as mathematical reasons, it is interesting to study sequential processes in which the random variables in the parts are independent and are added together to yield the whole.

Convolutions

Let U and V be two component random variables, and $T = U + V$. For compactness, short names are introduced:

$$u_k = P(U = k), \qquad v_k = P(V = k), \qquad t_k = P(T = k).$$

Assume, as in the case of temporal variables, that $k = 0, 1, \ldots$ in the present experiment. Then

$$T = 0 \text{ if and only if } U = 0 \text{ and } V = 0,$$

whence

$$t_0 = u_0 v_0.$$

$$T = 1 \text{ if either } U = 0 \text{ and } V = 1, \text{ or } U = 1 \text{ and } V = 0.$$

Therefore

$$t_1 = u_0 v_1 + u_1 v_0.$$

In general, $T = k$ if there exists a $j \leq k$ such that $U = j$ and $V = k - j$. Therefore, in general,

$$t_k = \sum_{j=0}^{k} u_j v_{k-j}. \tag{15}$$

Thus Eq. (15) is a way of composing a probability distribution $\{t_k\}$ from two others, $\{u_k\}$ and $\{v_k\}$. The process is so commonly used that it is given a special name and symbol: $\{t_k\}$ is the *convolution* of $\{u_k\}$ and $\{v_k\}$, and is written

$$\{t_k\} = \{u_k\} * \{v_k\}. \tag{16}$$

In general, if random variable T is the sum of independent random variables U and V, then the distribution of T is the convolution of the distribution of U and V.

Algebra of convolutions. The general idea and notion of a convolution are helpful in permitting one to generalize the idea to assemblies of more than two components. Let $D_1, D_2, \ldots$, etc., be various distributions. It is easy to show that

$$D_1 * D_2 = D_2 * D_1, \tag{17}$$

for the two expressions have the same sum computed in opposite orders. Furthermore,

$$D_1 * (D_2 * D_3) = (D_1 * D_2) * D_3; \tag{18}$$

that is, the process of forming convolutions is associative. These facts make it sensible to use expressions such as

$$\mathop{*}_{j=1}^{N} F_j$$

to express the convolution of N distributions.

Of particular interest are many convolutions of the same distribution with itself; the result of adding a number of random variables, all of which have the same probability distribution. It is conventional to write

$$D * D = D^{*(2)}$$

and, in general,

$$D * D * \cdots (N \text{ times}) \cdots * D = D^{*(N)}$$

is the N-fold convolution of a distribution D with itself.

Binomial as a convolution of Bernoulli distributions. Consider a Bernoulli distribution in the form (p, q), where $q = 1 - p$. Call this distribution β. Then

$$\beta * \beta = (p, q) * (p, q) = (p^2, 2pq, q^2),$$

as is seen by direct application of Eq. (15). The result is binomial distribution with parameter $n = 2$, and will be called bin_2. Now

$$\text{bin}_2 * \beta = (p^2, 2pq, q^2) * (p, q) = (p^3, 3p^2q, 3pq^2, q^3)$$

or a binomial distribution with parameter $n = 3$, bin_3. By informal induction, it appears that the binomial distribution is the convolution of n Bernoulli distributions. This makes sense; in the coin-tossing examples, the Bernoulli is the distribution of heads in a single toss, and the binomial is the distribution of the number of heads in n tosses.

Proof of the assertion progresses by mathematical induction, proving that the convolution of bin_n and β results in bin_{n+1}. Let $P_n(k)$ be the probability of k heads in n tosses, or more exactly, the probability that the total random variable takes the value k when it is composed of n component Bernoulli-distributed random variables. Then take the convolution of bin_n with β, and the result at the value k is

$$P_{n+1}(k) = P_n(k-1)p + P_n(k)q \tag{19}$$

by application of Eq. (15). Substituting the binomial expressions,

$$P_{n+1}(k) = \binom{n}{k-1}p^k q^{n-k+1} + \binom{n}{k}p^k q^{n-k+1}$$
$$= \left[\binom{n}{k-1} + \binom{n}{k}\right]p^k q^{n+1-k}. \tag{20}$$

It is not difficult to show that

$$\binom{n}{k-1} + \binom{n}{k} = \binom{n+1}{k} \tag{21}$$

as follows:

$$\frac{n!}{(n-k+1)!(k-1)!} + \frac{n!}{(n-k)!k!}$$
$$= \frac{n!}{(n-k)!(k-1)!}\left[\frac{1}{k} + \frac{1}{n+1-k}\right]$$
$$= \frac{n!(n+1)}{(n-k)!(k-1)!(n+1-k)(k)} = \binom{n+1}{k}$$

When this result is combined with Eq. (20), the result is

$$P_{n+1}(k) = \binom{n+1}{k}p^k q^{n+1-k},$$

which is the kth term of the binomial distribution bin_{n+1}.

Thus the convolution of bin_n with the Bernoulli distribution β yields bin_{n+1}. It was shown above that $\beta * \beta = \text{bin}_2$, and the two facts together show that, in general, by mathematical induction,

$$\beta^{*(n)} = \text{bin}_n$$

as was to be proved.

A similar argument, not given here, shows that the *n*-fold convolution of the geometric distribution yields the negative binomial or Pascal distribution.

GENERATING FUNCTIONS

An important mathematical technique for dealing with distributions is the generating function or a similar "operational function" such as the moment-generating function, characteristic function, and Laplace transform.

The awkwardness of working with probability distributions arises from the fact that each entity or distribution is a sequence rather than a number, and in many applications these sequences are infinite. The main mathematical operation on sequences is convolution, and though it is well defined, it is relatively laborious to perform. The proof of the elementary fact that the binomial distribution is the *n*-fold convolution of Bernoulli distributions was not particularly easy to handle directly, and we were forced to study a particular element of the sequence intensively, and then generalize.

Generating functions change the form of the problem. Since a sequence of numbers is difficult is handle, find a corresponding function of a real variable. To each sequence of numbers there corresponds a polynomial or power expansion, for the elements of the sequence are simply used as coefficients of the various powers of some variable *s*. The variable *s* has no significance, and is always removed from consideration in some way before any final conclusions are drawn from the calculations. All the variable *s* does is to bind the terms of the sequence into a single function, with which various manipulations can then be performed.

If

$$A = (a_0, a_1, a_2, \ldots)$$

is a probability distribution, then its generating function is defined as

$$A(s) = a_0 + a_1 s + a_2 s^2 + \cdots$$

$$= \sum_{i=0}^{\infty} a_i s^i. \tag{22}$$

There is precisely one generating function for each sequence of numbers.

Examples. Since the Bernoulli distribution is $\beta = (q, p, 0, 0, \ldots)$ its generating function is

$$B(s) = q + ps. \tag{23}$$

The binomial distribution bin_n has a generating function

$$B_n(s) = q^n + \binom{n}{1}pq^{n-1}s + \cdots + \binom{n}{k}p^k q^{n-k}s^k + \cdots + \binom{n}{n}p^n s^n,$$

or, using the binomial expansion, this is

$$B_n(s) = (q + ps)^n. \tag{24}$$

The generating function of the geometric distribution, $k = 1, 2, \ldots$, is

$$G(s) = ps + qps^2 + q^2 ps^3 + \cdots$$

$$= ps \sum_{i=0}^{\infty} (qs)^i = \frac{ps}{(1 - qs)}. \tag{25}$$

Fundamental theorem. If $\{a_k\}$ and $\{b_k\}$ are probability distributions with generating functions $A(s)$ and $B(s)$, and $\{c_k\}$ is their convolution, then the generating function $C(s) = \sum c_k s^k$ is the product

$$C(s) = A(s)B(s). \tag{26}$$

Again, only a heuristic proof can be given, restricted to the discrete probability distributions. However, by writing out the two generating functions $A(s)$ and $B(s)$ and multiplying, collecting terms with like powers of s, the result is

$$
\begin{array}{cccccc}
 & & & A(s) & & \\
 & a_0 & a_1 s & a_2 s^2 & a_3 s^3 & \cdots \\
\hline
b_0 & a_0 b_0 & a_1 b_0 s & a_2 b_0 s^2 & a_3 b_0 s^3 & \cdots \\
b_1 s & & a_0 b_1 s & a_1 b_1 s^2 & a_2 b_1 s^3 & \cdots \\
B(s) \quad b_2 s^2 & & & a_0 b_2 s^2 & a_1 b_2 s^3 & \cdots \\
b_3 s^3 & & & & a_0 b_3 s^3 & \cdots \\
\vdots & & & & & \cdots \\
\end{array}
$$

As one looks down a column, say, the column with s^3 appearing as a common factor, one notes the terms $a_3 b_0$, $a_2 b_1$, $a_1 b_2$, and $a_0 b_3$. These terms, if added together, are c_3, the third term of the convolution sequence. In the product of $A(s)B(s)$ they are added together and multiplied by s^3, and this process produces $C(s)$.

DERIVATION OF COMPOUND DISTRIBUTIONS

Using generating functions, some of the relationships seen above are now proved in very simple ways. First, note that the n-fold convolution of Bernoulli distributions yields a binomial distribution:

$$B(s) = q + ps, \qquad B_n(s) = (q + ps)^n$$

from the observations above. Since the generating function of the binomial is indeed the product of n generating functions of the Bernoulli, the result is proved.

Now consider the n-fold convolution of geometric distributions, a problem which was postponed as quite laborious without generating functions. First calculate the generating function of the negative binomial distribution [Eq. (8)] as follows:

$$N_k(s) = \left(0 + 0 + \cdots + p^k s^k + \binom{k}{k-1} p^k q s^{k+1} + \binom{k+1}{k-1} p^k q^2 s^{k+2} \cdots \right)$$

$$= p^k s^k \sum_{j=0}^{\infty} \binom{k+j-1}{k-1} q s^j = \left(\frac{ps}{1-qs} \right)^k. \tag{27}$$

This, however, is clearly the kth power of the generating function of the geometric distribution, given in Eq. (25). Hence the negative binomial distribution is the n-fold convolution of geometric distributions.

In psychological theory, one might now produce a model in which an interesting random variable is the sum of certain other random variables having various distributions. Consider, for example, a given problem which requires that two difficulties be overcome, and the trials to mastery of each part are described by a geometric distribution. The two parts, of course, have different parameters. Let

$$g_1 = p_1, p_1(1 - p_1), p_1(1 - p_1)^2, \ldots$$

and

$$g_2 = p_2, p_2(1 - p_2), p_2(1 - p_2)^2, \ldots$$

be the two geometric distributions. Their generating functions are

$$G_1(s) = \frac{p_1 s}{1 - (1 - p_1)s}$$

and

$$G_2(s) = \frac{p_2 s}{1 - (1 - p_2)s},$$

so that the generating function of the convolution is

$$G_{12}(s) = \frac{p_1 p_2 s^2}{1 - (2 - p_1 - p_2)s + (1 - p_1 - p_2 + p_1 p_2)s^2}.$$

Now one may ask, what use does this information have? What is needed is an expression for the distribution itself, not its generating function.

The following theorem is sometimes helpful. If

$$A(s) = a_0 + a_1 s + a_2 s^2 + \cdots,$$

then

$$\frac{d}{ds} A(s) = a_1 + 2a_2 s + 3a_3 s^2 + \cdots$$

$$\frac{d^2}{ds^2} A(s) = 2a_2 + 3 \cdot 2a_3 s + \cdots,$$

and, in general, the nth derivative is

$$\frac{d^{(n)}}{ds^n} A(s) = n!\, a_n + n + 1!\, a_{n+1} s + \cdots$$

and all the terms to the right contain higher powers of s. Evaluate this nth derivative at $s = 0$ and

$$\frac{d^{(n)}}{ds^n} A(0) = n!\, a_n.$$

Now, the nth term of the probability distribution arises from the generating function by the relationship

$$a_n = \frac{d^{(n)}}{ds^n} A(0)/n! \tag{28}$$

The result in Eq. (28) has theoretical interest in that it shows that the probability distribution can be calculated from the generating function. However, unless some particularly simple method of performing the successive differentiations comes to hand, the process may be relatively laborious. If numerical values for the parameters of the component processes are at hand, and differentiations can conveniently be performed on a computer, then this direct approach may be useful in deriving a new distribution.

A more promising approach is to develop a series expansion of the generating function itself. Suppose that various psychological considerations have led to defining the random variable T as the sum of certain other random variables, U, V, W, etc., each of which has a known form of distribution.

The generating functions of U, V, W, etc., are computed, a step that is usually not very difficult, and these generating functions are multiplied together. The result is a relatively complicated function of s. To find a series expansion is to find a sequence of coefficients $t_0, t_1, \ldots$, etc., such that

$$T(s) = t_0 + t_1(s) + t_2(s^2) + \cdots$$

The method of differentiating the function n times to find t_n is, now, seen to be merely an application to Taylor's expansion. The other most useful method, taught in intermediate algebra courses, is that of the partial fraction expansion.

The above discussion will not enable the reader to solve difficult problems in compound process models, but may be sufficient to indicate those areas of classical mathematics that will be most useful. The remarks here are intended to show how one gets from typical psychological models, and the probability distributions developed from psychological theory, into more complicated structures.

A RANDOM NUMBER OF COMPONENTS

In the models discussed above, it was assumed that the total process consisted of some fixed number of subprocesses. The binomial distribution gives the probability of the number of heads in n trials, where n is fixed. The negative binomial case gives the probability of requiring n trials when waiting for a fixed number k of heads.

Now consider a simple sort of model of reaction time. The subject samples the stimulus situation. If he does not detect the stimulus, he consumes a random number of milliseconds readjusting, then resamples. After the stimulus has been turned on, the subject might detect it on any of his samples of the situation, and there is a given probability distribution that he detects it on the k sample.

The number of milliseconds until the stimulus is detected is found to be the sum of all the random delays between samples. However, the number of delays is also a random variable, for that is the number of samples taken before detection.

Now let $d = (d_0, d_1, \ldots)$ be the distribution of delays before a given sampling of the situation, and let $f = (f_1, f_2, \ldots)$ be the probability distribution of the number of samples taken.

To denote the probability that a random variable, having distribution g, takes the value k, write g_k. The probability that the total time is k, given three samples, is then the convolution of d three times, and is written

$$(d * d * d)_k.$$

In general, the probability that the reaction time is a total of k milliseconds is given by

$$r_k = f_1 d_k + f_2 (d * d)_k + f_3 (d * d * d)_k + \cdots \tag{29}$$

This is true because the k milliseconds may be the result of a single delay of k and only one sampling (joint probability $f_1 d_k$), or the result of two samplings, in which case the probability of taking k milliseconds is $(d * d)_k$, the kth term of the convolution of two delay distributions, etc.

Let $R(s)$ be the generating function of r and $D(s)$ be the generating function of d. Taking the generating function of both series, a typical member of which is given in Eq. (29), we have

$$R(s) = f_1 D(s) + f_2 D(s)^2 + f_3 D(d)^3 + \cdots \tag{30}$$

Now let

$$y = D(s) \tag{31}$$

and

$$R(s) = f_1 y + f_2 y^2 + f_3 y^3 + \cdots \tag{32}$$

By the definition of a generating function given in Eq. (22), this is the generating function of f,

$$R(s) = F(y) \tag{33}$$

or, substituting Eq. (31),

$$R(s) = F[D(s)], \tag{34}$$

a compound function.

This result is particularly useful because it permits a simple solution for the generating function of a process that seems, at least at first, relatively complicated.

An example is in the simple Bower model of learning. Suppose that with probability p the subject makes an error on any trial, given that he has not learned. This gives a Bernoulli distribution β with generating function $B(s) = q + ps$. The number of errors on n trials, without learning, is the binomial distribution bin. The number of trials before learning is itself a random variable; in Bower's model, there is probability c of learning after each guess, so the probability of n trials without learning is

$$f_n = (1 - c)^{n-1} c, \qquad F(s) = \frac{cs}{1 - (1 - c)s}.$$

Let r be the distribution of total errors before learning. Following the argument as in Eq. (29),

$$r_k = f_1 \beta_k + f_2 (\beta * \beta)_k + \cdots$$

and the generating function of the total errors is

$$R(s) = F[D(s)]$$

$$= \frac{CB(s)}{1 - (1 - c)B(s)}$$

$$= \frac{c(q + ps)}{1 - (1 - c)(q + ps)} .$$

This result can be obtained in other ways, but the general approach is more powerful and permits an approach to much more complicated structures than have been studied, at least intensively, in mathematical psychology to date.

TYPES OF APPLICATIONS

These methods have several possible lines of application.

1. Given direct measurements of the distribution of certain subprocesses, as from control or "calibration" groups of an experiment, the problem is to calculate a prediction of performance on a more complex task. The above methods permit a combination of this known information, and the calculations are usually fairly straightforward.

2. Given a complex process and data concerning a complex output (i.e., measurements of a random variable T), one may speculate as to component processes, construct a model, and then attempt to analyze the random variable T into components U, V, W, etc. This is an extremely difficult process, and often simply is not possible if one suffers from much uncertainty as to the parameters, number, and specific rôles of the subprocesses. Efforts to analyze reaction time into components, using powerful analytic tools, result in some uncertainties until experimental work is done, varying the task and observing the specific changes in distributions, providing the investigator with a solid and detailed empirical basis. At that time, of course, the situation becomes more like situation (1) with known components.

3. Given the hypothesis that a certain probability distribution may arise as the combination of certain other distributions, the investigator can initiate a theoretical study to either prove or disprove this conjecture. Methods given in this chapter often lead to relatively compact and elegant methods for this purpose.

STOCHASTIC PROCESSES

In the simple examples given above, the probability of heads was constant from one trial to another—from this the binomial, geometric, and negative-binomial distributions were generated. Clearly, however, there is not sufficient mathematics for learning theory unless it is possible to deal with models in which $P(H)$ is not constant. When a random process is observed repeatedly, and the probability of the outcomes may be different from one trial to another, the system is called a *stochastic process*.

The simplest kind of stochastic process to describe is one in which a random variable has a different distribution at different times, trials, or stages of a process. Suppose that the probability of a certain response is p_i on trial i of an experiment. If that response is counted as 0 and any other response as 1, probabilities are obtained for the experimental sequence like

$$
\begin{aligned}
P(000) &= p_1 p_2 p_3, \\
P(001) &= p_1 p_2 (1 - p_3), \\
P(0101) &= p_1 (1 - p_2) p_3 (1 - p_4),
\end{aligned}
\tag{35}
$$

etc. Very little can be done with a system like this, unless the change in p follows some reasonably simple law. For example, it might be assumed that p was a decreasing function of the trial number according to the law

$$
p_n = \theta^{n-1} p_1.
\tag{36}
$$

Then

$$
\begin{aligned}
P(000) &= (p_1)(\theta p_1)(\theta^2 p_1), \\
P(0101) &= (p_1)(1 - \theta p_1)(\theta^2 p_1)(1 - \theta^3 p_1),
\end{aligned}
\tag{37}
$$

etc. A reasonably full analysis of this system is possible.[1]

A second kind of stochastic process occurs when the probability distribution depends directly on what has happened before, and therefore depends indirectly on trials or time. In the simplest case, the probability distribution on trial n depends only on the outcome of trial $n - 1$. This produces a Markov chain.[2]

Consider making repeated observations on a random variable X, so that a sequence of outcomes is $X(1), X(2), \ldots, X(n), \ldots$ The possible values of X (the range of X) is some specified set called the *states* of the system. The states might be "head" and "tail" in coin tossing, or $(1, 2, 3, 4, 5, 6)$ in dice throwing or "unlearned, learned" in a memorizing experiment. (The state space need not be finite as it is in these examples.) There are three phrases

---

[1] R. R. Bush and S. H. Sternberg, A single-operator model. In R. R. Bush and W. K. Estes (Eds.), *Studies in Mathematical Learning Theory*. Stanford: Stanford Univ. Press, 1959. pp. 204–214.

[2] For a more detailed analysis, it is possible to distinguish between a Markov process, where transition probabilities depend only on the current state but may differ from trial to trial, and a Markov chain, where transition probabilities are constant. See J. G. Kemeny and J. L. Snell, *Finite Markov chains*. Princeton, N.J.: D. Van Nostrand, 1960.

that mean exactly the same thing: (1) the *outcome* on trial n, (2) the *value of X* on trial n, and (3) the *state* on trial n. Each of these refers to the particular member of the state space which occurs on the nth trial of the experiment.

In a Markov chain, the probability distribution of X varies from one trial to another. The distribution on a particular trial n depends on the value of X on trial $n - 1$. Imagine a coin-tossing game where A wins on a head and B wins on a tail. A has a coin which comes up heads with probability 0.70, and B has a coin which comes up heads with probability 0.30. On each trial, the winner of the preceding toss gets to use his coin on trial n.

$$\text{If } X(n - 1) = \text{head, then } P[X(n) = \text{head}] = 0.70,$$
$$P[X(n) = \text{tail}] = 0.30.$$
$$\text{If } X(n - 1) = \text{tail, then } P[X(n) = \text{head}] = 0.30, \qquad (38)$$
$$P[X(n) = \text{tail}] = 0.70.$$

Another example is the strategy-selection theory of concept identification. The states of the system are

$L =$ correct hypothesis (problem solved),

$E =$ irrelevant hypothesis leading to an error, and

$S =$ irrelevant hypothesis leading to a correct response.

On each trial, the system is in one of these three states; in other words, L, E, and S are the possible values of a random variable $X(n)$. Using the assumptions given in Chapter 3, the following probability distributions are derived:

$$\text{If } X(n - 1) = L, \text{ then } P[X(n) = L] = 1.0,$$
$$P[X(n) = E] = 0, P[X(n) = S] = 0;$$
$$\text{If } X(n - 1) = E, \text{ then } P[X(n) = L] = c, \qquad (39)$$
$$P[X(n) = E] = (1 - c)q, P[X(n) = S] = (1 - c)p;$$
$$\text{If } X(n - 1) = S, \text{ then } P[X(n) = L] = 0,$$
$$P[X(n) = E] = q, P[X(n) = S] = p.$$

The examples make it clear that the main parameters of a Markov chain are conditional probabilities. If the system has k states, then there are k^2 parameters of the form

$$p_{ij} = P[X(n) = j \mid X(n - 1) = i]. \qquad (40)$$

These are called the *transition probabilities* of the Markov chain, and they are usually displayed in matrix form as the *transition matrix* **P**.

The transition matrix does not completely specify a Markov chain, because it does not tell how the process starts. In addition, there is the *initial probability* of each state, or the *initial vector* π. The elements of π are

$$\pi_i = P[X(1) = i]. \tag{41}$$

Note that the complete specification of a k-state Markov chain requires $k + 1$ probability distributions of the random variable X. One of these is the initial vector π, and the other k are the rows of the transition matrix $\mathbf{P}$.

This section on stochastic processes began by noting that the probability distribution of a random variable can be different from one trial to another. A Markov chain has this feature, but the change in the probability distribution over trials is not given by assumption. Instead, the trial-by-trial change in probabilities is derived from the assumptions.

The distribution of X for trial 1 is given by assumption—it is π. Obtain the distribution of X for trial 2 from π, $\mathbf{P}$, and the law of total probability. Let $A_1, A_2, \ldots$ be a partition of U, the whole universe. Then for any event B (which could be one of the A_i),

$$P(B) = \sum_i P(A_i \cap B) = \sum_i P(A_i)P(B \mid A_i). \tag{42}$$

By the definitions of π_i and p_{ij},

$$P[X(2) = j] = \sum_i \pi_i p_{ij}. \tag{43}$$

Note that the probability distribution on trial 2 is the vector $\boldsymbol{\pi}$ postmultiplied by the matrix $\mathbf{P}$. This can be generalized easily. Equation (43) is just a special case of the following recursion:

$$P[X(n) = j] = \sum_i P[X(n - 1) = i]p_{ij}. \tag{44}$$

Therefore the probability distribution of X on trial 2 is

$$\mathbf{P}_{X(2)} = \pi\mathbf{P}. \tag{45}$$

And the probability distribution on trial 3 is

$$\mathbf{P}_{X(3)} = \mathbf{P}_{X(2)} \times \mathbf{P} = \pi\mathbf{P}^2. \tag{46}$$

In general, the probability distribution on trial n is

$$\mathbf{P}_{X(n)} = \pi\mathbf{P}^{n-1}. \tag{47}$$

That is, the probability distribution of X on trial n is the product of the initial vector times the $n - 1$ power of the transition matrix.

Powerful and general methods are available for obtaining the powers of a matrix. With the use of Eq. (47), these can be applied to obtain the probability vector for any trial.

FUNCTIONS OF SEQUENCES

There is a stochastic process whenever a random variable X is observed repeatedly. Let U be the range of X. Then if X is observed n times, the set of possible sequences is observed:

$$V_n = U \times U \times \cdots (n \text{ times}) \cdots \times U; \qquad (48)$$

V_n is another universe whose elements are sequences. Call V_n the *outcome space* of the stochastic process.

The outcome space for the binomial distribution is of this kind. For example, $U = (0, 1)$, and $V_3 = (000, 001, 010, \ldots, 111)$. Now we can define a random variable S_n which maps V_n onto the set of integers $(0, 1, \ldots, n)$. For any sequence, the corresponding value of S_n is the number of zero's in the sequence. Then the probability distribution of S_n is the binomial distribution, given as Eq. (4).

Most of the calculations carried out in this book involve random variables defined on the outcome spaces of various stochastic processes. Uncertainty and information transmitted are defined as properties of sequences involving stimuli and responses. The learning curve, the number of errors before learning, and other common measures taken in a learning experiment are all random variables defined on the outcome space of stochastic learning models. Reaction time is a random variable defined on the outcome space of a stochastic process.

It is useful to distinguish two main kinds of random variables in the present context. One type depends on the whole sequence and can be called *global*. This includes such variables as the number of errors before learning, or the number of correct identifications during an experimental session. Other random variables depend on a feature of the sequence at a particular time, and may be called *local*. These random variables are indexed by trial number n or time t. Examples include error on trial n (0 or 1), or the magnitude of the nth stimulus in a detection experiment.

Collapsed Markov Chains

Another way to obtain a function of a sequence is to define a function of the state space of the stochastic process. Let $U = (S_1, \ldots, S_r)$ be the range of a variable X. And let $U' = (C_1, \ldots, C_q)$ be the range of a variable Y, such that $q < r$, and U' is a function of U. In other words, each C_i is really a collection of states from U, and the outcome space of sequences of Y is a function of the outcome space of sequences of X.

Examples are easy to construct. Suppose that X is the number of spots showing on a die. Then $U = (1, 2, 3, 4, 5, 6)$. Now let Y be 0 if an even number is thrown, and 1 if an odd number is thrown. Then $U' = (0, 1)$, and the two sets are connected by the function

$$f(2) = f(4) = f(6) = 0,$$
$$f(1) = f(3) = f(5) = 1.$$

A sequence of observations of X like 4, 2, 5, 5, 1, 6, . . . , would correspond to the observations of Y: 0, 0, 1, 1, 1, 0, . . .

It is common for psychological models to involve collapsing of the kind described here. This happens whenever it is assumed that the same response will be made even though the subject may be in a different psychological state. In a learning experiment, subjects will give correct responses (a) when they have learned, or (b) when they have not learned, but have guessed correctly. In a detection experiment, according to the theory of signal detectability, subjects will say "yes" whenever the stimulus input exceeds a certain criterion level. In this case we do not distinguish between perceived inputs which differ a great deal in intensity.

As these examples show, it is common for psychological models to include more states than can be distinguished in an experiment. Thus the psychologist often assumes that his data may consist of observations of a collapsed random variable. This situation has been investigated for the case in which the underlying process is a Markov chain.

The first question involves properties of the observed sequence—the sequence of values of Y. The question is whether the sequence $Y(1)$, $Y(2)$ is a Markov chain. Burke and Rosenblatt[3] showed that this depends on the transition probabilities of the underlying chain. Let $f^{-1}(C_j)$ be the inverse mapping of C_j in U—in other words, the collection of states in U which correspond to C_j. Then the collapsed process will be a Markov chain if for every j and k there is a constant p_{jk} such that for every $S_i \in f^{-1}(C_j)$,

$$P[C_k(n) \mid S_i(n - 1)] = p_{jk},$$

where p_{jk} is independent of i. In other words, all the members of each collapsed class have the same transition probabilities into the collapsed classes. Kemeny and Snell[4] noted that the Burke and Rosenblatt condition is necessary if the Markov property of the collapsed sequence is to hold for an arbitrary choice of an initial vector.

The second question involves inferences that can be made about the

[3] C. J. Burke and M. Rosenblatt, A Markovian function of a Markov chain. *Annals Math. Stat.*, 1958, **29**, 1112–1122.
[4] Cited above.

underlying Markov chain, based on observations of the collapsed chain. Since it is not possible to distinguish all the states that are assumed to exist, the amount of information that can be obtained about the parameters of the underlying process is limited. This gives rise to the problem of identifiability for Markov models, which is discussed in Chapter 10.

EXERCISES

1. Assume for a learning experiment that u_i is the set of possible response sequences for an individual item. What is U, the set of possible outcomes for k items? Assume that the number of errors per item has the geometric distribution, and that items are identical and independent. Let S be the summed number of errors over k items. What is the distribution of S? How could this calculation be used to test the assumption that the items were identical and independent?

2. What are the ranges of (a) the number of spots showing on a single die? (b) the number of spots showing on two dice (assuming that the dice are distinguishable)? (c) the number of errors made before solving a problem? (d) the amount of time taken to make a response?

CHAPTER NINE

Estimation of Parameters

All-or-none learning theory says that the probability of learning is θ, and this is constant from one trial to another. It does not say what numerical value θ will take. A cue-selection theory says that the probability of learning is the probability of selecting a cue from the set of relevant cues, but does not say how large the set of relevant cues will be. The linear learning model says that in probability-learning experiments, the probability of response A_1 will approach the probability π of the corresponding event E_1, but does not say what the latter probability must be. In adaptation-level theory, the situation is made up of parts, each having a value (e.g., a reflectance) and a relative weight w (an attention value); but the theory does not give these quantities.

The symbols θ, π, and w are parameters of the theories; in any experiment, when all detailed calculations have been carried out, there must be numbers to substitute for the variables.

The values of some parameters, the independent variables, are controlled or fixed by the experimenter, whereas others are free and are not known in advance of observing the dependent variables of the experiment. For example, θ, the learning-rate parameters of the linear model, is a typical free parameter, whereas π, the probability of event E_1, is fixed by the experimenter.

In some experiments it is possible to affect a free parameter strongly by varying some fixed parameter. For example, the parameter h, the probability of short-term memory in a paired-associates list, can be made very small by increasing the number of items intervening between study and test presentations. By making the study-to-test interval long enough, it is possible to drive the parameter h to zero. This indicates that the parameter is indirectly under the control of the experimenter. This does not make it a fixed parameter—it is still free, but it is predictable.

LOGICAL STATUS OF PARAMETERS

Some important relationships between free and controlled parameters can be understood by an analysis using logical quantifiers. Recall the logical notation: A simple sentential function of the form $F(x)$ can be turned into a sentence either by substituting a constant a for x, or by quantifying. The sentence $F(a)$, read "a has the property F," is about an individual. The sentence $(\exists x)F(x)$, read "There is an x that has the property F," asserts that an instance of F exists in the domain. The sentence $(\forall x)F(x)$, read "Every x has the property F," asserts that F is a property of all objects in the domain.

The domain of a parameter is the parameter space, and the elements in the domain are all the numbers that might possibly be the value of the parameter.

Ordinarily, a theory is written without quantifiers over the parameters. For example, if

$$Y = \text{number of errors,}$$

a theory may say that

$$P(Y = j) = (1 - d)^j\, d. \tag{1}$$

The assumption of all-or-none learning is that a single probability d applies after each error. However, d is usually a free parameter; this means that the theory merely asserts that some value of d (between zero and one) applies. The assertion is expressed explicitly by the sentence

$$(\exists d)(\forall j)[P(Y = j) = (1 - d)^j\, d]. \tag{2}$$

Let L stand for the trial of the last error in a concept-identification experiment. Then in the usual notation,

$$P(L = k) = (1 - d)(1 - qd)^{k-1}q\, d. \tag{3}$$

The idea is that some single value of d and a single value of q apply on all trials, and d and q are free parameters. Explicitly,

$$(\exists d)(\exists q)(\forall k \geq 1)[P(L = k) = (1 - d)(1 - qd)^{k-1}q\, d]. \tag{4}$$

Both of the above examples have involved free parameters, quantified under $\exists$. A fixed parameter, on the other hand, may be replaced by a constant. The experimenter may present E_1 and E_2 events, in probability learning, with probabilities $\pi = 0.7$, $1 - \pi = 0.3$. Then the equations which include π can be written using the constant. For example,

$$P(n) = \pi - (\pi - P(0))(1 - \theta)^n \tag{5}$$

becomes

$$P(n) = 0.7 - (0.7 - P(0))(1 - \theta)^n.$$

The above formula is intended to hold for *any* value of π the experimenter might choose. If the learning rate θ is the same for any value of π, then the explicit formula is

$$(\exists\theta)(\forall\pi)[P(n) = \pi - (\pi - P(0))(1 - \theta)^n].$$

Fixed or experimenter-controlled parameters are given universal quantifiers; free parameters receive existential quantifiers.

The order of quantifiers clarifies certain important aspects of assumptions. Chapter 2 derived the geometric waiting-times distribution from the assumption

$$P(X = n \mid X \geq n) = c, \tag{6}$$

where c is a constant over trials. The idea that c (whatever it is) is constant over trials, is expressed

$$(\exists c)(\forall n)[P(X = n \mid X \geq n) = c] \tag{7}$$

and reads, "There is some c such that for every n, . . ." Note the difference between the preceding and

$$(\forall n)(\exists c_n)[P(X = n \mid X \geq n) = c_n]. \tag{8}$$

Equation (8) would assert little or nothing—it would merely say that there was some probability of learning on every trial, but that each different trial could have a different probability.

The order of quantifiers also clarifies assumptions about the invariance of parameter values across different experimental conditions. Bower and Trabasso conducted an experiment in which different groups solved concept-identification problems with different numbers of responses. The assumption tested was that a single value of d could be applied to the two groups differing in q. Let i index the experimental groups. Then, for example, the distribution of trial of last error would be stated as the sentence

$$(\exists d)(\forall i)(\exists q_i)(\forall k \geq 1)[P(L_i = k) = (1 - d)(1 - q_i d)^{k-1} q_i d]. \tag{9}$$

That is, the distribution of the trial of last error is expected to differ between the groups, though each of them must have the almost-geometric distribution.

Equation (9) says that the groups were not expected to differ in the distributions of the number of errors, since the parameter q does not influence this variable. That is,

$$(\exists d)(\forall i)(\forall j)[P(Y_i = j) = (1 - d)^j\, d].\qquad (10)$$

Another problem, clarified by the use of quantifiers is called the "π, θ" problem of probability learning experiments. The problem arises in experiments where different groups predict lights occurring in random sequence, with differing values of π. The original theoretical proposal was the linear model (see Chapter 1) with a single value of the learning-rate parameter, θ. That is,

$$(\exists \theta)(\forall \pi)(\forall n)[P_{(n+1)} = (1 - \theta)P_{(n)} + \theta\pi],\qquad (11)$$

where π is a fixed parameter which differs among groups.

In the experiments, it turned out that θ was not invariant across groups differing in π, and the best theory possible was

$$(\forall \pi)(\exists \theta_n)(\forall n)[P_{(n+1)} = (1 - \theta_\pi)P_{(n)} + \theta_\pi\pi].\qquad (12)$$

(For a continuation, see Exercise 3.)

THE PARAMETER SPACE

In the theoretical description of an experiment, the possible combinations of parameter values can be visualized as the points in a space which has as many dimensions as there are parameters. If a certain theory has only one parameter θ and it is a probability, then the space is the unit interval $[0, 1]$. If there are two independent parameters θ_1 and θ_2, both of which are probabilities, then the parameter space is the unit square. Sometimes relationships within a theory impose further restrictions; for example, θ_1 may be the probability of a correct cue and θ_2 the probability of a correct color cue. Now, since the sets referred to are one within the other, $\theta_2 \le \theta_1$. The parameter space is a triangle. These three possibilities are shown in Fig. 9.1.

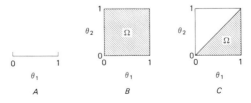

Figure 9.1

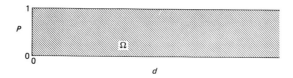

Figure 9.2

In other examples, the parameter space may include a distance and, say, a probability. If the distance is d, the probability is P, and they are independent, then the probability space is the strip shown in Fig. 9.2.

Two parameters are said to be independent if the possible values taken by one are unaffected by the value of the other. The two parameters are independent in Fig. 9.1(b) and Fig. 9.2, but they are interrelated and not independent in Fig. 9.1(c). It is often possible and desirable to reformulate a theory so that its parameters are independent. For the situation in Fig. 9.1(c), it is possible to substitute for θ_2 a new parameter ϕ, where

$$\theta_2 = \phi\theta_1 \quad \text{and} \quad 0 \le \phi \le 1.$$

This gives the same set of values of θ_1 and θ_2 as does the restriction leading to Fig. 9.1(c), but has the independent parameters θ_1 and ϕ.

If all the parameters of a theory can be controlled experimentally, a single point in the parameter space is specified when the experiment is set up. If the theory is correct, then all features of the data can be calculated from knowledge of the experimental conditions alone.

If a parameter must be estimated, it is as though an experimenter has set up the conditions of his experiment, but has not specified everything he needs to know. If all the parameters except one are controlled, specifying the experimental conditions determines a line in the parameter space. The problem of estimation is to select a point on that line as a reasonable estimate of the free parameter, basing the choice on the results of the experiment.

If there are two parameters to be estimated, then the experimental conditions specify that the combination of parameter values lies somewhere on a two-dimensional surface in the parameter space. If there are three parameters to be estimated, then the specified experimental conditions determine only a three-dimensional space of possible parameter values. The data of the experiment must be used to select a point in the parameter space before calculations can be carried out to apply the theory to data. The estimation problem can be understood as the selection of a point from a space whose dimensionality equals the number of free parameters.

The total parameter space of the theory includes points which specify all the possible experiments to which the theory might apply. The parameter space for the cue-selection theory of concept identification has (at least) two dimensions, corresponding to the parameters d and q, as in Fig. 9.3.

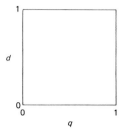

Figure 9.3

If q has a fixed value known in advance of running the experiment, then there is only one parameter to be estimated, so that the parameter space is restricted to a line through the unit square, as in Fig. 9.4.

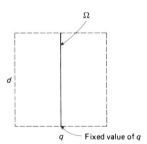

Figure 9.4

In Bower and Trabasso's two and four response concept-identification experiment, there were three free parameters, but it was necessarily expected that q_4, the probability of an error before learning in the four-response condition, would be less than q_2, the corresponding error-probability in the two-response condition. The parameter space for the experiment has three dimensions, but one of the parameters must be greater than another, as shown in Fig. 9.5.

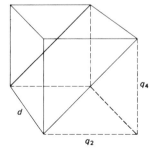

Figure 9.5

For a given experiment, each *free* parameter is quantified under Ǝ in a complete statement of the assumptions about the experiment. Then the number of dimensions of the parameter space within which that experiment lies is equal to the number of parameters that are quantified under Ǝ.

METHODS OF ESTIMATING PARAMETERS

If there are r free parameters, the theory says, "There exist $\theta_1, \theta_2, \ldots, \theta_r$," and the problem of estimation is to find such a set of numbers in the parameter space. It is important that estimation procedures should not arrive at any point outside the parameter space, such as a negative probability.

There are many methods of estimating parameters. It is often difficult to get any estimate at all, and special methods often are devised on the spot. However, the common methods can be classified as (1) method of partial data, (2) method of matched statistics (of which the method of moments is cited most often), (3) methods of minimum discrepancy, including least squares and minimum chi square, and (4) the method of maximum likelihood.

Method of Partial Data

This method uses the data from part of the experiment. For example, the responses to some of the stimuli may be used for estimation, and the resulting parameter values are then used to predict the responses to other stimuli. Or the data from the first few trials may be used for estimation, and the theory is then tested by its agreement with the data from the remaining trials by extrapolation.

An example is provided by Bush and Mosteller,[1] who used the method of partial data as a solution to some fairly knotty estimation problems. The problem is avoidance learning in dogs. The probability of getting shocked on trial 1 is 1, i.e., $p_1 == 1$. If the dog is shocked (makes an error) on trial n, then $p_{n+1} = ap_n$. If the dog is not shocked (makes an avoidance response) on trial n, then $p_{n+1} = bp_n$. In this model, $1 - a$ and $1 - b$ are learning rates, where $1 - a$ is the rate on shock trials and $1 - b$ is the rate on successful trials.

The raw Solomon-Wynne data are shown in Table 9.1. Note that, following the assumptions of the model, all animals were shocked on trial 1, so $p_1 = 1$ is tenable. Since all animals were shocked on trial 1, it follows that for all animals, $p_2 = ap_1 = a$. Bush and Mosteller noted that the proportion of shocks on trial 2 is an estimate of p_2, hence of a. The estimation equation is

$$\hat{a} = f_2,$$

[1] R. R. Bush and F. Mosteller. *Stochastic Models for Learning*. New York: Wiley, 1955.

Table 9.1 Solomon-Wynne data

Dog	Trial
13	S* S O S O S
16	S S S S S S S O S S S S S S
17	S S S S S S O O S O O S S O O S O S
18	S O O S S O O O O S O S O S
21	S S S S S S S S
27	S S S S S S O O O O S S O S
29	S S S S S O S S S S S S
30	S S S S S S S O O S S
32	S S S S S O S O S O O S O S S S O O O O O S O O S
33	S S S S O S S O O S O S
34	S S S S S S S S S S O O O O O O O S
36	S S S S S O O O O O S S
37	S S S O O S O S S
41	S S S S O S O O S
42	S S S O S O O S
43	S S S S S S S
45	S O S O S S S O S O O O O S
47	S S S S O S O S
48	S O S S S S O S S S
46	S S S S O O S O S O O S O S
49	S S S O O O O O S
50	S S O S O S O O O O O O O O O O S S
52	S S S S S S S
54	S S S S S S S S S O O O S O S S S O O S
57	S S S S S S O S O O O O S O S
59	S S O S O O O S O O S
67	S S S S O S
66	S S S O S O S O O O S O S
69	S S S S O O S S O O O S O S O S O S
71	S S S S O O O O O O S O S

Total	30	26	18	14	10	9	4	4	3	1	0	0	1
		27	25	18	12	7	11	8	3	2	0	1	0

* *S* signifies a shock (error).

where f_2 is the relative frequency of errors on trial 2. Since 27 of 30 dogs were shocked on trial 2, $f_2 = \frac{27}{30} = 0.90$. This is an estimate by the method of partial data—only the frequency of shocks on trial 2 is used.

The 27 animals shocked on trial 2 have, at trial 3, a probability $p_3 = a^2$ of being shocked again. In fact, 24 of 27 animals were shocked on trial 3. The natural estimator equation is

$$\hat{a^2} = \tfrac{24}{27},$$

whence

$$\hat{a} = 0.943.$$

Bush and Mosteller continued their discussion and obtained several estimates of a. Their best estimate was 0.923, which is close to being half-way between the two estimates obtained above.

The characteristics of the method of partial data should at once be apparent. By singling out data which bear on just one parameter of the model, it is often possible to get a very easy estimate. In fact, as above, there may be several such estimates possible, using different parts of the data or different amounts of data. When one has several estimates of the same parameter and they differ (as they almost always do), what is to be done? One estimate of a parameter is very good to have, but two estimates are distinctly troublesome, and the method of partial data has the drawback that it leads to several estimates of the same parameter.

Another example of the use of partial data is in the set of data given in Table 9.2, and summarized in Table 9.3. These are the results of 160 discrimination problems given one monkey (number 11) in a study of learning set formation by A. J. Riopelle.[2] All problems were made up of pairs from a set of four objects used repeatedly in all six combinations, with the correct object chosen at random. Animal 11 had had 56 discriminations before the present set of data began.

Using the cue-learning or strategy-selection theory, assume that the probability of a correct response on trial 1 is 0.5, and that with probability d the monkey learns and makes no more errors. Alternatively, the subject may not learn at trial 1, and is assumed to adopt some cue. If it is not the correct cue (probability $1 - d$), then he holds that cue as long as his responses are rewarded, but resamples any time he is not rewarded. Thus, on an error trial, there is probability d that the subject masters the problem.

Now, for the method of partial data, notice that the probability of no errors past trial 1 is, theoretically, d. This yields an estimator

$$\hat{d} = f(\text{no errors past trial 1}). \tag{13}$$

---

[2] Personal communication. A. J. Riopelle, 1960.

Table 9.2 Discrimination learning by one monkey, Riopelle data, animal 11, Problems 57–216

0001*	1	10 01001	01
1	1	0	01
01	1	0100100001 1001	0
0	0	0101	000011
0	101	10001	100011
0	1101	1010000100 1	00001
00100011	1	1100001	0
01	1	10100011	001
0	11	1	1
101	1	101000111	11
1	00001	010011	0
1	0	101	0
0	01	101	0
1	01	1	1
110001	1	0	0
1011	1	0	1
1	111101111	1	11
01	10011	01010001	0
001	01	1	0001001
1	10001	100011	101
100110001	11011	1	0
01	00001	1	11
01	0101	0	1
11	1	0	0
11	1101	1	0
1	0001001	01	0
1	1	01	01
1	10100001	1	0
001	011	0	
1101	1001	0001010000 1	
0	001	11	
0	10000101	00011	
1	101	001	
1	101	0	
110001	0	0	
1	0001	1	
000101	1001	0101	
0	000101	10001	
01	1010001100 0110100001 1001	0	
1	0110001	101	
1	010010001100001	0	
1	001	11	
11	101	0001001	
0	1001001	1	

* 1 is an error, 0 is a correct response. Five in a row correct at the end are not shown.

Table 9.3 Riopelle data summary, animal 11, Problems 57–216

Total errors		Trial of last error	
k	Frequency	Trial	Frequency
0	34	0	34
1	64	1	39
2	34	2	23
3	19	3	16
4	4	4	11
5	3	5	9
6	0	6	8
7	0	7	7
8	1	8	5
9	0	9	3
10	1	10	0
		11	2
		. . .	
		14	1
		15	1
		. . .	
		24	1
Mean = 1.49		Mean = 2.88	
Variance = 2.01			

There are 73 problems with no errors past trial 1, whence

$$\hat{d} = \tfrac{73}{160} = 0.46. \tag{14}$$

Consider this model with an unknown parameter p, the probability of a correct response given the subject is using an incorrect cue. Using partial data, note that the proportion of successes on trial 1 is p, since no learning can have taken place. This leads at once to the partial-data estimator,

$$\hat{p} = f(\text{success on trial 1})$$

which is

$$\hat{p} = \tfrac{77}{160} = 0.48. \tag{15}$$

Method of Matched Statistics

A time-honored method of estimating the parameters of a probability distribution is through its moments. Consider the distribution $F(\theta_1, \theta_2)$, a function of two parameters. It is usually quite easy, mathematically, to derive formulas for the mean and second moment, μ_1 and μ_2 of a distribution. Call the random variable X. If the observed mean and second moment are

$\bar{X}$ and $\bar{X}^2$, then the method of moments results from writing the estimation equations

$$\hat{\mu}_1(\theta_1, \theta_2) = \bar{X}$$

and

$$\hat{\mu}_2(\theta_1, \theta_2) = \bar{X}^2.$$

These two equations in two unknowns make it possible to obtain estimates for the two parameters.

When estimating from a given frequency distribution, the statistician can, in principle, always find enough equations to estimate any number of parameters from the successive moments. Since moment-generating functions are available for probability distributions, the estimation equations can often be written out quite easily. Of course the equations may not solve easily, and may lead to quite a bit of numerical calculation. In the example given, there is no such problem, since the calculations are very easy. The method of moments may be inefficient if the various moments do not have a sufficiently independent bearing on the parameters.

The illustration of these points uses the Riopelle data and the cue-selection theory. In the theory, the probability that the subject will make exactly k total errors (where T is the random variable of total errors) is

$$P(T = k) = \begin{vmatrix} (pd), & k = 0, \\ (1 - pd)d(1 - d)^{k-1}, & k > 0. \end{vmatrix} \tag{16}$$

Therefore

$$E(T) = \sum_{k=0}^{\infty} kP(T = k) = (1 - pd)d \sum_{k=1}^{\infty} k(1 - d)^{k-1}$$
$$= (1 - pd)/d.$$

This is the theoretical μ_1 written as a function of p and d, the two parameters. Rather than the second raw moment, use the variance

$$\text{Var}(T) = \sum_{k=0}^{\infty} (k - \mu_1)^2 P(T = k)$$
$$= \frac{(1 + pd - d)(1 - pd)}{d^2}. \tag{17}$$

This is the theoretical second moment about the mean, written as a function of p and d.

The obtained values for mean and variance were $\bar{T} = 1.49$ and $s^2 = 2.01$. This leads to the pair of estimation equations

$$\frac{(1 - pd)}{d} = 1.49, \tag{18}$$

$$\frac{(1 + pd - d)(1 - pd)}{d^2} = 2.01. \tag{19}$$

From Eq. (18),

$$pd = 1 - 1.49d$$

which, substituted in Eq. (19), gives

$$[1 + (1 - 1.49d) - d][1 - (1 - 1.49d)] = 2.01d^2$$

or

$$2.98 - 3.71d = 2.01d, \qquad \hat{d} = \frac{2.98}{5.72} = 0.52,$$

which gives an estimate of

$$\hat{p} = \frac{0.224}{0.521} = 0.43$$

when the estimate of d is substituted in Eq. (18). The estimates are of the same order of magnitude as those obtained by the method of partial data as applied earlier, but the difference is not negligible.

Instead of the higher moments of one statistic, the method of matched statistics can use the means of several statistics to estimate several parameters. One use of such a theory can be suggested very simply. Total errors, T, in the example above, depend on both parameters, but mainly (as can be seen from numerical trials) on d, the probability of learning. Since the subject can learn only on errors, the total error score is almost independent of the probability of a correct response before solution. The trial of last error should be somewhat more sensitive to the presolution probability p.

The distribution of the random variable L (trial of last error) is given by

$$P(L = k) = \begin{vmatrix} pd, & k = 0, \\ (1 - p)d, & k = 1, \\ (1 - d)[1 - (1 - p)d]^{k-2}(1 - p)d, & k > 1, \end{vmatrix} \tag{20}$$

and

$$E(L) = (1 - p)d + \frac{(1 - d)(1 + d - pd)}{(1 - p)d} \doteq \bar{L}. \tag{21}$$

From the data, $\bar{L} = 2.88$.

Equations (18) and (21) are simultaneous equations in two unknowns. Calculations result in a quadratic equation in d, and the estimates

$$\hat{d} = 0.49, \qquad \hat{p} = 0.53. \tag{22}$$

Again, the estimates are of about the same magnitude as those of other estimates. Three attempts have yielded estimates of d equal to 0.46, 0.52, and 0.49, and estimates of p equal to 0.48, 0.43, and 0.53.

Method of Minimum Discrepancy

The general problem of estimation is to select a point in the parameter space—in other words, to select one of the many special cases of the theory—in accord with the outcome of an experiment. The point in the parameter space is selected so that the theory will agree with the data in some way, and different methods of estimation employ different criteria of agreement. The methods of partial data and of matched statistics require that we select some portion of the experiment or some partial description of the data and choose parameters to ensure that the theory will agree exactly with the data for the selected statistics. The difficulty with these methods is that there is no fixed rule to guide the choice of statistics. Different properties of data can be chosen, and different estimates will result. Then the investigator does not have a reasonable basis for choosing among the various estimates. In this sense, the methods of partial data and matched statistics are *arbitrary* estimation methods.

The methods of minimum discrepancy and maximum likelihood have the advantage of providing a criterion for selecting statistics in the data to be used for estimation. Like the methods discussed earlier, these *criterion* methods result in the selection of a point in the parameter space, but the selection is based on all the data from the experiment, combined to make the overall agreement between the theory and the data as good as possible.

The general case is illustrated in Fig. 9.6. The data points in the two panels represent a hypothetical set of experimental results.

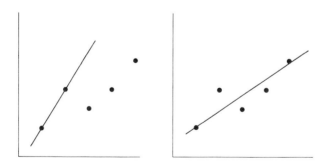

Figure 9.6

The theory is that these points fall on a straight line. The method of partial data could estimate the parameters of the straight line from any two points—say, the first two. Then the theoretical line would agree exactly with the first two data points as in the left panel of Fig. 9.6, but the fit to the remaining points might be bad. It would be more reasonable to select parameters that would take all the data into account, and give a theoretical curve like that in the right panel of Fig. 9.6. The line on the right does not agree exactly with any of the data points, but it represents a balanced use of all the data points, and it gives a result which appears to agree quite a bit better with the total set of data.

The method of minimum discrepancy works from some index of overall difference between the theory and data, and selects parameters which make that index as small as possible. There are two indices which are used frequently: the mean square error and chi square. The two indices use data of different kinds, and ordinarily one or the other will be more natural for a given set of data, because of the form in which the data are collected.

The method of least squares selects parameters to fit some function in the data, in this example, the learning curve, given as the probability of an error on trial n:

$$P(E_n) = \begin{cases} q & (n = 1), \\ (1 - c)(1 - qc)^{n-2}q & (n \geq 2). \end{cases} \tag{23}$$

The method of least squares is especially convenient and accurate if the function to be fit is linear. If the given function is nonlinear like Eq. (23), the method of least squares can be applied to the rectified function. The learning curve given in Eq. (23) is rectified quite easily:

$$\log P(E_n) = \begin{cases} \log q & (n = 1), \\ \log [(1 - c)q] + (n - 2) \log (1 - qc) & (n \geq 2). \end{cases} \tag{24}$$

The data transformed appropriately become y_n, the log of the proportion of errors on each trial. It is convenient to ignore the first trial. Let

$$a = \log [(1 - c)q], \qquad b = \log (1 - qc). \tag{25}$$

Then if the experiment is carried for N trials, the mean squared error (MSE) is

$$\begin{aligned} \text{MSE} &= \sum_{n=2}^{N} [y_n - a - (n - 2)b]^2 \\ &= \sum_{n=2}^{N} y_n^2 + (N - 1)a^2 + b^2 \sum_{n=2}^{N} (n - 2)^2 \\ &\quad - 2a \sum_{n=2}^{N} y_n - 2b \sum_{n=2}^{N} (n - 2)y_n + 2ab \sum_{n=2}^{N} (n - 2). \end{aligned}$$

To minimize this function with respect to a and b, take partial derivatives and set them to zero:

$$\frac{\partial \text{MSE}}{\partial a} = 2(N - 1)a + 2b \sum (n - 2) - 2 \sum y_n,$$

$$\frac{\partial \text{MSE}}{\partial b} = 2a \sum (n - 2) + 2b \sum (n - 2)^2 - 2 \sum (n - 2)y_n.$$

Table 9.4 Riopelle data, learning curve and logarithmic
transformation

Trial	Proportion correct	Log p + 3
2	0.244	2.387
3	0.169	2.228
4	0.144	2.158
5	0.119	2.076
6	0.062	1.782
7	0.062	1.782
8	0.062	1.782

The partial derivatives equal zero when

$$\hat{a} = \frac{\sum (n-2)^2 \sum y - \sum (n-2) \sum (n-2)y}{(N-1) \sum (n-2)^2 - [\sum (n-2)]^2},$$

$$\hat{b} = \frac{\sum (n-2) \sum y - (N-1) \sum (n-2)y}{[\sum (n-2)]^2 - (N-1) \sum (n-2)^2}.$$

(26)

The values of c and q which give the least-squares fit to the rectified learning curve are then obtained from the estimates of a and b:

$$\hat{q} = 1 + \log^{-1}(\hat{a}) - \log^{-1}(\hat{b}),$$

$$\hat{c} = \frac{1 - \log^{-1}(\hat{b})}{1 + \log^{-1}(\hat{a}) - \log^{-1}(\hat{b})}.$$

(27)

The technique may be illustrated with the Riopelle data (also see Chapter 1). Ignoring trial 1, the proportions of errors are as shown in Table 9.4. Calculating from the tabled values,

$$\sum (n-2)^2 = 91, \qquad \sum (n-2) = 21,$$

$$\sum (n-2)y = 39.502, \qquad \sum y = 14.195.$$

These yield

$$\hat{a} = 2.358 - 3 = -0.642, \qquad \hat{b} = -0.110.$$

And substituting into Eq. (27),

$$\hat{q} = 0.452, \qquad \hat{c} = 0.496.$$

(28)

The estimates obtained in this way agree well with those obtained from one of the methods of matched statistics described earlier. The difference is that in the present case, there is a definite criterion for a "good" estimate. The values obtained by least squares will provide the best possible agreement with a certain function—in this case, the log learning curve. There still is some arbitrariness in the estimation method, since different functions could be selected, and a criterion other than the squared discrepancy is possible, but still there is some basis for the selection of these parameter estimates.

Another method of minimizing the discrepancy between data and a set of theoretical quantities is the method of minimum chi square. The value of chi square indicates the discrepancy between a theoretical probability distribution and the corresponding observed frequencies. The method of minimum chi square simply is the selection of parameter values that yield the smallest possible value of chi square.

As an illustration, consider the first three trials of each problem as learned by Riopelle's monkey. There are eight possible sequences of correct responses and errors in these trials. The obtained frequencies and theoretical probabilities of the sequences are:

Sequence	Frequency, f_0	Theoretical probability, $f_e/160$
000	47	$pc + p^2(1 - c)c + p^3(1 - c)^2$
001	7	$(1 - c)^2 p^2 q$
010	21	$(1 - c)pq[c + (1 - c)p]$
100	51	$qc + qp(1 - c)c + qp^2(1 - c)^2$
011	2	$(1 - c)^2 pq^2$
101	15	$(1 - c)^2 pq^2$
110	16	$(1 - c)q^2[c + (1 - c)p]$
111	1	$(1 - c)^2 a^3$

The minimum chi-square estimates are values of p and d, which minimize the function

$$\chi^2 = \sum \frac{(f_0 - f_e)^2}{f_e}. \tag{29}$$

Usually the method of minimum chi square is practical only when a computer is available enabling a high-speed search of the parameter space. The technique involves calculating chi square over and over, using different values of the parameters, and gradually narrowing the search to regions of the parameter space where chi square has low values. Programs for this purpose are available at most university computing centers.

Method of Maximum Likelihood

Suppose that a man takes four marbles from a bag containing 38 red marbles and 62 black marbles, sampling one at a time with replacement. An investigator who knew the proportion of red marbles could calculate the probability of any sequence of draws—for example,

$$P(RBBR) = (0.38)(0.62)(0.62)(0.38),$$

or

$$P(BRBB) = (0.62)(0.38)(0.62)(0.62).$$

(30)

Now suppose that an investigator observes the outcome, $RBBR$, but does not know p, the proportion of red marbles in the bag. He can entertain various hypotheses, that p is 0.10, that p is 0.20, etc. According to the hypothesis $p = 0.10$,

$$P(RBBR) = (0.10)(0.90)(0.90)(0.10) = 0.0081.$$

According to the hypothesis $p = 0.20$,

(31)

$$P(RBBR) = (0.20)(0.80)(0.80)(0.20) = 0.0256,$$

etc.

The "likelihood" of a set of data is the probability or probability density based on a parameter. In this sense, the calculations in Eq. (31) represent likelihoods, denoted

$$L(RBBR; p = 0.10) = 0.0081,$$
$$L(RBBR; p = 0.20) = 0.0256.$$

(32)

The method of maximum likelihood is to select the value of the parameters which gives the highest possible value for the likelihood of the experimental result.

For a given value of p,

$$L(RBBR; p) = p^2(1 - p)^2,$$

and the problem is to maximize L by selecting the optimal p. It is almost invariably easier to maximize log L, and since the logarithm is a monotonic function, the value of p that maximizes log L will also maximize L.

$$\log L = 2 \log p + 2 \log (1 - p).$$

Differentiating with respect to p,

$$\frac{\partial}{\partial p} \log L = \frac{2}{p} - \frac{2}{1 - p}.$$

When this is set equal to 0, the solution is

$$\hat{p} = \tfrac{1}{2}.$$

The second derivative is negative, so this value of p is the maximum.

Now consider the method in general. Let X stand for a particular experimental outcome, and let $\theta_1, \theta_2, \ldots, \theta_n$ stand for the parameters of the theory. The likelihood function is

$$L(X; \theta_1, \theta_2, \ldots, \theta_n). \tag{33}$$

The maximum-likelihood estimate of θ_1 is that value of θ_1 which maximizes L. If L is differentiable with respect to all the parameters and has an analytic maximum with respect to each parameter, then the maxima are obtained by solving the n equations,

$$\frac{\partial}{\partial \theta_1} L(X; \theta_1, \theta_2, \ldots, \theta_n) = 0,$$

$$\frac{\partial}{\partial \theta_2} L(X; \theta_1, \theta_2, \ldots, \theta_n) = 0, \tag{34}$$

$$\frac{\partial}{\partial \theta_n} L(X; \theta_1, \theta_2, \ldots, \theta_n) = 0.$$

An example of a *maximum likelihood estimator* (MLE) will be developed using the cue-selection theory and Riopelle's data (Table 9.2). Assume that successive problems are independent and that the same parameters p and d apply to all problems. Recall that there is only one subject.

Now consider the first problem shown, which gives the outcome 0001. In the theory, learning occurs only after errors, so the subject learned after trial 4. Then the probability of 0001, according to the model, is

$$p(1 - d) \cdot p \cdot p(1 - p) d = p^3(1 - p)(1 - d) d.$$

The second problem had the outcome 1. The probability of just an error on the first trial is $(1 - p) d$. The probability of 01 is $p(1 - d)(1 - p) d$. The probability of 0 is pd. The probability of the seventh problem data, 001000011, is

$$p(1 - d)p(1 - p)(1 - d)pppp(1 - p)(1 - d)(1 - p)d$$
$$= p^6(1 - p)^3(1 - d)^3 d.$$

Notice that the probability of any sequence depends solely on the number of ones and zeros shown, on trials up to the last error. The order of 1's and 0's is immaterial except for trial 1; an error on any trial after trial 1 signifies failure to learn on a previous occasion, probability $1 - d$; but an error on trial 1 has no such significance. Suppose that on the ith problem there are G_i correct responses and T_i errors up to and including the last error, and let T_i' be the number of errors *after* trial 1. Then, following the rules of the model as exemplified above,

$$L(X_i) = p^{G_i}(1 - p)^{T_i}(1 - d)^{T_i'}d.$$

On the assumption that successive problems are independent, it follows that the joint probability of all the sample of data on N problems is

$$L(X) = \prod_{i=1}^{N} L(X_i) = p^{\sum_{i=1}^{N} G_i} (1 - p)^{\sum_{i=1}^{N} T_i} (1 - d)^{\sum_{i=1}^{N} T_i'} d^N. \tag{35}$$

Taking the logarithm, to obtain a more convenient function having its maximum at the same parameter values,

$$\log L(X) = \sum G \log p + \sum T \log (1 - p) + \sum T' \log (1 - d) + N \log d. \tag{36}$$

Recall further that $(\partial/\partial x) \log u = (1/u)\partial u/\partial x$. Therefore

$$\frac{\partial}{\partial p} \log L(X) = \frac{\sum G}{p} - \frac{\sum T}{(1 - p)},$$

$$\frac{\partial}{\partial d} \log L(X) = - \frac{\sum T'}{(1 - d)} + \frac{N}{d}. \tag{37}$$

Set each of Eq. (37) equal to zero and solve for the parameters. The result is

$$\hat{p} = \frac{\sum G}{(\sum G + \sum T)}, \tag{38}$$

$$\hat{d} = \frac{N}{(N + \sum T')}. \tag{39}$$

In the Riopelle data on animal 11,

$$\sum G = 223, \quad \sum T = 238, \quad \sum T' = 155, \quad N = 160.$$

From these values,

$$\hat{p} = 0.484, \quad \hat{d} = 0.508,$$

which are both within the parameter space. In fact, notice that from the form of Eqs. (38) and (39) and the fact that $\sum G, \sum T, \sum T'$, and N must be nonnegative, it follows that the maximum will always be between zero and one, hence allowable. In this theory, maximum-likelihood estimates can always be obtained in this simple way.

Notice how this calculation cuts through the various questions which arose in using the method of partial data, method of moments, etc. The first-trial data are used differently from the remainder of the data, in that the first trial has no bearing on the estimate of d. It is shown that [dividing Eq. (38) through by N]

$$\hat{p} = \frac{\bar{G}}{\bar{G} + \bar{T}}.$$

Since $G + T = L$, the trial of last error, it follows that

$$\hat{p} = \frac{(\bar{L} - \bar{T})}{\bar{L}}. \tag{40}$$

Similarly,

$$\hat{d} = \frac{1}{(1 + \bar{T}')}, \tag{41}$$

where trial 1 is excluded from T'. The estimators use the mean total errors and the mean trial of last error as the basic statistics.

PROPERTIES OF ESTIMATORS

For this discussion, let θ be the parameter (logically a variable), let θ_0 be the true value of the variable, that is, the number which if inserted in the theory would actually give the probabilities on the sample space; and let $\hat{\theta}$ be any estimate of θ. Let X_n be a data sheet resulting from a sample of n independent observations, and let U_n be the sample space of samples of size n. Now,

$$\hat{\theta} = F(X_n),$$

and F is the estimator function. There is a probability function on the sample space U_n which depends upon the form of the theory and on the number θ_0. Call this probability function (measure) $P(X_n; \theta_0)$, and since the estimator $\hat{\theta}$ is a function of X_n, it is a random variable and has a probability function defined on it. Suppose that $S_n(\hat{\theta})$ is the set of all data sheets which yield estimate $\hat{\theta}$. Then

$$P(\hat{\theta}; \theta_0) = P[S_n(\hat{\theta})].$$

What this means is that there is a distribution of values of $\hat{\theta}_n$ for samples of size n. Generally speaking, if the estimator is of any use at all, this distribution of $\hat{\theta}$ is relatively narrow and is centered, in some sense, near θ_0. The best estimator yields the narrowest possible distribution centered perfectly around θ_0. These descriptive phrases, although they give an idea of a general sentiment or intention, are imprecise, and must be replaced by specific properties.

Unbiasedness and Consistency

If for every sample-size n, the expected value of $\hat{\theta}_n$ is equal to θ_0, then $\hat{\theta}$ is called an unbiased estimator of θ_0.

The concept of an unbiased estimator is a stricter version of another notion—that of a consistent estimator. If $\hat{\theta}_n$ is consistent, the distribution of $\hat{\theta}_n$ converges to the point θ_0 as n becomes large. Therefore, any unbiased estimate is consistent. But an estimate may be biased for finite n and still be consistent. The distinction is illustrated in Fig. 9.7.

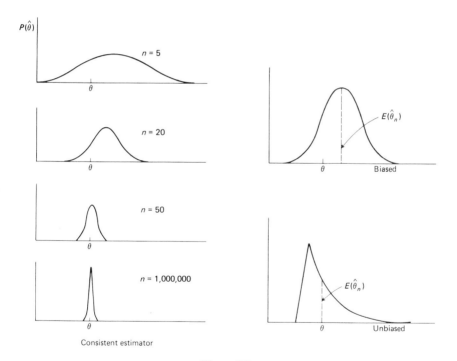

Figure 9.7

The estimate of d in the cue-selection theory is consistent but biased. Note that

$$P\left\{d_n = \frac{d}{n+k}\right\} = P\left\{\sum T' = k\right\} = \binom{n+k-1}{n-1}(1-d_0)^k d_0^n, \quad (42)$$

whence

$$E(\hat{d}_n) = \sum_{k=0}^{\infty} \left[\frac{n}{n+k} \right] \binom{k+n-1}{n-1} (1-d_0)^k d_0^n$$

$$= d_0 \sum_{k=0}^{\infty} \left[\frac{n}{n+k} \right] \left[\frac{k+n-1}{n-1} \right] \left[\binom{k+n-2}{n-1} (1-d_0)^k d_0^{n-1} \right]. \quad (43)$$

The terms in the square brackets are the terms of a negative binomial distribution; hence the sum is the expectation

$$E \left[\frac{n}{n+k} \right] \left[\frac{k+n-1}{n-1} \right],$$

every term of which is greater than one for $k > 0$. This is so because $n/(n-1) < (k+n)/(k+n-1)$. Therefore

$$E(\hat{d}_n) = d_0 E \left[\frac{n}{n+k} \right] \left[\frac{k+n-1}{n-1} \right] > d_0. \quad (44)$$

However, the estimate of d is consistent, for as n and k increase without bound, $n/(n+1)$ and $(k+n-1)/(k+n)$ both converge toward unity, so that

$$\lim_{n \to \infty} E(\hat{d}_n) = d_0. \quad (45)$$

Efficiency of Estimates and Correlations between Estimates of Different Parameters

Estimates of parameters are random variables, and have not only expectations but also variances and covariances.

An estimate is efficient if it has small variance, and will lead to similar values of the parameter if the experiment is repeated many times.

If a theory has several parameters to estimate, the variance of any single estimate tells how much that estimate will fluctuate because of random variation. Random variation might influence the estimates of two parameters in the same direction or in opposite directions, or random variation might also have independent effects on the estimated values of two parameters.

These questions are answered by considering the variances and covariances of parameter estimates given in the *covariance matrix*. If the free parameters of a theory are

$$\theta_1, \theta_2, \ldots, \theta_i, \ldots, \theta_r,$$

then let

$$\sigma_{ij} = \begin{cases} \text{Cov } (\hat{\theta}_i, \hat{\theta}_j) & \text{if } i \neq j, \\ \text{Var } (\hat{\theta}_i) & \text{if } i = j. \end{cases} \quad (46)$$

For maximum likelihood estimates based on large samples, the covariance matrix is the inverse of another matrix whose elements are the negative expected values of the second partial derivatives of the log likelihood. Let

$$d_{ij} = -E\left[\frac{\partial^2}{\partial\theta_i\,\partial\theta_j}\log L\right]. \tag{47}$$

Then let D be the $r \times r$ matrix of these negative expected second partial derivatives. Let Σ be the covariance matrix. Then the asymptotic distribution is the r-dimensional normal with variances and covariances

$$\Sigma = D^{-1}. \tag{48}$$

The above results belong to mathematical statistics and will not be proved here. A numerical example gives valuable information about the estimates of p and d in the cue-selection theory of Riopelle's experiment. Differentiating Eq. (37) a second time,

$$\frac{\partial^2}{\partial p^2}\log L = -\frac{\sum G}{p^2} - \frac{\sum T}{(1-p)^2},$$

$$\frac{\partial^2}{\partial p\,\partial d}\log L = 0, \tag{49}$$

$$\frac{\partial^2}{\partial d^2}\log L = -\frac{\sum T'}{(1-d)^2} - \frac{N}{d^2}.$$

The expectations of these second derivatives depend on the expectations of T, T', and G.

$$E(\textstyle\sum T') = \frac{1-d}{d}N,$$

$$E(\textstyle\sum T) = \frac{1-pd}{d}N, \tag{50}$$

$$E(\textstyle\sum G) = \frac{(1-d)p(1+qd)}{qd}N,$$

$$-E\left[\frac{\partial^2}{\partial p^2}\log L\right] = \frac{1-pd-q^2d^2}{pq^2d}N,$$

$$-E\left[\frac{\partial^2}{\partial p\,\partial d}\log L\right] = 0, \tag{51}$$

$$-E\left[\frac{\partial^2}{\partial d^2}\log L\right] = \frac{N}{d^2(1-d)}.$$

Inverting the matrix, we have

$$\Sigma = D^{-1} = \begin{vmatrix} \dfrac{pq^2d}{N(1 - pd - q^2d^2)} & 0 \\ 0 & \dfrac{d^2(1 - d)}{N} \end{vmatrix}.$$ (52)

Thus the estimates of p and d are uncorrelated, since the covariances are zero. Variances are estimated by substituting the parameter estimates into the above. From the earlier results,

$$\text{Var}\,(\hat{p}) = \frac{(0.484)(0.516)^2(0.508)}{(160)[1 - (0.484)(0.508) - (0.516)^2(0.508)^2]} = 0.000598,$$

$$\text{Var}\,(\hat{d}) = \frac{(0.508)^2(0.492)}{160} = 0.000794.$$

From these results, it is possible to infer that in the Riopelle data, p was estimated with a standard error of about 0.024, and d with a standard error of about 0.028.

Sufficient Statistics

A statistic is a random variable. It is some function of the outcome of an experiment, such as mean errors to solution, trial of last error, proportion of successes before last error, etc. An estimator is also a random variable that takes a value near some parameter. It may be a function of some other well-known statistic; in the cue-selection theory of learning, for example, if $\bar{T}$ is mean total errors to solution, the maximum likelihood estimator of the parameter d is $1/(1 + \bar{T})$. Thus $\bar{T}$ is a statistic upon which the estimate of d is based.

An important question about estimators is, how well chosen is the statistic used? The best answer, if true, is to identify what is called a sufficient statistic.

Recall that in cue-selection theory, learning can occur only on errors and then with probability d. If the problem has not been learned, there is probability p of a success and $1 - p$ of an error. A natural conjecture is that though d can be estimated from mean total errors, the estimate might be slightly improved if account was also taken of the trial of last error. However,

$$P(\text{TLE} = 1 \ \& \ \text{TE} = j) = \binom{k - 1}{j} p^{k-j}(1 - p)^j(1 - d)^j d$$

and

$$P(\text{TE} = j) = (1 - d)^j d,$$

whence from the definition formula of conditional probability,

$$P(\text{TLE} = k \mid \text{TE} = j) = \binom{k-1}{j} p^{k-j}(1-p)^j. \tag{53}$$

The conditional probability in Eq. (53) is not a function of the parameter d. Given total errors, the parameter d has no bearing on the distribution of trial of last error, and conversely, trial of last error can have no bearing on the estimate of d. Therefore it is said that the statistic total errors is sufficient relative to the trial of last error, for the estimation of parameter d.

The general idea of sufficiency is as follows: Let t and u be two statistics of samples, and θ the parameter of theoretical interest. It is said that *t is a sufficient statistic for parameter θ with respect to u* if the conditional distribution of u given t,

$$P(u \mid t; \theta),$$

does not depend upon θ.

A first generalization is to say that *t is a sufficient statistic* (no qualifiers) if t is sufficient with respect to θ for all statistics.

A second generalization deals with several parameters and statistics at once. *A set of statistics $t_1, \ldots, t_m$ is sufficient for the parameters $\theta_1, \ldots, \theta_n$* if the conditional distribution of any u given $t_1, \ldots, t_m$, namely,

$$P(u \mid t_1, \ldots, t_m; \theta_1, \ldots, \theta_n)$$

does not depend upon any of the parameter θ_i.

It is a theorem of statistics that maximum likelihood estimates are functions of sufficient statistics. A formal proof of this fact will not be given here, but it is quite easy to see intuitively why this is so. The derivation of a maximum likelihood estimate works from the probability of the complete outcome of the experiment, providing a built-in guarantee that all the relevant information in the data will be taken into account. The fact that maximum likelihood estimates are always based on sufficient statistics provides one major argument favoring their use whenever it is practical to do so.

Different methods of estimation may use the same statistics. Suppose, for example, the experimenter obtains independent judgments of N different stimuli sorted into m categories. The problem is to estimate the marginal probability distribution on the judgments; the parameters are $p_1, \ldots, p_m$. Let $N_1, \ldots, N_m$ be the numbers of stimuli which are judged to be in the various categories. The likelihood of the data is

$$L(N_1, \ldots, N_m; p_1, \ldots, p_m) = p_1^{N_1}, \ldots, p_n^{N_m}. \tag{54}$$

The maximum likelihood estimates are

$$\hat{p}_i = \frac{N_i}{N}. \tag{55}$$

In other words, the sufficient statistics for the parameters are the frequencies of the several judgments. Of course, these are exactly the statistics needed to compute estimates using the method of minimum chi square, minimizing

$$\chi^2 = \sum_{i=1}^{m} \frac{(N_i - p_i N)^2}{p_i N}, \tag{56}$$

which has its minimum value (zero) when

$$p_i = \frac{N_i}{N},$$

exactly the same estimates that are derived using the criterion of maximum likelihood.

A theorem by Cramér[3] says that for any parameters estimated from data in the form of frequencies, the maximum likelihood estimates and the minimum chi-square estimates will converge to the same value for large samples. Similarly, if a theory has linear equations in observable and theoretical variables, and has as parameters the coefficients of the variables in the equations, Hurwicz[4] and Koopmans[5] have shown that under the usual assumptions of the analysis (namely, that the variables are distributed normally with equal variance), the methods of maximum likelihood and least squares lead to estimates which are asymptotically equivalent.

EXERCISES

1. The cue-learning theory applied to the Riopelle data has in it the symbols p, d, n (trial number) and N (problem number). What are the proper quantifiers over these variables, and in what order should they appear before the sentences which define the theory? (You need not work out the theory.)

2. Chapter 5 described an experiment reported by Michels and Helson, where a number of gray disks of different reflectance were judged when they were placed on

[3] H. Cramér, *Mathematical Methods of Statistics.* Princeton, N.J.: Princeton Univ. Press, 1946.

[4] L. Hurwicz, Prediction and least squares. In T. C. Koopmans (Ed.), *Statistical Inference in Dynamic Economic Models.* Cowles Commission Monog. No. 10. New York: Wiley, 1950, pp. 266–300.

[5] T. C. Koopmans, The equivalence of maximum-likelihood and least squares estimates of regression coefficients. In T. C. Koopmans (Ed.), *op. cit.*, pp. 301–304.

backgrounds which also differed in reflectance.   Assume that the weights of the backgrounds, the disks, and the stimuli in the subject's memory are constant throughout the experiment, and write a sentence in which the formula for the adaptation level is the sentential function.

3. In probability learning experiments, it typically results that estimates of the learning parameter θ are obtained from the data in different blocks of trials.   Let m be the index for blocks of trials, and assume that $\theta_{i,m}$ is the learning-rate parameter applying during the mth block of trials for a given fixed value of θ, θ_i.   Modify Eq. (12) to take into account the difference in θ during different stages of learning.

4. It won't fit too well, but consider the following model for the Solomon-Wynne data.   The subject starts in state S_0 (and is shocked with probability 1), then moves to state S_1 with probability c.   In state S_1 the subject has probability p of being shocked.   Finally, the subject moves to state S_2 with probability d and is never shocked.

You have three parameters, c, d, and p, to estimate.   What parts of the data would you try to use for each?   (It is not necessary to work out estimators, though it can be a sobering experience.)

5. Consider N independent trials, where p is the probability of success; and let S be the number of successes that are observed.   Obtain estimates of p using the method of maximum likelihood, the method of minimum chi square, and the method of least squares.

6. Chapter 2 considered Estes' miniature paired-associate experiment, including items given a single study trial followed by two tests.   The probabilities of response on the two tests are

$$P(00) = c + (1 - c)g^2,$$
$$P(01) = P(10) = (1 - c)g(1 - g),$$
$$P(11) = (1 - c)(1 - g)^2.$$

Consider the estimation of c, with g given a fixed value.   Let $p(00), p(01), p(10)$, and $p(11)$ stand for the observed proportions of responses.   Show that the maximum likelihood estimate is

$$\hat{c} = \frac{p(00) - g^2}{1 - g^2}.$$

Find the least-squares estimate of c, and show that the minimum chi-square estimate is that value of c which satisfies the equation

$$\frac{p(00)^2}{c + (1 - c)g^2} + \frac{p(01)^2 + p(10)^2}{(1 - c)g(1 - g)} + \frac{p(11)^2}{(1 - c)(1 - g)^2} = 1.$$

7. Relatively simple calculations show that the statistics used in the maximum likelihood estimates for the cue-selection model are sufficient for the parameters with respect to the statistics used in the minimum chi-square and least-squares estimates.   Show that for a single sequence, the statistics T, T', and G are sufficient for the parameters d and p with respect to (a) the probability of a three-trials sequence at the beginning, 001, and (b) the probability of an error on trial 2.

8. Find an unbiased estimator of d in the cue-selection theory.

9. Is the estimator (again from the same cue-selection theory),

$$p_n = \frac{\sum\limits^{n} G}{\left(\sum\limits^{n} G + \sum\limits^{n} T\right)},$$

biased or not? [*Hint:* it may be useful to determine the bias for a given fixed value of $\sum T$ first.) If you find a bias, find an estimator based on n, $\sum G$, and $\sum T$ which is unbiased.

10. Consider a highly simplified psychophysical experiment, in which the same weak signal is presented repeatedly, where the subject responds "yes" or "no" depending on whether he thinks he senses the signal on each trial. Assume that the subject's response on trial n depends on his response on trial $n - 1$ according to the matrix

$$P = \begin{array}{c} \\ 0 \\ 1 \end{array} \begin{array}{c} 0 \qquad 1 \\ \left[\begin{array}{cc} p_0 & 1 - p_0 \\ p_1 & 1 - p_1 \end{array} \right], \end{array}$$

where "0" stands for the response "yes." Let π be the probability of response 0 on the first trial. Let $N(i)$ be the number of sequences in the data which have response i on the first trial, let $n(jk)$ be the number of occurrences of response k following response j, summed over sequences. (a) Write the likelihood function for the data as a function of the parameters π, p_0, and p_1, and the statistics $N(i)$ and $n(jk)$. (b) Obtain maximum likelihood estimates of the parameters. (c) Derive the covariance matrix for the parameter estimates.

CHAPTER TEN

Identifiability

The problem of *estimation* arises when there is too small a *number* of observations. Infinitely many observations could usually specify the parameter values exactly. The problem of *identification* arises when an experiment yields the wrong *kind* of observations. If the observations are not sufficiently detailed in certain specific ways, then they will not yield estimates of all the parameters, and could not do so even if they were based on infinitely many observations.

Consider an example: Suppose that there are two urns, A and B, and each contains red and white marbles. The proportion of red marbles in the two urns are r_A and r_B, respectively. On each trial a random device selects one of the urns: urn A is selected with probability p, urn B with probability $1 - p$. After an urn is selected, a marble is drawn at random from that urn. The urn selected and the marble drawn are independent from one trial to another.

The system will generate a sequence of red and white marbles drawn on successive trials. Suppose, now, that observation during each trial is limited to the color of the marble, and one cannot tell which urn the marble came from. The system has three parameters—p, r_A, and r_B. However, there is only one identifiable parameter,

$$P(R) = pr_A + (1 - p)r_B, \qquad (1)$$

the overall proportion of red marbles drawn.

The parameters are not all identifiable, because different combinations of values of p, r_A, and r_B would all lead to the same probabilities in the observations. Consider the following three possibilities:

i) $p = 0.40$, $r_A = 0.10$, $r_B = 0.60$;

ii) $p = \frac{2}{3}$, $r_A = 0.20$, $r_B = 0.80$; $\qquad (2)$

iii) $p = 0.90$, $r_A = \frac{1}{3}$, $r_B = 1.00$.

All three lead to the same value of $P(R)$, namely, 0.40. Now suppose that an experimenter observed a very long sequence of red and white marbles and decided that the value of $P(R)$ was really 0.40. He would have no way of knowing whether the parameters were those of case (*i*), (*ii*), (*iii*), or any other combination of numbers that could give $P(R) = 0.40$. In general, a model is said to be nonidentifiable whenever different sets of parameter values lead to identical probabilities of the events observed.

Before giving a rigorous and general discussion, three important aspects of the identifiability problem can be introduced with the urn example. The first aspect involves *identifiable parameters and testable assumptions*. The data yield a well-defined estimate of the quantity $P(R)$; that is, $P(R)$ is an identifiable parameter of the system. Of course, this means that hypotheses about the value of $P(R)$ could be tested in the data. In addition, there are other testable assumptions about the system. Recall that the urn selected and the marble drawn are assumed to be independent from one trial to another. This implies that the sequence of red and white marbles will be independent, that is,

$$P(R_{n+1} \mid R_n) = P(R_{n+1} \mid W_n) = P(R), \qquad (3)$$

where the subscripts refer to trial numbers. The quantities in Eq. (3) can be identified, and so the implied equality can be checked.

The second aspect of the problem of identifiability involves *identifying restrictions*. Equation (1) states a functional relationship between the parameters of the theory and the parameter which can be identified. If appropriate restrictions are placed on some of the parameters, values for the remaining parameters can be determined. For example, it might be assumed that all the marbles in urn A were red and all the marbles in urn B were white. That is, the parameters r_A and r_B are assumed to have the values

$$r_A = 1.0, \qquad r_B = 0.0. \qquad (4)$$

Then Eq. (1) becomes

$$P(R) = p,$$

and since $P(R)$ can be identified, p can also be identified. An identifying restriction is an hypothesis about the parameters of the system, but it cannot be tested in the data of the experiment in which it is applied. Therefore it is important to devise ways to obtain independent evidence from other experiments regarding the accuracy of the assumptions which are used as identifying restrictions.

Finally, the problem of identification can be solved by an appropriate *experimental manipulation*. Suppose that it were possible to remove the randomness from the selection of the urn, perhaps by causing the first urn to be selected after each trial in which a red marble was selected, and by causing the second urn to be selected after each trial when a white marble was selected. The trial outcomes would no longer be independent (unless $r_A = r_B$), and we could identify the parameters r_A and r_B:

$$r_A = P(R_{n+1} \mid R_n), \qquad r_B = P(R_{n+1} \mid W_n). \tag{5}$$

General Definitions

The problem of identification was formulated in a general way by econometricians in 1950.[1]

It is important to give careful definitions to some terms that have ambiguous references in ordinary usage. The term *model* will refer to a theory about a specific kind of experiment. It includes statements about the experimental conditions, specifications of free and controlled parameters, and a statement about which dependent variables will be observed. The model contains free parameters as variables, and (possibly) numerical values for controlled parameters. The term *structure* will stand for the theory after numerical values have been substituted for all the parameters. A structure, then, is a specific case of a model. That is, the model is a class of structures.

When all parameters have numerical values (i.e., when a structure is specified), the probabilities of all the possible outcomes of an experiment can be calculated. Thus a structure is said to *generate* a probability distribution of the dependent variables of the experiment.

Now consider the set of structures of a model, and consider the set of possible probability measures for data which are consistent with the theory. For each structure there is just one probability measure. However, several different structures may generate a single probability measure. If that is the case, then even if the probability measure were known exactly, one could not tell which structure of the model generated it.

An identifiable model is one in which there is a one-to-one correspondence between the structures of the model and the permitted probability measures within the data. If there is a many-to-one correspondence between structures and probability measures, then the model is not identifiable.

Recall, in the example, that the several different sets of parameters in Eqs. (2) all gave the same value of $P(R)$, and $P(R)$ generates a probability measure on data. In the present terminology, each of those combinations is a different structure, but the different structures listed in Eqs. (2) all generate the same probability measure for data.

---

[1] See articles by L. Hurwicz, Generalization of the concept of identification, in T. C. Koopmans (Ed.) *Statistical Inference In Dynamic Economic Models*, Cowles Commission Monograph No. 10. New York: Wiley, 1950, pp. 245–257. A. Wald, Note on the identification of economic relations, also in T. C. Koopmans (Ed.), *op cit.*, pp. 238–244. And T. C. Koopmans and O. Reiersöl, The identification of structural characteristics. *Ann. Math. Statist.*, 1950, **21**, 165–181. The terminology used here is closest to that of Hurwicz.

The set of all the structures of a model can be considered as being divided into subsets so that all the structures in a subset generate the same probability distribution. Then all of the structures listed in Eqs. (2) would be in a subset along with all the other structures giving $P(R) = 0.40$. The situation is pictured in Fig. 10.1: M is the model, and it is pictured as a set of structures; P is a family of probability measures, and its members are all the probability measures which are consistent with the model; and G_i is a subset of M, such that if a structure S is in G_i, then S generates the probability measure P_i for the data.

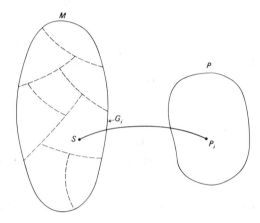

Figure 10.1

Suppose that the estimation problem is solved—that is, the experimenter can select the correct probability measure P_i. This allows him to specify a class of structures G_i. If there is just one structure in each subset G_i, then there is a one-to-one correspondence between the structures and the probability measures, and the model is *identifiable*. However, if each subset G_i contains many structures, selecting the correct P_i does not specify which structure in G_i generated the probability measure that was observed, and the model is *nonidentifiable*. If there are some subsets containing single structures, then there are some probability measures that allow identification of the model, and we say that the model is *locally identifiable*. This intermediate case is not usually found.

Now a general definition of *identifiable properties* will be given. Consider the structures in one of the subsets G_i. These structures will differ in some ways and will be alike in others. In the urn example, the structures have different values of p, r_A, and r_B, but they are all alike in the value of the function $pr_A + (1 - p)r_B$. An identifiable property is one which is shared by all the structures which generate any single probability distribution.

Sometimes such a property is the value of an *identifiable parameter*, such as $P(R)$. In other cases, an identifiable property is a *testable assumption* of the model, such as the independence of responses from one trial to another. If the model is identifiable, then all its properties are identifiable.

Finally, we generalize the concept of *identifying restrictions*. Consider a new class of structures built by selecting just one point from each of the subsets $G_1, G_2, \ldots$ There are many subsets like this. Let m_j stand for a typical subset. It can be formed by placing appropriate restrictions on the parameters of the model. For example, Eq. (4) gives such a restriction, since there will be exactly one point in each subset of the model for which $r_A = 1.0$ and $r_B = 0.0$. Such a subset is a special case of the original model, and the special case is an identifiable model, since there is just one structure in the restricted model corresponding to each possible probability measure. The situation is pictured in Fig. 10.2, where we have represented two of the many submodels which could be formed by making different identifying restrictions. Note that each probability measure P_i in P corresponds to just one structure in m_1 coming from S_i in M, and also to one structure in m_2, a different point from S_i in M.

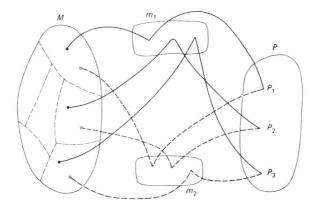

Figure 10.2

Any identifying restriction is an assumption about the parameters of M, and is therefore a property of some of the structures of M. However, it cannot be a property which is shared by all the structures in a class S_i which generates the same probability measure. Therefore an identifying restriction is *not* a testable assumption in the data of the experiment for which M is formulated. In other words, the data give no way to determine which of many identifying restrictions should be selected to identify the model.

Evidence about the identifying restrictions of a model can only be obtained by changing the experiment in some appropriate way. Thus a new experiment is needed which involves the same processes as those studied in the first experiment, but it must permit identification of the values of the relevant parameters. Strictly speaking, the new experiment requires a new model, and, in order to be suitable, the model for the new experiment should be identifiable (or at least the properties that we want to examine from the original model should be identifiable).

Consider the example once more. An identifying restriction is $r_A = 1.0$, $r_B = 0.0$. Given the data of the experiment, there is no way to check whether this identifying restriction is correct. However, a modified experiment was also suggested. If the modified experiment were carried out, then the parameters r_A and r_B could be estimated, and the earlier identifying restriction would be an hypothesis to be tested in the second experiment. Of course, other restrictions such as $r_A = r_B$, $r_A = 1 - r_B$, etc., could also be checked in the modified experiment, and the data from the modified experiment could be used to help decide which of several alternatives is closest to the truth.

Observable States[2]

In the example involving two urns, it is clear that the parameters of the system are not identifiable, and it is easy to find the single identifiable parameter of the system. Many systems are not as easy to analyze. Theories with observable states are sometimes useful in analyzing more complicated cases. The idea will be introduced in connection with the urn example.

If the observer could see which urn was used on each trial, the outcome on each trial would be one of our alternatives:

$$R_A: \text{red marble drawn from urn } A,$$
$$W_A: \text{white marble drawn from urn } A,$$
$$R_B: \text{red marble drawn from urn } B,$$
$$W_B: \text{white marble drawn from urn } B.$$

These can be used as states of a Markov chain. The initial and transition probabilities are

$$P[R_A(1), W_A(1), R_B(1), W_B(1)] =$$
$$[pr_A, p(1 - r_A), (1 - p)r_B, (1 - p)(1 - r_B)];$$

$$P = \begin{array}{c|cccc} & R_A(n) & W_A(n) & R_B(n) & W_B(n) \\ \hline R_A(n-1) & pr_A & p(1-r_A) & (1-p)r_B & (1-p)(1-r_B) \\ W_A(n-1) & pr_A & p(1-r_A) & (1-p)r_B & (1-p)(1-r_B) \\ R_B(n-1) & pr_A & p(1-r_A) & (1-p)r_B & (1-p)(1-r_B) \\ W_B(n-1) & pr_A & p(1-r_A) & (1-p)r_B & (1-p)(1-r_B) \end{array} \quad (6)$$

---

[2] The concepts presented in this section were developed by J. G. Greeno and T. E. Steiner, Markovian processes with identifiable states: general considerations and applications to all-or-none learning. *Psychometrika*, 1964, **29**, 309–333. Also see their comments on this article in *Psychometrika*, 1968, **33**, 169–172.

The system is nonidentifiable because we cannot observe the differences among the states in Eq. (6). If a red marble is drawn on a given trial, we know that the system was either in state R_A or R_B, but we do not know which. And if a white marble was drawn, we know only that the system was either in state W_A or W_B. In other words, the system has four states, but only two states R and W are observable.

This situation involves two kinds of sequences. The system produces sequences of the states of Eq. (6). These are of the form

$$x = R_A\ R_A\ W_A\ W_B\ R_A\ W_B\ W_B\ W_B\ R_B\ W_A,$$

where the length of the sequence is determined by the experimenter. On the other hand, the observer sees sequences of the form

$$y = R\ R\ W\ W\ R\ W\ W\ W\ R\ W.$$

An important characteristic of the situation is that if x were known, y would also be known. Imagine a set having all possible sequences like x; call this set X. And imagine a set having all possible sequences like y; call it Y. For each $x \in X$, there is just one $y \in Y$. In other words, there is a function which maps the set X onto the set Y.

The relationship between X and Y is a special kind. Each state in a sequence like y corresponds to two states in x. On any trial n, if x has state $R_A(n)$ or state $R_B(n)$, then y has $R(n)$; and if x has state $W_A(n)$ or state $W_B(n)$, then x has $W(n)$. Keep in mind that the sequences in X are composed of the states R_A, W_A, R_B, and W_B. The states that compose sequences in Y are R and W. And the states that compose sequences in Y correspond to a partition of the states that compose sequences in X.

The sequences in Y are the sequences that can be observed. An important question is whether or not these sequences can be considered products of a Markov chain. This question was investigated first by Burke and Rosenblatt[3] and given the name "lumpability" by Kemeny and Snell.[4] For the case at hand, the sequences in X certainly are products of a Markov chain. The chain that produces them is given in Eq. (6). The question is whether the sequences in Y have the properties of Markov sequences. If they do, then Eq. (6) is lumpable into a Markov chain with states R and W.

To investigate this question, Burke and Rosenblatt considered transition probabilities based on the original chain [Eq. (6) in the present case] and

[3] C. J. Burke and M. Rosenblatt. A Markovian function of a Markov chain. *Ann. Math. Statist.*, 1958, **29**, 1112–1122.
[4] J. G. Kemeny and J. L. Snell, *Finite Markov chains.* Princeton, N.J.: D. Van Nostrand, 1960. The material referred to here can be found in Chapter 6.

on the partition of the states. Equation (7) lists the relevant quantities:

$$P' = \begin{array}{c|cc} & R(n) & W(n) \\ \hline R_A(n-1) & pr_A + (1-p)r_B & p(1-r_A) + (1-p)(1-r_B) \\ R_B(n-1) & pr_A + (1-p)r_B & p(1-r_A) + (1-p)(1-r_B) \\ \hline W_A(n-1) & pr_A + (1-p)r_B & p(1-r_A) + (1-p)(1-r_B) \\ W_B(n-1) & pr_A + (1-p)r_B & p(1-r_A) + (1-p)(1-r_B) \end{array} . \quad (7)$$

These quantities are the conditional probabilities of the new states, given states in the original chain. The dashed lines separate sets of states that are grouped together in the new chain. Now the question is whether the states R and W behave like states of a Markov chain. In other words, does the probability of state R on trial n depend on events in the sequence before trial $n - 1$?

Equation (7) shows that in the present case, the states R and W must have the Markov property. In this case, the probability of $R(n)$ is the same regardless of what happened on trial $n - 1$, as well as all earlier outcomes. As the reader knows, in a Markov chain the probabilities of states on trial n can depend on the state during trial $n - 1$, but not on earlier outcomes.

The Markov property is satisfied if all the probabilities in each rectangle are equal. In that case, the probability of either state on trial n depends only on which of the observable states occurred on trial $n - 1$—not on which of the original states gave rise to the observable state that occurred. And if the probability of an observable state on trial $n - 1$ depends only on the observable state on trial $n - 1$, the sequence of observable states has the Markov property. Since this is the case, the observations can be analyzed as though they were produced by the Markov chain:

$$P^* = \begin{array}{c|cc} & R(n) & W(n) \\ \hline R(n-1) & pr_A + (1-p)r_B & p(1-r_A) + (1-p)(1-r_B) \\ W(n-1) & pr_A + (1-p)r_B & p(1-r_A) + (1-p)(1-r_B) \end{array} . \quad (8)$$

The relationship between Eq. (6) and Eq. (8) is important. Since the observation on each trial consists only of a red or a white marble, all the sequences produced by Eq. (6) can also be produced by Eq. (8). But the fact that Eq. (6) is lumpable into Eq. (8) says something more. Since the states of Eq. (8) have the Markov property, there is no way in which sequences produced by Eq. (6) would differ from sequences produced by Eq. (8). Once it is known that the sequences produced by Eq. (6) can be described by a Markov chain with just two states, it is immediately clear that Eq. (6) can have at most two free parameters. This is true because any two-state Markov chain has the form

$$P = \begin{array}{c|cc} & S_1 & S_2 \\ \hline S_1 & a & 1-a \\ S_2 & b & 1-b \end{array}.$$

(9)

And in the case of Eq. (8), the values of the two parameters happen to be equal for all values of p, r_A and r_B; hence the system has only one identifiable parameter.

The idea of observability will now be defined in a general way. Let X be the outcome space of an experiment in which each outcome is a sequence of the theoretical states of some model. And let Y be a set of sequences that could be observed in the experiment; that is, each member of Y is a sequence of observable responses. It is convenient to consider only cases in which each $x \in X$ corresponds to just one $y \in Y$. This restricts the discussion to theories that are formulated in enough detail to specify the sequence of observations exactly, given that the sequence of theoretical states is known. This condition means that there is a function f that maps the theoretical outcome space into the space of observable sequences, as in Fig. 10.3.

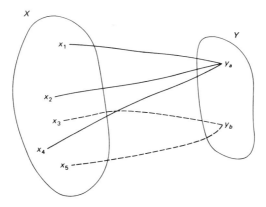

Figure 10.3

The situation in Fig. 10.3 is similar to the example involving urns; the model specifies many different ways in which a given sequence of observations might be produced. For example, suppose that observations on the first two trials of an experiment were R, W. The system could have produced these outcomes in any of four ways: R_A, W_A; R_A, W_B; R_B, W_A; or R_B, W_B. In other words, from a sequence of observations, it is impossible to tell what the sequence of theoretical states was. However, if the function mapping X onto Y were a one-to-one function, then a sequence of observations would correspond to just one sequence of theoretical states. *A model is said to have observable states* in a given experiment if the function that maps its theoretical outcome space into the outcome space for that experiment is one-to-one.

A model with observable states can be constructed as a tool to help solve problems of identifiability and estimation for a psychological theory that is not identifiable. Of course, when a theory with observable states is to be used for such a purpose, the observable-state theory has to be related in a close way with the psychological theory. The relationship that is required is called *implication*.

Recall the earlier discussion of identifiability. A model is a class of structures, each structure corresponding to a point in the model's parameter space. Let two models be denoted M_1 and M_2; M_1 implies M_2 if every probability measure generated by a structure of M_1 is also generated by at least one structure of M_2. In the example with urns, Eq. (6) implies Eq. (8), since every structure obtained by substituting numbers for the parameters of Eq. (6) corresponds to a structure that would be obtained by substituting the same numbers for parameters of Eq. (8).

Application[5]

In the areas of experimental psychology treated in this book, the problem of identifiability seems to have first been raised formally in connection with the theoretical question discussed in Chapter 3. The question is whether simple all-or-none learning involves formation of new associations or selection from a set of strategies of hypotheses available for accomplishing a task. The simplest systems of association formation and of selection lead to similar models of the learning process. In fact, it is easy to write a general model in which the difference between the theories becomes a difference in parameters. There are three states: L (learned), E (error), and S (correct response before learning). The transition probabilities are

$$P = \begin{array}{c|ccc} & L & E & S \\ \hline L & 1 & 0 & 0 \\ E & d & (1-d)q & (1-d)p \\ S & c & (1-c)q & (1-c)p \end{array}. \qquad (10)$$

The initial probabilities will depend on experimental procedures—for example, if a test precedes any information given to the subject, then the system will never be in state L at the start. However, if the subject studies each item before being tested, or has one opportunity to select an hypothesis, then there is a chance that the system will be in state L the first time we take an observation. In order to avoid lengthy consideration of different

---

[5] This section presents a special case of an analysis given by J. G. Greeno, Paired-associate learning with short-term retention: Mathematical analysis and data regarding identification of parameters. *J. Math. Psych.*, 1967, **4**, 430–472.

procedures, let the initial vector be free:

$$P(L_1, E_1, S_1) = \langle t, (1 - t)r, (1 - t)(1 - r) \rangle. \tag{10a}$$

A main theoretical interest centers on the values of c and d. A theory of association formation should predict that c and d are about equal, perhaps with c slightly larger because of the additional reinforcement effect of being confirmed in a correct response. However, an hypothesis theory predicts that c should be less than d, because learning is a trial-and-error process which occurs with some probability when the subject samples from the set of possible hypotheses. He always samples after an error, but not after some correct responses based on short-term memory or irrelevant hypotheses.

On the face of it, this difference in predictions about parameter values should make it easy to settle the issue between the association and hypothesis theories. However, there is a problem of identifiability which makes a direct solution impossible. This can be shown by an analysis of the recurrence probabilities of state E, the error state.

Let e_i be the probability that the first error in a sequence occurs on the ith trial:

$$e_i = \begin{cases} (1 - t)r & \text{for } i = 1, \\ (1 - t)(1 - r)[(1 - c)p]^{i-2}(1 - c)q & \text{for } i \geq 2. \end{cases} \tag{11}$$

Similarly, let f_j be the probability of a correct response on trials $n + 1, \ldots,$ $n + j - 1$, and an error on trial $n + j$, given an error on trial n. That is, given any error, f_j is the probability that the next error will occur exactly j trials later:

$$f_j = (1 - d)q[(1 - c)p]^{j-1}. \tag{12}$$

The values of the e_i and the f_j completely determine the probability distribution of the possible response sequences. If the errors were not recurrent events, this would not necessarily be true; but since the error corresponds to just one state of a Markov chain, the sequence must have the property that nothing which happens before a given error can affect the probability of anything which occurs after that error. Thus the recurrence probabilities are sufficient to generate a complete description of the probabilistic behavior of the system.

There are five parameters in the theory: $t, r, c, d,$ and p. However, Eqs. (11) and (12) show that only four quantities are needed to determine the entire set of recurrence probabilities. Let

$$\begin{aligned} \alpha &= (1 - t)r, \\ \beta &= (1 - t)(1 - r)(1 - c)q, \\ \gamma &= (1 - d)q, \\ \delta &= (1 - c)p. \end{aligned} \tag{13}$$

Then

$$e_i = \begin{cases} \alpha & \text{for } i = 1, \\ \beta\delta^{i-2} & \text{for } i \geq 2, \end{cases}$$
$$f_j = \gamma\delta^{i-1}. \qquad (14)$$

The situation here is exactly like that involved in the introductory example about urns and marbles. There are n parameters in the theory, and fewer than n quantities are needed to specify the probability distribution in the data. In the urn example, different structures could lead to the same value of $P(R)$ and hence to identical probabilities in the marble experiment. In the learning theory, different combinations of values of t, r, c, d, and q would lead to the same values of α, β, γ, and δ, and hence would be indistinguishable in a learning experiment.

The representation in terms of α, β, γ, and δ gives us a convenient way of showing that the model is not identifiable, but a model with observable states is more suitable for further analysis. In Eq. (10), state E is observable, since every error that occurs corresponds to an occurrence of state E. However, state S and state L are not observable. We know that each correct response before the last error corresponds to an occurrence of state S, but after the last error there will be an indefinite string of occurrences of state S before the system will go to state L, so that neither of these states is observable.

In analyzing the identifiability of the present model, it is convenient to construct a second model, which is implied by Eq. (10) and has observable states. The observable-state model may or may not have a reasonable interpretation as a psychological process—usually it will not. However, the observable states correspond in a direct way to the events that are observed in data sequences. This leads to considerable simplification in many calculations and analyses.

In experiments that can be analyzed using Eq. (10), there are sequences of correct responses and errors, and at some point in each sequence there is a last error. Correct responses can be put into one of two categories—those occurring before the last error, and those occurring after the last error. Then one observable state is A, which applies on all trials after the last error, or on all trials in a sequence which has no errors.

Each time there is an error in the data, the system must be in state E. In other words, occurrences of state E are observable. In the observable-state model, the error state is called R.

Finally, the data will contain sequences of correct responses interspersed with errors. Define a series of observable states $S_1, S_2, \ldots, S_j, \ldots$, and say that the system is in state S_j on trial $n + j$ given that there is an error on trial n and correct responses on trials $n + 1, \ldots, n + j$, but the last error occurs after trial $n + j$. Similarly, for correct responses at the beginning of the sequence, define states $B_1, \ldots, B_i, \ldots$, and say that B_i is the state on trial i given that there are correct responses on all the first i trials, but there is an error after trial i. This gives the state space of a model, and these states have two important properties. First, the states give a complete description of the possible outcomes of the experiment. Second, from a sequence of observations, one can tell exactly which of the observable states occurred on each trial.

The observable states of the new model are defined mainly on the basis of the observations that are available. The original model can be used to calculate the initial and transition probabilities for the observable states. This will guarantee that the model with observable states will be implied by the original model. From state R, the system can go to any of three states on the next trial. If there are no more errors, the system will go to state A. Refer back to Eq. (12), and let

$$f = \sum_{j=1}^{\infty} f_j; \tag{15}$$

that is, f is the probability that there will be an error sometime later in the sequence. The probability of going from R to A is the probability of no errors later in the sequence, so

$$p_{RA} = 1 - f = \frac{(1 - d)pc}{q + pc} + d. \tag{16}$$

The probability of going from R to R is just the probability of an error following an error:

$$p_{RR} = f_1 = (1 - d)q. \tag{17}$$

The probability of going from R to S is the probability of a correct response following an error, and an error sometime later in the sequence. This is

$$p_{RS_1} = (1 - d)p\frac{(1 - c)q}{q + pc} = f - f_1. \tag{18}$$

Next consider transitions out of state S_j. Recall that S_j is defined so that it applies only before the last error. Therefore, by definition,

$$p_{S_jA} = 0. \tag{19}$$

Now calculate p_{S_jR}, the conditional probability of an error on the $j + 1$ trial after a preceding error, given j correct responses and an error later in the sequence. The probability of the sequence of correct responses and the error is f_{j+1}. And the probability of the sequence of correct responses and some later error is

$$P(S_{j,n+j} \mid R_n) = (1 - d)p[(1 - c)p]^{j-1} \frac{(1 - c)q}{q + pc} = \sum_{i=j+1}^{\infty} f_i.$$

Therefore

$$p_{S_jR} = \frac{f_{j+1}}{\sum\limits_{i=j+1}^{\infty} f_i} = q + pc. \tag{20}$$

It is important to note that p_{S_jR} (hence, $p_{S_jS_{j+1}}$) does not depend on j.

Now, we can calculate the initial probabilities of the observable states. The probability of zero errors is

$$P(A_1) = t + (1 - t)(1 - r) \frac{c}{q + pc}. \tag{21}$$

The probability of an error on the first trial is

$$P(R_1) = (1 - t)r, \tag{22}$$

and the probability of an initial correct response followed by at least one error is

$$P(B_1) = (1 - t)(1 - r) \frac{q(1 - c)}{q + pc}. \tag{23}$$

Finally, the probability of an error on trial $i + 1$, given i initial correct responses and an error sometime, is

$$p_{B_iR} = q + pc.$$

Since the transition probabilities from all the S_j and B_j to the other states are constant and independent of j, all the S_j and B_j states can be lumped together and considered as a single state S. This gives a new theory with states A, R, and S, whose initial and transition probabilities are

$$P(A_1, R_1, S) = \langle \pi, (1 - \pi)\theta, (1 - \pi)(1 - \theta) \rangle,$$

$$P = \begin{array}{c} \\ A \\ R \\ S \end{array} \begin{array}{c|ccc} & A & R & S \\ \hline & 1 & 0 & 0 \\ & u & (1 - u)v & (1 - u)(1 - v) \\ & 0 & v & 1 - v \end{array}, \tag{24}$$

where

$$\pi = t + (1 - t)(1 - r)\frac{c}{q + pc},$$

$$\theta = \frac{r(p + pc)}{q(1 - c) + rc},$$

$$u = 1 - \frac{(1 - d)q}{q + pc}.$$ (25)

$$v = q + pc.$$

The symbols π, θ, u, and v stand for a convenient set of identifiable parameters for the theory. One reason for the convenience is the ease in which these parameters can be estimated. The parameter π is estimated as the proportion of perfect sequences, and θ is the proportion of imperfect sequences with errors on the first trial; u is estimated as the proportion of errors which are followed by no later errors; and v is the proportion of trials, before absorption, that are errors.

The identifiable parameters π, θ, u, and v can be considered as empirical quantities which can be measured (estimated) from experimental data. These are not enough to determine the values of the five theoretical parameters. However, some of the theoretical parameters have greater interest than others. Perhaps a reasonable assumption about one of the initial probabilities (t or r) would be sufficient to determine the remaining parameters.

It turns out that this will not work, but it is important to see why. One natural assumption about r is that it is just the probability of an error before learning occurs, $r = q$. If this is substituted in Eq. (25), the result is

$$\theta = q + pc = v.$$ (26)

This means that two of the empirical quantities have to be equal. Of course, this may or may not be the case. If it is not, then $r = q$ has to be rejected. If it is, then the restriction is not a means to get estimates of the remaining four parameters, because there are only three empirical quantities left to work with.

Another possibility can arise. In some experiments, r and q will not be equal, but r will equal a known guessing probability g. If, on the first trial, the subject has to guess on items that he does not know, so that $r = 1 - g$, then it is natural to assume that the probability of learning on that trial is d. That is, the subject will know that he does not know the answer, even if he gives a correct response, and the trial will have the same effect that later trials have when errors occur. In that case,

$$\pi = t + (1 - t)g\left[d + (1 - d)p\frac{c}{q + pc}\right] = t + (1 - t)gu, \quad (27)$$

$$(1 - \pi)\theta = (1 - t)(1 - g),$$

and u and v are as given in Eq. (25). It can be shown that

$$\theta = \frac{1 - g}{1 - gu}, \quad (28)$$

and since g is a known constant, Eq. (28) states a functional relationship between θ and u which must be satisfied in the data to permit the assumptions about r and the first-trial probability of learning.

We have examined two assumptions about r that could be satisfied in experiments. Neither of these identifies the model—that is, both are testable assumptions, rather than identifying restrictions. It turns out that the same is true of reasonable *a priori* assumptions about t. (See Exercise 3.) Therefore, in order to identify the model, it is necessary to impose a restriction on the parameters c, d, and q. One possibility is that learning never occurs after a correct response. If $c = 0$ is assumed, then Eqs. (25) can be solved to obtain the estimates

$$\hat{t} = \pi, \quad \hat{r} = \theta, \quad \hat{d} = u, \quad \hat{q} = v. \quad (29)$$

Another possibility with attractive simplicity is the assumption that $c = d$. Then the parameter estimates are

$$\hat{t} = 1 - \frac{(1 - \pi)(1 - \theta)}{1 - u},$$

$$\hat{r} = \frac{\theta(1 - u)}{1 - \theta u},$$

$$\hat{c} = uv, \quad (30)$$

$$\hat{q} = \frac{(1 - u)v}{1 - uv}$$

Experimental Manipulation

The preceding discussion has presented detailed information about the identifiability of Eq. (10). Equations (29) and (30) are related to two identifying restrictions, and these in turn are related to the theoretical question for which Eq. (10) was devised—the question of association formation vs. selection of strategies. The model presented in Chapter 3 and studied by Bower and Trabasso[6] includes the assumption that $c = 0$; that is, learning occurs only following errors, because learning is a process of selection. The discussion leading to Eq. (29) points out that $c = 0$ is an identifying restriction for the model when it is applied to an ordinary experiment. Therefore there is no way of testing the assumption unless a special experiment is performed.

Evidence relevant to the assumption $c = 0$ was obtained by Bower and Trabasso in an experiment where groups had different numbers of responses. Two groups were given stimuli to classify, with four different values of the stimulus dimensions (shape, color, etc.), but one group had two response categories and the other group had four. It was assumed that the difference in responses did not affect the difficulty of the problem, but did affect p. That is, if c_2, d_2, and p_2 are the parameters for the two-response group, and c_4, d_4, and p_4 for the four-response group, then it was assumed that

$$c_2 = c_4, \quad \text{and} \quad d_2 = d_4,$$

but that

$$p_2 \neq p_4.$$

In the experiment, subjects guessed on the first trial, and then were told which category was correct for the first stimulus. The most reasonable assumption to initialize the system was that $r = 1 - g$, ($\frac{1}{2}$ or $\frac{3}{4}$), and that an hypothesis was sampled after the first correct response was given. The subjects had no way of knowing the correct solution to the problem at the start, so $t = 0$ was assumed. These assumptions lead to the restrictions

$$\pi = gu, \qquad \theta = \frac{1 - g}{1 - gu}. \tag{31}$$

Thus, there are just two parameters for each group that are identifiable: u and v. Assuming single values of c and d,

$$u_2 = \frac{q_2 d + p_2 c}{q_2 + p_2 c}, \qquad u_4 = \frac{q_4 d + p_4 c}{q_4 + p_4 c},$$

$$v_2 = q_2 + p_2 c, \qquad v_4 = q_4 + p_4 c.$$

---

[6] G. H. Bower and T. R. Trabasso, Concept identification. In R. C. Atkinson (Ed.) *Studies In Mathematical Psychology*. Stanford, Calif.: Stanford Univ. Press, 1964, 32–94.

From the two groups, it is possible to obtain estimates of all four of the parameters. They are

$$c = \frac{(u_2 - u_4)v_2v_4}{(1 - u_4)v_4 - (1 - u_2)v_2},$$

$$d = 1 - \frac{(1 - u_4)v_4(1 - v_2) - (1 - u_2)v_2(1 - v_4)}{v_4 - v_2},$$

$$p_2 = \frac{(1 - u_4)v_4 - (1 - u_2)v_2}{(1 - u_4)v_4 - \left(\dfrac{1 - v_4}{1 - v_2}\right)(1 - u_2)v_2}, \tag{32}$$

$$p_4 = \frac{(1 - u_4)v_4 - (1 - u_2)v_2}{\left(\dfrac{1 - v_2}{1 - v_4}\right)(1 - u_4)v_4 - (1 - u_2)v_2}.$$

Estimates of the identifiable parameters can be derived using the method of maximum likelihood. Let N_A, N_R, and N_S denote the numbers of sequences starting in the three observable states, and let n_{RA}, n_{RR}, n_{RS}, n_{SR}, and n_{SS} denote the numbers of transitions from one state to another, summed across sequences. Then the likelihood function is

$$L = \pi^{N_A}(1 - \pi)^{N_R+N_S}(\theta)^{N_R}(1 - \theta)^{N_S}(u)^{n_{RA}}$$

$$\times (1 - u)^{n_{RR}+n_{RS}}(v)^{n_{RR}+n_{SR}}(1 - v)^{n_{RS}+n_{SS}}. \tag{33}$$

If one first makes the substitutions given as Eqs. (31), which are required by the assumptions about the initial trial, then finds log L, takes partial derivatives with respect to u and v, and sets them equal to zero, the result is the set of estimates

$$\hat{u} = \frac{N_A + n_{RA}}{N_S + n_{RR} + n_{RS}}, \qquad \hat{v} = \frac{n_{RR} + n_{SR}}{n_{RR} + n_{SR} + n_{RS} + n_{SS}}. \tag{34}$$

From Bower and Trabasso's data,

	Two response	Four response
$N_A + n_{RA}$	22	22
$N_S + n_{RR} + n_{RS} = n_{RR} + n_{SR}$	283	273
$n_{RR} + n_{SR} + n_{RS} + n_{SS}$	558	381

These lead to the estimates

$$\hat{u}_2 = 0.0777, \qquad \hat{v}_2 = 0.507$$
$$\hat{u}_4 = 0.0856, \qquad \hat{v}_4 = 0.674$$

Substituting these numbers in Eqs. 32, we calculate

$$\hat{c} = -0.005, \qquad \hat{d} = 0.090,$$
$$\hat{p}_2 = 0.485, \qquad \hat{p}_4 = 0.318.$$

Of course, the negative value of $\hat{c}$ should not be permitted, and the best admissible estimate of $\hat{c}$ is zero, consistent with the identifying restriction $c = 0$, and with the strategy-selection idea.

In summary, the problem of identifiability exists when different versions of a theory cannot be distinguished in the result of an experiment. In some cases the inaccessible information is the value of a parameter. In the case discussed here, the problem was solved by finding an appropriate method of enriching the data so as to provide the information lacking at the outset. Thus the problem of identifiability is really just the problem of finding appropriate experiments for obtaining evidence relevant to certain theoretical questions. The formulation of the problem as a precise mathematical question, however, makes possible a clearer understanding of just what information is missing, and a definite decision as to whether a proposed experiment actually supplies the needed information.

Observable States and Models

The preceding discussion has illustrated the use of a theory with observable states for investigating questions about identifiability. The theory is useful in two additional ways, and these uses will be described in the present section. These further uses are related to the idea of *sufficient parameters*.[7]

Recall that the design of an experiment determines the set Y of possible outcomes. A model of the experiment has a parameter-space θ of which a typical point is $(\theta_1, \theta_2, \ldots, \theta_r)$. The parameters $\theta_1, \ldots, \theta_r$ are a sufficient set of parameters if they determine a probability measure on the outcome space Y. In other words, the model must specify a function from θ to the set of probability measures. This is not true of all psychological models; for example, the adaptation-level models do not specify probability distributions on the whole outcome space, but instead only predict mean judgments without any probability distributions.

It is perfectly possible to have a model with parameters that are sufficient but not identifiable. Each point in the parameter space θ corresponds to a structure of the model, and it is possible that different structures may correspond to the same probability measure. The parameters are all identifiable

[7] Formal discussions of this idea are given by E. Barankin, Sufficient parameters: solution of the minimal dimensionality problem. *Ann. Inst. Statist. Math.*, 1960, **12**, 91–118, and R. Shimizu, Remarks on sufficient statistics, *Ann. Inst. Statist. Math.*, 1966, **18**, 49–55.

if there is a function from the set of probability measures to the points in the parameter space.

If the parameters are sufficient but not identifiable, it is desirable to find a new model with a new set of identifiable parameters $(\theta_1^*, \ldots, \theta_r^*)$, also sufficient, and such that there exists a function from θ to θ^*. This new model is implied by the old one, and can be said to be an identifiable representation of the original model.

Estimation of parameters. It often happens that construction of a model with observable states provides a direct and manageable method for finding an identifiable representation of a model. This makes the model with observable states useful for investigating identifiability, as illustrated in the discussion earlier. It also can be used to facilitate estimation of parameters.

Recall that observable states for a model are defined on the basis of the kinds of observations that are available. By definition, the occurrences of states are events which can be observed directly in the data. For this reason, the parameters of the model with observable states will be relatively easy to obtain. This is because the parameters are either observable frequencies or are directly related to observable frequencies.

The point is hard to see in the abstract, but easy to see in examples. Consider Estes' *RTT* experiment,[8] as described in Chapter 2. Assume a theory with two states, L and U, $P(L) = c$, and the following response rule:

$$P(0 \mid L) = 1.0, \qquad P(0 \mid U) = g.$$

Then the probability of data sequences is

$$\begin{aligned}
P(00) &= c + (1 - c)g^2, \\
P(01) &= P(10) = (1 - c)g(1 - g), \\
P(11) &= (1 - c)(1 - g)^2,
\end{aligned} \tag{35}$$

where g can be considered as a free parameter. The model is identifiable. There is a testable assumption; namely, $P(01) = P(10)$. However, optimal estimates of parameters are not particularly easy to obtain. Maximum likelihood estimates are obtained as the solution of the following equations:

$$\frac{[n(00)](1 - g^2)}{c + (1 - c)g^2} = \frac{n(10) + n(01) + n(11)}{1 - c}, \tag{36}$$

$$\frac{2[n(00)]g(1 - c)}{c + (1 - c)g^2} + \frac{[n(10) + n(01)](1 - 2g)}{g(1 - g)} = \frac{2[n(11)]}{1 - g}.$$

The equations can be solved, but only with difficulty.

---

[8] W. K. Estes, Learning theory and the new "mental chemistry." *Psych. Rev.*, 1960, **67**, 207–223.

By contrast, consider the following model with observable states, Z and Y. Assume $P(Z) = u$ and the following response rule:

$$P(00 \mid Z) = 1.0,$$
$$P(10 \mid Y) = P(01 \mid Y) = w,$$
$$P(11 \mid Y) = (1 - 2w).$$

This model can be shown to be implied by the one used by Estes. It can be seen immediately that the model has observable states, the assumption $P(10) = P(01)$ is present and testable, and again there are two parameters. The probabilities of data sequences are

$$P(00) = u,$$
$$P(10) = P(01) = (1 - u)w, \qquad (37)$$
$$P(11) = (1 - u)(1 - 2w).$$

Maximum likelihood estimates are obtained as simple frequencies:

$$\hat{u} = \frac{n(00)}{n(00) + n(01) + n(10) + n(11)},$$
$$\hat{w} = \frac{n(10) + n(01)}{2[n(01) + n(10) + n(11)]}. \qquad (38)$$

Note that the estimator equations in Eq. (38) have only data values on the right side, and only simple parameters on the left; also, only one parameter appears in each equation. Thus the estimates are obtained directly rather than by solving complicated simultaneous equations. It is often much easier to estimate the parameters of a model with observable states than the parameters of a corresponding model without observable states.

The calculations given above illustrate an important and general principle, based on properties of sufficient parameters and maximum likelihood estimates. Consider a meaningful psychological model M_1 with parameters that are identifiable, and a second identifiable model M_2 implied by M_1, but with observable states. Since M_1 implies M_2, the parameters of M_2 are a sufficient set of parameters for M_1.

The method of maximum likelihood, working with model M_1, selects the point in M_1's parameter space that produces the probability measure assigning the maximum possible likelihood to the observed data. There must exist, for model M_2, a corresponding point in its parameter space, that produces the same probability distribution over outcomes of the experiment. There are two possible cases. The more frequent case is one where the corresponding set of parameters for M_2 is the maximum likelihood estimate for M_2's parameters. Since M_2 has observable states, it is usually easier to estimate the parameters of M_2 than to obtain direct estimates of M_1's parameters. When M_2 was found, however, the technique involved defining the observable states in the data, and then calculating the values of M_2 on the basis of the assumptions of M_1. Thus the parameters of M_2 are known functions of the parameters of M_1. If these functions have inverses, then estimation of the parameters of M_2 leads at once to estimates for M_1.

Consider the example of the *RTT* experiment again. For fixed values of c and g, Eq. (35) assigns a likelihood to any set of data. The same likelihood comes from Eq. (37) if

$$u = c + (1 - c)g^2,$$
$$w = (1 - c)g(1 - g)/(1 - u) = g/(1 + g). \tag{39}$$

The parameters u and w are easy to estimate, using Eq. (38), giving maximum likelihood estimates. But that means that maximum likelihood estimates of c and g result from using Eq. (38) to estimate u and w, and then obtaining values of c and g using the inverse of Eq. (38), namely

$$g = \frac{w}{(1 - w)}, \qquad c = \frac{u - \left(\dfrac{w}{1 - w}\right)^2}{1 - \left(\dfrac{w}{1 - w}\right)^2}. \tag{40}$$

Of course, the numbers that result have to be the same as those obtained by solving Eq. (36) to estimate c and g. The advantage of the observable-state method is that some hard calculations are avoided.

In cases like the one used here, the maximum value of the likelihood function for the psychological model is the same as the maximum value for the model with observable states. Therefore the maximum-likelihood estimates obtained with one model can be used to calculate the maximum-likelihood estimates for the other model. There are cases in which this procedure will not work. One such case was discussed above; in the two- and four-response experiment of Bower and Trabasso, the data were used to obtain maximum-likelihood estimates of the parameters of a model with observable states. The function relating these parameters and those of the psychological model is given by Eq. (32). When this function was used to work back to estimates of the original parameters, one of the probabilities was found to be negative. This means that the parameter point of maximum likelihood for the model with observable states did not correspond to any point in the parameter space for the psychological model. The true maximum likelihood estimates for the psychological model were not given, but it is clear that they must correspond to some point in the observable-state model's

parameter space that is not optimal for that model. In cases like this, computer search routines often are needed to find the optimal parameter point in a restricted parameter space. However, such cases are relatively rare, and it is usually possible to obtain the parameter estimates of a model using the estimates of a set of sufficient parameters obtained through the method of observable states.

Testing goodness of fit. In preliminary stages of research on a problem, students may ask only about the goodness of fit of a model. In later stages of research, when questions arise about the values of parameters, it is still necessary to investigate the model's fit in order to evaluate the validity of the parameter estimates as measurements of psychological properties.

To test the goodness of fit of a model, one needs a list of quantitative predictions to be compared with experimental results. Parameter estimates are needed in order to calculate the predictions. However, predictions can be calculated and statistical tests can be carried out using the model with observable states. The calculations will usually be simplified considerably, because the observable states are related closely and directly to events that are easily counted in the data. In most cases, tests using the model with observable states can be carried out without translating its parameter values into the parameters of the original model. This is especially helpful if the original model is not identifiable, in which case tests using the model with observable states can be used to decide whether any of the identifiable versions of the model are consistent with a given set of data.

Observable States and Identifiability

In closing, a remark will be made to clarify the relationship between observable states and identifiable models. An identifiable model is defined as one whose structures are in a one-to-one correspondence with the permitted probability measures. A model with observable states has the property that from a sequence of observed responses, the sequence of theoretical states can be specified completely.

These two concepts are really separate notions; neither condition implies the other. First, consider a model with the following transition matrix:

$$P = \begin{array}{c} \\ L \\ E \\ S \end{array} \begin{array}{c} \begin{array}{ccc} L & E & S \end{array} \\ \left| \begin{array}{ccc} 1 & 0 & 0 \\ c & (1-c)q & (1-c)p \\ c & (1-c)q & (1-c)p \end{array} \right. \end{array} .$$

The model is identifiable, as seen earlier. However, its states are not observable, since correct responses occur in both states L and S, and after the last error, there will be an indeterminate number of trials in which state S occurs before the terminal string of L begins.

Next, consider a model with the following transition matrix:

	L	E	S
L	1	0	0
E	ad	$(1 - ad)q$	$(1 - ad)p$.
S	0	q	p

This model has observable states, since state S occurs only on trials before the last error, and state L only on trials after the last error. However, as the model is stated, it has three parameters, and we know that only two parameters can be identified for a model of this kind. Thus the model is nonidentifiable, even though it has observable states. The conclusion is that identifiability of the model, and observability of the states, are separate concepts.

It might be supposed that if a model with observable states is shown to be implied by a psychological model, then the parameters of the model with observable states are identifiable and sufficient for the psychological model. This will often be true, but it is possible for the parameters of the observable-state model to be nonidentifiable. If there is any question about this, it can be resolved only with a proof that the probabilities of observed outcomes determine the values of the parameters.

EXERCISES

1. Consider an extension of the example described at the beginning of this chapter. Suppose that on the trial after a red marble is drawn, urn A is selected with probability p_r, and after a white marble is drawn, urn A is selected with probability p_w. Now there are four parameters for the system: p_r, p_w, r_A, and r_B. How many parameters are identifiable, and what are their functional dependencies on the four theoretical parameters?

2. Show that Eq. (6) implies Eq. (9), but not conversely.

3. For the model of Eqs. (10) and (10a), find the restrictions on the identifiable parameters which are implied if it is assumed (a) that $t = 0$, and (b) that $t = d$. [Examine each of these (*i*) as a single hypothesis, and also in conjunction with (*ii*) $r = q$, and (*iii*) $r = 1 - g$.]

4. For the model of Eqs. (10) and (10a), show that if $r = 1 - g$ and the probability of learning on the first trial is d, then t is an identifiable parameter. What is the estimate of t in this case?

5. The notions of sufficient parameters and identifiability have been discussed here with respect to all the data of an experiment. The notions can be defined almost as easily for any set of statistics from an experiment.

a) Regarding Eq. (24), it was shown that π, θ, u, and v are sufficient and identifiable for the data from a learning experiment. Suppose that only the distribution of total errors is available. Show that π and u are sufficient parameters for this distribution, by showing that for fixed π and u, the distribution of total errors is not affected by variation in θ and v. Also show that π and u are identifiable from the distribution of total errors.

b) Find which of the parameters of Eq. (10) and (10a) are sufficient for the distribution of total errors. Is the obtained set also identifiable from the distribution of total errors?

c) In the discussion leading to Eq. (5), an hypothetical identifying experiment for the hypothetical urn model was proposed as an illustration. Suppose in that experiment, you were only told the total number of red marbles that were drawn in n trials. State a parameter which is sufficient and identifiable for that statistic.

6. Obtain maximum-likelihood estimates for the parameters of Eq. (24), and use them to derive maximum-likelihood estimates for the parameters of Eq. (10) and (10a), under the identifying restrictions (a) that $c = 0$; (b) that $c = d$.

Index

Index

U-shaped distributions, 166
Unbiased estimator, 321, 328
Uncertain recurrent events, 85
Uncertainty, in detection, interval of, 173
 in information theory, 196–206
Unconscious inference, 132, 141, 167
Underwood, B. J., 57, 60, 101
Union of sets, 74, 258
Uniqueness, 217
Units, physical, 121
Universal quantifier, 251, 301
Universe, 251–253, 274
 of discourse, 251
 of an experiment, 274–275
Unknown parameters, 84
Unusable redundancy, 204
Urn model, of accumulative learning, 8–9
 of replacement learning, 3, 25
Usable redundancy, 204
Utilities, paired, 229
Utility, existence of, 231
 numerical, 230
 ordinal, 234
 strict, 236, 239
 weak, 235–237
Utility model, 207, 235

v-scale, existence of, 216
Valence, 224–225
Value, of money, intrinsic, 229
 of the self-adaptation parameter, 157
 true, 220, 320
Values, of objects, 231
 scale, 229
Variable, index, 42
 random, 42–43, 50, 275, 278–279, 284

Variables, controlled, 300
 logical, 254–268
 sum of a sequence of random, 43, 284
Variance, binomial, 43
 of a distribution, 283
 normal distribution, 283
 of total errors, 50–54
 of total errors in linear model, 44
Vector, initial, 296
Verbal conditioning, 2
Verbal theory, 261
Veridical judgments, 133
Vocabulary, learning, 1
Von Neumann, J., 240

Wage, fair, 224
Waiting times, distribution of, 280–282
Waveform, likelihood of, 185, 189
Weak ordering, 230
Weak stochastic transitivity, 232
Weak utility, 235–237, 242
Weaver, W., 195
Weber's law, 190–194, 204
Weight, judgment of, 174–177
 of cues, 87
Weighted average, 121
Weighted geometric mean, 121
Well-formed formula, 245, 252
White noise, 161
Winet, M., 235
Woodworth, R. S., 175, 177
Wrong codes, 111
Wrong strategy, 83

z-scores, 46–47, 175
Zinnes, J. L., 219